The Quest for the Golden Trout

DOUGLAS M. THOMPSON

The Quest for the Golden Trout ~

Environmental Loss
& America's Iconic Fish

UNIVERSITY PRESS OF NEW ENGLAND ~ HANOVER & LONDON

University Press of New England

www.upne.com

© 2013 Douglas M. Thompson

All rights reserved

Manufactured in the United States of America

Designed by Eric M. Brooks

Typeset in Adobe Jenson by Passumpsic Publishing

University Press of New England is a member of the
Green Press Initiative. The paper used in this book meets
their minimum requirement for recycled paper.

For permission to reproduce any of the material in this book,
contact Permissions, University Press of New England, One Court
Street, Suite 250, Lebanon NH 03766; or visit www.upne.com

Library of Congress Cataloging-in-Publication Data

Thompson, Douglas M. (Douglas Marshall)

The quest for the golden trout: environmental loss and
America's iconic fish / Douglas M. Thompson.

    pages cm

Includes bibliographical references and index.

ISBN 978-1-61168-319-6 (cloth : alk. paper) —

ISBN 978-1-61168-482-7 (ebook)

1. Stream channelization — Environmental aspects —
United States. 2. Fish habitat improvement — United States.
3. Stream conservation — United States. 4. Golden trout
fishing — United States. I. Title.

QH545.S8T46   2013

639.2'757 — dc23   2013011037

5 4 3 2 1

Contents

Acknowledgments

I want to thank my wife, Rebecca, for her support and patience throughout the research and writing of this book. She was gracious enough to read multiple versions of chapters that were fortunately not nearly as boring as most of my writings. Our daughter, Haley, was a critical partner in crime on many clandestine research expeditions and helped me see issues through the next generation's eyes. My mother heartened me with her questions about how the book was proceeding. More importantly, she understood my early love of rivers and gave me the freedom to explore my surroundings, no matter how muddy I got. My sister joined me on several early trips to rivers and encouraged me to immerse myself in my passion, clothing and all. Finally, my dad taught me the ways of the angler and introduced me to the rivers I love. Although he may not always agree with my views on angling, I deeply appreciate the support he always provided in my search for knowledge.

The publication of a book requires the careful scrutiny of many sets of eyes. Ellen Wohl provided encouragement and strategic suggestions that greatly improved the entire book. Jed Wright asked the tough questions that needed to be asked and provided invaluable sources to include. Derek Turner was kind enough to provide his thoughts on the chapter, "To Serve a Higher Soul," and suggested important philosophical issues for me to consider further. Stephen Hull walked me through the process of publishing a book and answered my many dumb questions. Gary Hamel and Peter Fong provided a careful review during editing. And finally, Mildred Nash joyfully turned editing into a much-needed, thankfully painless grammar lesson.

The Quest for the Golden Trout

In Search of Gold

We fished the canyon the way you do when
you're prospecting a new place.
~ JOHN GIERACH, 2005

$\mathcal{A}$t select little rock and mineral shops dotting the countryside, especially in regions where the history of resource extraction runs deep, a curious game of deception calls to old and young alike. For a few dollars, eager children can take their chances at panning for gold. One day I decided to let my daughter give it a go. Unlike the original placer miners who sought hidden riches from untamed mountain brooks, I used money to buy both the equipment needed to search and the gold she ultimately sought. Of course, the entrepreneur of this business already did calculations to ensure that the prize we would leave with today was worth much less than the fee already collected. In the back of my mind I understood this seeming folly, but the economics of the situation was of no real consequence. The point of all this activity was entertainment, not profit.

For a few dollars, we were handed a pan and a small bag of dirt and directed to walk outside to an artificial waterway that was carefully constructed to ensure the treasure could not escape capture. As I realized, but my daughter did not, carefully concealed inside the bag, among all the sand and gravel, were small golden trinkets. Of course I noticed that a bucket of identical minerals existed inside the shop door. I knew that maybe the same novelty could be obtained for less at the register, but this was more fun. For my child's sake, I played the role of the straight-faced poker player. The trick was to conceal the ace up my sleeve for as long as possible because I knew the waterway contained no valuables of its own. Everything of worth must be carried over and poured there first from our bag of dirt.

We carefully emptied the contents of the bag into my daughter's pan, placed the pan in the water and the game began. With a graceful flex of her thin wrists, the swirling waters began to slowly wash away the soil between small hands. Soon the shimmering bounty was revealed. Tiny fingers eagerly reached into the cool water to extract the objects of all these theatrics. The pan was neglected now; there were no more spoils to be had. As we knew all along, each bag contained only a few rewards. The waters held nothing more of interest. My daughter looked on in amazement at the precious nugget still dripping in her hand.

At this point, I imagined an exchange that I dreaded but knew would come. She would look at me wide-eyed and breathless for clarification: "Is it real gold, Dad?" I would want to maintain the illusion, preserve the magic of the moment. As gently as possible, I could explain that it was a mineral called pyrite made of a combination of iron and sulfur. However, these responses would do little to answer her question. I would be confronted with silence and a confused look. Finally, I would be forced to say the words I hoped I would not have to utter, knowing the sheer disappointment it would bring. "No, it is not real. It is just fool's gold."

~ ~ ~ In countless rivers and streams in the United States, this same game is played with trout. The methods are more complex; the challenges somehow seem more real. But, in the back of our minds we know it is ultimately just an illusion. We are all fishing for fool's gold.

It is not about economics, at least not personal economics. All of us need to purchase gear and fishing permits. The trout we catch could have been obtained from the supermarket with much less cost and effort. If we are lucky, we might have a young partner in crime to accompany us on our trout-mining expedition. Excitement is palpable as we head off to prospect the canyon and see what the swirling waters will reveal.

Although the river probably looks natural enough to the untrained eye, it is very unlikely to have escaped the ravages of humans. Unfortunately, the waters were probably fished out of native trout long ago. Perhaps they never even existed here in the first place. Pollution, construction, and destruction rearranged both the river and the inhabitants. Without constant intervention, the waters would contain no more treasures. In most cases, the shimmering trout sought were placed there a short time before by hatchery staff to maintain the fantasy of an untamed environment. Perhaps the banks and bed of the river were modified to enhance the fishing experience: an artificial waterway like the sluices of the placer miners.

We begin early in the morning to beat the other birds to the worm. We stake claim to a promising section of water and stone, and start the search. Every fisherman needs to wear special sunglasses to cut through the glare of sunlight on water. As we prospect for elusive gems, the warm hue of the lenses blocks out the reflection of the terrestrial world, and our vision penetrates into the realm of the trout. We take out our tools, our rod and reel, and prepare to sieve through the water searching for gold.

We know that proper casting technique requires a graceful flick of the wrist. With patience, skill, and a little luck, we receive our first strike. A slight tug on the rod lets us know the cards have been dealt. The bluff worked, and now it is time to cash in with the ace up our sleeve. The hand is revealed to the unsuspecting fish: the hook is set. After a moment or two, the foe can be reeled in, battered and exhausted. We reach into the cool water with long fingers and gently lift the bounty into the gleaming sunlight.

Perhaps the child looks on in glowing admiration at his mentor and the sleek fish in hand. Trout are truly beautiful creatures. It is hard not to be impressed by the silver glimmer and colorful spots that resemble so many sparkling crystals in a precious stone. The inevitable question surfaces: "Is it a brook trout, Dad?" The tutor patiently explains that it is a brown trout. Maybe even adds that brown trout originally came from Germany and were brought here to provide additional angling opportunities. Maybe, if the poker face is good enough, the magic of the moment will be preserved.

~ ~ ~ Perhaps it is worth asking the question whether it matters that trout fishing has largely become a bit of scientific theater. Do we need to hear about another environmental problem when this issue does not really sound that bad in comparison to global warming, acid rain, or tropical deforestation? It is undeniable that catching a fish brings enjoyment and pleasure to thousands of people each day. I love just seeing trout swimming in crystal-clear water. Trout anglers are also some of the most vocal advocates for clean and healthy rivers. Consequently, few people question methods used to produce good fishing, and many welcome the results. But we must take off our rose-colored sunglasses if we are to see rivers for what they have truly become. The reflection of the human world on the water's surface is as real and dangerous as the rocks hidden below the waves. Perhaps it is time to think long and hard about what we are trying to accomplish when we take the very necessary steps to save our country's rivers and streams.

This book is about looking at our nation's rivers with a more critical eye and asking more questions about both historic and current practices in fisheries and river management. If nothing else, people need to be aware of the story of our trout-filled waters. Some people may read this book and decide they are happy enough with the present situation. Others will read the book and call for change. In my mind, change is needed. Because of my own love for rivers and all the things they naturally contain, especially trout, I write this book to inspire people to initiate change. As with many people drawn to rivers, my vision is surely clouded by an emotional reaction that trout create. With these biases in mind, I hope you will join me and hear a story that is fascinating, frustrating, and perhaps even inspiring: a story of rivers and all that is done to them for the love of trout.

CHAPTER ONE

Controversy over the Salmon's Migration

*The spirit of the Atlantic salmon is truly unquenchable, and if
any fish deserved the epithet "Brave Heart," then this is it.*
~ JOHN BAILEY, 1998

$\mathcal{T}$o understand the role trout play in driving management decisions it helps to first talk about a related fish and a place that borrowed its name. For a century and a half, beginning about 1809, the people of Connecticut faced the awkward question: "What happened to the salmon of the Salmon River?" The once impressive salmon migration had stopped. The year I was born, 1967, groups of volunteers, scientists, concerned citizens, and politicians decided to correct this situation. Thanks to their efforts, stocked salmon returned to the river and ended decades of embarrassment. Unfortunately, as part of restorative efforts to return fish, provide better trout angling opportunities, and appease landowners along the riverbanks, there is currently a fight to end migration of a different kind. Rock and wood are the weapons of choice as attention now focuses on a battle against the river itself.

Salmon capture the imagination and inspire people, myself included. But despite our admiration, we have not seen fit to keep species out of trouble on both the eastern and western coasts of the United States. The eastern version, Atlantic salmon, is slowly disappearing from much of New England as it once did from the Salmon River. As a kid I always wanted to see a salmon, but I was instead forced to search for other species in rivers near my home, which had lost their salmon generations before. Carp that had been introduced somehow provided a constant lure to bring my friends and me back to the river. Their gray flowing forms would appear in beams of sunlight that penetrated the water, like apparitions spied through the window of some haunted house. They were not particularly good looking or valuable, but intriguing just the same. We used rods and reels in a vain attempt to provide flesh to these ghostly creatures. Day after day, the only salmon we saw were in our imagination.

As time passed, family vacations brought me to other eastern towns that still held salmon. I always relished chances to explore new places pointed out by a rod and reel. Every stream was an adventure. To find source and destination I would walk up and down banks, or if possible, cross channels on logs and stone. Steep mountain brooks with large rounded boulders offered the delight of rock-hopping. Perhaps the reason I chose to study rivers as an adult is because I still loved the challenge of crossing cold waters on the tops of so many round stony islands. Each rock offers a small refuge from swift current. Large boulders provide a place to catch a quick breath and scout my route. Smaller stones offer the riskier prospect of a momentary readjustment of momentum. Each successful crossing is a small victory won. It is much the same feeling of satisfaction I once found with reeling in fish.

Throughout my early years, trout were common acquaintances on small streams, rivers, and lakes. However, I never happened upon the iconic fish that embodies power, persistence, and mystery. I was well into my fourth decade before I finally caught a glimpse of an Atlantic salmon. It was still a small fish that had yet to venture into the deeper waters of the ocean that gives it half a name. Perhaps three inches long at best, it skimmed along near the rippled surface. It was in the Salmon River, appropriately enough, that I sighted this fish, a waterway that holds great promise, fascination, and a good deal of sadness for me. It is both my playground and workplace. It teaches me lessons and serves as my classroom. It is a river with a fascinating history and remains a symbol of wildness and natural beauty for many.

Truly wild and natural rivers provide amazingly diverse environments for fish. Fallen trees, undercut banks, and periodic shifts in river path provide a complex array of habitats that support a myriad of different aquatic organisms. For millennia these organisms survived together in a symbiotic tangle of life histories. Each species occupied a particular habitat and performed an invaluable function in an unorchestrated symphony of life and death. Haphazard changes in rivers create new niches to occupy, such as when erosion around an introduced log or deposition on the inside curve of a new bend reshuffles the balance of habitat types. Rivers are interconnected to floodplains in ways that allow vital nutrients to flow into aquatic ecosystems. Natural processes of change reinvent rivers each time floods rework channel beds. These mechanisms provide resilient means to refurbish older habitats. Species find their own balance of numbers in response to availability of food and habitable environments. In many of these healthy ecosystems, young salmon used to swim in and around complex channel forms, finding food to eat and places to hide from danger. Occasionally they would catch a glimpse of their own futures when a massive adult swam by on its way to spawn. It is hard to imagine any way to improve on the complex interdependencies among different species and varied physical places that exist in wild and natural river systems. Unfortunately, the Salmon River is no longer truly wild, and in many ways it is now unnatural.

Connecticut's Salmon River is one of several in this country that took its name from the amazing fish that splits its time between cool, freshwater rivers and wide oceans. This river does not officially begin in some secretive spring on a tucked-away hillside, as we might perhaps imagine. This Salmon

River suddenly pops up on the map as a full-grown entity. Of course, in reality, the river does not just appear on the landscape; it is more of a cooperative effort. The Blackledge and Jeremy Rivers end their separate voyages and join to give birth to the Salmon. I see it as a bit of an insult to the various rivers involved that this naming convention obscures the rivers' relationship. Perhaps I am overly sensitive because the Sudbury River, my favorite haunt as a kid, is unknown to most people until it is arbitrarily renamed the Concord River, which is nationally known as a birthplace of the American Revolution and a favorite haunt of Henry David Thoreau.

The Salmon River actually results from the cumulative offerings of many smaller rivers and creeks in a network of drainages that reach into a watershed occupying more than a hundred square miles. The river drains to the Connecticut River and is part of the nation's first "blueway," a watershed-scale designation signifying that local, state, and federal agencies are collaborating to better manage aquatic environments in the basin. The more than ten-mile-long Salmon River can be traced north to a source seventeen miles farther upstream along the Blackledge River. In this place and numerous others in the watershed, raindrops and melted snowflakes quietly thread their way through an endless maze of cracks and crevices in soil, then emerge into the light once again. This supply of water from underground helps maintain cooler water temperatures and a more constant flow when sunlight chases away rain clouds. As water seeps from soil, it stops being called groundwater, is momentarily valued as a spring, and quickly evolves into runoff. This water maintains an aquatic ecosystem for an amazing array of animals, and beckons people across the region to come and visit.

The Salmon River is many things to many people. The surrounding state forest lands offer excellent mountain biking, hiking, and hunting opportunities. I often join people exploring Airline Rail Trail, which parallels the Salmon and Jeremy Rivers. A cinder-covered pathway is all that remains of the Airline Railroad and an ambitious but ultimately failed attempt to provide a direct route from Boston to New York City. The river becomes visible to travelers along this route as they traverse one of numerous high trestles that crisscross the waters. The deep valley is best appreciated farther along the way from atop the Rapallo and Lyman viaducts that rise steeply above tributary dales, which offer breathtaking views to the south. People explore other trails on horseback and ATVs. The river also provides good swimming holes that quickly sprout inflatable floatation devices, toy boats, and nearby lawn chairs when temperatures rise. I taught my golden retriever to swim in one pool below a picturesque covered bridge over a decade and a half ago. Later she joined me on research adventures and carefully perched between the tripod legs of survey equipment my students and I used to catalog sections of the watershed. For whitewater enthusiasts, the river offers the thrill of piloting a kayak or canoe among boulders during high water when navigation becomes more about reading strong currents and less a game of pinball. The water itself is a drinking source for individual homes and whole communities. The Connecticut Department of Energy and Environmental Protection, or DEEP for short, established its Eastern District Headquarters in the watershed along the banks of the Blackledge River. Further downstream at the mouth of the Connecticut River sits the department's Marine Fisheries headquarters, where biologists ponder the fate of anadromous fish migrating past on spawning runs.

To anglers, the river is an irreplaceable source of excellent trout fishing. Here is a place where a carefully placed fly can entice a long, iridescent fish to play a game that has captivated humans for hundreds of years. As anglers wade in water surrounded by green-scaled trees and smoothly worn boulders, they excitedly anticipate a flash of their prey. An electric tug on a rod gratefully signals that their hours of patient pursuit have not been futile. For some, fishing is addictive. It involves an instinctual fight for survival, an opportunity to spend time in a beautiful natural setting and a chance to demonstrate a prowess with a rod that many people will never master. For true fanatics, it is hard to think of the Salmon River as anything but a coldwater fishery for trout. However, the river has a much older and more diverse story to tell.

As the Salmon River flows south, it crosses a landscape steeped in geologic history. Black ledges in the upper watershed were once the bed of an ancient ocean. Over four hundred million years ago, shifting plates in Earth's crust and upper mantle caught the Iapetous Ocean in a massive vise. The continents of North America, Africa, and Europe conspired against an ocean that bore the mythological name of Atlas's father and slowly squeezed together, crushing marine sediments in their grasp. Sediments were thrust upward and transformed into a line of mountains with a twisted core of metamorphic bedrock. Salty water rushed away to find new ocean basins to fill. Evidence of this once great sea was erased to all but geologically inclined daydreamers like me.

Today, the Salmon River methodically works to dismantle evidence of past geologic construction and destruction, and cleverly sweeps clues under the waters of Long Island Sound. Once impressive mountains are now worn to nubs. Still, the persistent river plucks off flakes of mica, pries loose grains of quartz, and dissolves away darker amphibole and pyroxene minerals. When flows rage, bedrock breaks into larger chunks that I occasionally hear bouncing along the riverbed. During these seemingly tumultuous times, the river adopts the role of a master sculptor and works to soften lines in stone by rounding each pebble. When flows recede, I drink in a scene with a riverbed heavily populated with smooth cobbles and boulders. The remaining rock fragments are not discarded, but are themselves reused as part of a never-ending polishing process comprised of countless minuscule collisions of sand and rock. When resting, these smaller grains do their best to hide from currents as they reside at the feet of their bigger cousins. Most of this sand is quartz, but a small portion is comprised of tiny red crystals of garnet that likewise become dislodged and huddled together in quiet swirling waters behind boulders. When I bring students to the river, I usually try to extract a handful of these minute gems for inspection. We momentarily marvel at the beauty contained in this tiny detail of a landscape. Then, with an agenda in mind and a schedule to keep, I immerse my hands in the river and wash away the crimson specks, knowing that eventually these grains will find their way into the current to continue their intermittent march to sea. By the time they arrive, the human world will look very different and the fate of the salmon will be decided.

When I first arrived in Connecticut, I explored the Salmon River with both the enthusiasm of a young boy exploring a new place and the dispassion of a scientific observer quietly sizing up a place for its potential as a research subject. Every bend in the river called for me to explore a little farther. Each rapid and deep pool was an answer in need of a question. Each glance down a new reach promised to reveal a treasure previously unseen in miles of water already traversed. As I passed down along the river, I encountered old stone abutments for bridges that marked important routes of commerce long since abandoned. Stone walls led away from these sites and bookended locations of roads that once held ruts from horse-drawn wagons. These abandoned country lanes now serve as collection sites for leaves discarded each autumn by trees that send roots to reclaim previously well-trodden routes. Stone walls contain spurs that run perpendicularly away from old lanes to highlight important property boundaries, which subsequently lost their significance when the state took over the land in 1934. The surrounding forest contains a balance of deciduous and coniferous trees that is best appreciated in fall when nature highlights select species with bold yellow, orange, and red flashes. Once winter takes hold, tall hemlocks and white pine do their best to add color to an otherwise gray and muted landscape. With leaves gone, more of the region's colonial past and suburban present can be seen from afar. It is a watershed where nature is trying to erase a history of human habitation, but those marks are still much too numerous to ignore.

One big impact to the watershed occurred as a result of massive deforestation with the arrival of European settlers. Trees began to disappear as agriculture and grazing activities took over the region. Other newcomers targeted trees themselves as a resource. Hemlocks attracted tanneries, which established themselves in the watershed to turn livestock hides into shoes, harnesses and a myriad of other utilitarian items. Bark was peeled, dried and turned into a powder for use in the tanning process. Wastewater spilled back into streams. Trees, normal building blocks for a healthy aquatic ecosystem, had become a source of pollution. After manufacturing methods changed in the mid-nineteenth century, hemlocks began to make a comeback. But other trees were sought for paper, lumber, railroad construction, and firewood. The overall impact was a landscape with fewer trees to obscure the growing outlines of wooden buildings, and a corresponding increase in runoff and erosion.

In many areas, valley walls along the Salmon River are steep by Connecticut standards. Anyone like me who has biked along Route 16 knows the harrowing descent as you approach the river, the brief opportunity for respite along the narrow floodplain, and then the long painful climb up the other side of the valley. Alternatively, as a hiker along one of the many trails, I have peered down to a thread of water from above. On hot days, I must decide if these cool river waters are ample compensation for a slippery descent and sweat-inducing ascent back up to my perch. Unfortunately, the steep and narrow valley is highly prone to erosion when trees are removed. Valley walls act like a funnel and direct tons of sediment toward the aquatic realm of salmon and trout. For the last fifteen years, I have brought students to one particular section of the river that remains treeless to estimate the size of a missing lump of sediment that tore itself free during a rainstorm and hit the river as a muddy and rocky flow. Undergraduates cling to weeds as they take measurements. Backpacks occasionally make a break for it, rolling down toward the river. Nearby, scars of landslides hint at a history of similar erosive events along previously denuded valley walls. It is amazing that any fish survive at all.

Although I usually approach the Salmon River by college van, car, bicycle, or foot, it can also be reached by boat. Approximately 16.5 miles inland from Long Island Sound, tucked away on the eastern banks of the mighty Connecticut River, hides a small inlet called Salmon Cove. The cove marks the mouth of the Salmon River and an important stairway for many fish species. As in many coves along this stretch of the Connecticut River, wild rice plants grace the shores of this quiet backwater area. Flora is gently flushed twice a day by freshwater tides as the ocean backs up New England's premier river and sends surges of nutrient-rich water up riverbanks. The Salmon River supplies additional nutrients and rocky chips and fragments from its artistic endeavors. If tides are low and the Salmon River is flowing with gusto, sediments are deposited farther downstream, closer to the Connecticut River. If tides are high and the Salmon River is struggling to pull much water from countless microscopic crevices, sediment begins to fill in the cove further upstream. Slow filling is an inevitable consequence of the imperceptible sea-level rise that pushes tides further inland each year. Still, local property owners grow concerned and call for measures to halt this deposition.

DEEP responds to concerns about sedimentation by identifying short upstream sections of river where banks erode. They then design solutions to what is a natural process of river evolution. Usually, a river will slowly migrate across its floodplain by eroding away sediments on outer banks of a meander bend and depositing those same sediments on insides of curves further downstream. These changes create channel complexity, which is a much appreciated attribute of healthy aquatic ecosystems. Unfortunately, projects engineered to "fix" river migration solve few environmental maladies and instead entail attempts to pin in place and neuter the river. In one place along the outer edges of a reconfigured bank on the Jeremy River, angular boulders unlike those on the riverbed rest on wooden shelving units submerged below the waterline. These wooden devices are called lunkers, intended, strangely enough, to shelve trout for anglers. These devices sit on an isolated piece of land surrounded by private property and backed by a field for horses with one lonely barn. Even after many years of existence, the bank is largely devoid of vegetation except for a few invasive vines that poke through riprap. Half a mile away on the Blackledge River, the state planted logs with their trunks in the ground and roots exposed. Boulders were placed between roots along a 440-foot section to halt bank erosion and provide a different home for trout.[1] The $120,000 project looks slightly more natural even with overturned trees, but bank erosion persists. In both cases the state won publicity battles by taking action, but tons of sediment is still released throughout the watershed as tractors till agricultural fields, sand trucks make icy roads passable and hundreds of homeowners undertake small landscaping projects. Ultimately, it is highly doubtful that any sediment particles carefully incarcerated in these banks by the state will be missed among millions of similar-sized grains miles downstream in the cove or anywhere else along the river. It is also likely that the influx of sediment to the cove was more heavily influenced by the lowering of a local dam that trapped sediment for approximately two hundred fifty years.[2] It was at this dam that the government spent about $1 million in 2005 to install thirty-two concrete and stone teeth in the riverbed to break up ice flows that were damaging several homes located too close to the river. As part of the never-ending battle against the Salmon, the U.S. Army Corps of Engineers also dredged the channel to trap sediment that would normally pass through this area.

Although people seem intent on continually plastering the banks of the Salmon River with band-aid projects working toward some type of romanticized riverine Egyptian mummy, it is best to remember that the river has thousands of potential places to erode and endless time to achieve its goal of evicting sediment. This is an easy lesson to miss. As an adolescent, I was often arrogant enough to try and impose my will on local streams. My carefully carved and painted boats, complete with pencils for outriggers, were raced against other youths' nautical designs down narrow rock-lined channels crafted to resemble the most terrifying rapids of the mighty Colorado River. In preparation, I launched a thousand twigs looking for the right path to take. Pebbles were rearranged and revisited to see if summer showers could wash away my handiwork. Once, a best friend and I even tried to dam the neighborhood brook. We built an interlocking structure of brick and mud in our desire for control. We did not give up easily and worked to perfect a design, which was desperately needed for some unidentifiable purpose. Luckily, streams are more persistent than little boys, and much more powerful too. The bricks were eventually discarded on the shore and our footprints led away to more promising adventures. I still feel a twinge of guilt for my adolescent attempts to impose my will on water, and I am grateful for my failure as an engineer. Even today the desire to tinker, to repair some perceived flaw, is ever present. I now have training to build dams to restrain water and design riprap revetments to fix rivers in place. However, I realize that rivers should flow unrestrained to the sea to allow salmon, shad, and even homely lamprey to complete their life's voyage. After all, with more than 75,000 large dams already in this country, do we really need another? I now appreciate that, despite my strong will and determination, a river's persistence will always win out and destroy anything I could build to constrain it. Ultimately, saving a river like the Salmon is probably more about planning a careful strategic human withdrawal than reengineering the system to meet our lofty expectations.

Historically, salmon in the Connecticut River watershed represented a population at its farthest southern extreme. As one of the closest tributaries to Long Island Sound, the Salmon River was always at the margins of the species range. The forceful Hudson and other rivers further south along the Eastern Seaboard did not contain salmon in historic times. Unfortunately, New England was the birthplace of the American industrial revolution, and waterpower drove economic engines of the region. Because of a combination of a lack of concern and understanding, here and throughout the Connecticut River watershed, salmon became extirpated in the nineteenth century. Impressive runs of other anadromous fish also dwindled to a small trickle. Shad, river herring, and sea lamprey managed to maintain viable populations, but at much lower levels. Even American eel survived to uphold a reduced reverse commute, spawning in saltwater and maturing in rivers. However, Atlantic salmon vanished from the entire Connecticut River basin. Standing in their way and barring upstream passage to all fish were massive dams at Turners Falls and Holyoke, Massachusetts.

Both dams still exist and continue to fuel owners' bank accounts. Droplets carefully collected and ushered downstream by the river are corralled and funneled through large pipes known in the industry as penstocks. Water impeded by dam impoundments and penned up in penstocks finds its way to the ocean temporarily blocked by a whirling dervish of rotating metal fins. To young fish headed to the ocean, these spinning blades must resemble a gigantic food processor. However, it is probably the dramatic drop in water pressure associated with turbines that ultimately kills many fish. Pressure differences develop as each molecule of water releases its potential energy and sacrifices its momentum for the sake of turbine motion. Each rotating turbine, in turn, is connected by a sturdy metal rod to large magnets surrounded by coils of copper wire. Turbines spin magnets to create a product few understand, but we all rely on: electricity. A series of wooden poles and heavy wires leave buildings and carry this precious product to feed the grid. Here and throughout the country, we plug in our cell phones, televisions and laptop computers and slowly suck life from our nation's rivers.

Hydropower holds an uncertain future as a long-term source of power. Electricity that emanates from hydropower plants is hailed as a solution to global warming by some, and, by others, reviled as the most hideous environmental disaster perpetrated on rivers. To companies and managers tasked to meet the cumulative demands of a connected populace, hydropower is a critical weapon in their arsenal of production facilities. Hydropower plants provide a supply of electricity that can rapidly respond to the needs of a population. Every morning when we wake to switch on coffee makers and toaster ovens, the electrical grid is taxed. Often it is hydropower to the rescue. Lonely power plant operators and computer-operated control systems sense our electrical needs and respond by slowly opening gates at thousands of dams throughout the country. Like stoking the fire of a giant steam locomotive, their actions supply the fuel that turn the wheels and power the system. As more water rushes past turbine blades, more electricity is produced. When we finally settle in and use our remote controls to unplug for the night, huge gates close and turbines spin to a halt. In the morning, turbines are revived by the same call of alarm clocks that beckons a nation to rise. Water molecules begin their morning commute and push through turnstile-like turbines to help ensure their human masters can ride subways to work.

The hydropower facility at Holyoke Dam currently has a system to let anadromous fish pass and, in a reversal of fortune, was a critical cog in the restoration engine that has a future as tenuous as the salmon's. Dams on smaller tributaries contributed spawning fish that made their way up various fish ladders in the watershed. However, Holyoke was the principal place where returning adult salmon were nabbed and introduced to a broodstock program to help restore populations. During spring runs of anadromous fish, a lift system originally installed in 1955 operates to raise one of two gigantic water-filled buckets crammed with fish. It is quite a sight to see and the power company that owns the facility runs an educational program for anyone who wants to drop by when fish are migrating. Visitors, many on school fieldtrips, and fisheries biologists watch through large glass windows as hundreds of shad, sea lamprey and their friends pass upstream. These spectators desperately search for returning salmon. In previous years, when one was spotted, the facility went into lock-down mode; gates were closed and staff sprang into action until the fish was safely detained for breeding purposes. Unfortunately, it is unclear what will happen when a salmon is spotted in the future because the stocking program is in jeopardy.

In 2012, I was fortunate to be present on a banner day. A total of forty-one Atlantic salmon were captured, which represented more than half of the fish observed at the facility, and one-third of all salmon captured in the entire watershed that year. I was lucky enough to see three individuals, the first adult Atlantic salmon I had ever seen returning to spawn. Even though the surroundings were artificial, it was very exciting, but tempered by the realization that a hundred-odd fish is not many for a watershed that covers eleven thousand square miles of New England. In fact, the numbers of returning salmon on the Connecticut River were so low that no wild breeding was expected. It was for this reason that salmon were carefully removed and trucked to waiting hatcheries. It is also worth pointing out that Holyoke Dam, far upstream of the mouth of the Salmon River, cannot account for the loss of the fish on this small Connecticut river. So why had this waterway lost its source of inspiration?

Not surprisingly, the Salmon River has its own history of dams. In places, there are piles of rocks along the shore that give hints of a more industrious past. By the mid-1700s, waterpower facilities dammed the Salmon River and greatly reduced the flow of anadromous fish.[3] One site occupied a small falls along the river where slices of ancient bedrock jut through water at low flow. Students and I frequently visit here and observe large blocks of cut stone that remain along both shores of the river. An opening in the stone wall divulges a place where water was once ushered down a canal to a hungry waterwheel. Nearby resides a shell of a building that now resembles a bombed-out European factory from the 1940s. The roof has collapsed and workers and windows are gone. However, the legacy of the building, its dam and the death it inflicted can still be read in the waters of the river. Salmon no longer leap the small falls to complete their journey.

The Salmon River watershed contains a host of other dams, most notably downstream at Leesville. This is a modern-looking structure, but it has existed in various forms since 1763. The impoundment is no Grand Coulee Dam, but even a twelve-foot wall of concrete is enough to end a fish's search for home. Luckily for salmon and its anadromous friends, the dam at Leesville contains a fish ladder that provides a glimmer of hope for those adult fish able to decipher the secrets of this manmade contraption. This fish ladder and hundreds like it on other dams throughout the region are the result of efforts by state and federal fisheries biologists, lobbying by environmental groups, and urging by fishing organizations. Many of these folks would have preferred to rip the dam out, but that was not possible.

Most of the benefactors of the fish ladder are not salmon, but one of the most repulsive-looking animals on the planet, the last thing a parent and toddler wading in the river's swimming holes would want to see. One look at the nearly yard-long, dark-olive, snakelike fish with its concentric rings of teeth would send any unsuspecting child screaming from the water. Several times even I had to fight the urge to abandon the river when I looked down and saw this overgrown leech of a fish slowly undulating between my rubber-clad feet. In truth, I had little to fear from a lamprey completing its reproductive cycle. My defensive instinct was unwarranted as I suspiciously watched a fish that was in the midst of putting my own parental sacrifices to shame. The once-menacing parasite of the seas was slowly disintegrating in the freshwaters as it worked its way up the Salmon River through the fish ladder, under the covered wooden structure of Comstock Bridge, up past small falls and into the quieter waters of its birthplace where I eventually encountered it. Here it used its mouth and deteriorating teeth to move pebbles as it quietly prepared a bed for its offspring. After it laid its eggs and completed its reproductive mission, it would silently siphon in its last breath and its lifeless body would gently float back downstream with the rest of its returning class and undoubtedly wash up on downstream banks. It is usually in this sad final state that my student companions and I find lamprey. Intellectually we might know to marvel at these creatures, but it is still hard not to shudder at the sight of one. We usually poke the lifeless body with sticks, turn it over to gawk at its hideous mouth and kick it back into the river in a hopeless attempt to erase it from our memory. Despite the remarkable life history of this fish, it is not the type of organism that rallies strong support to save a river. In fact, people's reaction to the fish is so negative that the U.S. Fish and Wildlife Service contracted out for a publication to try to educate people about the ecological value of the species.[4]

In contrast, the Atlantic salmon secures multitudes of private donations and heaps of government protection. Fishing clubs and environmental groups sound the war cry and carry the flag for this fish. Hundreds of school children learn about salmon life cycles and sit on green vinyl seats in yellow buses trekking to isolated places where the fish can be occasionally spotted making its return. And thanks to hard work by numerous state and federal fisheries biologists, researchers in private and public labs, and countless volunteers supplied by nonprofit organizations like Trout Unlimited, American Rivers, and the Nature Conservancy, salmon began trying to stage a comeback in the Connecticut River watershed. Those efforts brought back a little credibility to the promise in the name of the Salmon River, which once again contained salmon. And as in the days before the dams made their mark, those salmon were swimming to the ocean as wide-eyed youth and returning to the river as well-traveled adults. Personnel from DEEP and the U.S. Fish and Wildlife Service carefully stood guard along the way. Signs posted on trees pointed out distinguishing features between young trout and salmon to educate anglers and ensure release of the elusive anadromous artifact. Members of local chapters of Trout Unlimited tried to avoid these salmon as they cast their flies at trout, and they carefully released any salmon unlucky enough to participate in the fishing game. They also spent spare time educating others about the value of salmon, fought to remove dams, worked to improve water quality, and lobbied to restore salmon to the watershed. The Atlantic salmon is a fish with many friends.

The return of the Atlantic salmon follows much the same life history as the lamprey, but with a slightly less fateful end on many occasions. Salmon belong to the biological family *Salmonidae*, which has inhabited Earth for at least one hundred million years.[5] Eggs are laid in nests of rocks swept clean of silt and other small sediments by the tails of caring mothers. Young emerge after six weeks from between golf ball–size stones and proceed to spend one to three years as juveniles in their freshwater home. Eventually, fingerlings turn into smolt and race downstream against internal biological clocks to reach saltwater before their bodies complete a complex transformation. Once at sea, these fish feed and grow, usually for two years, before returning to rivers in spring. These fish do not immediately reproduce, but instead wait until autumn. After females lay eggs and males fertilize them with milt, both attempt to recondition themselves and return to sea. Eventually, they may return to the same place and repeat the spawning process. It is an amazing story, and each adult salmon has to overcome million-to-one odds to tell it.

Unfortunately, the numbers of adult salmon annually returning to the river that bears its name left a great deal to be desired. Biologists used observation windows and cameras to search desperately for the prized symbols of the region's healthier past. In some years no adults scaled the fish ladder. In other years, like 2011, only a single mature salmon was observed in the Salmon River. It is very difficult for a single adult salmon to reproduce successfully — but, surprisingly, it is not impossible. While juvenile females are not yet strong enough to produce eggs, an adult female can have her eggs fertilized by a juvenile male who has yet to learn about the secrets of the deep ocean. The chances of this happening, however, are not good. In fact, the probability of success is so low that fisheries biologists decreed that scientific intervention was needed. Salmon that made their way to the Leesville fish ladder were carefully trapped and trucked to one of the region's hatcheries. Caution dictated that only through carefully manipulated and monitored reproduction could salmon be restored to the Connecticut River watershed. Unfortunately, the restoration effort was mostly a story of science fiction.

Salmon returns were so disappointingly low that in July 2012 the U.S. Fish and Wildlife Service announced a discontinuation of salmon stocking in the Connecticut River watershed and a reevaluation of their efforts in the Merrimack River watershed to the east.[6] This is part of a movement that suggests species protection efforts should be focused in the watersheds where success is most likely.[7] Salmon restoration in the Connecticut River was just not sustainable. The authorities were forced into their decision because Tropical Storm Irene, perhaps fueled by global warming, demolished a key hatchery on Vermont's White River in 2011. Scientists previously voiced concerns that global warming would render the Connecticut River watershed uninhabitable for salmon, but nobody predicted climate could devastate restoration efforts in such dramatic fashion. It now appears that salmon will once again disappear from the watershed and the Salmon River.

Brook trout are a distant relative of Atlantic salmon and a fish known to most freshwater anglers. Brook trout are native inhabitants of northeastern waterways, including the Salmon River. They are closely related to lake trout, and both types of fish are actually misnamed, because in fact they trace their lineage to the char family of fish. Char inhabit cold freshwater like true trout. They genetically diverged from Atlantic salmon more than five million years ago.[8] Today they occupy only a portion of their range in many watersheds because of competition from two introduced species of trout. Brown trout are more closely related to Atlantic salmon, but were not found on this continent until enterprising anglers introduced them from Germany and Great Britain at the end of the nineteenth century. Brown trout were also followed by immigrants from the West Coast in the form of rainbow trout. Rainbow trout are also genetically dissimilar to Atlantic salmon, and their family history is linked to various types of Pacific salmon species found in northwestern United States and Canada. Like char, they were genetically independent from Atlantic salmon more than five million years ago.[9] Unlike the great biologic gathering of dinosaurs that occurred with the geologic formation of Pangaea, it took human hands to formally introduce these various salmonid species. Hatcheries sprouted up all over the region by 1900 and poured fish into every conceivable waterway, spurred by hopes that brown trout and rainbow trout would provide exciting new angling opportunities. Soon rainbow and brown trout took over larger rivers, and native brook trout became a marginalized species in places where they once thrived. Scientists now report that "a growing body of evidence suggests nonnative trout can substantially change ecosystems wherever they are present."[10] Each year, hatcheries pour out millions of exotic invasive brown and rainbow trout to meet demands of rod-toting citizens. Because of perceived differences in the level of ease with which brook, rainbow, and brown trout are caught, many anglers express preferences that have little to do with environmental realities. Although anglers still catch trout in large numbers, for brook trout and many other native species, brown trout and rainbow trout are alien invaders that disrupt the ecological balance that once existed. As a result, Atlantic salmon, brook trout, and lamprey of the modern Salmon River live in a very different reality from their forbearers.

If salmon are ever to make a full comeback, large numbers of stocked young must survive and prosper. Unfortunately, rainbow and brown trout can be aggressive feeders. As an author of one fishing book stated, "Wherever it travels, the rainbow proves to be a good colonist, adapting itself to hostile conditions and alien food stocks."[11] Unfortunately, the term "alien food stocks" refers to the propensity for these trout to eat species unfamiliar to rainbows but native to the environment. They compete against each other, their own young, brook trout, and salmon. They are also known to directly feed on small salmon fry and eggs. Young salmon raised in hatcheries a short time and stocked along the Salmon River for restoration purposes battled against brown and rainbow trout that were fed in hatcheries for much longer and reached larger sizes. If we compare national salmon-stocking to trout-stocking efforts, more than twice as many salmon are introduced, but they account for less than half the total mass of the trout-stocking effort.[12] That's because although salmon are a larger species when fully grown, hatchery trout placed in the nation's waters are on average almost six times as large as most released salmon. More effort and food resources are expended on growing trout to support game fisheries than salmon. At times, young salmon stocked to rivers become meals for newly stocked adult trout that may only live one or two weeks in the watershed. These stocked trout are continuously resupplied as part of a complex system of river management designed to placate anglers and benefit the state's economy. The same agencies tasked with reviving the annual ascension of salmon upriver, compete against their own efforts by stocking trout that reduce the chances that salmon young will survive to adulthood. Salmon are stocked to feed our imagination about the future possibility of a wild river restored, while brown and rainbow trout are stocked to feed an insatiable hunger for good angling opportunities here and now.

~ ~ ~ The Salmon River and its numerous tributaries offer an amazing outdoor classroom to learn about geologic history, forces of nature, and the power of flowing water. Students are usually happy enough just to get off campus and enjoy a little sunshine, but the river leaves a more lasting mark on most. One of the more memorable of these trips occurred on a cool spring day. The warmth of the sunshine made cold meltwater seeping from the banks just bearable. The plan for this lab was to collect and catalog various macroinvertebrates and assess the life the river held. Although the list of aquatic critters found would seem commonplace to fly anglers, most of the students had never looked carefully at life hidden below the undulating surface. It was as much fun watching students scour the stream bed as it was analyzing what they found. Several students excitedly plunged their arms into the flow to extract rocks carpeted with a thin veneer of dark green growth. Eyes carefully searched nooks and cracks in cobbles for tiny aquatic bugs clinging to lunch spots. Various types of stoneflies, mayflies and caddis flies soon lined the base of several stainless steel bowls. Other students showed much more trepidation. They pointed to strange creatures in the bottom of smooth bowls, but quickly withdrew fingers at the first sign of movement. Boredom was nonexistent. Various lab groups vied in an unspoken competition to collect the greatest number and variety of species. Their thoroughness was both entertaining and utilitarian.

One important lesson learned from the day's haul told of the general status of the aquatic ecosystem. In ecology, macroinvertebrates serve as a bit of a canary in a coal mine when it comes to riverine health. Various species are referred to as indicator species because they have a high sensitivity to pollution and other types of human disturbance that soon shrink or swell populations as conditions vary. Our survey of the relative abundance of macroinvertebrates told us that the Blackledge River was a fairly healthy place to grow up as an aquatic insect. The presence of freshwater mussels was an even better sign. As you can imagine, an animal like a mollusk that spends its time living in and among sand and gravel, filtering water through its body and slowly absorbing dissolved nutrients to make a shell, prefers a world free of pollution. They also disappear in places where massive volumes of sediment rapidly bury the channel bottom. We spotted a few freshwater mussels here and there as further evidence that whatever was interfering with salmon recovery, it was probably not chemical pollution or instability of the river's bed and banks. Although freshwater mussels are a good sign, concerns still persist about excessive erosion, which plays a factor in how governments approach river management. It also heavily influenced past thinking.

One of the first projects I initiated when I arrived in Connecticut as a raw recruit from graduate school was to visit rivers and streams throughout New England to measure dimensions of pools. I knew it was a simple project, easy to get going and had the added benefit of exposing me to many local brooks and creeks. Veteran's Fishing Area in the middle of the Salmon River watershed was one of many sites I saw that year for the first time. It is one of the most heavily stocked and fished half miles of stream in Connecticut.[13] As the name implies, it is a place where expert anglers, some with war experience, happily take on waves of new trout draftees born and bred for battle. At that point in my career, I was unaware of a complex history of river manipulation that involved decades of efforts by anglers, fisheries biologists, and engineers. And as luck would have it, Veteran's Fishing Area is not just some random trickle of water; it is a place on the Blackledge River with a deep history and tradition with regard to river restoration.

Four years before America entered World War II, G. W. Hunter, a little-known and largely forgotten researcher from nearby Wesleyan University, contacted two scientists from the Connecticut State Board of Fisheries and Game with an idea.[14] He was concerned about a previous state fisheries survey that indicated two-thirds of all stocked trout failed to survive winter. He also followed massive federal developments in the nation and wondered how devices installed in the 1930s by the Civilian Conservation Corp, or CCC for short, and the U.S. Forest Service impacted rivers. He later stated that despite a lack of substantiation, "it has been considered self evident that these devices did, indeed, improve conditions for trout."[15] In 1937, he proposed a project. Shortly before the German Blitzkrieg exposed the inadequacy of static defensive positions along the Maginot Line to withstand mobile attack, workers from a CCC camp a few miles downstream from Veteran's Fishing Area on the banks of the Salmon River began to install immobile wood and rock dams, current deflectors, and habitat cover structures to battle the ever-migrating river. Then he and his partners tested the scheme to see if it worked. They published one of the first studies in the country that systematically looked at the impact of these instream structures on macroinvertebrates. The study took place just a few hundred yards downstream from where my students scoured the bed on their own macroinvertebrate scavenger hunt. The results showed promising signs with apparent improvement in temperature, oxygen levels, and macroinvertebrate populations. Although I did not learn about this study until several years after I first visited the site, remarkably I stumbled upon the exact structures the CCC installed. Somehow the devices survived six decades, and now I too began to wonder how they impacted the river.

Habitat-improvement structures like the lunkers recently placed in the Jeremy River have a design life of about twenty years, but in the 1930s ten years was the goal. The estimate is based more on an economic justification for a project than field experience. Engineers and project managers need to deliver something that lasts more than a year or two to secure funding, but do not want to promise too much. Practitioners historically settled on design lives somewhere in the decade or two range and then did their best to estimate the size of flood that would be expected within that time frame. Structures they devised were built to withstand those size floods. If the project lasted the full lifespan, engineers fulfilled their technical promise. However, structures can survive for longer, occasionally more than one hundred years. Perhaps that suggests taxpayers are getting more bang for the buck. But although structures might survive, that does not mean they are functioning as they were initially intended. A wounded structure may do more harm than good. The river might alter course and attack the device from an exposed flank. A stationary bank project can later turn into a major river blockage when and where the channel shifts. Today, Veteran's Fishing Area is left with a decaying assemblage of static structural soldiers still fighting a battle against a migrating river that employs fluid tactics. It is a situation that should have ended long ago. Unfortunately, no one was standing guard.

As I began to poke around I noticed several different structural designs. I eventually found a 1992 U.S. Forest Service manual that showed blueprints of identical structures and explained their purpose.[16] But the structures outdated the manual by more than fifty years. I did more digging and eventually stumbled upon federal design manuals from 1969, 1952, 1936, and 1935.[17] I saw almost identical designs throughout the years. It was apparent that not much had changed design-wise in more than half a century. But more than sixty years of active service on the river had certainly worn on the structures' wood and stone.

When river restoration was first proposed in the mid-1880s, there was a concern that loss of streamside plants resulted in a loss of fish habitat along riverbanks. In the 1930s, the solution to the problem was to build dual-purpose revetment and cover structures. Logs were driven into banks perpendicular to flow. Planks were then placed on top of the logs and nailed in place with giant steel rods to form a long line of shelves protruding from the banks into the water. Wooden shelves provided cover for trout to utilize, but they could not withstand the onslaught of floods. To stabilize the wood and fortify banks, angular rocks were placed on top of planks and extended back into the banks. These designs were used along the outside curve of natural meanders that existed in the area. If this layout reminds you of the shelved lunker structures installed in the watershed by the state more than sixty years later, perhaps you won't be surprised that, in general construction and design of purpose, they are almost identical to the modern devices a few miles away. Plywood replaced planks, but otherwise there are few differences.

When I studied the treated meanders, I noticed that the underlying sediment was highly compact and erosion-resistant material deposited by glaciers seventeen thousand years earlier. I questioned whether these banks needed to be protected from erosion in the first place. I also paid attention to the structures themselves. The planks were now mostly AWOL. A few decayed sawed remains were all that were left to suggest the original design. In contrast, the support logs and steel rods mostly survived and now threatened to impale any clumsy angler unlucky enough to stumble upon them. Sadly, rocks that once supplied stability, now posed the main problem. Without the wooden planks, stones collapsed into the channel and formed an angled buttress of rock. Few trees rooted among the boulder rubble further up on the banks. The result of the CCC effort was to create long sections of bank that contained none of the trout cover naturally supplied by roots and overhanging banks.[18] Ultimately, these stream-improvement structures had destroyed the specific habitat they were built to provide. Sadly, lunkers installed more recently probably will create similar long-term problems.

Just upstream from the CCC lunkers, the state relocated the entire river when it completed a highway in the 1950s. Although this was not uncommon, the state did take some remarkable steps for the era, trying to compensate for lost habitat by creating a rock-lined carbon copy of the meander bend that held the 1930s structures. However, rivers are hard to tame and changes in gradient and curviness, the river's sinuosity, can create unintended con-sequences. Eventually, during a major flood in the 1980s, the river blasted through a wall of stone designed to divert it and abandoned the artificial course.[19] Now, the Blackledge River flows through a strange assortment of reaches that date to different historic times, and long sections of engineered river lay derelict. The site is still a favorite for trout anglers, but it is hard to find much that is natural in the aquatic landscape of today.

Almost ten years after I published two articles describing the discouraging processes at Veteran's Fishing Area, I took my graduate school mentor, Ellen Wohl, on a tour. The 1930s structures were still there, but something had changed. When I first collected data on these structures at the turn of the millennium, I noticed one enormous tree with undercut roots along a sec-tion of river that had thankfully been spared a stony revetment. It provided splendid cover habitat, but the tree did not look long for this world. I noticed the river slowly whittling away the earthen bank and was amazed that roots resisted the ravages of gravity. Ten years later, as we approached the site of the hemlock, it was evident that the stately old tree had finally surrendered. It now sat with roots clinging to one bank and its top limbs clawing the far side of the floodplain. Nevertheless, the riverine felling was far from a disas-ter. On the contrary, the tree formed the deepest pool and best cover habitat on that two-mile stretch of river. Even with good water clarity, it was impos-sible to see the eerily deep channel bed. Branches provided numerous places to hide, with ideal sanctuary for macroinvertebrates. I knew of at least forty stream-improvement structures in the same area. Ironically, the simple act of river erosion had accomplished stream improvements that scientific minds of the 1950s and ccc laborers in the 1930s could not. Erosion of banks was the solution to good aquatic habitat at this place, not a cause for its decline.

The Salmon River continues to supply me with these valuable learning opportunities. One fall semester, I took a group of eight students to the head of the Salmon River on a typical outing. Here was where the Blackledge and Jeremy Rivers both weave their way across a mostly flat expanse of land. As they each snake their way along, they both turn a blind corner and seem-ingly bump into each other by sheer good fortune. Downstream, the Salmon River shows little initial inclination to abandon these old wandering ways. It works its way in three gentle bends before striking smack into a hunk of bedrock that marks a change in attitude and altitude for the lower reach. It was just downstream from this peninsula of rock that we parked college vans and disembarked on our learning adventure.

My plan for the day was to show students around the river confluence, explain processes of lateral migration, look at meanders as they slowly eat away the outer edges of banks, and see how these changes are compensated for by new deposits of sediment on the inside of bends and on the floodplain. The undergraduates had geomorphic terms like *oxbow lake, meander bend, point bar, slump block,* and *paleostage indicator* floating in their minds as we arrived. My intent was to convince them that rivers are living entities with movements that involve not just currents, but sediments and the path of the eroded channel itself. Rivers constantly remake landscapes with daily changes that seem trivial at first. Flood waters carry pebble after pebble to new locations in a leisurely process that is only appreciable on a grander scale and longer time frame. Together these processes create channel complexity that houses the biodiversity of a healthy aquatic ecosystem. Little did I suspect that we would see more evidence for relocation of the river channel than for repositioning of its scaly inhabitants.

As soon as we reached the river, we peered into the depths of a pool formed by a stubborn stony impediment. The pool was lit by the low-angle sun of a clear mid-autumn afternoon. The golden light revealed trout slowly undulating below the surface in the cool waters of a living river channel. Their shapes were just visible above a chocolate brown bed in areas where reflections of red, orange, and yellow clad trees was faintest. Perhaps this would seem like a perfect advertisement for wild New England, but something was amiss. Despite water temperatures and flow conditions ideal for trout survival and dispersal, we saw not two or three trout, but close to a hundred. In a channel no wider than an abandoned country road hidden in the woods sat an assemblage of similar-sized, mindless bodies clustered together in an aberrant rectangular procession. The only other time I had seen so many trout all swimming together fin to fin was at a hatchery. If we could transport a lengthy hatchery run in its entirety into the river and magically dissolve away the cement walls, it is unlikely that the trout would be any better organized than the congregation before us. These fish were clearly unable to think outside the box!

Most good fishing stories pit the wise angler against a wily trout. But a cast into this pool was more likely to foul hook a trout than entice one to bite. Even the presence of nine dark silhouettes standing just along the shore did little to disperse this peaceful assembly. Eventually I coaxed everybody to follow me upriver to our appointed destiny with sediment and sinuosity. We immediately spotted an angler trolling the next upstream pool and privately chuckled at his poor choice of location. When we eventually returned to the site of our initial amazement, the trout were still there. Each fish was apparently content to search for sustenance surrounded by all its closest rivals.

As soon as I returned to campus, I called the local state hatchery and learned that these fish were stocked two weeks earlier as part of the 16,000 trout placed in that section of the river each year.[20] I had actually given the hatchery trout more credit and assumed they had been freed perhaps a day or two before our arrival. In hindsight, I should not have been surprised that approximately eighty weeks' worth of experience at the hatchery was not erased in a mere two weeks' time. Survival of these trout seemed doubtful if they did not quickly learn to disperse and find natural sources of food. Given the short life expectancy of a hatchery trout stuck in a river with a valley full of hungry anglers, it seems questionable if any of these fish would ever understand their wilder surroundings. I decided my spring class would include a fieldtrip to the hatchery where these trout were born and raised.

A few months later, many of the same students and several of their friends took a class titled River Environments and joined me on a short drive north of campus to one of the state's factories of fish. Quinebaug Hatchery contains several large buildings that house eggs, fry, fingerlings, and broodstock, and produces approximately six hundred thousand trout annually. Although the state fisheries agency claims to supply trout to meet demand, it is hard not to detect a sense of salesmanship in the display area open to visitors. The hatchery proudly displays a map with hundreds of blue, red, orange, and yellow pins that depict various stocking locations within the state. Each pin represents either five hundred or one thousand stocked trout. The map would shame even the martyred Saint Sebastian with the number of times it has been impaled. Further along the wall, the "Connecticut Fishing Wall of Fame" showed thirty-nine pictures of trophy fish proudly displayed by various anglers. A sign claimed that four hundred thousand freshwater anglers spend $140 million in Connecticut each year. The "Freshwater Fishes of Connecticut" exhibit held ten mounted fish including introduced brown and rainbow trout, and coho and kokanee salmon from the Pacific. Curiously missing was the indigenous Atlantic salmon. An adjacent wall contained a three-foot-long, twenty-six-pound hatchery brown trout mounted and displayed with a complete life history. A nearby sign read "Try fishing sometime yourself!"

The first time I visited the hatchery was actually one year earlier when my daughter and I were on our way to pan for fool's gold at Dinosaur State

Park run by the same agency. About the time we were poking around, trout stocking made the news on public radio. During a WNPR radio interview, the director of the Inland Fisheries Division for Connecticut said, "The reason the state stocks fish prior to opening day is because the demand for trout fishing exceeds the ability of wild populations to reproduce." But a quick survey of the hatchery and free publications it distributed revealed that to suggest the state plays no role in creating demand is misleading. For example, Connecticut stocked special trout parks with easy access to fishing for children, giving new meaning to the phrase "'hook 'em while they're young." In 2010, the state introduced the "Connecticut Hunting and Fishing Appreciation Day," cosponsored by three commercial outfitting companies and five sportsmen organizations. Fun activities for all ages included three instructional talks on angling, bait and fly-fishing coaching sessions, and kids' arts and crafts setups. One year earlier the director and his agency had hosted the "First Annual Trophy Fish Award Ceremony" to recognize anglers for catching freshwater and saltwater fish of qualifying size. The timing of the event was surprising, given the poor economy and general talk of funding cuts within Connecticut and the nation. The director was quoted on the associated state government website: "Fishing is an activity that can be enjoyed by the entire family and it can be done close to home. These awards demonstrate the excellent fishing opportunities that we have right here in Connecticut."[21] However, to provide excellent trout fishing requires massive stocking from this facility and its sister complex to the west. That sounds a bit like a circular argument to me: a bureaucratic version of whirling disease.

The real whirling disease is a parasite that infects trout, especially the widely introduced rainbow trout, and eventually forces the fish to swim round and round until they die from starvation or predation. The disease itself was accidentally imported from Europe along with brown trout. Stocking that serves as a salvation to anglers, may also lead to the ultimate demise of trout.

Although I had previously toured the public visitor section of Quinebaug Hatchery with my daughter, I had never been beyond the chain-link fence and locked doors to the heart of the facility. Because I called ahead and arranged a tour for educational purposes, a friendly hatchery manager was nice enough to lead us around. The first stop was just beyond the display area in a rather unassuming office space complete with wood paneling. The room contained one of the most crucial pieces of equipment for the entire facility, an inauspicious-looking computer intricately linked to the trout's food chain.

The hatchery feeds an average fish for approximately eighteen months before release. Consequently, this is a good place to watch about one million trout cumulatively eat approximately one ton of trout pellets per day. It was fascinating to learn how hatcheries feed these multitudes. The search for efficiency resulted in a system of computer-controlled, automatic feeders. At Quinebaug Hatchery, managers use a computer-mouse to remotely flip switches on 110 separate feeders. The only feeders not controlled by this silicon network are those for fry, which are raised in forty-eight hatch house tanks below smaller, mechanically controlled feeders. We could see their tanks through a large window in the office. The all-important broodstock who give birth to all the other trout rely on old-fashioned hand feeding from buckets. For the rest of the fish, it is high-technology fast food.

After hearing about the impressively efficient electronic food network, we passed through a series of doors and peered at a huge backup generator that serves as the trout's only salvation in the event of an electrical blackout. The hatchery manager explained that he lived at the facility to man the genera-tor because these trout were entirely reliant on flow provided by electrically powered, groundwater pumps on site. The water supply is ideal from the hatchery's perspective because the temperature remains consistently cool year round, providing optimal growing conditions. Following our brief encounter with the notably large but otherwise rather uninspiring diesel generator, we left the oily maintenance area, walked past racks where eggs are hatched and nosed around a few tanks designed to hold inch-long fry after their egg sac is absorbed. After glancing at a few thousand diminutive trout, we were off to see some bigger fish.

A short stroll outside from the main building, past the parking area for the hatchery trucks, sat a key component of the complex: a large building housing a total of thirty round tanks, each twenty feet in diameter and rearing approximately thirty thousand trout. Every tank contained a large blue inflow pipe and one automatic feeder. The sheet-metal structure was poorly lit by a series of fluorescent lights hung from steel girders. The walls and ceiling had a general beige and gray appearance. Large blue barrels of disinfectant lined one wall. The overall atmosphere was stark and dull look-ing, a far cry from the scenic beauty people often associate with trout. The building, erected to eliminate loss of fish to birds by enclosing the treasure for as long as possible, holds trout that never see the sun for the first half of their existence. These trout spend more hours per day in buildings than the anglers who use them as an excuse to escape their own indoor captivity.

When visitors enter this structure, they are required to step on a chemically treated mat to help ensure no diseases are transported inside. My fourteen students and I all dutifully wiped our feet upon arrival. The group showed a combination of excitement and skepticism. The rearing tanks were sunk into the floor with no railings and only about a one-foot lip showing. I watched as my students leaned over and peered down to see the fish, anxiously but unnecessarily imagining the fallout if someone fell in.

After inspecting the sunken tanks we were shown a large food storage area stacked with hundreds of bags of pellet food. The facility relied on a brand of aquafeed called Nelson's Sterling Silver Cup Fish Feeds. The storage zone smelled fishier than the room with trout — each bag, we learned, contained mostly processed herring. Briefly we stared at the reconstituted remains of millions of marine fish neatly wrapped in large tan paper sacks: the trout version of a brown-bag lunch. Soon, two hatchery personnel arrived and began the endless task of refilling automatic feeders. They slowly swung each feeder to the side and poured the contents of pellet bags into hoppers. After each device was set back in place over the trout, workers tested it to ensure that everything was ready. Trout quickly responded to the offering of pellets made visible by a radial pattern of splashes. Fins poked out above the surface and water splashed as the trout fought for a handful of pellets released in this tantalizing test run. Once the feeding system checked out, it was on to the next tank. We went on to the next building.

The next dimly lit room was the highlight of the fieldtrip. Weak lighting was automatically controlled and adjusted to control the spawning cycle for broodstock contained within long rectangular raceway walls raised about three feet above the cement floor. We were invited to lean over and look into one of many pens. The hatchery manager was an experienced tour guide who knew how to get a rise. As soon as we were all lined along the side of a tank full of rainbow breeders, he tossed a handful of food in. The upstream end of the concrete run erupted with fish spraying water and students in all directions. Heads ducked and bodies lunged for cover. The sound emanating from the students was a bit like the reaction on a rollercoaster when people hit the first big drop off. Soon students began to venture forward again with cell-phone-mounted cameras at the ready. The class observed the circus show at tanks that held brook and brown trout. Each time, the combination of splashing pellets, churning water, exposed flapping tails, musty smells, camera flashes, and student screams was priceless.

After our visit to the breeding stock, we enjoyed the slightly drizzly and gray weather that awaited us outside. The majority of the production area for the hatchery was outdoors, devoted to forty, fifty-foot-diameter tanks that hold fourteen thousand trout each. These individuals were beefier blokes than all but the broodstock. They were almost prepared to take DEEP's public transportation system from the trout version of a crowded inner city out to the suburbs of Connecticut. The outdoor pens were covered with an elaborate netting and fencing arrangement. We were informed that without netting, losses from birds could approach a hundred thousand fish a year. With a combined capacity for more than a half million fish outside alone, an efficient feeding system was a must for this part of the operation. Each tank got two automatic feeders. The rotating motion of the feeders closely resembled broadcast-fertilizer spreaders that many suburbanites push endlessly back and forth across their lawns to ensure the grass is not greener on the other side of the street. Overuse of fertilizers on lawns and agricultural fields constitutes a nonpoint source pollutant negatively impacting water quality in many of our nation's watercourses, like the Salmon River. Back at the hatchery, the spray of reconstituted marine species likely created a similar problem.

The constant cool temperatures of the water from the local groundwater aquifer result in remarkable trout growth at the hatchery. The manager informed us that surface-water hatcheries require up to twenty-six months for trout to reach stocking size, but here fifty-two-degree water and oxygen generators designed to maintain seven parts per million of dissolved oxygen can grow fish in just eighteen months. The associated survival rate for fish is 85 percent. Water is used and reused five times in various tanks before it passes under the fence. The other big facility in Connecticut manages to recycle water six times. The manager reported that the approximate food-to-fish conversion is 1.2 pounds of pellets per pound of trout. That means that more than 300 pounds of food fed to trout each day is not absorbed and could exit the runs as nutrient waste. Small settling tanks are used to extract some of these nutrients from the water. The hatchery also uses a sludge pond on-site to settle out other solids from rearing tanks, but nets and fences do not protect this area from wildlife. When we visited, the settling pond contained a swan and looked remarkably like a wetlands area. After passing through the settling tanks, water and any dissolved nutrients flow as runoff directly to the Quinebaug River, which lends its name to the facility. Based on the conversion of food to pounds of trout, over the course of a year, the facility could easily dump tons of excess nutrients into the local ecosystem beyond the fences.

The following spring, three students from the previous year's class asked me to help them escape from campus to do some river wading. I was more than happy to oblige, and we traveled back to the Salmon River to check out a few sights. Midway through the trip we pulled into the parking lot at the newly reconstructed Comstock Bridge just in time to see trout we visited the previous year at Quinebaug Hatchery discover the wilds of Connecticut. The lot was mostly full when we pulled in: three hatchery trucks, a small bus for volunteer stockers, and a bevy of automobiles from onlookers and eager anglers occupied most spots. We immediately noticed a man on top of a hatchery truck use a long-handled net to scoop out large trout. He then handed the net off to a line of volunteers who had established a bucket brigade just below the bridge to haul fish down a steep embankment. Once the net reached the water, trout were unceremoniously dumped into the Salmon River and allowed to orient themselves into the flow. We watched a few large fish gather their senses and slowly work their way up current. Meanwhile, just upstream of the bridge a pair of fly flingers gracefully looped long lengths of brightly colored floating filament and tossed temptations to trout underneath the covered span. Despite the anglers' clear talent for finding fish, the newly stocked trout did not immediately take the bait, either because they were too disoriented or because they still only recognized food in pellet form. However, later that day farther upriver, we saw bait fishermen haul in trout that perhaps had been in the water for an hour or so. Ironically, these anglers ended up spending more time in the watershed that day than the trout they caught.

Shortly after the spring Quinebaug Hatchery trip, my class and I drove through the gates of the most scientifically impressive hatchery I have ever visited. It was also the smallest facility and by far the least imposing. Most motorists on Route 32 in Palmer, Massachusetts, probably drive right past without much thought. A white-shingled hatchery building looked more like a house than a government facility. A small cluster of outside hatchery pens was easy to miss under an open-walled shelter. The sign for the Roger Reed State Fish Hatchery was small and inconspicuous. Perhaps drivers see the "No Visitors" warning and chain-link fence but not much else. The reason things were so different at Roger Reed was that the focus was not on sport fisheries; the spotlight was on Atlantic salmon and the associated restoration efforts. People who wanted to see a big, state-administered trout hatchery with a public visitor center continue a few miles down the road. However, we wanted to learn about hatchery genetics, state-of-the-art restoration work, and the life of an anadromous fish. Therefore, Roger Reed was the perfect place to start.

We were greeted by the manager, Dan Marchant. He was friendly, knowledgeable, and very happy to share his insight. He was the type of person who immediately impressed me with his intelligence and compassion. We learned that, unlike many trout hatcheries, Roger Reed placed a strong premium on encouraging wild traits in salmon broodstock. All were either captured on their spawning runs or were first-generation descendants of sea run fish. If a salmon or its parent had not displayed the genetic ability to swim to the ocean, survive for several years, and return to the watershed where it originated, the hatchery did not want it. There were strict regulations on how salmon were stripped of their eggs to avoid damage to the broodstock. There was also a conscious effort to avoid overcrowding broodstock, and the extra space was obvious when we peered into tanks. The salmon were large and notable. They swam continuously and shied away from us. The extra care and effort was due in large part to the small number of salmon the state and federal agencies had to work with. With so few anadromous fish to choose from, it was important to make each breeding pair count. In the past, every fish that made it to one of several capture stations, especially Holyoke Dam, was gingerly removed and transported to a system hatchery. The goal was to take all the genetic stock for the entire watershed and utilize it with scientific efficiency. If there is a salmon in the Connecticut River system, it is almost certain that it came from a hatchery like this one.

The hatchery building housed several small tanks where fry were looked after. The water supply passed through a series of ultraviolet and sand filters before pouring into tanks. The ceiling was a tangle of pipes that separately carried surface water and groundwater to each tub. Pollution levels in the effluent water were calculated based on food and metabolism to maintain concentrations dictated by a discharge permit. Still, nutrients left the site as a potential source of pollution. The number of fish per tank was small, and the degree of caretaking was high. When Dan Marchant talked, he made the fish sound less like a product. The broodstock were valued for their uniqueness, not their size and total egg output. I was impressed.

Soon after a potential breeder arrived at the hatchery it was evaluated. Each breeding fish was carefully checked for diseases. With small numbers of fish there was a danger that a malady would cripple the entire population. Therefore, state and federal hatcheries had, on occasion, tossed an entire year's worth of eggs to protect the remaining stock. After fish passed their physicals, they had a fin clipped for DNA analysis. Each fish was then mated with the most distant relative available. Scientists believed the best chance for Atlantic salmon was to produce a genetically viable subspecies that evolved for the specific challenges of each watershed. Watershed-specific adaptation for salmon was nothing new, but in the Connecticut River basin scientists needed to start from scratch. The crops of salmon were actually descendants from fish that returned to the Penobscot River in Maine. However, those transfers ended in 1993, and all salmon in the Connecticut River watershed currently originated from parents within the same drainage area. The hope was that almost twenty years of life in the new basin had started to rub off on salmon. Scientists ultimately anticipated that future offspring could learn to be better equipped for life in their specific environment than their parents. Ideally, every new generation became less like their Penobscot River ancestors and more like the Connecticut River fish of yore.

Unfortunately, small returns of Atlantic salmon with such a large federal and state investment raised concerns. Was it worth spending millions of dollars for a species that might never exist in large numbers in the river again? Was this an example of a failing government system? Surprisingly, it was our guide at Roger Reed who suggested that restoration efforts were about more than just salmon. Without the powerful image of this fish to support fish passage projects at dams, restoration work at impacted segments of river, and watershed-scale pollution control efforts, other anadromous species would be in much tougher shape. Shad runs might be in the hundreds instead of the hundreds of thousands. Even homely sea lamprey would be in decline. So, much like the panda bear, the California condor and the African lion, Atlantic salmon served as a bit of a loss leader for a restoration effort that was about much more than one species. Now that the U.S. Fish and Wildlife Service has bowed out of the effort and left it in states' hands, it will be interesting to see what future awaits the salmon and their friends with wanderlust.

Each year fish return to breed, and now our attention should also return to the Salmon River. We must realize that the breadth of attitudes on how best to use the river is as far ranging as the anadromous fishes' nomadic paths. Should we take an active role in undoing physical damage to the river wrought by centuries of human development or let the river slowly and unpredictably work to erase these scars? Should governments work to bring back species of trout and salmon that may be inevitably doomed in the ever-warming watershed or let invasive species of trout continue to act as a shoddy replacement for lost fish? Do we invite as many people as possible to enjoy this special place, even if it spells the end for some aquatic species? If access is restricted to the river for ecological reasons, who is allowed to enter and what are they permitted to do? This list of questions is just a small sampling of the types of issues that face this and other rivers nationwide. Often, the quest for trout plays a major role in how these rivers are managed. The story of the Salmon River is told time and time again across the country: damages done, species lost, and an uncertain understanding of how to best secure a promising future for these thousands of special places.

CHAPTER TWO

First-Class Entertainment

*The quality of the trout fishing — not of the fish — has sadly deteriorated
in some of our moorland rivers to which the "working-man angler" has found
his way in vastly increasing numbers. I do not want to appear to take up a
snobbish attitude . . . but if we are to deal with plain facts there is no blinking
the truth that the "working-class angler's" indifference to the best possibilities
of trout fishing is, in many instances, ruining possibilities for others.*

~ W. CARTER PLATTS, 1927

*I*f I happen to stand by a river some day and hear two well-clad anglers talk about poached salmon, chances are they will not be exchanging recipes. Wealthy anglers have concerned themselves about the "theft" of fish from "their" streams for centuries. In fact, laws prohibiting poaching have existed since the sixteenth century in some countries. Similarly, when I hear a particular river is "first-class trout water," it might apply in more than one way. The fishing might be great for all to enjoy, or good fishing might be reserved solely for the upper crust. Often both situations pertain and the fishing is fantastic if one has the means to enjoy it. Beginning in the nineteenth century, battles over public access to fishing and poaching reached new heights in America. As railroads connected more people to more places, blocks of land were increasingly withdrawn from development by wealthy urbanites as their summer retreats. Today, some people claim these were the first acts of environmental visionaries, while others see it as proof that class has its advantages. Either way, the story of how wealth is expressed through fishing is worth a careful examination.

On Long Island sometime between 1823 and 1827, Daniel Webster, the famed senator from Massachusetts and future secretary of state, caught the world's largest brook trout at an impressive fourteen and a half pounds near Sam Carman's inn, which specialized in housing anglers from Manhattan, on Carman's River in South Haven, New York. Webster was reportedly obsessed with this fish and made numerous trips to catch it.[1] Webster finally caught the behemoth — after he was summoned from the middle of a church service by a slave who had been instructed to watch for the fish. The trout was eventually immortalized in story and also as a wooden-replica weathervane atop the church where Webster had impatiently waited for word of the fish. I can imagine the big impression the world's largest brook trout had on other anglers living in Manhattan. People soon made pilgrimages to see the trout-topped church and the famed river of the legend's birth.

Although Webster had caught his prize, his desire was not quenched. The incident, in fact, prompted Webster and his friends — future president Martin Van Buren, railroad pioneers John and Edmund Stevens, and industrialists Philip Hone and Walter Browne — to buy fifteen hundred acres and Carman's Inn.[2] This effort evolved into the Suffolk Club in 1858, the region's first officially organized sporting club with grounds, facilities, and nonresidential membership. The fifteen-member association owned the three-story clubhouse and a hatchery. It was considered the wealthiest fishing club in the country for its size.[3] Original members of the club included the son of President Van Buren as well as William Butler Duncan II, president of the Mobile and Ohio Railroad. With a site easily accessible to New York City by way of the Long Island Railroad, the Suffolk Club enticed visitors, including Theodore Roosevelt in 1915.[4] The club even spurred a local boom for palatial estates to support angling and hunting outings.[5] It was the start of a trend where wealthy urbanites used fishing and hunting as a way to establish their social credentials and escape the ills of cities. A century after revolutionaries evicted the hand of English monarchs from American soil, the wealthiest and most powerful families in this young country were desperately trying to emulate the aristocratic ways of the old empire.

Once social status and fishing prowess became linked, it was a race to keep up with the Joneses. Speaking of which, William Floyd-Jones was a member of that well-off family of Joneses who inspired the phrase.[6] He was also an angler who, before 1850, controlled a seven-mile section of Massapaqua Creek on Long Island near New York City. He stocked the creek and millpond and kept the public out. Farther to the east, approximately midway between Massapequa Creek and Carman's River, is a watershed that best exemplifies the role that exclusive clubs played during the late 1800s. The Connetquot River is not particularly long or large, which made it attractive as a trout fishing destination for wading anglers. Just above the head of tide sat a small gristmill, erected in 1750, accompanied by a long arcing pile of earth and stone that dammed the river and damned its anadromous inhabitants from migrating to the sea. Seventy years later, a second building, known initially as Snedecor's Tavern, was added. The inn specialized in housing anglers and was situated a long cast from the large millpond. With a railway line to New York City just through the woods, the location was ideal for urbanites to quickly escape for hunting and fishing. However, in Snedecor's old tavern where Webster once stayed on his eastward quest for the great trout, changes were about to take place.

A group called the South Side Sportsmen's Club emerged immediately after the Civil War with fishing and hunting on their minds. When the inn became too crowded, these men bought it outright and quickly amassed almost thirty-five hundred acres in the hamlet of Oakdale. The river provided fish and waterfowl, and the surrounding land had the upland bird habitat the club members wanted. The old mill was closed, but the building and dam were retained because they added a nice rustic charm to the postcard view members wanted. Apparently, the loss of anadromous fish, which included trophy sea-run brook trout, was offset by the advantages of having a large reservoir where trout could grow large and waterfowl would tend to gravitate. The most eminent original member of the club was Charles Lewis Tiffany, founder of the famed jewelry store.[7] He was eventually joined by some of the most powerful men in the country; the list included Andrew Carnegie, J. P. Morgan, and William Vanderbilt. Frederick William Vanderbilt was another member best known for his financial exploits as director of three transportation giants, the New York Central Railroad, the Pittsburg and Lake Erie Railroad, and the Chicago and Northwestern Railroad. Other members, whose names are not as well known, were just as rich and powerful: John Steward Kennedy, a childless railroad mogul and financier who gave away roughly half of his $60 million fortune, about $1.5 billion in today's dollars, upon his death in 1909; Bayard Cutting, another railroad manager, financier, and lawyer; Fredrick Gilbert Bourne, president of the Singer Sewing Machine Company; and finally, Henry Baldwin Hyde, founder of the world's largest insurance company, The Equitable Life Assurance Society of the United States.

The club invited other prominent individuals to visit, including then president Ulysses S. Grant and General William Tecumseh Sherman.[8] Future politics were influenced through the tangled web of the Roosevelt clan. In 1870, the highly cultured South Side Sportsmen's Club began the culturing of trout. First they tried a hatchery below the gristmill, then one on an adjacent creek. They finally decided on an impressive set of runs and buildings a mile north of the clubhouse, which were used to raise brook, brown, and rainbow trout and Pacific salmon at one time or another. They invited the founder of the New York State Fish Commission, Robert Barnwell Roosevelt, to see the process.[9] Roosevelt, an early conservationist, was at different times a U.S. congressman, treasurer of the Democratic National Committee, and minister to The Hague. He also heavily influenced his nephew, Theodore Roosevelt. James Roosevelt Sr. was another club member and father of Franklin Delano Roosevelt, the other future president. His older half-brother, James Roosevelt Roosevelt, joined the club in 1899. As time would show, the two Roosevelt presidents tremendously impacted the manner in which rivers in this country were managed.

The club followed an old English aristocratic practice of hiring keepers to monopolize property resources and keep the public at bay. These keepers, or watchers, were essentially a combination of gardener and armed guard more than happy to use violence when the need arose. After the club was founded, the surrounding area became an enclave for millionaires. Bourne owned a mansion with a thousand acres, and William Vanderbilt established a nine-hundred-acre estate called Idle Hour a short carriage ride from the clubhouse. It sat near the club's private railroad station across the river from Cutting's impressive summer place, where I found it a fun challenge to count the number of chimneys. I tallied about seventeen examples. Both Vanderbilt's and Cutting's summer getaways are places built to impress: places that make ordinary people feel small.

The Suffolk Club and South Side Sportsmen's Club spawned other Long Island clubs, including the Wyandanch Club and Nissequogue Club, both located a few miles north on the Nissequogue River. All four clubs selected rivers with millponds and, in some cases, built their own impoundments. When fishing was less than perfect, they built hatcheries and stocked exotic species of game fish. They also began to physically modify their river to improve fishing. They often fished their river in the English style from wooden platforms that extended over water like small docks, the common etiquette for the period for people with uncommon wealth.[10]

These Long Island examples highlight a basic pattern for the spread of fishing clubs. Pioneering city anglers with time and money to spare braved long, bumpy wagon rides, hired local guides, and lived for a few weeks in rustic conditions to fly fish for trout. Inevitably, they had great fishing success because few others could afford to match their outlays. In various social clubs in New York City and new sportsmen's journals sprouting up, they bragged and published their exploits, which increased interest in these adventures. More and more gentlemen anglers with Izaak Walton's famous book, *The Compleat Angler*, in one hand and a fishing rod in the other tried to establish themselves by catching the largest number or biggest specimen of trout they could find. Soon inns popped up on famous fishing waters to house these wealthy wanderers. When the crispiest of the upper crust arrived years later and found inns packed and streams crowded with city dwellers, they bought the establishments and surrounding lands for themselves and kicked everyone else out. The most affluent often organized themselves into exclusive clubs to rub elbows with those of a similarly high social status. Decades later, these clubs were canonized for protecting streams and the trout they contained, which is a claim that needs a bit more scrutiny.

Motivated by the desire to save large catches for members, clubs bragged that they prevented overfishing and preserved watersheds with private ownership. However, it was the fish, not the rivers, they wanted to safeguard.

Dams they owned or built usually blocked anadromous fish passage, even including large sea-run brook trout similar to Webster's behemoth. But from an angler's perspective, dams with screened outlets prevented large stocked fish from leaving watersheds and monopolized trout for better year-round fishing. Almost all clubs built their own hatcheries and began to plant exotic species of trout even after watersheds were supposedly saved from overfishing by the masses. Why hatcheries were needed when club memberships were often extremely low is a question that will unfortunately remain unanswered. In three cases, clubs owned the land until a growing tax burden outstripped the desire for trout, so they sold the land to New York and only then was the public welcome. In response, clubs are credited with saving rivers from the market forces of development. In reality, club actions were not part of some grand aspiration of members to save the wilderness for future generations, especially not generations of hoi polloi. Land was held until it was no longer valuable to them, then it was discarded. It was a trend also common with logging businesses in the nineteenth century.

Today there is a major misconception about the state of the land left behind that seems to be perpetuated by modern-day anglers. Nick Karas wrote *Brook Trout* in 2002 and credited the South Side Sportsmen's Club with land preservation and said; "only a private club, with its wealth, could afford to maintain the river and its surrounding lands in as pristine a state as when it had been purchased."[11] It is clear that much of the land would be covered with houses if wealthy Manhattanites had not invested in hunting and fishing. But the word "pristine" carries a good deal of weight that needs justification. When I visited the Connetquot River State Park Preserve with my daughter, we saw the primary reservoir. Upstream, a second concrete dam and reservoir supplied water to the hatchery via a channelized river that ended in a complex series of concrete spillways and chutes. As we walked the grounds, abandoned concrete channels and earthen canals connected forest and river and were part of an even more extensive hatchery system in the past. Both upstream and downstream sections of the Connetquot River included wooden platforms for fishing and banks with well-worn trails. Riverbanks were very uniform, probably because they were reworked to provide ease of passage. The middle of the sacred river contained stone dams and half-dams, similar to CCC structures in the Salmon River watershed, to scour out more places for trout to reside. Trees were secondary growth with occasional open fields and wide grassy lanes penetrating the woods perpendicular to the hatchery road. These manufactured habitats benefited upland birds and hunters who sought them. Even Karas admitted the club's grounds contained "well-manicured banks, trimmed trees, man-made pools."[12] My definition of a pristine river does not include modified banks, wooden platforms, small dams, and stocked exotic invasive species.

The misrepresentation of the Connetquot ecosystem is not a solitary example. Karas praised the multi-dammed Nissequogue River and claimed that "like the Connetquot, it has been preserved in near-pristine state."[13] According to dictionary definitions, *pristine* should describe an area uncorrupted by civilization. But, once again, Karas's use of the term refers solely to the quality of trout angling. Coincidently, *corruption* and *civility* were terms associated with many of the millionaire club members. Their business approaches often negatively impacted watersheds, a fact raised by contemporaneous anglers in fishing magazines. Rivers in Long Island were just another holding in club members' massive portfolios, and their actions to remake landscapes produced exclusive retreats that were anything but pristine.

~ ~ ~ If remodeling rivers was an isolated practice on Long Island, perhaps it would not bear mentioning. However, finding the perfect trout stream soon became an obsession for many, and then a management project. North of Manhattan rests the famed Catskill and Adirondack regions, while the Poconos lay slightly west. With most good Long Island waters in private hands by the 1850s, new generations of anglers turned to these more distant hills to repeat patterns already set. Native American groups that fished for trout for subsistence using traditional netting methods were displaced by early European settlers who tried to scratch out an agricultural living and also caught trout for food via a myriad of methods. Eventually, urban anglers explored these distant waters and documented every trout caught. Books are littered with accounts of small clusters of men catching hundreds of fish in a matter of days, seemingly recording every single large fish caught over the last two hundred years.[14] Local entrepreneurs soon opened inns and hotels that catered to anglers. As access to fishing waters expanded with improved road and railroad networks, pressure on fish populations increased. Eventually, the wealthiest anglers monopolized resources using business tactics perfected in the industries and railroads they commanded. They kicked out the masses, squeezing them onto a dwindling supply of public waters. Soon the few remaining public places were overrun with so many anglers that fishing declined dramatically. Fishing advocates complained about declines in fish stock as a result of overfishing and asked for legal catch limits. Clubs pointed to these declines, reaffirmed their role in protecting trout by excluding public fishing, and instigated artificial propagation to rebuild fish populations on their waters. Stocking of exotic species caused additional unintended consequences, often changing species distributions of native fish, especially brook trout. Each time a new place was ruined by overexploitation, anglers would hear of huge trout and large hauls of other fish on some new distant river. And each time they did, they swarmed this new area until the fishing was ruined there too. Then their attention would again shift to new waters. Here and elsewhere the process was expedited by advertisements posted by railroads eager to fill trains and railway hotels. Owners of these railroads made more money and privatized more land, pushing more people to fewer community waters open to the public. It was a vicious circle and a tragedy for the commoners.

In the Adirondacks, railroads were serving the area by the 1840s. The process of privatization began with the formation of the Piseco Lake Trout Club in 1842. It was followed by the North Woods Walton Club in 1857, with members including future vice president James S. Sherman. Just a little farther south, privatization reached the Catskills in 1868 with the formation of the Willowemoc Club.[15] The club consisted of just twenty members, who quickly purchased and leased three of the most famous ponds and more than four miles of river in the upper Willowemoc River watershed. Unfortunately, the most famous Catskill rivers, the Beaverkill, Willowemoc, Neversink, Rondout, and Esopus, can only conjure approximately a hundred miles of trout stream.[16] As on Long Island, it would not take long for well-to-do individuals to obtain the majority of good fishing in that region. In Maine, the eleven members of the Oquossoc Angler's Association initiated a privatization wave in 1868, and subsequently attracted visitors including Theodore Roosevelt and Herbert Hoover.[17] In Pennsylvania, the Blooming Grove Park Association was established in 1871 by jeweler Fayette Giles and publisher Charles Hallock, who would go on to found *Forest and Stream* magazine, later renamed *Field and Stream*.[18] The club acquired twelve thousand acres, leased two thousand more, and crisscrossed fourteen miles of forest with telegraph wires to ensure that members could access the latest New York Stock Exchange prices.[19] The club's overall approach to fisheries management was inspired by European nobility game parks at Baden and Fontainebleau: the state even gave the club permission to enact its own game laws, including a fine for poachers of approximately $50 per fish in today's currency.[20]

For most families in America, the 1870s was not a happy time. The panic of 1873 was followed by a depression that lasted until 1879. Still, by 1878, twenty-five thousand people belonged to approximately six hundred private hunting and fishing clubs in the United States.[21] More importantly, one year after the Great Railway Strike of 1877, where private guards and U.S. troops were employed to protect railroad property, James Van Cleef and another member of the Balsam Lake Club hired watchmen to keep away poachers from their valuable assets: their trout.[22] During a difficult economic time when locals might have needed fish as a source of food, they were turned away by paid guards both at work and at trout streams. The pattern of the 1870s was later repeated in the 1890s. The panic of 1893, partially fueled by speculation on railroad expansion, was the worst depression the country had witnessed to date, with unemployment rates approaching 20 percent and an economic recovery delayed until 1897. During this period and at a time when many in America were fighting for their economic futures, members of Peekamoose Fishing Club, comprised of a group of seven prosperous businessmen, fought a publicized internal battle over who would control access to club grounds.[23] Their choice to focus their attention on the pursuit of trout instead of the country's economic turmoil, illustrates how totally out of touch club members were with the hardships of the day.

Wealthy fishing clubs and individuals increased the use of stream watchers in the 1880s and 1890s at a time in the nation's history when the Pinkerton National Detective Agency made news for forcefully breaking up strikes by poorly paid workers. The best known incident involved Pinkerton detectives at the Homestead Strike from June to November of 1892. Henry Clay Frick, working on behalf of Andrew Carnegie, used the agency, barbwire-topped fences, sniper towers, and water cannons capable of spraying boiling hot water, to wage battle against a well-organized collection of strikers and their small navy of rowboats. The battle came to a head on July 6 when three hundred Pinkerton men attempted an amphibious landing at Homestead Steel Works to open it for non-striking workers. They were met by an armed mob of approximately five thousand. Nothing less than a small war broke out, killing men on both sides. When the carnage subsided, Carnegie and Frick prevailed—not the first time their wealth and power worked to their favor.

In his book, *The Johnstown Flood*, David McCullough describes one of the most horrific events in U.S. history.[24] In 1881, Frick organized the South Fork Fishing and Hunting Club in western Pennsylvania. Carnegie and his friend Robert Pitcairn joined approximately sixty other members. Pitcairn had previously taken over from Carnegie as Pittsburg Division Superinten-dent of the Pennsylvania Railroad, and played a key role in squelching the Great Railroad Strike of 1877, where National Guard troops killed dozens of workers protesting wage cuts. Other club members included famous banker Andrew Mellon as well as Samuel Rea, who eventually served as president of the Pennsylvania Railroad. The group, also called the "Bosses Club," pur-chased South Fork Dam and some surrounding lands from the Pennsylvania Railroad, and then fenced the area.[25] The dam was in bad shape with a large gap from a previous failure. The club plugged this rupture with mud, straw, and manure, neither reinstalling an outlet valve nor providing oversight by a qualified engineer. It was a decidedly unsophisticated and inadequate repair supervised by men famous for their technological innovations. They then refilled the previously empty reservoir for their fishing and boating resort. People living downstream in Johnstown expressed many concerns about the safety of the dam, but the club did nothing. The dam eventually burst on May 31, 1889, when heavy spring runoff exacerbated by deforestation of the surrounding landscape raised the reservoir level, overtopping the structure and rapidly eroding through the repaired section. A flood of twenty million tons of water ran downstream, ripping through multiple riverside towns and piling remains of wooden structures against a railroad bridge in Johnstown. The tragedy intensified when fires somehow ignited flood debris. The Johns-town flood of 1889 drowned and burned more than twenty-two hundred people — the single biggest loss of life due to river flooding in our country's history. One factor exacerbating the dam failure was a fish screen installed by the club that caught flood debris and raised water levels at the reservoir. The region's richest men modified the spillway to prevent fish from escaping, but were too cheap to fix the dam properly and install an outlet valve. After the flood, only one club member ever returned to the property; almost all remained silent about the event, and member names remained secret for more than a year. Despite a clear case of negligence, the club avoided serious legal consequences and paid no damages when courts ruled the flood was a "visitation of providence" and an "act of God."[26] In reality, this deadly flood was more a violation of prominence by an act of Angler!

When I think about wealth in America, the name Rockefeller certainly jumps to mind. William Avery Rockefeller Jr. was famous for his success in oil refining, mining, railroading, and finance. In 1899, he mirrored actions of many of his millionaire colleagues and acquired fifty thousand acres in the Adirondacks for hunting and fishing. He even bought the entire town of

Brandon except for one parcel of land owned by holdout Oliver Lamora.[27] Rockefeller used armed guards set up in watchtowers around the perimeter of his estate to protect his trout and game. He also brought a lawsuit against Lamora for trespassing on the preserve and fishing a section of the Middle Branch of the St. Regis River. The defendant argued that the trout he sought were stocked by the state and could not be privatized, a legal right supported by state legislation. He argued that he was entitled to follow fish onto Rockefeller's private estate to catch them. The lower courts agreed, but Rockefeller pursued several appeals, and the case soon gained public attention. Blooming Grove Park Association founder Hallock published an account on the front page of his July 11, 1903, issue of *Forest and Steam* amid numerous stories about the pleasures of camp life.[28] The periodical sided with Rockefeller, who won a retrial based on the assertion that state stocking could not be proved. However, Rockefeller later suffered another defeat in court. Despite these legal rulings, the December 26 issue of *Forest and Stream* continued to defend the right of private landowners to exclude the public. It was not hard to guess the financial credentials of most of the periodical's readers. When I thumbed through the pages of that issue, I saw blueprints for a fifty-seven-foot yacht, a smaller sailboat, and a launch for the readership to contemplate. Finally in 1906, as reported in the *New York Times*, the multimillionaire prevailed in court, winning his much-sought-after monopoly on the Middle Branch of the St. Regis River, and being awarded a $790.49 settlement to add to his massive portfolio.[29]

The trend of privatization continued into the next century and incited even more interest in fishing in New York City. Clubs were formed and people raced to join the elite. In 1905, The Anglers' Club of New York suggested that "anglers are almost as thick in New York City as flies or Jersey mosquitoes."[30] The club, just getting started, was destined to become one of the most exclusive and secretive clubs in the country. As a clear statement that fishing was wholly about sport, The Anglers' Club of New York rules precluded anyone who earned money fishing, as a guide or manufacturer of fishing equipment from becoming a voting member.[31] Meanwhile in Massachusetts, The Old Colony Club, Monument Club and Boston Single Hook Club were all established. In the Lake Superior region, the Baptism River Club purchased 352 acres in 1886 and attracted James Jerome Hill, "the Empire Builder," as a member. Founded in 1890, Huron Mountain Club had fifty members and twenty-four thousand acres of land in the Upper Peninsula of Michigan. Even Henry Ford had to swindle his way into a club membership by buying adjacent land and blocking a state highway scheduled to cross the club's estate. Imagine how important membership must have seemed if the person most responsible for mobilizing America with cars decided to block highway construction, which his product required. The Wigwam Club established a private hatchery on the South Platte River in Colorado and created a bit of a stir in the early 1920s: "Fishermen naturally didn't like the idea of a bunch of rich guys closing off part of their river, while a privately published history of the club suggests that at least some of those rich guys considered it their responsibility to close as much of the river as possible to the common rabble."[32] As privatization expanded westward, it inevitably created problems with other people.

Americans crossed our northern border to establish clubs and private estates throughout Canada. The same year as the Stock Market Crash of 1929, James Drummond Dole, a native of Jamaica Plain, Massachusetts, began an endeavor in British Columbia that exemplified a disregard for indigenous rights.[33] Dole, known as the "Pineapple King," was the wealthy founder of Dole Foods Industry. He first commissioned a search for the perfect fishing retreat in an untouched wilderness setting, then masterminded a takeover of an aboriginal fishery at Pennask Lake to turn it into an elite fly-fishing club for roughly fifty American and Canadian members. The year before Pennask Lake Fishing and Game Club was formed, 430 aboriginal people caught more than 45,000 trout for subsistence. To privatize key fishing grounds, Dole purchased land without the knowledge of the tribe or the Bureau of Indian Affairs, and then used an Indian agent to enforce his right to privacy. When tribe members arrived that year to prepare their food stores for winter, they were turned away empty handed. Eventually, even aboriginal names for various creeks and coves were renamed to honor club members. By conveniently wiping away signs of an indigenous way of life that had persisted for centuries, the club created a sense that they were pioneers in an untamed wilderness.[34] This club, which eventually hosted a visit by Queen Elizabeth II, serves as a perfect symbol of twentieth-century colonialism in North America.[35]

In 1936, during the Great Depression, Pennsylvania Fish Commissioner Oliver M. Deibler complained that clubs excluded the public from one-seventh of the state's "most worth-while streams" with public fishing shrunk "to less than one-quarter of what they formerly were."[36] If we jump several decades ahead, we see trends of the late nineteenth century and early twentieth century continued. By 1974, only a little more than a thousand miles of New York's roughly seventeen thousand miles of trout streams were in public ownership.[37] For more than a century, the best trout fishing waters in many states were reserved for those individuals with the most money. As history shows, the more that fishing was regarded as in vogue, especially by the New York elite, the more that affluent people tried to monopolize it—and the more new devotees it seemed to attract.

~ ~ ~ The whole time I read modern accounts of the late 1800s and early 1900s, I was uneasy with assertions in many books that wealthy anglers were saviors. When I finally connected my two childhood fascinations, fishing and railroads, a major hypocrisy became clear in my mind. Many members of the famed Suffolk Club, South Side Sportsmen's Club, and other similar organizations made their money in railroad ventures. The Vanderbilts, James Hill, J. P. Morgan, John Kennedy, William Cutting, Robert Pitcairn, and many others managed and owned rail networks. Elsewhere, railroad mogul Jay Gould was a Catskill native who fished the region as a wealthy man.[38] His son eventually purchased 3,000 acres in the Catskills and fenced it off.[39] Decades later, the family still owns title to that land. William Seward Webb was the son-in-law of Cornelius Vanderbilt and the president of the Wagner Place Car Company, builder of railroad cars. Webb owned a 200,000-acre game preserve in the Adirondacks and built the first railroad to cross the heart of the region. He also teamed with Collis Huntington and J. P. Morgan as board members on the shortest standard-gauge railroad in the world, built to transport themselves and other wealthy passengers to massive summer camps in the Adirondacks on Raquette Lake.[40] In addition to owning and running railroads, Carnegie and Frick gained fortunes supplying iron rails, bridges, and other steel needs of the lines. Their mills provided rails for some of the seventy-three thousand miles of railway laid down in the 1880s alone.[41] Bradford Lee Gilbert was an angler, railroad architect, and engineer. FDR's father was a railroad executive, and relatives married into the Aspinwall and Howland families made rich partly in railroad businesses.[42] It seems impossible to decouple the fortunes of trout estates from railroad tycoons.

During the nineteenth century, trout definitely needed to be saved, but we need to remember why. If we inventory the ills of the land that necessitated trout preservation, we find pollution, deforestation, and overfishing topping the list. Pollution was partially the result of deforestation, chemical industries, and tanneries. Mining, steel, and oil industries also contributed to contamination of America's rivers. For example, Deibler reported in 1936 that three-quarters of the mileage along Pennsylvania rivers was affected by coal mines.[43] Ironworks also had direct impacts. South Side Sportsmen's Club member Abram S. Hewitt supplied iron to railways; his Long Pond Iron Works used both hydropower-driven bellows and charcoal-fueled furnaces.[44] Hydropower meant the construction of dams on local streams, while charcoal creation consumed prodigious numbers of trees. This facility and similar charcoal-powered plants in the Adirondacks each devoured approximately one thousand acres of forest a year.[45] Meanwhile, major logging drives to supply railroad ties for expanding iron-railed empires consumed additional timber nationwide. Webb's rail system in the Adirondacks contained many spurs to help deforest the region.[46] The logs here and elsewhere were transported by railroads or floated down rivers cleared of obstacles using dynamite on a wave of high water supplied using splash dams. Families like those of Gifford Pinchot made fortunes supplying wood to railroads and eastern markets. Pinchot's eventual ascension as leader of the U.S. Forest Service was prompted by the poor state of the nation's eastern forests, where logging companies reneged on taxes and abandoned land after the saleable timber was removed. Even construction of large rustic retreats used hefty volumes of lumber with at least one Adirondack camp requiring fifteen hundred trees for its assembly.[47] The forests of the East were not the only ones to suffer. Much of the forest of the Front Range in the towering Rocky Mountains of Colorado and Wyoming was cut to supply railroads and mines.[48] Railroads used these ties to create wood-bedded transportation networks. Rails carried locomotives that often burned wood and pulled lines of cars made of lumbered boards and steel. Locomotives even sparked numerous forest fires as embers cast from their stacks ignited local trees. Large-scale deforestation helped fuel the manufacturing and transportation industries of many affluent club members. For them, money *did* grow on trees and rivers suffered the consequences.

The impact of railroads extended beyond their role in clear-cutting the nation's forests. After railway lines were completed, railroads used special railway cars and company hatcheries to stock numerous routes with nonindigenous species. Railroads worked with state agencies, through cooperation of men like Robert Roosevelt, to expand the range of trout with the more heat-tolerant species, brown and rainbow trout. The resultant loss of brook trout in eastern states is a problem that persists today. Railway executives were profit driven with a desire to increase ridership for angling-minded clients. Their expanding networks greatly improved access to fishing regions nationwide. They heavily advertised fishing opportunities along their routes, running angler specials as a means to boost ridership. New trout trains carried large numbers of both anglers and fish for stocking, bringing lots of money for railroad tycoons and greatly exacerbating overfishing problems. Of course, Henry Ford's contributions to transportation later played a role too. Railroad and automobile men used wealth accumulated through encouraging both deforestation and overfishing to buy private and club estates that would protect small segments of property from the general destruction they helped cause on landscapes. Privatization schemes thus created a nasty spiral of environmental problems linked to railroads as a diminished supply of public fishing areas became increasingly dependent on stocking by trains. Meanwhile, railroad men simply attached their private railway cars to the ends of these trains to take themselves to their private estates. It seems hypocritical to consider these wealthy industrialists as saviors of trout, since they were only saving trout for themselves from themselves.

~ ~ ~ At the turn of the century, conservationist and preservationist camps originated with opposing views on how to manage public lands. The preservation movement gained traction under John Muir and Aldo Leopold, attracted wealthy backers, and was often aligned with privatization. The conservation movement was best exemplified by Theodore Roosevelt's formation of the U.S. Forest Service, where trees on public lands were simply considered a different type of crop, which explains why the Forest Service was embedded in the Department of Agriculture. During Roosevelt's term, the area of forest reserves quadrupled, and numerous rivers were afterward managed as public resources. So where do we place wealthy anglers of this era?

Many influential anglers, even those who privatized large tracts of land, regarded river management as akin to farming, not a simple act of protection. Stocking, biological manipulations, and physical modifications were acts of conservation, not preservation. The Forest Service and conservation movement of the day had its capable leader in the form of Pinchot. Pinchot's most important friendship was with Theodore Roosevelt, which directly led to his role as the first chief of the Forest Service. Pinchot was born a short distance from the Catskill region and was, as fate would have it, an avid fisherman.

Pinchot was born in Simsbury, Connecticut—to a family of affluent merchants, landowners, and politicians—just four months after the end of the Civil War. A graduate of Yale University, he spent a good deal of his youth at his family's estate, Grey Towers in Milford, Pennsylvania. His family owned several miles of Sawkill Creek, where Pinchot fished for trout. His grandfather was a land speculator of great success who used profits from his store to amass large land holdings in Pennsylvania, New York, Michigan, and Wisconsin.[49] He used his lands to produce lumber for sale, which made the family a great deal of money but left the landscape denuded and eroded. Pinchot's father, James, made his living principally selling furniture in New York City, and was involved in a gentrification movement in Milford. His son was named after close friend, Sanford Robinson Gifford, a well-known artist from the second generation of Hudson River School painters.[50] Sanford Gifford, a passionate angler like many Hudson River School artists, was one of America's earliest salmon fishers and spent many summers fishing in the Catskills.[51] In 1866, Sanford Gifford painted *Hudson River Twilight*, a post–Civil War piece, which profoundly impacted Gifford Pinchot because it depicted a landscape laid waste by clear cutting.[52] This artist was an early role model who influenced not only Pinchot's passion for forestry, but his hobby as an angler.

During Pinchot's stint directing the Forest Service he wrote *The Relation of Forests to Stream Control*, which carefully laid out the role that a forested landscape plays in hydrology.[53] More than one hundred years later it is hard to find fault with the natural processes described. Pinchot carefully explained how a canopy of trees and forest litter intercepts falling raindrops, lessening their impact on the ground and reducing erosion. He talked about the role decayed roots, dead leaves, and needles play in the percolation of rainwater. He illustrated how roots hold and bind soil particles and rocks together to prevent sediment removal by flowing water. These various processes initially help to limit erosion, but, as he correctly surmised, they also slow the passage of water across a landscape, thus reducing the size of floods. The prevailing scientific thought at the time was a belief that modifications in vegetation cover strongly influenced rainfall totals. Pinchot did not discount this possibility but countered, "The greatest influence of the forest is not upon the amount of rain which falls, but on what becomes of the rain after it falls."[54] Once again, his intuition and scientific training is spot on. Deforestation created larger floods, more erosion, and dried up springs because less water remained in soil after rains ended. Most amazingly, Pinchot prophetically warned that then-current rates of erosion were unsustainable for agricultural lands because "the formation of soil through underground decay of the rocks cannot keep pace with such a rate of erosion."[55] Even today, scientists warn that observed rates of erosion on agricultural fields are too high and could ultimately lead to a complete loss of soil critical to crop growth.[56] Pinchot's article is a joy to read and an impressive contribution to our understanding of what modern scientists call forest hydrology. With it, Pinchot made a strong argument for his vision of a more scientifically managed system of forest lands to replace the haphazard clear-cutting of the past.

Pinchot also wrote a book on fishing simply titled, *Fishing Talk*, which accurately sums up the book.[57] I must admit that I could not wait to get my hands on Pinchot's book because of his importance in American conservation. To say I was disappointed would not do my feelings justice. The story was predictable. He had an early start trout fishing with his dad, requisite references to Izaak Walton, boastful accounts of the largest fish landed, and few quotes of any note. It quickly became obvious that Pinchot simply liked to catch and admire as many different types of fish as possible in his home waters of New England, Pennsylvania, and New York, as well as during adventures to the Florida Keys, Oregon's Pelican Bay, San Clemente Island, the Galapagos Islands, the Marquesas Archipelago, and Tahiti. He was enamored with harpoons, *Moby Dick*, and the lives of whalers. He detailed his success harpooning sharks and manta ray. He even helped Theodore Roosevelt set up with a guide for the president's own manta ray harpooning escapade. Pinchot clearly disliked sharks and said, "No shark ever struck my hook and got away alive with my consent."[58] He had a similar thing against pickerel and dispatched those fish whenever possible. Conversely, he was adamant about fishing for trout only with barbless hooks. Overall, I found the three consecutive chapters on harpooning porpoises most excruciating. He talked about the clear intelligence of these animals, but still joyfully discussed harpooning them and marveled as wounded animals dragged him around in his little Old Town canoe. Eventually, these impaled porpoises tired and Pinchot dispatched them with a .45 revolver. Somehow, I had a difficult time rectifying fishing accounts written by Pinchot with his earlier contributions on hydrology.

Although Pinchot influenced future trends in the nation's management of forested trout streams, another lesser-known, affluent man of the same region and period played an equally large role. No single person better exemplified what it means to be a first-class angler than Edward Ringwood Hewitt. Hewitt, born the year after Pinchot, was an avid fly fisherman and wealthy industrialist who lived much of his life in Gramercy Park, New York City. Hewitt knew Pinchot and learned his method for releasing hooked trout.[59] Hewitt once tried to impress Pinchot by catching a three-pound trout by hand, but Pinchot apparently responded, "No! That is no gentlemen's way to fish; put him back."[60] Why Pinchot believed that harpooning and shooting a porpoise was gentlemanly while catching a trout by hand was not is beyond me!

According to fishing legend Lee Wulff, Hewitt was one of the most influential Catskill anglers.[61] He developed innovative ways to fish for trout and salmon and introduced new flies that became highly touted. He ran a private hatchery most of his life, developed ways to physically modify habitat in streams, and published several widely read books. Hewitt's eventual impact on how streams are managed is hard to overestimate. He is also a story unto himself. It was only after I read Hewitt's 1943 book, *Those Were the Years*, that I truly began to understand what it must be like to be born with every privilege in life and be free to follow any whim.[62]

Hewitt's middle name derived from his family's twenty-two-thousand-acre summer estate in northern New Jersey, Ringwood Manor. Edward was one of six children. Hewitt's grandfather, Peter Cooper, began life as a poor, shoeless child in Peekskill, New York, but accumulated significant wealth as an iron and glue manufacturer and mine owner. He built the first American steam locomotive, laid the first transatlantic cable, invented gelatin from horses' hooves, and founded Cooper Union in New York. Hewitt's uncle, Edward Cooper, expanded the family wealth and served as mayor of New York in 1879 and 1880. Hewitt's father was Abram Hewitt, the steel manufacturer from New York. Abram was a member of the famed South Side Sportsmen's Club and owned the New York and Greenwood Lake Railroad where Edward occasionally served as engineer. His father's story was another rags-to-riches affair made possible when he won one of only two scholarships to Kings College, now Columbia University, in a competition against thousands of other New York City pupils. He eventually teamed with Cooper's son and together they supplied most of the gun iron for Union troops in the Civil War. Abram eventually sold the company to J. P. Morgan and served briefly on the board of U.S. Steel Corporation. He then entered public life and served stints as chairman of the Democratic National Committee, a five-time member of the U.S. House of Representatives, and mayor of New York. He knew to varying degrees Presidents Lincoln, Grant, Hayes, Garfield, and Cleveland, and was even mentioned as a potential cabinet appointee under the Cleveland administration.[63] He also allowed Pinchot to convince him to put thousands of his forest acres in New Jersey and West Virginia under management of the U.S. Division of Forestry in 1898.[64] Of course, the land around the New Jersey mine and ironworks was not much of a forest anymore because it largely lacked trees.

Edward Hewitt's older brother, Peter, was another successful tinkerer; he invented the mercury vapor lamp, which made fluorescent bulbs of today possible. Together they formed quite a pair in their youth. Their early life was one of great opulence as they created long wooden tracks for sliding, lassoed calves from the family herd, built a steam-powered boat for the estate pond, produced a gladiatorial show in the piazza with a family goat, played with their pet black bear cub and, of course, raised trout in their private hatchery.[65] Edward was rebellious, mischievous, and destructive as a youth. He proudly outlined his numerous pranks, and bragged that the police eventually put a watchman in Gramercy Park outside his family's home to keep an eye on him and his siblings. Regrettably, the young Hewitts scared off this policeman by essentially blowing up the sentry box with fireworks. Hewitt tells tale after tale of similar antics that usually went unsolved and unpunished, and persisted through his undergraduate years at Princeton University, surviving into a period of graduate study at Berlin University.

Hewitt eventually quit his doctorate in Germany and returned to New York to work as a chemist in the family glue business. He was not in the business for long when circumstances altered his career path and he established Hewitt Motor Company, which eventually merged with Mack Truck. He subsequently served as a consulting engineer to the company until well into his eighties.[66] Despite early business success, Hewitt lost much of his fortune in the stock market crash of 1929. This financial setback probably encouraged several commercial endeavors, including selling trout food, running a fishing camp in the Catskills, and producing various chemical goods under the label Hewitt Products of Liberty, New York. None of these activities brought Hewitt the fame he appeared to desire. According to Hewitt's own seemingly humble words, "none of [my patents] has proved of fundamental importance," "my scientific work has been a minor character, and my success in business was not large."[67] He later stated, "I do not regret not having made a great success of anything."[68] He then used the rest of his two autobiographies and numerous books on fishing to convince the reader that he was one of the most interesting, inventive, and original people that ever lived.

Hewitt's autobiographies read a bit like a fantasy novel or Disney movie. Stories ranged from childhood dinners with Red Cloud of the Lakota Sioux to meals in Constantinople at the sultan's palace.[69] He received two years of fencing instruction from Von Taube, who reportedly killed a governor of Kiev in a duel. He owned a steam-powered car early in life called the Locomobile, which slightly resembled "Chitty Chitty Bang Bang." He visited the home of Baron von Richthofen and met his young son Manfred Albrecht, the famed Red Baron. He caught a fish he referred to as a barbell at the request of Kaiser Wilhelm I and fish for Emperor Franz Joseph of Austria-Hungary while the latter monarch talked politics with Hewitt's father. As an adult he stayed in an eighty-bedroom mansion in Gloucestershire and in Invergarry Castle, among other palaces. He dined with the Duke and Duchess of Marlborough, and other English aristocracy. For four summers, he rented Lairds Palace in Balnakiely, a seventeen-bedroom retreat with a whole staff of servants. He showed fishing movies to Lord Davidson, Archbishop of Canterbury, with twenty-one bishops in attendance and claimed one of the bishops stole his hat. He told a tale of a private dinner party with a very drunken Buffalo Bill. The Honorable William Lyon Mackenzie King, prime minister of Canada, was a close friend who reportedly credited Hewitt's wife with his political ambitions. Hewitt fished for salmon in the Duke of Athol's private haunts in Scotland. He was also invited to fish for salmon in Spain at the bequest and with financial support of His Excellency, General Francisco Franco of Spain. Afterward, Hewitt defended Franco's desire for "limited" monarchy and touted Franco's role in helping to win World War II. Hewitt's preference for European aristocracy is easy to infer.

Hewitt was a staunch believer in tea at 5:00 PM, a practice he credited to his mother.[70] Hewitt married Miss Mary Ashley in 1892 with a honeymoon at Niagara Falls immediately followed by the couple's first fishing trip to Canada. He proudly proclaimed that he never had a quarrel or cross word with his wife in fifty-three years of marriage.[71] He was fond of shooting upland birds. He built his own fishing reels. He also collected and repaired antique musical instruments. He had an extreme abhorrence of modern music, modern poetry, and modern art, considering them a degeneration of civilization. Once, he and his wife even held a dinner party for several modern art critics, at which they displayed art painted by insane mental patients as a way to fool and hence discredit the experts. The party and paintings were a great success, and he seemed immensely impressed with himself over the ruse. Luckily, Hewitt's son-in-law painted society portraits in oil following the more classic style. Later in life, Hewitt took lunch at the Dutch Treat Club on Tuesdays, the Angler's Club of New York on Wednesdays, the Coffee House Club on Fridays, and the Century Club on Saturdays. Throughout his life he was surrounded by servants as he seemed more than happy to report. He was clearly born with a silver spoon in his mouth, which he metaphorically fashioned into a silver fishing hook.

Hewitt was almost as adept at dropping names as he was at delicately placing flies. He mentioned contacts with Mark Twain and famous scientists who included Lord Kelvin, geologist Clarence King, and Dr. Casimir Funk. He was best friends with Dr. Nicholas Murray Butler, president of Columbia University. Hewitt knew J. P. Morgan, Charles M. Schwab, Henry Phipps Jr., and James Hill, and met many of the famous inventors of the day including Westinghouse and Edison. In a single act of either restraint or poor penmanship, he mysteriously talked about a Mr. and Mrs. M___ in his 1943 book. Carnegie was a close family friend, whom he described as "a little man, resembling the bust of Socrates."[72] Hewitt visited Carnegie at his Skibo Castle in Scotland, where he hunted grouse delivered in panniers on horseback and impressed Carnegie by catching a dozen trout by hand, using the technique known as guddling—the method that later offended Pinchot.[73]

As these stories document and others confirm, Hewitt was a braggart.[74] His fishing stories always seemed to show him catching trout as no one else could, or making observations that everyone else missed. He also claimed many firsts. Hewitt worked with Hiram Maxim, the man who modernized warfare with the invention of smokeless powder and gas-recoil powered machine guns, and Hewitt suggested he was one of the first to fire the new weapon of mass destruction.[75] Together they worked in Bexley Park and developed an early airplane capable of achieving flight before the Wright Brothers' success in 1903. Hewitt declared he was the first person outside the research labs to try both modern pressure-cuff blood pressure instruments with Dr. Rouleaux in Germany and vitamins with Dr. Funk. Hewitt even allegedly developed the world's first multivitamin. He claimed that at his suggestion, Nikola Tesla took the first X-ray for medical purposes with a Geisler tube when a needle became imbedded in Hewitt's wife's foot. He said he initiated the common practice of getting up immediately after abdominal operations in 1941, and developed different cures for the onset of both cataracts and Paget's diseases. At age ninety, Hewitt credited his longevity to numerous healthy habits he developed.[76] At this point I will remind readers that anglers are infamous for stretching truths in the tales they tell.

If those stories are not sufficient to label Hewitt a colossal boast, some stories earlier in his life take on a real sense of the surreal. As a graduate student he was apparently mistaken for a German spy and arrested in France. Hewitt claimed he cooperated with his captives by accurately predicting the strategy Germany would later use to invade France in World War I. He then referred to himself as an "American prince," and demanded to be put in touch with the American Consul, which successfully prompted his release.[77] At roughly the same time in his life, he claimed to have written anonymously a hoax article on a reorganization of the German Army. It was picked up by ninety-six newspapers in Germany and provoked a response by the General Staff. He then anonymously authored a second farce article recommending distribution of beer through pipelines, and claimed this article was run all over Germany and caused a great storm. Of course, Hewitt recounted the stories during World War II and was probably touchy about his German education. He was far less critical of Germans in his 1957 book; instead he focused on a critique of Russians. It is hard to verify these stories. Possibly the two autobiographies themselves represent just elaborate fabrications designed to trick gullible readers by a man devoted to deceiving fish with flies he concocted.

Hewitt possessed eyes that still stare confidently through a photograph or painting and directly challenge the viewer. His hair parted down the middle and his clean-shaven face more closely resemble a bird of prey than the trout he adored. Wulff wrote, "He was loved, revered, disliked and feared by those around him" and was "crusty and sometimes hard to take."[78] In 1930, Hewitt admitted "no doubt, I was quite rude, as I often am."[79] In supposed tribute to Hewitt, Wulff recalled an incident where he asked Hewitt to write a forward to his book, *Leaping Silver*, but was rebuffed because Hewitt did not support Wulff's equipment or technique. However, when Wulff spoke to the Anglers' Club of Philadelphia to promote his book, Hewitt was invited to introduce Wulff with "a word or two."[80] Instead, Hewitt spoke for twenty minutes and stole material from Wulff's book. Still, Wulff loved and respected Hewitt and credited him as a master who overshadowed even fishing greats George La Branche, Theodore Gordon, George Parker Holden, and Preston Jennings.

As his self-anointment as an "American prince" might attest, Hewitt had strong ties and affinities to the upper class and a disdain for the masses. In 1943, Hewitt recalled a childhood incident when Mrs. Fish drove one of the first electric cars over an African American man, backed over him and then ran over him again, all in an apparent accident. Hewitt seemed quite amused by the incident, which luckily did not kill the man. A second tale brings to mind a famous scene in *Monty Python and the Holy Grail* when Michael Palin, playing the role of Dennis the Peasant, yelled, "Come and see the violence inherent in the system. Help! Help! I'm being repressed." In Hewitt's account, his friend Maxim jumped from their car and beat a tramp who was taking thatch from a roof on Maxim's property.[81] Hewitt immediately warned Maxim that he would surely get a visit from the constable. Maxim, as predicted, was brought before a local magistrate but produced an original deed from Henry VIII that specifically granted property owners the right to flog beggars. Maxim and Hewitt exited the courthouse without reprimand while Maxim joked that he had always wanted to test the legality of his deed. Remarkably, the victim of the beating was lectured by the magistrate to avoid trespassing. Hewitt tells the story without a hint of remorse. He displays little obvious regret that his friend automatically treated a man of lesser means like an inferior.

Despite Hewitt's isolated stories of intended and unintended violence against lower-class workers, I remained unsure if it was unfair to categorize him as an elitist until I read a quote in his last book, which explained how he thought people become king:

> If both the father and mother come of able stock for a number of generations, the offspring, on average, will be far superior to that of ordinary people. . . . After the fall of the Roman Empire and during the Middle Ages, small groups formed in order to have protection to survive. These groups were led by those who had the greatest physical vigor and ability and these families became the ruling aristocracy of Europe. They intermarried and continued to produce superior individuals who were capable of leading. From this came the respect which most Europeans still have today for aristocracy. When these families came to intermarry more for the acquisition of estates than for physical vigor and stamina, the aristocracy largely deteriorated to the common level, or often below, as was the case with the Bourbons.[82]

It is hard to read those lines and not picture a Monty Python skit with a few descendants of the Capetian dynasty stewing in the background.

Near the end of his last book, Hewitt offered an interesting observation of economic progression in prosperous families. He believed the first generation of English industrialists was largely comprised of frugal men who reinvested in their own ventures, and ultimately wanted a better life for their sons.[83] These sons were competent businessmen, spent more money in living, and reinvested fewer profits. They wanted their sons to be gentlemen and follow aristocratic ways. This third generation hired managers for businesses and kept most profits for their own personal expenditures. The resultant businesses were ill-prepared to deal with competition, especially from American mass-production facilities. Hewitt's grandfather, Peter Cooper, definitely fell under the first generation of American industrialists, which would place Hewitt in the analogous third generation of somewhat selfishly inclined men. In keeping with that generation, he was more interested in travel, hunting, and fishing than business. He admitted his early automobiles were undercut on price by Henry Ford's mass-production entry into the market. However, do not give Hewitt credit for self-reflection and criticism. Shockingly, his quotes are directed almost exclusively to English families, and he does not mention any similarities to his own life. I wonder if Hewitt considered the inability to recognize one's own faults as a common characteristic of the generation of greatness two times removed.

Hewitt provides an interesting tale of a well-to-do man, but he is still best known for fishing, which is why he is of interest in my book. As a young man, Hewitt visited the three-thousand-acre Catskill estate of Clarence Roof and fished along Roof's five miles of the Neversink River.[84] Roof and his Neversink Club friends angered local residents when they purchased and closed most of the west branch of the Neversink River to public fishing and hired heavily armed, stream watchers to guard their prize. Years later, Hewitt was a member of the Willowemoc Club with five others, and he was a controversial Neversink property owner of his own. The hullabaloo surrounded his purchase of five thousand acres and more than 4.5 miles of the lower Neversink River shortly after it was logged. Hewitt looked for and found a property that was easy to protect because of the lack of public roads. However, access from downstream was probably a headache because the land bordered on Black Hole, a famous rendezvous for anglers.[85] Initially, Hewitt permitted area residents to fly fish on his property with a limit of twenty fish per day. He later claimed that anglers caught two thousand eight hundred trout from his property in one year. He abruptly closed the area and hired a private watchman to keep the public out.[86] This action provided an ironical twist of fate when we remember that public funds were earlier used in New York City to hire police to keep an eye on this mischievous youth's private whereabouts. On the property, he built and later rebuilt a hilltop seven-bedroom, five-bathroom summer home complete with servant quarters and constructed a second camp within sight of one of the better fishing pools. He usually resided there from May until late October. He even hosted an Angler's Club of New York annual outing in 1929. Perhaps it was after that year's stock market crash and the loss of much of his fortune that he began renting the house as a fishing camp.[87] He further used his fishing knowledge in other commercial endeavors. Although these activities would make him ineligible to be a voting member of the Angler's Club of New York, how could they remove their most famous and princely associate?

The local community was furious about various restrictions Hewitt imposed and the incident helped force the state to search for public fishing areas.[88] Interestingly, Hewitt simultaneously complained that trout stocking for fee-paying sportsmen was only utilized by state fish commissioners because they did not control enough land to manage resources effectively.[89] Hewitt was particularly concerned with problems of overfishing by the public and suggested use of government fees and restricted access to improve fisheries. In perhaps the biggest case of irony, to better handle overfishing, the few state-owned, public-fishing areas were later modified using stream-improvement techniques publicized by Hewitt and financed by the public fishing license fees he backed.

Hewitt's impact on American rivers was not confined to the Catskills. In general, he heavily relied on technology and heavy-handed land management practices to try to perfect his day of trout fishing. He developed a photographic technique to make fishing leaders more invisible to trout and built a Pitot tube to measure current velocities to determine the speed of flow preferred by trout.[90] He was one of the first anglers to use a polarizing filter fitted inside opera glasses, called a Nicol prism, to cut down on glare to see fish. He developed new flies and casting techniques, and pioneered hatchery methods and selective trout breeding for size. In this last procedure, fast growing trout were carefully screened out of tanks and growth rates of hatchery fish were checked with microphotographs of scales. Livers of hatchery trout were also inspected to assess impacts of various hatchery diets. He even experimented with radium in his hatchery to observe its influence on fish. Hewitt invented, borrowed, and promoted structural approaches to create habitat in rivers. Singularly focused on modifying river environments to improve sport fishing, Hewitt expected these various investments to pay off in the form of better angling. Hewitt was clearly a conservationist, not a preservationist.

Hewitt's memberships included the Anglers' Club of New York, the Willowemoc Club, and the Tuscarora Club. By 1946, the Tuscarora Club controlled seven miles of stream on what is considered by many the most beautiful trout stream in the Catskills.[91] A friend of Hewitt's and another important member of both the Anglers' Club of New York and the Tuscarora Club was Henry Andrews Ingraham. In many ways the two men could not seem more different. Ingraham was a naturalist and an attorney in Brooklyn who walked each morning across that famous bridge to Wall Street.[92] His wife was active in civic work in New York.[93] Their only daughter, Mary Ingraham Bunting-Smith, went on to become a prominent microbiologist and the fifth president of Radcliffe College. Her picture graced the November 1961 cover of *Time* magazine.[94] Ingraham owned a weekend and summer home on a forty-acre lot in Northport on Long Island, close to the Wyandanch, Nissequogue, and South Side Sportsmen's Clubs.[95] In 1926, he published a book with the Anglers' Club of New York, which resembles the work of a scientist more than a lawyer.[96] It advocated for more science in the management of streams and contained chapters on stream ecology, geology, temperature and climate, reforestation, and pollution. The first chapter hints at why his daughter was drawn to the life of a microbiologist. Ingraham made a strong case for reforestation and suggested that deforestation was the primary culprit in stream deterioration. Perhaps inspired by Pinchot's writings, Ingraham discussed the role that forests play in limiting erosion, reducing flood peaks, supplying low flow and cooling temperatures. He also mentioned the seriousness of flood-induced erosion on the Neversink, Beaverkill, and Willowemoc Rivers in the Catskills. Ingraham argued for protection of natural processes and restoration of riparian vegetation. In contrast, Hewitt was more inclined to engineer a solution to a perceived problem. In the subsequent decades, it was Hewitt's approach that inspired fisheries managers.

Not all of Ingraham's ideas were novel or a strong departure from historic club practices. He justified privatization of fishing waters with the continued claim that wealthy landowners provided conservation of resources for the benefit of all. He suggested that public fishing of these same areas would lead to a depletion of populations. He believed governments should purchase large tracts of headwaters and prevent fishing on these small streams because of their importance as rearing areas for young trout. However, he argued against similar fishing restrictions on private streams because of their anticipated unpopularity. In suggesting this approach, he failed to acknowledge that, politically speaking, far more voters would be impacted by fishing regulations on public lands than private ones. Although he recognized the need for public fishing areas, Ingraham suggested that it was government's role to supply them. He even proposed the establishment of an English approach to leased fishing rights, where farmers maintained and sold admission to their rivers. Ingraham regarded trout primarily as a sportsman's fish, not a food source, and wanted laws prohibiting the sale of trout in order to close markets to poachers and reduce the theft of fish from clubs and private estates. He similarly advocated for severe punishment of trespassers. As a fitting tribute to this figure and perhaps in a bit of a paradox, his former summer residence on Long Island was recently turned into a nature preserve, named in his honor, for all to enjoy.

~ ~ ~ Many early clubs were inspired by European game preserves. Conversely, a tradition more firmly founded in the United States is our particular take on the administrative branch of government. After the struggle to free our nation, the revolutionary fathers designed the Constitution to eliminate concentration of power and ensure a president's rule was not unlimited. Still, the institution of the presidency represents a position of great power and prominence. Of course, presidents are people, not institutions. Unlike a real institution, they can take a day off and go fishing. Many Americans fished, so it is perfectly predictable that presidents, and even some first ladies, would too. However, some presidents took fishing to its highest level as strong advocates for the sport.

Fishing with the Presidents, by Bill Mares, is a fascinating look at the importance that angling played in various lives of our nation's leaders.[97] According to Mares, our first commander in chief, George Washington, started the precedent of fishing presidents. Unlike many of those that followed him, though, he fished commercially and for profit. Although Washington is often considered above reproach, members of the angling clubs of the nineteenth and twentieth centuries would have ostracized him for his meat fishing. Washington was followed by more recreational anglers in John Quincy Adams and Martin Van Buren, who was a founding member of the Suffolk Club in New York.[98] Although there is evidence that some of our most famous presidents, for example Abraham Lincoln and John Kennedy, fished as youths, they were not active participants in the sport during their presidential years. In contrast, except for Woodrow Wilson — who preferred golf — the period from 1881 until 1961 was dominated by rod-wielding presidents. Many of these fine leaders preferred fly fishing. The more serious anglers were Chester Arthur, Grover Cleveland, Theodore Roosevelt, Herbert Hoover, Calvin Coolidge, Franklin Roosevelt, and Dwight Eisenhower. Arthur held a record for the largest salmon caught on the Cascapedia River in Quebec. Cleveland was such an intense angler he fished through thunderstorms and hail. Theodore Roosevelt grew up with an uncle who was a fly-fishing legend. Teddy also visited prominent fishing clubs during his presidency and was a member of Tahawus Club, a hunting and fishing group that controlled ninety-six thousand acres in the Adirondacks. In fact, he was in the Adirondacks when he received word that he needed to be sworn in to replace a dying President McKinley.[99] Cleveland and Hoover wrote fishing books, a practice revived when Jimmy Carter wrote *An Outdoor Journal*[100] and George Bush wrote the article, "The Thrill of Northern Fishing."[101] Angling was such an important aspect of Hoover's life that the Herbert Hoover Presidential Library and Museum houses a life-size diorama of this leader fly fishing.[102] Coolidge occasionally used worms, but relied on flies when the press buzzed around. He was undoubtedly aware of the prevailing attitude of many toward bait fishing as expressed by one English author of the era: "The growing evil is indulged in without hindrance, and the degenerate influence spreads through the adjoining fisheries, to a great extent changing the natural habits of the trout and transforming them from solitary surface-feeders into gregarious gravel-grubbers."[103] If you believe these sentiments, President Coolidge was a degenerate spreader of evil and creator of gravel-grubbers. Franklin Roosevelt was an avid angler and fly fished in his youth, but was forced to fish mostly from boats after polio limited the use of his legs. When in office, he used U.S. Navy and Coast Guard vessels for his angling adventures. To a lesser extent, Ulysses Grant, Benjamin Harrison, Warren Harding, and Harry Truman fished during their terms, but they were not consumed by the sport. Finally, Eisenhower was a dedicated fly fisherman. Altogether, the First Office held lots of love for fish.

Fishing entered a dark period in the White House beginning with President Johnson. Eisenhower tried to teach Vice President Richard Nixon to fly fish but with little success.[104] Nixon's replacement, President Ford, fly fished as a youth with his father, but Gerald never caught the bug. Carter temporarily reversed the downward trend and set aside an office in the White House for fishing-related activities. However, his successor, Ronald Regan, did not follow suit. Both Bush and his son were anglers of the primarily saltwater variety, although the senior Bush fished some for salmon during his presidency, and after his term became "an enthusiastic, even a fanatical, fly-fisherman."[105] Bill Clinton was not known for angling, but was spotted in an Orvis shop in Florida at least once.[106] The latest commander in chief, Barack Obama, fly fished in Yellowstone and Grand Canyon National Parks with his daughters. One website even reported he adopted an artificial green pupa as the official fly of the White House.[107] When we consider that fishing organizations, most notably Trout Unlimited, actively lobby government to promote fishing, it is interesting that political support appears to extend right up to the top.

Some presidents made great efforts to fish while in office. During his term in office, President Arthur trekked three hundred fifty miles on a hunting and fishing trip in 1883, accompanied by a seventy-five-man cavalry escort and 174 pack animals.[108] Cleveland, who was married in the White House in 1886, packed his fly rods for his honeymoon. He and J. P. Morgan both used beloved guide Alvah Dunning on fishing trips to the Adirondacks. Coolidge took long vacations to fish; he set up temporary executive offices in the Rapid City High School and White Pine Camp during summer fishing vacations to the Black Hills and Adirondacks, respectively. Eisenhower fished more than forty times during his presidency, traveling as far as Argentina to pursue the sport. He even fished with Hoover on one very public occasion. Hoover had purchased a 164-acre site in Virginia for a retreat during his tenure and, in 1929, built several pools by hand in the headwaters of the Rapidan River. During the war years, when fishing offshore was considered a security risk, Roosevelt looked for an inland location with good trout fishing. He selected an old CCC camp that he originally renamed Shangri-La; later it became better known as Camp David. Carter performed incredible acts of diplomacy there with the Camp David Accords, and used the presidential retreat as a weekend fishing resort and base of departure for clandestine fishing trips to Spruce Creek, Pennsylvania. Reportedly, Carter and First Lady Roselyn arrived by helicopter at Camp David, waved to the press, waited for them to leave and hopped right back on the chopper for a short ride north. They fished in relative peace on a private farm and returned to Camp David for a well-documented departure to Washington by the same helicopter. Unlike the trout Carter targeted, the press never caught on.

Several presidents frequented private fishing estates seeking solitude. Coolidge fished at Henry Clay Pierce's four-thousand-acre Cedar Island Estate near Lake Superior, which featured a hatchery and was guarded by an eight-foot wire fence and two lookout towers.[109] Pierce made a fortune in oil and was considered one of the richest men in the country. Cleveland was president during some of the tumultuous strike years of the 1880s and 1890s. During the time between his two presidencies, he bought Gray Gables, a house on a one-hundred-acre plot of land in Buzzards Bay, Massachusetts.[110] He later fished there and elsewhere with well-known railroad pioneer John Murray Forbes and railroad financier Elias Cornelius Benedict. In one strange incident, Cleveland secretly had surgery on Benedict's seventy-ton yacht, *Oneida*, in Long Island Sound to hide a health ailment at the start of his second term.[111] Cleveland even gave a speech to a collection of anglers at the Old Colony Club in Buzzards Bay.[112] Eisenhower fished Aksel Nielsen's Byers Peak Ranch in Colorado, which controlled access to three miles of the St. Louis River. Nielsen made his money in real estate and mortgage financing and was president and then chairman of the board of the Mortgage Investments Company. Lastly, Carter made more than a dozen of his clandestine helicopter trips to visit Wayne Harpster's farm in Pennsylvania.

At the taxpayers' expense, both Secret Service and hatchery trucks often preceded presidential fishing trips. Hoover stocked his Rapidan River retreat with rainbows. Roosevelt fished in Hunting Creek at Camp David for brook trout secretly stocked without the president's knowledge.[113] In Vermont, Furnace Brook was heavily stocked for President Eisenhower from a nearby federal hatchery. Most embarrassingly, Coolidge fished for trout especially stocked and confined by wire-mesh booms within a section of river in the Black Hills as part of a covert Secret Service operation. These special efforts kept presidents happy and surely contributed to political support for state game-management practices.

Perhaps it is understandable that fishing and politics will mix. With more than sixty-five million licensed anglers in the country in the 1990s, Mares suggested that anglers are the nation's second-largest voting bloc.[114] Presidential candidates recognize this fact and arrange photo opportunities designed to appeal to anglers. However, at times politics becomes so personal it raises questionable outcomes. In one strange instance, a man convicted of manslaughter had his ten-to-fifteen-year sentence commuted to one and a half to five years after he supplied excellent batches of artificial flies, first to the state governor and then President Eisenhower.[115] Carter was a big supporter of Trout Unlimited and the Federation of Fly Fishers. He and his chairman of the Federal Reserve both helped fund-raising efforts for Catskill Fly Fishing Center in Livingston Manor, New York. Carter also helped to raise funds to support the International Fly Fishing Center in Montana. After his term in office, Carter used his political·pull to convince the U.S. Customs Service to modify a law governing the labeling of imports to specifically exclude artificial flies. None of these should be considered acts of treachery, but these stories certainly add to the sense that fly fishing somehow enjoys a political status above its true value as an activity of leisure.

In summing up, no single political or environmental outlook characterized the early class of affluent anglers, but to deny the importance of social status would be uninformed. Because of their station in life, these groups of anglers had major impacts on how rivers would be managed into the future. As we take stock of the country's current state of rivers, we may find some solace that a few rivers and plots of land in Long Island and elsewhere exist for public use directly or indirectly because they once served as game preserves for the über-rich. In other places, No Trespassing signs persist, but large chunks of relatively intact forest survive because individual millionaires and collections of prosperous anglers continue to fight off developers. Even presidents have taken advantage of private lands and elite fishing clubs where fishing stories and political ideas were surely swapped in equal measure. How these specific experiences impacted political thinking and action is hard to verify, but it is equally difficult to suggest that national decisions are unaffected by these fishy encounters.

CHAPTER THREE

Fish Factories Feed Lots

*The production of ecologically viable individuals is not part of the hatchery
equation because the production of large quantities of fish, rather than natural
history, behavior and ecology, largely guides hatchery practices.*

~ CULUM BROWN AND RACHEL DAY, 2002

*A*lthough it may be stupid to feel empathy for an animal that may itself be beyond reason, hatcheries are sad places for me. The preordained fate that awaits trout seems unfair. It is hard not to see these places as prisons with little for the fish to do but grow fat and long. Each tank contains uniformity of shape and size. Countless bodies clad in identical prison clothing march in a never-ending, undulating fitness program. Fin constantly touches fin among innumerable similarly aged brethren. Various segments of the hatchery pens resemble large cellblocks where each fish is destined to serve the same length term. Each detainee mirrors every other's confinement. Trout with worn fins hover just above the cement floor waiting, always waiting, for that dark human silhouette that will appear and refill the automatic pellet feeders that supply life-giving nutrients.

The lack of physical features within most hatcheries differs dramatically from the types of habitats fish encounter when they are released. As two conservation biologists from the University of Cambridge reported: "For the most part, hatchery environments are completely devoid of structure. They tend to comprise of a featureless, monotonic enclosure with no opportunity to escape from conspecifics [other trout] or display any other natural behavior. They bear no resemblance whatsoever to the fish's natural environment and densities can be up to 100 times greater than those in nature."[1] Hatcheries contain countless masses sluggishly swimming in concrete pens with nothing to anticipate but the next food pellet dispersed by machine. They are protected from avian and terrestrial predators by tall fences and overhead wires. Hatchery fish are raised mostly to supply pleasure, and few trout will be used to fill human's nutritional needs. These trout are a product, not a functioning member, of an ecosystem.

When their sentence finally ends, the fish will be transported miles away by trucks waiting just outdoors and delivered to rivers that appear to have no bounds. As I saw on the Salmon River, many of these parolees cluster together and mill around as they take in their new exercise yard. A few of the clever ex-cons disperse — in case hatchery wardens decide to revoke these mass paroles. Each fish's hundred shadows eventually disappear. One true silhouette remains, a shadow becoming the new dark friend that was previously lost amid hundreds of indistinguishable outlines on murky concrete floors. In all respects, it is alone for the first time in its life.

Food does not drop as pellets from the heavens at timely intervals in rivers. It must be sought in the form of strange new morsels that float by.

After a day or two, a growing sensation of hunger must become the fish's one central focus. Eventually, a familiar silhouette appears above the water's surface. Then, a tiny splash that reminds of countless pellet lunches. The shape of the meal is unfamiliar, but in this strange new world everything must be tasted to see if it is edible. Suddenly, the fish senses a new unpleasant metallic taste and feels a yank on its jaw. It fights using muscles that were never properly developed in the confined, barren walls of the hatchery run. Tattered fins cannot propel the fish to safety. An invisible force pulls the fish slowly and inevitably toward the surface. A net appears and the fish feels the full weight of gravity on its body. No longer a nurtured pet, the fish can finally look with unblinking eye into the face of its creator. The creator's face is attached to a familiar silhouette that was previously known only in blurred form, a face that continuously watched this fish slowly grow from egg to fry to fingerling to prized possession.

With luck, the fish will be admired and dropped back in a stream to repeat the horror at the end of another's line. How many times a fish can fight this battle and live is anyone's guess. If the fish survives long enough in the wild to endure the harsh conditions brought by winter ice, it will probably end up on someone's plate the next season. If it is a real trophy, it will be immortalized on a plaque above a fireplace mantel. So ends the life of a hatchery-raised trout. The waterway is temporarily depleted, but next week a truck will come back to add a new Cracker Jack prize to the stream.

~ ~ ~ For more than a hundred years, Americans stocked trout originating from distant seaboards in order to supply fishing demands. Other fish, including several species of carp, were imported, while rainbow trout and salmon were exported overseas. Despite limited knowledge about the number of fish that could be supported by native waters, it became standard procedure to stock large numbers of fish during the late 1800s and early 1900s.[2] Little changed in the next century, and by 1948 there were 522 state-run hatcheries and 99 federal facilities that employed more than three hundred trained biologists.[3] Despite this apparent technical knowledge base, biological mistakes were made. Before the scientific discovery of the function of DNA in 1943, state and federal hatcheries unknowingly altered the genetic makeup and biodiversity of our nation's waters with aggressive rearing activities. As early as the 1940s, concerns were raised that the process of natural selection was circumvented by hatcheries trying to boost survival rates. According to a 2004 scientific paper, breeding practices that ended more than forty years earlier continue to create genetic problems in modern trout.[4] These concerns stem from activities, including a series of experiments from 1919 to 1930 conducted by a Cornell University professor at Hacketts-town Hatchery in New Jersey, to try to produce disease-resistant strains of trout. Eventual inbreeding produced trout with higher growth rates and increased egg output for less food.[5] Fish stocked by hatcheries today are not genetically equivalent to those that lived in rivers more than a century ago, but boy are there plenty of the new version!

The number of trout stocked in this country's rivers every year is stagger-ing. In 2011 alone, New York State introduced more than 7.2 million trout and salmon, a population that rivals the number of people in the great port city itself.[6] These were not little fry that required a magnifying lens to see. Most stocked fish were above the legal limit with an average length of more than six inches. If we lined up these stocked trout nose to tail, they would stretch a length of more than seven hundred miles, the approximate dis-tance from New York City to Indianapolis. More than 80 percent of these stocked fish are nonindigenous species that originated in Europe and the western United States. Even without including massive stocking efforts to restore anadromous Atlantic salmon, the six New England states contrib-ute an additional five million trout and non-migratory salmon every twelve months.[7] Additions from just Maine, Massachusetts, and Vermont would stretch nose-to-tail from New York City to Portland, Maine. All six New England states stock nonnative brown and rainbow trout; three of them also add tiger trout, a sterile hybrid of introduced brown and native brook trout that exist only because of constant restocking. They are attractive to fisheries managers because they obtain a high growth rate and do not waste energy on reproduction. Maine does not participate in those efforts but does add splake, a hybrid combination of a male brook trout and female lake trout. Splake can reproduce but rarely do. Spurred by ecological concerns, almost 85 percent of the state's remaining stocking effort centers on native species of trout and landlocked salmon. The other New England states stock between 37 and 87 percent exotic species, which compete with native Atlantic salmon, brook and lake trout.

Continuing south, Delaware, Maryland, New Jersey, and Pennsylva-nia add almost six million trout each year.[8] One hatchery in New Jersey produces approximately one hundred miles of trout a year. Delaware does not add many fish, but those trout face a grim future as the state admitted: "Since Delaware stream temperatures are marginal at best for trout survival in the summer, and no reproduction has been noted, stocked fish are meant to be taken, not caught and re-released."[9] Despite problems with native species, almost 60 percent of trout introduced in the Garden State and greater than 80 percent of trout in the Keystone State are nonindigenous species. Maryland and Pennsylvania even stock a novelty fish called golden rainbow trout. Golden rainbow trout (*Oncorhynchus mykiss*), not to be confused with California's golden trout (*Oncorhynchus aguabonita*), are trout with a genetic flaw that produces a gold-orange colored fish. Along the fish's sides, Creamsicle-orange bands stand out against a background of more muted hues reminiscent of cheap beer. These trout were selectively bred as a special treat for anglers. Talk about fool's gold in an artificial sluiceway. The pyrite-like, golden rainbow trout is the clearest example of ecological compromises adopted to support trout-driven economics. Pennsylvania produced a slightly less brilliant version called the palomino rainbow trout. In contrast, the true golden trout evolved in the wild in the state known, fittingly enough, for its famous gold rush. In the West, introduced brook and brown trout compete with and eat the California golden trout, and human stocking efforts with hybridized rainbow-golden trout push the pure genetic strain to the edge of extinction.[10] Meanwhile, in the East, the pyrite-like, golden trout competes with native brook trout. Clearly, efforts to spread trout to new waters come with unwise costs.

As part of my research's due diligence, I visited several hatcheries. My first exposures came during family outings and Cub Scout excursions. Although children do not often visit factories or feedlots to see the engines of mass production, hatcheries appear to be a general exception to the rule. No hatchery visit was more anticipated than my recent quest for golden rainbow trout. Children's literature contains accounts of powerful fish that are caught by some lucky soul and that subsequently agree to grant the fortunate angler any desire imaginable. These stories describe chance encounters with seemingly impossible odds of occurrence. I must admit I felt a bit like a kid as I headed out on my adventure, but unlike in the magical quest of yore, I knew just where to find the supernaturally radiant fish of my dreams. I was on my way to the Albert Powell Hatchery in Hagerstown, Maryland. I mused, where else would I go to find an enchanted fish but in a land of merry? I planned to work my hatchery visit into a separate research project in Virginia; an investigation of a decades-old erosion-control project that had done more harm than good. I decided to head down I-81 on my way to conduct my field research and hit any hatcheries on the way. Albert Powell

Hatchery was on my list, but was not the closest to home. I would have to wait for the big prize.

The golden rainbow trout I sought were selectively bred from a single female observed in a West Virginia hatchery pen in 1955, but golden trout have also been produced in other states, Poland, Japan, and elsewhere.[11] Meanwhile, genetically independent populations of pigmentless and subsequently whiter albino rainbows were created in at least eight university, federal, and state hatcheries in Pennsylvania, South Dakota, Utah, Montana, Idaho, and Washington.[12] Perhaps it seems a perfect contradiction in terms, but I could catch a colorless rainbow. In addition to breeding efforts for rainbows, populations of albino brook trout were maintained in at least Pennsylvania, Utah, and Washington.[13] In Michigan, approximately 1 percent of lake trout raised and stocked from the Jordan River National Fish Hatchery are albino,[14] which seems like an unnaturally high number. Back in West Virginia, the 1950s yellow-mottled female soon earned the nickname "Little Camouflage,"[15] which was both an accurate description and a warning. Had the original fish been born in the wild, its genetic mutation would have doomed her to an early death. As the big bad wolf might say, "The better to see you my dear." However, hatchery staff quickly recognized a marketing opportunity when they peered down and saw gold staring back. The oddball female differed from a true albino in color as well as in its normal eye coloration. Eggs from this one fish were fertilized with milt from a single male and approximately three hundred light-colored fingerlings were produced from nine hundred eggs.[16] These funny fry were not true golden trout yet; they were half-breeds or palominos, but later pairings of palominos produced 24K gold in about one-quarter of the offspring.[17] Offspring of golden rainbows then retained their purity. It took eight years of careful breeding to remove the nasty tendency of golden fish to be undersized, but eventually a large enough population existed at Spring Run Hatchery in Petersburg for public consumption.[18] When it was first introduced to rivers in West Virginia it was called a centennial trout in honor of the state's one hundredth anniversary. California stocks a similar-colored trout they call the "lightning rainbow."[19] But, golden rainbow trout is the more common name for this bizarre creature.

Rainbow trout can take on a rainbow of different colors, with at least seven color variations in total—highlighted by albino, golden, green, and blue end members.[20] I eventually discovered almost thirty journal articles describing one color variation or another. According to these publications, the various fish have flaws. Golden rainbow trout are often more lethargic than their darker cousins, and more sensitive to sunlight.[21] Slow growth is also an issue. Future generations outperformed their dull, multicolored rainbow brethren in Pennsylvania,[22] although these results differed in a Polish scientific study.[23] Survival rates of golden and blue rainbows are lower than common rainbows, and the cobalt version apparently suffers from the typical American afflictions of obesity, liver disease, and kidney problems.[24] These last unsavory traits were very disappointing to researchers — it had been hoped that the silvery blue color would be a useful marketing trait for production trout.

Selective breeding that promotes recessive genes and hereditary mutations are prime examples of genetic monocultures, which worry conservation biologists and environmentalists. Here are fish known to be genetically inferior in the wild from a "survival of the fittest" perspective. Still, for more than fifty years these fish were bred by the thousands each year and annually introduced to multiple streams and ponds. Utah alone stocked more than ninety-five thousand or 13.5 miles of pigmentless brook trout in 2011.[25] The golden version is also widely distributed.

So now I was off to see this precocious fish. I headed out the door June 1 and eventually made my first stop in Pennsylvania at the Huntsdale Hatchery. I knew that Pennsylvania's Fish and Boat Commission stocked golden rainbow trout, but not knowing what to expect, I felt a palpable sense of anticipation as I arrived. As I walked up to the very first pen, I knew I had hit pay dirt. Swimming in front of me were hundreds of foot-long, trout-shaped goldfish or goldfish-colored trout. I could not decide. Despite the fact I had seen pictures and knew what I was looking for, I was still a bit bewildered. Frankly, I think a more descriptive name for this fish would be the "what-the-hell-is-that" trout. I can only imagine my reaction if I had been unaware of these bizarre nuggets and seen one in a stream. Inside the pen was a mass of golden trout of similar size and a few rainbow trout with more usual coloration. As I watched a few darker rainbows caught in this sea of orange fins, I wondered if these "normal" rainbow trout had any idea who was the real oddball. I soon noticed another anomaly. The only younger trout in the pen was blue. I suspect this abnormal fish was scooped up from one of the other pens and added to the freak show. I was quite sure the hatchery staff had big plans for that bluish being.

Over by another line of tanks, two staff members were scrubbing scum off of the bottom of one run. They chatted with a small group of older visitors. I heard them mention the netting that surrounded the pens; they complained about fish lost to grackles. I noticed black birds with tiny fish in their beaks. They had easily snuck through small holes in the netting. Meanwhile, a concrete drainage channel emanating from the hatchery held trout fugitives that had apparently escaped captivity. These trout seemed happy enough to continue living surrounded by artificial walls despite the fact that they were essentially free. They probably fed off of waste emanating from the hatchery before it flowed into the local stream.

The noise of a thousand splashing fins had initially caught my attention. I noticed a pickup truck with a large hopper and quickly surmised that this setup was used to dispense the day's nutrients. As I watched the truck slowly drive down a long line of pens, a shower of pellets shot out into the water. Just behind the truck it looked as if someone had turned on a Jacuzzi. Water erupted into a sudden frenzy of writhing rainbows. Pen after pen burst into action as the truck crept on. I walked over to investigate and saw how this trout churning was so intense that flotsam and jetsam swirled around like the dance of leaves in a strong autumn breeze. Even though the water was only a few feet deep, it was impossible to see the bottom. I could just barely make out the outline of even foot-long rainbows below. The bubbling filth-filled water certainly did not conjure up images of crystal-clear mountain streams. In fact, the closest image I could invoke was a teenage experience sailing on the Charles River in Boston in community sailboats. Near the Community Boathouse a large bubbler situated on the bottom of the river kept organic waste from sucking all the oxygen out of the water. One day my friend and I were fumbling around at the helm of our borrowed, four-yard yacht when we were caught by a gust of wind. As novice sailors, even that little puff was enough to upset our world. We failed to release the mainsail, tilted too far and quickly swamped the boat. Jumping onto the bow and fearfully looking into the cockpit I saw brown, flotsam-filled water, made famous in song, swirling around my shipmate's feet. Decades later, as I peered into the murky depths of the hatchery pen, the lyrics "I love that dirty water" came to mind — but certainly did not invoke my true feelings.

As I patiently observed the trout, they quieted down after the food vanished. Eventually, I began to perceive an occasional gentle clinking sound, a pleasant tone a bit like a wind chime or perhaps a tiny doorbell. A bit confused at first, I looked for the source of the tune. It took me a minute to conclude that trout were nudging against the grate on the upstream end of the runs. Pipes tenderly bumped against steel brackets that confined these trout, creating a metallic ringing. Some musicians were looking for a way out. But what I initially interpreted as a jingle was, in fact, part of a rowdy ruckus. Unruly inmates were rattling their cages! It reminded me of an old movie cliché of a prisoner raking his tin cup along the bars of his cell. I pictured Jimmy Cagney or perhaps Humphrey Bogart screaming for guards to go get the warden. I wondered what this trout had to say that was so important. My curiosity about the origin of the noise satisfied, I quietly moved along. I would not play accomplice to any jailbreaks today.

After I walked around outside to see the inmates, I strolled over to the visitor center and went inside to see exhibits on outdoor fishing. I immediately noticed a large mounted golden rainbow trout above the doorway to the main portion of the visitor center and snapped a picture. The same fish that greeted hundreds of hatchery visitors now emblazons the back cover and frontispiece of this book and invites readers to join my quest. It is a fish that is strangely beautiful and grotesque at the same time. The body is oddly warped, perhaps to recreate a single moment in time when the fish was unnaturally yanked from the water. The pose suggests both excitement and sadness. This event signaled the fish's death, but in no way characterizes its previous existence. The belly looks bloated from too many hatchery meals. The coloration is artificial but strangely familiar. The mouth opens perhaps because it holds a fly, is gasping for breath or is desperately trying to tell the visitor something important about its life. It was clear to me that this fish is a symbol for much of what is wrong with coldwater fish management. This fish is just one of millions of carbon-copy "what-the-hell-is-that" trout manufactured for humans' amusement. For me, it was the Holy Grail, albeit with a bit of Monty Python thrown in.

Inside the visitor's center were displays showing different types of fish, historic hatchery practices, and two large tanks with live specimens in case the outdoor fish weren't enough. One sign caught my attention. It was titled, "An Angler's Dream" and showed all the different kinds of trout in the state including the golden rainbow trout and albino brook trout. Another sign touted "The Non-Native Fish of Pennsylvania." The commission was quick to put a good spin on exotic invasive species: "Pennsylvania streams in the year 1800 hadn't the variety of fish that we find today. The specimens illustrated here have been so successfully introduced into the state's waters over the years that they seem to have been here all the time." All the species pictured were game fish. The commission is not as cheery about other specimens such as sea lampreys, which do not need intentional introductions to make themselves successfully at home in Lake Erie, where they prey on trout and salmon. Major efforts are now underway to eradicate the lamprey from the Great Lakes.

In one display case I noticed a huge artificial fly tied on a hook that was perhaps eight inches long. Below the hook was written, "A Fisherman's Prayer," followed by a little poem.

> May the good lord grant
> That some day
> Even I
> Might catch a fish
> On a make-believe fly

Putting the separation of church and state issue aside, I thought these words seemed out of place. I wondered why an agency with restoration as part of its stated goals promoted fishing to such a degree? But here resided the poem, located in a building devoted to altering the genetic makeup of a non-native fish simply so that people could fish for a novelty. On second thought, I realized I was out of place. The terms "angler's dream" and "make-believe" certainly seemed to characterize my entire hatchery expedition. After snapping a quick picture of the giant hook, I decided this claim was all played out, and it was time to prospect farther south.

After I had my fill of Keystone fish, I jumped back into my pickup and rambled an hour down to Albert Powell Hatchery near Hagerstown, Maryland. The hatchery is located immediately off and within sight of I-70. I wondered how many trout leave their hatchery raceways and begin their journey to the wild racing at 65 mph along this same highway. The hatchery was smaller and much more subdued than its northern cousin. There were no other visitors, no visitor center and few signs. The only outdoor display had a few educational tidbits, a No Fishing sign and a stocking schedule. Behind the display sat the heart of the facility: each pen was a long cement channel with a mixture of normal and golden rainbow trout. These were not big fish; they would surely need a few more meals before they were released. Many trout sat motionless in the runs while they waited for their turn to speed along the interstate beyond the tree line. I noticed this hatchery had forgone bird netting and, predictably, a great blue heron sat three hundred yards away in a large dead tree overlooking the fish. It could surely see the glowing delicacies even from that distance, but it seemed more interested in me. I went to get a picture, but as soon as I lifted my camera to take the shot, the bird flew off. Too bad — that would have made an interesting picture!

The heron reminded me of an incident almost twenty years earlier. At the time, I worked as a consultant at a small firm in Massachusetts which investigated groundwater contamination. In the back of the office building was a little pond where someone had thrown goldfish years back. Nobody seemed to care much for these fish, but somehow they survived to produce several different-aged clusters of fish. All that changed one day. Some lucky heron, probably flying to a much larger body of water, was fortunate enough to look down. To herons, goldfish must be like a dream come true. Here is a fish marked with a highlighter. The heron landed and stayed for a week. By the time it finally flew away, only a few goldfish were left. Back in Maryland, this heron was probably just as eager to exploit the hatchery's bright anomalies that nature never would have let spin so completely out of control.

I was a little disappointed as I walked along raceways and saw only smaller fish. They were interesting enough, but hard to photograph — though, I am sure the heron and other smaller birds flying around thought these miniature morsels were just spellbinding. As I started to walk along a different row of tanks, I noticed a strange phenomenon. Fish all seemed to be frantically swimming toward me, not away. I looked down and noticed an open bucket of food pellets at the corner of each pen. The scientist in me was curious now, and I methodically observed each group of fish as I approached their cell. Ten times in a row, fish all raced toward me and clustered in the corner near the food bucket. Even my golden retriever hardly showed that much enthusiasm when I came home. Apparently these trout could tell the shape of a human silhouette, but could not tell the difference between an official hatchery uniform and my white T-shirt.

I finally found big broodstock fish in a separate pen built a bit like a maze. It was long, rectangular and could be separated into different sections, but was open so the fish had full access to many different areas. They didn't care. They only wanted to hang out by two automatic feeders. A green plastic box comprised the main body of the feeders with a set of tiny brass gears in a clear plastic enclosure attached to the end. Shiny-yellow cogs constantly turned and, as I sat by the tank, pellets occasionally dropped into the water. Fish suddenly came to life fighting for floating morsels. I began to realize that the trout's entire life cycle moved to the rhythm of those tiny sprockets. Each extra gram of fat and incremental increase in length was a result of the progress of these metallic cogs. What a crazy way to live! I dismissed this thought, glanced at the hands of my watch, and realized that I needed to grab lunch.

As I walked back to my truck, I noticed the heron back on its roost near the top of the barren tree. I lifted my camera for a shot and once again the heron took flight. I must say I found it very interesting that the bird was terrified of man, but the trout at the same facility would have jumped into my hands if given the chance. I wondered if the heron was just tense or perhaps had learned from experience to be extra cautious near the hatchery. The trout clearly knew nothing of the fate that awaited them. As I pondered this situation, I headed back onto the highway to focus my attention on the field research that awaited me in Virginia.

After my research in Virginia, I worked my way back north. However, if I had explored around Virginia and farther south into North Carolina, South Carolina, and Georgia, I would have found some of their 2.4 million stocked trout each year.[26] With the Eastern Seaboard covered, I then could have drifted west like the pioneers of old. Crossing the Appalachian Mountains provides no real barrier to me or trout. Kentucky receives approximately 800,000 or 113 miles of trout annually with 97 percent exotic species from Wolf Creek National Fish Hatchery alone.[27] The Tennessee Wildlife Resources Agency stocks roughly 325,000 or 53 miles of trout each year, and a report indicates the U.S. Fish and Wildlife Service released 1.1 million rainbow trout in the state in 2004.[28] Unfortunately for these creatures, many are intentionally stocked in waters where summer temperatures are too high for their continued survival. Ohio, Illinois, and Indiana toss in more than 600,000 specimens monopolized by exotic species.[29] The northern strongholds of Michigan, Wisconsin, and Minnesota plant roughly 10.8 million mostly nonnative trout and salmon each year.[30]

I have driven across the country several times in my life. When I first traveled west over the Mississippi and across the desolate expanse of the Great Plains, I had no idea that trout surrounded me on my journey. But it is impossible to cross this part of the country and not find a state that stocks trout. Iowa, Missouri, and Arkansas place more than five million trout per annum.[31] I usually think of those places as agricultural regions, but thanks in part to agreements made with the federal government when many of the region's rivers were dammed, these states now grow more than just corn. Here and elsewhere, U.S. Fish and Wildlife Service hatcheries are located adjacent to reservoirs and help supply the district's trout. In this previously troutless region, trout are obviously introduced species and are mostly tossed into impoundments and tailwater portions of rivers downstream of dams. Further west, regardless of whether I cross the Great Plains through North Dakota, South Dakota, Nebraska, Kansas, Oklahoma, or Texas, I can't avoid the approximately 1.6 million trout stocked annually.[32] Trout in these six states are all as foreign to the native landscape as the rusted windmills and grain towers that dot the area. In modern times, trout-filled reservoirs replace rusted windmills and trout displace native aquatic species.

As the dusty voyage through the Great Plains nears its completion, a distant mirage of snow-capped peaks grows into a new reality. I am approaching the promised lands for trout, with more than 3.3 million rainbow trout stocked each year.[33] Somehow, Colorado offers more than 570 miles of catchable rainbow trout alone. Here and elsewhere, fishing is allowed even in national parks — while the remaining wildlife is carefully protected. The state also stocks millions of cutthroat, brown, brook, lake, and splake trout for the taking. When I imagine the faint outline of the Rocky Mountains beginning to appear on the horizon, I am reminded of my drive to Colorado to attend graduate school. I left the warm sheltered backwaters of New England to visit the mighty Colorado, Snake, Rio Grande, Missouri, and Columbia Rivers. Once I arrived, I spent many hours sitting along high mountain creeks watching water carve an underwater home for trout. I learned to read turbulent flows, not as an angler, but as a scientist. I waded in raging, near-freezing water, feeling the tug on my waders produced as tornado-like vortices and boils traveled downstream. At times I felt as if I had been struck by a solid object, only to look around and realize that the turbulent water was playing a game of tag and I was "it." Of course not all days were filled with drama. I spent many of my days penned up with other graduate students in a small drab cinderblock-walled room with one tiny window plus multiple desks and filing cabinets. Perhaps it is that experience in particular that makes me feel so sorry for the hatchery trout in their mundane pens.

One day, I was collecting measurements in Wild Basin on a rickety old footbridge, peacefully enjoying clear sunny skies in the mountains of Colorado. Below me a current-meter meticulously rotated to translate thousands of gallons of churning and twisting water into a single bland number. Although I was intent on science, I was not blind to beauty. I observed my surroundings as carefully as the metal instrument in my hand. Soon, a broad-winged hummingbird buzzed in and began to hover just above the water's surface.

I was used to hummingbirds in the area with their daring mating dives that surely inspired barnstormers of old. Male hummingbirds begin at flag-pole height and drop into power dives, pulling up just above the ground's surface. I would usually hear these maneuvers before I could spot the dare-devil. The bird's wings beat so fast they create a humming sound; hence the bird's name. The changing pitch of buzzing birds mimics the alternating tune a race car makes when speeding by. Occasionally, birds would zip in and inspect me if I happened to be costumed in crimson. I would clumsily turn my head in a futile attempt to follow the bird's flight, fully aware of the different paces of life we followed. I appreciated their visits, but was always too slow to mount a worthwhile response.

On this occasion, I sat on the bridge as the bird came in low over the water. It cared little about my presence and was apparently transfixed by the play of light on the shimmering current below. I am not sure if the alpine aviator or I was more shocked at the sudden mass that shot out of the water. A rainbow trout, often acknowledged as an aerial acrobat itself, had made its move. If I had controlled the little feathered flier, another native species would have ended its life as lunch for a foreign trout. But hummingbirds are quicker than I, and danger was averted. In an instant, tiny wings carried the iridescent-green aeronaut off to safer airspace in some distant flowerbed. I knew I had witnessed an event that I was unlikely to ever see again. The incident forever impressed me with the ferociousness of a rainbow trout in search of a meal.

During my time in Colorado I often made short trips south, west, and north to visit national parks and scenic wonders in the region. In each direction hordes of trout waited. New Mexico, Colorado's southern neighbor, has a robust stocking program for native and introduced species. Northward, Wyoming discusses exotic species on their website and warns, "aquatic invasive species (AIS) are organisms that are not native and cause significant harm to an ecosystem when introduced."[34] The Department highlights five species: two mollusks, a plant, crayfish and the Asian carp. Despite these concerns, the state proudly reports the addition of nonnative species that include brook, brown, golden, rainbow, lake, and splake trout among the greater than 3.6 million trout and salmon stocked each year.[35] Historically, the state also stocked ohrid trout. To make it to the Cowboy State, this little-known trout completed a voyage all the way from Ohrid Lake, located in the Republic of Macedonia. It was brought to the United States by the U.S. Fish and Wildlife Service and shipped to a federal hatchery in Iowa and a state hatchery in Minnesota in the 1960s.[36] It was also introduced to neighboring Colorado and Montana, and more distant Tennessee. Meanwhile, in the fish-eat-fish world of the Wild West, it is the ironically named native cutthroat trout that cannot compete. Several subspecies of this trout are listed as threatened throughout the Rocky Mountain region. One of the primary reasons for population declines is competition with introduced species, especially rainbow and brown trout.

To the west of Colorado, Utah is an amazing destination with impressive mountains, panoramic views of red rock mesas and narrow slot canyons worn smooth by millennia of sporadic floods. The state places 7.3 million trout annually in this landscape, which tally more than seven hundred miles in length.[37] Approximately 80 percent of the fish are nonnative, and exotic fish stocked in Flaming Gorge Reservoir alone number almost 500,000 rainbow trout and kokanee salmon. The dam at Flaming Gorge resembles an overgrown Lego structure thrust into the rough rocky escarpments of a deep canyon. Pickup trucks parked at the base look like small toys from higher up on canyon walls. The reservoir and the other nonnative invasive game fish it contains create major problems with genetically unique fish that originally evolved in the Colorado River and Green River watersheds. In particular, bonytail chub, Colorado pikeminnow, humpback chub, and razorback sucker are all listed as endangered species partly because trout like to eat their young.

Further downriver in Arizona, rainbow trout prosper in Marble Canyon and the Grand Canyon within the nation's most easily recognized National Park.[38] Once again, these exotic invasive trout push native Colorado River species to the brink of extinction and trout are now themselves the target of an eradication program by the National Park Service.[39] Furthermore, Glenn Canyon Dam now traps most suspended sediment carried by the waterway and steals the water's associated red color that originally gave the river a name. Standing on the south rim of the canyon, I see how the bluish water stands in sharp contrast to the region's red cliffs. It is only because the dam has reduced sediment loads that trout survive. If the river was restored to its former muddier habits, trout would suffocate and die. In response to concerns about exotic trout and an invasion of quagga mussels at the Lake Mead Fish Hatchery, trout stocking was ended further downriver in the reservoir backed up by Hoover Dam.[40] Quagga mussels are mollusks from Ukraine, similar to exotic zebra mussels in the way they disrupt aquatic food webs.[41] Apparently, the Nevada hatchery was accidentally producing and stocking this nonnative species along with exotic rainbow trout. North in Nevada and Oregon, historic stocking of rainbow trout hybridized Alvord cutthroat trout into extinction.[42] This demised species was initially discovered in 1934 by one of the country's most famous ichthyologists, Carl Leavitt Hubbs. He pickled a few for his University of Michigan collection, which now serve as a genetic benchmark that current fish fail to attain. In Arizona, Verde trout are now extinct, and threatened Apache and endangered Gila trout are in rapid decline, largely because of stocking nonnative trout.[43] However, Arizona and Nevada remain generally undeterred and stock four million trout each year despite decades of problems with native trout.[44]

When it comes to visions of the West, many trout anglers immediately picture Montana and wild stocks of trout. To help protect the wild nature of both native and nonnative trout species found in the state, the Montana Fish, Wildlife and Parks agency discontinued stocking of rivers in the 1970s and continued to stock only lakes and reservoirs. Of course reservoirs are just dammed rivers, and state hatcheries are still busy producing just fewer than 7 million trout, salmon, and grayling.[45] Montana currently lists five species of introduced trout, along with four hybrid species; the five species of native trout include the Montana Arctic grayling. The stocked specimens add three hundred miles of trout and eighty-five miles of salmon and grayling to our nation's waterways. There is fishing even for bull trout despite the fact it is currently listed as a threatened species under the Endangered Species Act. It made the list because of historic competition from introduced rainbow, brown, lake, and brook trout. Despite these concerns and an overall focus on wild trout, the state planned to stock more than 3.3 million nonnative trout species in 2010, versus 620,000 of the native cutthroat species of trout.

Years ago I passed through Idaho's stocked waters as I traveled to Oregon and Washington. The more than 3.8 million trout stocked each year in those waters does not include the 10 million trout fry tossed in 2011.[46] In Washington, eastern brook trout become unwanted invaders and drive western species from their home waters. If I ventured south, I could finish my search for gold like thousands before me and rummage around the heavily stocked waters of California. In California, I will surely strike it rich with more than 50 million trout stocked in 2006 alone.[47] Imagine how much more alluring the California gold rush of 1849 would have been for early cross-country travelers if they could have found nuggets along the entire westward trip! In fact, I could easily line up our nation's annually stocked trout nose to tail as a continuous trail from Portland, Maine, all the way to Los Angeles and still have millions left over to fish for when I get there. And year after year the nation lines up a new annual crop of stocked fish and blazes a fresh trail of trout from a different eastern port to the shores of the Pacific Ocean. Imagine this annual cross-country voyage completed entirely on the backs of trout.

From California, I could catch a ship to Alaska. This state is renowned for its wild trout and salmon fishing. I have seen anglers elbow to elbow just off Route 1 in what has been called "combat fishing." Surprisingly, the state still adds more than 7.5 million trout and salmon to rivers each year to meet angler demand.[48] I now have only one place left to go on my westward travels. I will be sorely mistaken if I try to delude myself that I am safe from trout in Hawaii. Rainbow trout made it to this tropical paradise on the island of Kauai.[49] Of course, these fish are as exotic as the fancy drinks that greeted me on my sole visit to the islands. Trout, like the miniature umbrella-adorned beverages, were introduced to help draw more tourists.

All told, state and federal hatcheries currently supply almost one hundred fifty million trout annually from a subset of the more than one hundred federal and five hundred state hatcheries.[50] Private efforts from more than two thousand hatcheries of various kinds add an unknown additional number.[51] In fact, trout and salmon are the most extensively stocked, introduced and genetically altered group of game fish.[52] Furthermore, trout are now farmed in all fifty states, and the United States producers distributed fifty-seven million pounds of trout to consumers in 2007 alone.[53] The only states that do not appear to currently offer public trout stocking programs, mostly government sponsored, are Florida, Mississippi, and Louisiana. However, even these states have a history of stocking trout.[54] Trout stocked nationwide are mostly large catchable trout grown for short-term release and recapture. In Michigan this management policy has been termed "instant put-and-take trout fisheries."[55] Interestingly, instant put-and-take stocking has been around a long time.

The salmonid family includes not only trout, but several species of migrating salmon. Currently, millions of salmon are stocked for both restoration efforts and game fishing in the United States alone. Worldwide, the annual stocking estimate for Atlantic salmon is more than five billion, which begins to rival the world's growing human population.[56] While salmon stocking is often focused on efforts to save native fish runs, other plantings represent introduction programs of nonindigenous species. In the modern world, Pacific Chinook, coho, and pink salmon call the Great Lakes home. Unfortunately, wild populations of native lake trout are simultaneously vanishing from these waters. Meanwhile, Atlantic salmon finally managed to circumvent Niagara Falls by hitching a ride in trucks to visit Michigan. Pacific steelhead, a migratory version of rainbow trout, apparently found the elusive Northwest Passage and traveled all the way to Vermont. Most surprisingly, Colorado now supports the country's largest kokanee salmon run.[57] Little consideration seems to be given to the place of origin for many of these species. Adequate supply to support game fishing is the overarching goal.

In reality, fish do not line themselves up end-to-end in some nationwide parade of fin and tail designed to highlight massive fish stocking programs. Clearly this is just poetic license to create a sense of scale, migration, and movement. However, it is equally misleading to suggest that trout never leave their place of origin. Most fish that survive the rigors of their hatchery youth will eventually die miles from their place of birth. After all, fishing is strictly prohibited at hatcheries. Besides, anyone who has visited a hatchery and seen mature trout soon to be released will agree that the idea of casting into throngs of fish while they are still clumped together would seem unsporting. Today as in the past, trout are raised in concrete canals of numerous hatcheries as huddled masses not necessarily yearning to breathe free. To create the illusion of sport we must first transport these fish and liberate them in our nation's rivers and streams.

~ ~ ~ In centuries past, millions of people climbed into large containers of steel plate and rivet, and set out on endless waters in search of a brighter future in a new land. Some of these same ships carried brown trout to the New World. Today, millions of trout voyage on the backs of shiny steel trucks in pockets of wet surrounded by miles of dry. The vehicle of choice is a small six-wheeled truck with an odd square tank on the back and a state fish and game agency emblem on the door. States seem proud of these mass transit systems designed for trout. As the weekly fishing report for Colorado's Division of Wildlife proclaimed, "Among the earliest signs of spring in Colorado is a Division of Wildlife fish-stocking truck pulling up to a nearby lake or stream."[58] It seems that spring is nothing without a little diesel exhaust. Pick any working day during fishing season and it is likely that hatchery trucks are rolling. Because it is always trout season somewhere in the country, it is hard to find a time when our nation's stocking trucks are all parked.

During January, March, April, October, November, and December, trout are on their way to eager anglers in Iowa. Idaho conducts stocking March through November, apparently inspired by its state motto *"Esto perpetua"* or "Let it be perpetual." Trucks roll December through March in Texas. Arizona has trucks on the move April through September. In Pennsylvania, the big rigs are moving March through May and then again in October through December. In South Carolina, stocking programs run straight from February to November. In New Hampshire plantings occur from March through July. Oregon has a program running year round.

A pattern for widespread stocking is repeated throughout the country. North Carolina reports that six trucks from two different hatcheries cover sixty thousand miles each year alone.[59] In Wyoming, three trucks from just one of the state's ten hatcheries and rearing stations drive approximately fifty-two thousand miles to deliver up to two million trout a year.[60] Pennsylvania currently operates thirty-four trucks that are replaced every fifteen to twenty years when usage exceeds two hundred thousand miles.[61] These numbers suggest state trucks cumulatively drive three hundred fifty thousand miles or more each year. New York trucks drive more than five hundred thousand miles each year.[62] If you add up the hundreds of hatcheries nationwide and the millions of trout that need transportation, it is easy to see the cumulative impact of this aspect of hatchery operations. Hatchery trout need petroleum as much as they need water.

Like the U.S. Marines, fish and game departments launch a combination land, water, and airborne assault. Hatchery staff in Wyoming use backpacks and ATVs to distribute fish.[63] Even the cavalry is involved with horseback stocking to mountain lakes. Other locations more accessible by water have trout boated in. And as crazy as it might seem, fish are even flown to remote locations for aerial dispersal, a practice that dates back to just after World War II. In fact, one reason California golden trout are in difficulty is because California's Department of Fish and Game aerially stocked rainbow trout that unknowingly hybridized with golden trout.[64] It must be quite a sight for the native fish to look up and see the combination of trout and mist descending through the sky on a sunny day. Picture the rainbow trout gracefully descending through a true rainbow of droplet and sunshine. Perhaps this is what the author of one angling book meant when he called the rainbow trout a "fabulous aerial performer."[65] The idyllic picture of rainbows in the sky rapidly vanishes for native golden trout when hundreds of new competitors strike the water. If you are wondering if this airborne assault is some crazy anomaly, Alaska, Colorado, Georgia, Michigan, New Hampshire, New York, Oregon, South Carolina, Utah, and Wyoming are other states that did or do stock trout by airplane and helicopter. These tactics seem to add new meaning to the notion of a species invasion.

An article titled, "It's Raining Trout, Hallelujah," detailed Oregon's aerial stocking program.[66] The air time costs $3,600 per hour, with a total cost of almost $116,000 to drop three hundred thousand trout in a five-day effort. Rainbow, cutthroat, brook, and brown trout are released above about four hundred fifty lakes, including some in wilderness areas that otherwise ban motor vehicle and bicycle traffic. The vehicle ban is designed to preserve the wild nature of wilderness areas. Why the state stocks these regions with large numbers of exotic brook trout is anyone's guess. The high-tech aerial procedure involves GPS satellites and computer-generated flight paths to aid pilots and the aptly named bombardier in their mission. The author even described the canister and deployment device containing fish as something akin to the space shuttle. One fishery biologist was quoted, "You can't see much from the bombardier's seat. But doing this really makes me want to go fishing."[67] Somehow the idea of trying to catch a fish that was introduced to a pond as a skipping stone does not generate much enthusiasm in me. The story does conjure up young World War II bombardiers who shipped out to Europe and Asia to risk their lives. They were assigned the unenviable task of dropping death and destruction on those below. To native trout or macroinvertebrates and amphibians in previously fishless lakes, descending rainbow and brook trout might as well be explosives. Moreover, stocked trout are even more terrifying than simple ammunition because these invading trout are more intelligent than even our latest laser-guided smart munitions. Trout are able to conduct autonomous search-and-destroy missions, have endless numbers of reinforcements and will happily remain in the combat zone to mop up any survivors. The scene continues until the cavalry arrives. The crowd applauds as an ambitious angler gallops up on horseback and saves the day with rod and reel!

In Utah, the Division of Wildlife Resources drops brook, cutthroat, tiger, and splake trout from planes from July through September in a practice that dates back to 1956.[68] In their online publication explaining stocking activities, a fictional fisheries biologist provided a literary prop to give a sense of progress in fisheries management. The story begins by describing the old method of using pack horses and milk cans to access remote locations for stocking and then described the man's last trip. "The year is 1955. As he rides atop his horse, the old timer knows this will be his last trip. The new fixed-wing airplanes will replace him next year, and a way of life will be lost."[69]

When referencing the lost way of life, you might wonder if the Utah Division of Wildlife Resources was referring to native species that could be lost with continual stocking of exotic species, but alas no. After the presentation of some stocking data, the publication ends with another story of the old-timer: "Now it's time to take out his fly pole, and like an artist painting a masterpiece, catch his supper for the evening. He'll also survey the lake to see if it needs more fish next year, this time dropped from a plane in the sky."[70] Apparently the idea of fishing for hybridized tiger and splake trout that were raised in an artificial environment, flown in a Cessna 185 and dropped 150 feet into a lake below made the state agency envision famous Bierstadt paintings of high-mountain lakes. I have had a Bierstadt poster hanging over my desk for years, but I never noticed the outline of an airplane anywhere in the sky. Call me sarcastic, but I do not see the Division of Wildlife Resources' analogy to a Hudson River School masterpiece. Instead, I picture an old Xerox machine capable only of making endless numbers of cheap facsimiles.

Unfortunately, truck and aerial stocking efforts create their own environmental burden because of the need to transport fish and the associated water. Even back in the 1940s, Hackettstown Hatchery in New Jersey had a fleet of forty trucks to cover stocking in a radius of one hundred fifty miles around the hatchery.[71] Similarly, the main hatchery in Connecticut reported that it stocked six hundred thousand trout a year, and indicated that its trucks weighed more than eleven tons and carried approximately twenty-two hundred trout per trip. To transport trout to waiting anglers from the hatchery required at least two hundred fifty round trips a year with twenty-two hundred tons per mile per year when loaded. With only two state hatcheries to supply more than five thousand square miles of Connecticut, trucks must cover many miles annually. Not surprisingly, the facility has its own truck refueling station. Meanwhile, the same state agency in Connecticut invited me to participate in a special taskforce of scientists in 2009 to evaluate the possible impact of climate change on Connecticut rivers. One obvious recommendation would be to curb needless driving within Connecticut because it exacerbates greenhouse-gas emissions and global warming. This hatchery and annual stocking programs from other states represent millions of fish, collectively traveling thousands of miles in trucks mostly to distant waters. One possible impact from all the driving is to contribute to global warming to some unknown degree, which adds ultimately to the detriment of heat-intolerant trout.

Most people realize that it takes a fleet of trucks to keep our supermarkets stocked. For someone who does not understand the connection to arable land, it may be hard to imagine that without transportation, supermarkets would not be so super. Instead, stores would contain crowds of unhappy customers pushing around empty shopping carts while staring at bare shelves. Fewer people understand that without hatchery trucks many streams might also be largely devoid of fish. We could have groups of unhappy anglers wandering around with empty nets staring at barren waters. With stocking programs, many streams represent little more than cleverly disguised fish markets. When comparing recently caught stocked trout to purchased fish, a state hatchery employee from New York was quoted as saying, "it's the same as if you buy a trout dinner in a restaurant. Those fish are raised in hatcheries, and they taste all right."[72] In both cases we are talking about a factory product intended for economic consumption. One important difference is the added transportation cost of carrying hatchery trout and tons of water to a river versus the more efficient and environmentally friendly movement of cleaned, tightly packed, frozen fish to a local store. There is also less loss of edible food for market-bound fish compared to stocked trout that are often intentionally thrown back into the river to perpetuate the recreational benefit of the catch. Perhaps a main difference between fish in supermarkets and hatchery-raised trout caught in our nation's streams is the happy smile on an angler's face.

Much like signs at the ends of grocery aisles informing shoppers where to find various food items, state agencies appear compelled to provide clear notice on where trout can be found. Consequently, many state fisheries agencies proudly report stocking schedules on their websites. A sense of interstate rivalry between fisheries agencies vying for angler attention is obvious. Just type in "trout stocking" followed by a state name into your preferred web browser and you will probably see a state agency website appear near the top of the list. It is often easy to find detailed information on stocking programs. In many cases, advanced warning is provided for fish plantings. As a case in point, Pennsylvania provides an interactive database to help people cipher through a myriad of "stocking events." Pennsylvania's database includes the latitude and longitude of the reach of river, type of trout that will be stocked, the time for each stocking event, and a column called the "meeting place" that seems to specify locations anglers will be formally introduced to their quarry.[73] Such wording makes me imagine a lunch date. The state recommended, "If you would like to meet the stocking truck at the meeting location, we recommend that you arrive at least 30 to 45 minutes prior to the listed meeting time." Similarly, a Texas website promises to post a full schedule for the next winter stocking program by November of the preceding year.[74] With months to plan, it should be easy to attend to every possible detail. Oregon goes one step further and offers a handy e-mail service to provide their clientele with automatic updates of any changes in stocking schedules. Now anglers no longer need to fear being stood up on their big date. How embarrassing it is to get lost on the way to a scheduled rendezvous! Maryland and Oregon have solved this problem with handy links to Google Maps to show locations of stocking, while Delaware provides online topographic maps and Texas reports the date of each stocking on an interactive website that provides a link with directions to each site.[75] For the computer-savvy angler, each website provides one more tool to ensure the blind date ends in a perfect match.

All told, at least one-third of all states provide advanced warning of date and location for stocking efforts. Many other states provide information on the locations where trout were stocked as recently as the day before. An author of an angling book complained: "Millions of small rainbows are dumped into streams every year, many of them dead before they even hit the water. So-called anglers follow the trucks and catch their limit fast, because hatchery-raised fish are easy to catch after such a dumping."[76] State advertising programs seem to ensure this situation. Stocking trucks in Connecticut even have signs that read "Trout Onboard" and the date of opening day prominently displayed. Unlike signs on construction trucks that warn motorists not to follow, state hatchery trucks seem to invite an angler motorcade.

In 2009, Connecticut stocked four hundred thousand trout and expected two hundred thousand trout fishermen on opening day.[77] Twenty percent of the fish will be caught that day and by the end of the first two weeks of the season 58 percent of the fish will be gone.[78] According to a trout-tagging study conducted in West Virginia, 35 percent of the trout stocked were gone after one week.[79] Perhaps plantings are publicized because there is a perceived pressure on agencies to demonstrate that state monies are hard at work for citizens' benefit. Maybe it is just good business practice to let customers know the product they want is in stock. Possibly agencies hope fish are rapidly caught before they all die. In any case, trout will have almost no time to acclimate to their new surroundings before they are assaulted by web-savvy anglers.

As Pennsylvania implied for its stocking events, it is best to have a hook already in the water as new arrivals disembark because hatchery trout probably will not survive long. Luckily, stocking plans usually contain multiple trips at nicely spaced intervals to the same reaches of water so that plenty of hatchery-reared, predator-naïve trout, as scientists call them, will be available. Pennsylvania and New Hampshire stock many popular locations at least monthly during the season.[80] Texas stocks about twice a month.[81] Arizona, New Jersey, and West Virginia visit some sites on a weekly basis.[82] In 2011, the Utah Division of Wildlife listed 154 different stocking events in eleven months to Strawberry Reservoir outside of Provo to deliver more than 1.5 million trout and salmon.[83] In Oregon, the Rogue River above Lost Creek was stocked weekly with 2,250 rainbow trout per trip for a total of sixteen times from March 21 to September 9, 2012.[84] It is certainly interesting to ponder what happens to more than 2,000 trout a week in one of the more remote areas of the continental United States with its aptly named creek. Exactly where do they go?

CHAPTER FOUR

Educating the Masses

Rivers and the inhabitants of the watery element were made for
wise men to contemplate, and fools to pass by without consideration.
~ IZAAK WALTON, 1653

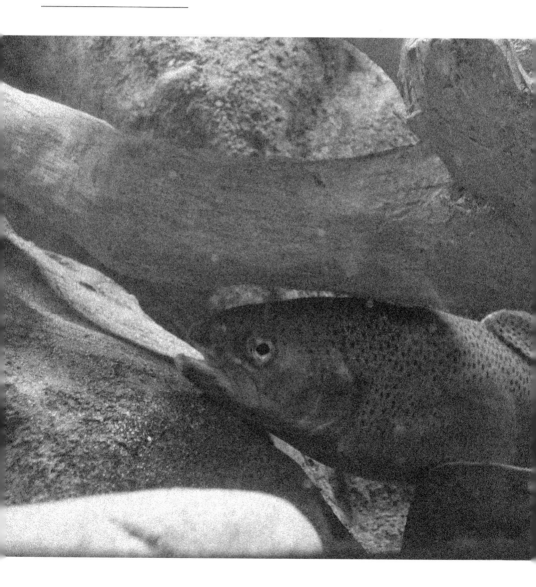

*O*ur nation is at a crossroads with our educational system. I spend sleepless nights wondering what is best for my daughter. Politicians and parents complain about low achievement in public schools. Private schools are scrutinized from social and economic perspectives. At places like the institution of higher education where I teach, tuition prices reach new heights that raise the ire of cash-strapped families. For-profit colleges surface with questionable classroom practices and requirements. People wonder if knowledge gains justify costs for various steps up the educational ladder. Does all this supposed knowledge equate to wisdom? The conclusion reached by many segments of the population seems to suggest that improvements are required. We need smarter kids and better schools. Congressional candidates talk about educational needs of future generations. Fixes are proposed, funds are allocated, and systems implemented.

The methods to improve student learning in elementary and middle schools revolve around national standards with high-pressure testing. The first big standardized test I faced occurred in high school. The SATs had both me and my fellow comrades shaking in our shoes. We knew that our own future would be heavily influenced by a few simple numbers produced by black and white ovals carefully filled in with yellow number two pencils. Now, my daughter and other elementary school children take tests that decide the fate of teachers and schools. Stories of educators systematically cheating to improve scores underlie the seriousness of the ordeal and types of extreme pressures placed on young minds; minds that really should be given more freedom to simply enjoy learning about something fun. The national outcome of all this poking and prodding of the immature intellect reveals disappointing results. News of failing schools blankets the media. Meanwhile, high schoolers feel the pressures of gaining access to the best schools. Entrance exams, personal essays, and admissions interviews loom large in their junior and senior years. Long lines of high school scholars and their parents arrive at colleges and universities to hear an official spiel. I often look out my office window and watch as they dutifully follow back-peddling college students around a preordained labyrinth of walkways designed to impress. Our campus and others they visit must seem as unearthly as the moon-walking tour guides with eyes in the backs of their heads. Few faces express the joy admissions staffers so desperately try to impart. The stresses of their undecided future weigh heavily on their expressions. Those who are accepted and admitted must then survive the last stage of educational sorting.

When the latest class of first-years arrives to the campus where I work, they face an entirely different set of challenges than they did in high school. Teenage rebellions are no longer necessary and parents' frustrated faces are secretly missed. New responsibilities and opportunities arise. A college experience currently represents much more than a simple list of classes. Collegians endure endless inner battles as they decide between spending more time with friends, joining a club with some idealistic mission, or working on assignments that must be completed. Peaceful moments of introspective reading and carefully crafted writing samples are contrasted with all-nighters and cramming. Momentary appearances in theater productions, singing groups, and sports teams compete for precious free time against parties, web surfing, and just hanging out. In the end, most complete their coursework and don a cap and gown. As they sit in the crowd of black robes on graduation day, they hear a learned orator talk about a bright but perhaps slightly vague future. Eventually, each graduate stands and walks toward a stage populated by dignitaries and board of trustee members, knowing that life will never be the same once they accept the diploma being offered them by the colorfully clad administrator. Remarkably, they knowingly extend their hands and take on the challenge. Row by row, I watch them sit back down with freshly minted, leather-framed documents on their laps. Most fidget slightly and watch fellow classmates bravely arrive at the same conclusion. All must silently wonder what the future holds. Did all the time and effort prepare them for the real world?

Hatchery trout certainly do not ponder their future in the way our nation's youth do at commencement. Still, the tests trout face when they are released are no less daunting. Unfortunately, research shows that hatchery-raised trout are very poorly prepared to live in the wild because they have almost no experience with natural river environments. Scientific studies suggest less than 1 percent of trout released by hatcheries survive in streams for a year or more.[1] As Art Lee, author of multiple books stated, "You can take the trout out of the hatchery, but you can't take the hatchery out of the trout."[2] There are far too few aquatic knowledge gains, and the fish equivalent of wisdom is completely absent. Hatchery systems fail generation after generation of graduating trout. The sad reality is that trout raised in concrete hatchery raceways are just plain dumb.

Because hatchery trout are daft, or at least poorly educated, they often fail to eat for a period of days or weeks following release. Hatchery feeding methods are a big part of the problem. Laboratory experiments confirm that food recognition and foraging behavior are learned activities.[3] In contrast, the menu at hatcheries is a bit limited: "Hatchery-reared fish are now routinely reared on a mundane diet of man-made pellet foods that require limited use of potential foraging behavioral repertoires as there is no variation in the timing, location, abundance or type of food on offer."[4] Manufactured pellets of ground-up ingredients might be convenient for aquatic farmers, but they do not teach fish life lessons. If I grew up eating chicken nuggets every meal of every day, even a hamburger would look baffling. A mayfly or stonefly would look otherworldly. Similarly, hatchery pens are certainly not the type of place where a trout can learn the important difference between an emerging nymph and an artificial fly lure. Maybe fly fishing itself only appears to require great skill because trout do not know they are supposed to eat real bugs!

Research shows that newly released fish adopt high-risk and energetically costly approaches to feeding. When I picture what it must be like to fight for food in a hatchery pen with hundreds of other similar-sized fish, it is easy to understand why hatchery trout might adopt these dangerous behaviors. Hatcheries would seem to reward individuals who are bold feeders. Trout that swim close to the surface and lunge without hesitation at any disturbance on the water surface will get the desired pellet. Without many true dangers, there is little reason for trout to show caution. Fish that do not hesitate to bite an obstacle floating by will consume more food than wary fish that demonstrate perhaps a bit more cynicism and mistrust. Trout that excel in these settings eventually get moved to broodstock tanks to spawn the next generation of feeders. Broodstock which my class saw at Quinebaug Hatchery certainly showed this inclination. Meanwhile, trout that hang further down in the water column will need to feed on leftovers. If they swim away from shadows of hatchery employees, they may never get fed. When they fail to grow fast enough, they end up as lunch for their cannibalistic classmates. The remaining individuals learn that consumption is growth and growth is survival. But much like warnings posted for various mutual fund investments, past performance does not guarantee future gains.

In rivers, trout that swim high in the water column and aggressively approach any type of disturbance on the surface will learn far too late that real rivers are dangerous places for dumb fish. Rivers have predators on the surface that are more than happy to grab an unsuspecting trout that makes itself easy prey. Even back in the 1930s Edward Hewitt complained: "The real fact is that hatchery fish are not as smart as fish raised in the stream and fall more easily prey to all kinds of vermin."[5] The subsequent eighty years of hatchery breeding has not helped. Failure to learn from past mistakes is certainly not a sign of intelligence in any species, and modern science has the potential to make a bad situation worse. In particular, the use of growth hormones is a major research topic as scientists work to boost weight gain for farmed fish. One interesting outcome from growth hormone use on rainbows is an increased risk of predation by herons and other birds.[6] Growth hormones actually influence feeding behaviors, with treated trout twice as likely to swim high in the water column where herons have better batting averages. Even after simulated heron attacks where a model bird head struck a tank where fish were swimming, hormonally high trout took more chances while feeding. That behavior is likely to result in larger losses of these technologically tainted trout.

Trout, like most organisms, learn necessary behaviors from experience. Basically, trout need to learn how to be trout. Unfortunately, evidence shows that hatchery fish cannot tell friend from foe. Obviously, it is a useful skill to recognize something that is trying to eat you. Research articles refer to this hole in a fish's understanding as being predator-naïve. A study completed in Spain explains that trout essentially reduce the risk of being eaten by decreasing their activity levels, avoiding hazardous areas and hiding.[7] Natural selection ensures that fish genetically disposed to danger become somebody's lunch. Over time, the population of trout adapts and becomes more immune to predation. It is an evolutionary tactic that ensures survival in the wild. In contrast, hatchery rearing almost entirely removes predation and creates both inexperienced and genetically inferior fish. When released, few fish survive long, with most of the mortality resulting from predation that occurs in the first few days. In comparison, even hatchery-raised juvenile brown trout whose parents were wild trout demonstrated better predator-avoidance skills than second-generation hatchery juvenile brown trout. This result shows the negative genetic impact of rearing fish in hatcheries: scientific evidence that we are selectively breeding dimwitted fish who do not know when to run and hide. From the angler's perspective, maybe it is better and easier if the trout remain stupid because anglers are the primary predator, and high-risk feeding behaviors increase chances of success with a rod and reel.

Viable wild populations need genetic variability, diverse habitats, and competition. Conversely, many anglers who buy licenses that help support hatcheries want bigger fish, not necessarily smarter or ecologically sounder ones. For example, tiger trout raised and released in many states are revered by fisheries agencies because they do not waste time breeding; they just get bigger. Joe Brooks, an author of multiple fishing books, discussed the value of crossbred trout: "While the crossbred fish cannot reproduce, the combination develops a big, healthy, extra-bright-colored and extra-hard-fighting fish."[8] The term "healthy" here is used exclusively as a means to describe the fish's ability to physically resist a rod and reel, but does a poor job of describing the ecological health of the trout. In addition, more subtle genetic problems arise.

Hatchery environments influence not only trout behavior; they impact the physical characteristics of the trout. Hatchery trout often abrade and round their fins on concrete walls and floor, which impacts the fishes' swimming ability. In addition, brook trout have a natural ability to adjust their coloration to best match surrounding aquatic environments. The camouflage technique takes a while to develop. When a trout grows up in a hatchery and is then placed in a river, the fish's coloring can be all wrong. It is like asking U.S. Army soldiers to fight in the deserts of Iraq wearing dark green uniforms. In both cases, the poor choice in clothing increases visibility to predators. In one study from Macdonald College in Quebec, hooded mergansers captured almost twice as many brook trout from a group of fish that had not had adequate time to adjust their coloration relative to a population that had eleven to twelve weeks to acclimate.[9] It is a bit astounding that even minor differences in color dramatically impact life expectancy. Just imagine how albino trout must fare. For the rest of the breed, three months to acclimate may not seem like a long time, but keep in mind that many hatchery trout never make it more than a week in a river. Slowly, both the problem and one of its potential causes becomes clear. To address this issue, researchers suggested that hatcheries should select backgrounds of color that will match the coloration of gravels where fish will be transplanted. However, trout from any single hatchery pen could be placed in a multitude of different rivers or streams that all may have unique habitat coloration. Therefore, a workable solution to the problem may be both costly and unmanageable for a hatchery that is more about numbers than quality control.

It is important to remember that many agencies responsible for stocking genetically modified fish are also legally responsible for the overall ecological health of rivers and streams in their state. They work for branches of government with names that include the Department of Environmental Conservation, the Department of Natural Resources, the Department of

Environmental Management, the Department of Wildlife, and the Department of Environmental Protection. These agencies walk a fine line between protection and promotion of aquatic resources. I have had the opportunity to interact with several of these types of state agencies as part of my research, especially here in Connecticut. Most individuals I had the pleasure to know are thoughtful, intelligent people who deeply care about the health of aquatic ecosystems. They talk about various species and are incredibly knowledgeable about threats to freshwater mussels, sea lamprey and other aquatic animals that often escape the public's eye. It is a little baffling when a collection of bright people come to a somewhat odd consensus, like the decision to stock exotic invasive species in the same rivers where Atlantic salmon are a major restoration goal. There is little doubt that invasive trout hurt salmon restoration efforts by eating native species. So why does stocking occur?

I am confident that the rivers and streams in my home state and elsewhere can be managed from a broader perspective when public support develops for a more balanced approach. I am less convinced that hatchery trout will ever learn to behave like a true river inhabitant. We have been raising trout in hatcheries for more than one hundred years in the United States and not much has changed with respect to knowledge gaps. Consequently, trout die in large numbers soon after they are stocked. You will understand my surprise when I learned that in response to these and other related concerns, fisheries biologists proposed a tutoring service for our finned friends. Has modern aquaculture finally decided to teach trout a lesson?

Connecticut College has a special program called CELS, which has nothing specifically to do with biology despite the name. The CELS acronym stands for Career Enhancing Life Skills. It is a program that essentially provides students with internship opportunities to gain real-world experience. Perhaps you can understand my initial confusion when I ran across an article titled, "Social Learning and Life Skills Training for Hatchery Reared Fish." I wondered if this was some type of internship opportunity for trout. Did trout need to submit a cover letter and resume? Actually, the article is part of a new scientific movement to try to train trout to act more like fish, and less like cattle.

As early as the 1960s, experiments used electric shocks to train salmon to avoid model predators. Electrifying fish may make an impression, but it is hardly an evolutionary survival strategy. Alternatively, more modern studies rely on the trout's own instinctual warning systems. One of the first studies of this type helped show that juvenile rainbow trout could detect chemical stimuli from northern pike and simultaneously be conditioned with warning signals to adopt instinctual antipredator behaviors.[10] These educated fish literally smelled trouble coming when they remembered their scents. When a whiff of a problematic predator wafted their way, trout began to hide and modify activity levels. The changes triggered included decreased foraging behavior, increased cover use and freezing activities by trout. These behaviors made a big difference in life expectancy of fish. In one study, trout remembered this instruction for three weeks, which suggests that periodic exposure to animal hunters is needed to drive home the point. Failure to learn these life lessons undoubtedly invites the pointy end of a predator's teeth or bill.

Hatchery trout gain a survival benefit when they learn about predators. The key was a natural evolutionary mechanism that preferences survival of an entire species over the continued existence of any one individual. One outcome of survival of the fittest is an ingenious adaptation where mistakes by one animal increase the chances of existence for its fellow kind. When trout fall victim to nasty marauders, the doomed individuals often provide warnings. In the case of aquatic species, many animals release chemical cues as part of this warning system that then teaches other organisms to associate danger with the particular circumstances. When a trout sees a predator and smells a doomed acquaintance, it automatically triggers avoidance behaviors. Scientists used this knowledge to conduct some experiments on 120 brook trout.[11] In particular, trout were exposed to chain pickerel odor at the same time they experienced alarm signals produced by damaged trout. After only a single exposure, hatchery trout learned that the smell of pickerel is a bad thing, and they remembered this lesson for at least ten days. When these trout were put to the ultimate test and asked to avoid a real pickerel with real teeth and a real healthy appetite, the trained trout exhibited increased survivability. Unfortunately, it is one thing to run a carefully constructed experiment on a relatively small number of fish. Scaling the educational experience up to address the needs of millions of trout each year with dozens of potential predators poses a different challenge. Likewise, it is unclear how this method could be used to educate juvenile fish about the dangers of cannibalistic adult trout. Still, hatchery trout can be trained to avoid some hunters. It will be interesting to see if trout are ever taught to avoid humans.

~ ~ ~ With so many dumb trout swimming around, perhaps it is not a surprise that another nationwide education effort exists called Trout in the

Classroom. However, this program is not geared to creating smarter trout; it is aimed at enlightening our nation's youth. The main goal is to stimulate K–12 students about the importance of aquatic environments and to help generate stewardship of local rivers and streams.[12] Trout eggs, and in some cases salmon eggs, are delivered to classrooms in various states. Teachers and students are then challenged to raise fish to fry stage when they can be released into the wild. Equipment and expertise are provided to local school systems when possible, with each tank and chiller setup costing approximately $1,000.[13] Officially, the program is less about stocking than it is about edification. Classroom activities focus not just on trout, but the river as a whole. In the ideal case, children learn about pollution problems, biodiversity and the interconnection of various species. It is easy to imagine students developing an emotional attachment to the tiny creatures they see grow in front of them. It is also easy to visualize these same students beginning to look at rivers and streams differently as they try to picture a future life for their minute adoptees. The program tries to bring into being a generation that cares about what gets flushed down storm drains, where pesticides from agricultural fields end up, and how construction activities along roads directly change river habitat.

Many state fish and wildlife agencies promote and manage the program with financial support provided by private organizations, companies, and foundations. Nationwide, the program is active in most states.[14] Kentucky lists twelve schools, while approximately forty-six schools with about three thousand students participate in Maryland.[15] Nevada's Division of Wildlife runs the program for thirty schools, and New York enlists two hundred schools.[16] The program dates back more than twenty years in New Jersey and involved eighty-nine schools and eleven thousand students in 2009.[17] More than seven thousand students and eighty-six classrooms alone were involved during the 2011–2012 academic year in Connecticut.[18] Pennsylvania maintains a digital map with about one hundred locations, and more than two thousand classrooms a year participate in California.[19] In Idaho applications from schools are so numerous that an annual waiting list is formed.[20] There is no doubt that the Trout in the Classroom curriculum influences thousands of young minds.

Because teachers need to learn the material first, instructors are provided DVDs, lists of books, and sample lesson plans. Some videos are high-class productions with sophisticated computer animations and live-action shots. On the official website, lesson plans are divided by general subject.[21]

Physical education lesson plans suggest fly tying, fly-fishing lessons, and fishing excursions for the class. Language arts lesson plans include creation of a trout journal and lists of literature. Books on trout and salmon abound. One social science exercise describes two classes with a total of forty-two students who were each given a different trout or salmon to research. Classroom visits from local anglers are encouraged. Fine arts lesson plans include, among other ideas, suggestions to write trout poetry, paint trout, or sing fish songs. Another suggested activity is called "Love Letters to the Trout," and recommends writing letters or Valentine's Day cards that can then be placed around the tank for their trout to see. Corny perhaps, but it does get the message across. The lesson plan also suggests students broaden the love letters to consider the entire watershed or Earth. Maybe even that seems a bit ridiculous, but the point is to create caring.

When I looked at lesson plans I was most interested in the science section, which includes a large list of learning opportunities. Various lesson plans focus on trout habitat requirements for items that include temperature, dissolved oxygen, and nitrogen. Other ideas include native trout mapping, matching invertebrate hatchings, and study of aquatic nuisance species. These are not only interesting subjects; they are useful skills for future anglers. One science teacher's packet includes the 1969 "conservation classic" film, *The Way of a Trout*. I watched the movie with great anticipation and saw it as a slightly grainy digital video. It was not hard to imagine the sound of an old-fashioned movie projector that would have spun the reel when the film was first released. Throughout the film a rainbow trout is portrayed as it survives numerous encounters with natural predators. Eventually, after several failed attempts, the actor/narrator manages to hook the fish on a self-tied fly. The short clip devotes a large portion of time to fishing technique and fly selection. The emotional conclusion of the film shows a long battle between angler and prey, and the eventual decision to release the trout to enable future reproduction by the fish. It is hard not to come away from the film with a clear theme that fishing for trout is just one of many predator-prey interactions in the normal trout life cycle of this Wisconsin river. Of course, neither the Caucasian-looking male nor rainbow trout are native to Wisconsin. The portrayal of this angler's eventual victory is used to imply wisdom relative to other predators. This view is reinforced by references to Izaak Walton and contemplation of nature.

It is worth noting that there are misconceptions in the science teacher's packets that result from the single-species focus of the program. For example, the "Dream Stream" packet states that a "healthy stream" has a "partially to fully rocky substrate and bed."[22] Although many streams suffer from human-induced sedimentation problems that buried gravel beds, rivers with muddy and sandy bottoms naturally existed in many places. For centuries they supported healthy ecosystems for many non-trout species. In some cases, the modern streams may show few impacts from humans and support wild indigenous populations of aquatic organisms. To suggest that these types of streams are unhealthy or less desirable simply because they aren't the type of habitat preferred by trout is dangerous. Some Trout in the Classroom films even show artificial structures used in restoration projects. These devices are clearly not a normal component of a natural stream, and may have negative consequences for other species and rivers as a whole. Aspects of the Trout in the Classroom curriculum pose the danger of encouraging students to value trout and their associated habitat over other species that might exist in their local area. These small misconceptions and overzealous desires for the perfect trout stream can lead to inappropriate restoration projects and management approaches designed to fix perceived deficiencies in an ecosystem. As the history of coldwater management demonstrates, efforts to improve upon nature often have the opposite impact.

Could an equally successful initiative focused on freshwater environments be created that does not focus primarily on trout or salmon? Sadly, the answer is probably no. Conservation and environmental groups discovered long ago that it helps to have a captivating character as a symbol of your cause. Perhaps no conservation mascot is more famous than Smokey the Bear, who has been protecting forest lands from fires for decades. Many folks in my generation also grew up with the other Forest Service icon Woodsy Owl and the catch phrase, "Give a Hoot, Don't Pollute." The World Wildlife Federation selected a panda for its logo. Its website highlights an adoption program with stuffed animals of more than one hundred charismatic species to choose from.[23] Monkeys, whales, cats, bears, birds, and fish fight for financial contributions. The list includes only four reptiles, two amphibians, and a single insect. Spiders, scorpions, leeches, cockroaches, clams, and lamprey are understandably absent from the World Wildlife Federation site. Let's face it; some animals are just easier to love. When it comes to rivers, freshwater mussels may be one of the most heavily impacted species, the most sensitive to pollution and physical disturbance, and more critical to overall ecosystem health. Mussels may represent the perfect canary in the coal mine. But, who is going to get excited about an animal that is often mistaken for a rock? So fish become a natural choice for a symbol of water purity and aquatic health. And if we are going to pick a fish, we might as well pick the species that many anglers believe is the most beautiful fish of all: trout.

Even state legislatures reflect an inclination toward trout. When it comes to selecting official state fish, there is definitely a common preference. If I ever find myself with a trivia question about the state fish for a particular location, my best bet is to retrieve my old number two pencil from high school and carefully fill in the entire oval next to the answer "trout." All told, almost half the states in the country think trout or salmon best represent the character of their state, with nineteen states listing trout and three selecting salmon as their state fish. Even Louisiana did not want to feel left out of the mix and lists the saltwater speckled trout as their favorite finned friend. The patterns thankfully mirror the native ranges of fish. Brook trout are particularly popular in the East with nine states laying claim to this species. Along the continental divide, seven states list one of the various species of cutthroat. Clearly, the continent is not divided on what fish it loves most.

I am fully in favor of any program that helps teach children to better protect aquatic organisms. However, my skepticism kicked in when I learned that national financial sponsors of the program included the hunting and fishing outfitter Cabela's Inc., and That Fish Place–That Pet Place, a pet supply company.[24] It is easy to see that in addition to the stated goal of fostering environmental awareness, there are secondary financial motivations for the sponsors. The Future Fisherman Foundation offers a different but similar program geared at kids. They offer grants up to $2,500 for K–12 educational programs focused on fishing and boating. The Future Fisherman Foundation organization itself is sponsored by a list of nearly one hundred industry partners and organizations.[25] Most are equipment manufacturers or suppliers. It is unlikely that most elementary-aged participants in the Future Fisherman Foundation grant or Trout in the Classroom program understand the idea of a national market force. Children do not comprehend that they are viewed as consumers as much as students.

Local financial sponsors and volunteers include numerous fly-fishing and angling clubs. An article describes a typical scene in California as a volunteer from Mission Peak Fly Anglers walks into a classroom with thirty rainbow trout eggs for students.[26] He represents a club that lists promotion of fly fishing as the first goal on its website.[27] We certainly should not demonize this volunteer and the countless others like him for helping to encourage protection of fragile aquatic environments. Anyone who tries to influence our youth because of a deep sense of caring should be admired. Neither, however, should we turn a blind eye to the hidden agenda embedded in the Trout in the Classroom initiative.

The main backer of Trout in the Classroom and the company that runs the official website is the private organization Trout Unlimited. I want to be very careful not to be overly critical of Trout Unlimited. Much of the progress made in improved water quality, protection of riparian areas along streams, and management of water levels in rivers would not have happened without political pressure. Countless dams were removed because Trout Unlimited paved the way. Members donate more than 500,000 hours a year in cleanup and educational endeavors.[28] Trout Unlimited has been a champion of trout, and many aquatic systems have benefited from those efforts. Trout Unlimited even lists inappropriate stocking of hatchery trout as a danger on its website. Ironically, the organization itself was founded on a river in Michigan that had no native brook, rainbow, or brown trout of its own, only the closely related Arctic grayling. But despite countless good outcomes that result from the group's efforts, the name of the organization itself suggests a certain bias when it comes to setting priorities in river management. And Trout Unlimited is very interested in helping to set priorities, with constant federal and state lobbying efforts on the behalf of anglers. In 2008 alone, the company spent almost $1.2 million on federal lobbying.[29] Trout Unlimited claims more than one hundred forty thousand members, and a staff of respected lawyers, policy experts, and scientists.[30] The website provides a section that states the organization's stance on various conservation legal matters.[31] There is also a handy search tool to help club supporters find their appropriate government representatives and persuade members to send letters encouraging favorable legislation. Most staff at state fisheries and game agencies could easily list a few key Trout Unlimited officials in their area. I have sat in many agency meetings with representatives from the group. Clearly, Trout Unlimited is a club that learned about pull and leverage from fishing, and applies that awareness to the political arena. Trout in the Classroom is just one of its successful endeavors with state fish and game agencies.

As part of my research for this book, I actually joined Trout Unlimited. Interestingly, it was a free membership that was literally attached to a pair of waders I purchased to conduct research on rivers. One of the strangest e-mails I received from Trout Unlimited in 2009 was from four individuals who included the director of Youth Education Programs and the vice president for Volunteer Operations and Watershed Programs. The e-mail asked me to support the No Child Left Inside legislation being considered by the House Education and Labor Committee. Why do they care so much about kids? According to the e-mail:

> The future of Trout Unlimited depends upon encouraging the next generation to become conservationists. No Child Left Inside is a huge step in that direction. TU programs such as Trout in the Classroom, our Youth Conservation Camps and First Cast, an instructional fly-fishing program for children, provide the kinds of outdoor activities and experiential learning that is at the heart of No Child Left Inside. Passage of this important legislation would not only encourage growth within these existing programs, it would also provide future opportunities for collaboration between TU volunteers and their local schools.

Although No Child Left Inside is a national movement sponsored by multiple environmental groups, Trout Unlimited's initiatives show that children are a major focus of theirs. The outer shipping cover of the Summer 2009 issue of *Trout* magazine, the organization's main publication, even had a picture of a boy holding a large trout and the words "We need them to love it too."[32] The inside pages talked about a new initiative aimed at recruiting young anglers. The organization's new *Stream Explorer* magazine and associated website aimed to "encourage kids to go outside and discover the magic on their nearby trout streams."[33] The latest initiative by the organization is called First Cast, which is designed to promote coldwater conservation by teaching kids to fly fish. With a current membership dominated by older white males, enrollment of young members is critical to the organization's future. Trout Unlimited's various activities are part conservation initiative and part enlistment effort.

Recruiting efforts reach directly into public classrooms. The May 2010 newsletter for Trout in the Classroom encourages students to join Trout Unlimited to battle what they call ETS or Empty-Tank Syndrome.[34] This apparent disorder occurs when the Trout in the Classroom program predictably moves onto a trout in the stream exercise. In one instance reported by the Blue Ridge Mountain Trout Unlimited chapter, a seventh-grade class in Georgia was so attached to their newly released fish that they serenaded them with "The Trout Song."[35] If this example provides any evidence, Trout in the Classroom appears to be a successful initiative.

I ask myself the difficult question, do I support Trout in the Classroom despite my concerns about trout stocking and the obvious promotion of trout angling? The begrudging answer is yes. My own daughter had animals in her classroom twice in seven years. On the first occasion a teacher supplied an aquarium tank of Madagascar hissing cockroaches. As the name suggests, these are nonnative to New England and do not necessarily encourage discussions about the local environment. Two years later, another nonindigenous species showed up in the form of two brown anoles. I must admit to a soft spot in my heart for these creatures, and I was an easy mark when my daughter asked if she could have a pet anole for herself. Still, there is a danger when classrooms use exotic invasive species as classroom pets. Predictably, pets need homes when the school year ends. Unfortunately, some animals are intentionally released into local environments with negative consequences. A colleague of mine helped to develop an educational program geared toward K–12 teachers to alert them to the ecosystem dangers of these types of practices. I would prefer to see my daughter raise rainbow trout, but I also want her to know the flip side of the coin associated with dumping more nonnative trout into our local rivers and streams.

Overall, we must remember to look at the big picture. Water is the most important liquid resource for the future of our world. People have survived for thousands of years without petroleum but won't make it a week without water. Existing management conundrums over competing uses for water will only intensify and increase the need to protect rivers from abuse. Trout in the Classroom at least gets kids to care about rivers, the first step in protecting all aquatic species and the rivers themselves. But that does not mean we should be satisfied with the current educational undertaking. It is easy to picture a better outcome with a class of students who each have a separate favorite native species to care about. Imagine what a great learning environment it would be if kids were chatting about different species' needs and interdependencies. They discover that simply planning for a single species might adversely harm the aquatic flora and fauna their friends care to save. The diversity of thought leads to a level of understanding that a single perspective could never hope to achieve. That approach would seem to be much better than what we have today. The current curriculum is a little too reminiscent of hatchery menus. It runs the risk of producing a class of like-minded individuals who have eaten only informational morsels supplied by friends of trout.

~ ~ ~ In another attempt to educate, Colorado redefines the term *game fish* by providing an electronic hatchery simulation for school children.[36] I took on the challenge. Disaster struck when a family of raccoons was supposedly able to eat ninety-five pounds of my fish in one night. Then, a flock of pelicans attacked my raceways and ate another four thousand medium trout. Those must be big raccoons and a sizable flock of pelicans! Mostly, the simulation required me to watch videos and then calculate how much food to throw in to my trout. I eventually accumulated a respectful 54,645 points by successfully raising nonnative rainbow trout in the simulated hatchery and subsequently dropping fifty thousand fish in an alpine lake by airplane. At least I hope it was a simulation. After seeing the electronic-feeding system at Quinebaug Hatchery and reading about space-shuttle-like airplane stocking that follows computer-generated flight paths in Oregon, who knows? Maybe I unwittingly served as mission control!

If running a fake hatchery is too intimidating, I can enroll in fly-fishing school. The Orvis Company runs a series of schools in fourteen different locations within twelve states. For a few hundred dollars I could take a one- or two-day class. If I wanted to spread the wealth, I could select from a large number of other private fishing schools across the country. These private guides would take me anywhere I want to go and teach me their trade. Then again, George Harvey was literally a professor of angling. He taught the first noncredit, and then the first accredited, university course on fishing in the country, instructing more than thirty-five thousand individuals in thirty-eight years of teaching at Pennsylvania State University.[37] Interestingly, Gifford Pinchot was governor of Pennsylvania when the university appointed Harvey to teach the first college-level courses on fly fishing. Harvey instructed President Carter and the First Lady; he tied flies for and fished with President Eisenhower.[38] Alternatively, The American Museum of Fly Fishing in Vermont, the Catskill Fly Fishing Center and Museum in New York, the Pennsylvania Fly Fishing Museum Association, the Fly Fishing Museum in Oregon or the Rangeley Outdoor Sporting Heritage Museum in Maine have plenty to teach me. Someday I might even travel to Henschel's Indian Museum and Trout Farm in Elkhart Lake, Wisconsin. Unfortunately, the Trout Museum of Art farther north in Appleton is named after a person, not the fish. Or, I could just be frugal and pick up an angling book and figure it out for myself.

Walton loved to use the terms "fool" and "wise" in connection with angling prowess, and he started a trend that carries on today. In modern books, experts represent the wise angler because they know all the tricks of the trade. Fly-fisherman author and psychologist Dr. Paul Quinnett joked that "fly fisherman [are] so loaded down with frontal lobes they have trouble balancing when they wade."[39] The term novice also becomes a bit of an insult in angling books. Experts complain that these folks do not appreciate the finer points of the sport. Readers need to absorb nuggets of information from experts if they also hope to be wise. Of course, these nuggets are not free and come with price tags ranging from the cost of the book to the outlay for private lessons on foreign shores. Writers describe fly fishing as an art form where style matters, while they simultaneously set themselves up as both masterful artists and critics. Undoubtedly, an air of elitism helps to sell books. Author and Catskill resident Art Lee, a member of the Catskill Fly Fishing Center and Museum Hall of Fame, complained about folks who come up from the city to fish: "The casting is jerky or mechanical, sometimes both. There is an underlying tension, competition, too much looking around to see what the other guy is doing, too much 'oneupsmanship.' It's as if the worst a person leaves behind in the city for a weekend away greets him again on the river."[40] Paying attention to people around you who share the same hobby should not be a sin. Rivalry is also an expected outcome for a sport that equates success and wisdom. Perhaps Lee might also want to remember it is unwise to insult the people who buy his books.

Many angling books are written by professional fishermen. In general, these people come in two breeds, those who keep their fish and those who do not. Among the former are commercial fishermen and rare fisherwomen who for centuries left from ports like Gloucester, Massachusetts, headed for the ocean's great fishing grounds. They risk their lives to catch fish for landlubbers. We still rely on these folks and their risky occupation to help feed the world. I wonder how long they would remain professionals if they fished just for fun and released everything they caught. I could only imagine what the reaction at the docks would be if a boat returned after a month at sea with nothing but good fishing stories. I suspect they all would be labeled with a four-letter word that begins with *F* and rhymes with *school*.

The catch-and-release professionals do not help feed anyone and seem to make money primarily to support their own angling activities. Lee, a self-proclaimed professional angler, bragged about fishing two hundred fifty days a year.[41] Most people in search of their annual fun need to make do with only fifty-two weekends and two or three weeks of vacation a year. With approximately two hundred fifty days a year spent at our jobs, it is hard to find time to master a hobby. Even many serious trout anglers average fewer than forty days fishing a year.[42] Many part-timers are just looking for temporary escapes from their jobs into more tranquil settings. They read books at night and practice casting in their backyard after work. When they hit the river, they glance toward adjacent anglers to pick up a few tips. They know it is unlikely they will ever reach the level of proficiency of masters who write fishing books. Regardless of how poor an angler these novices might be though, I would be loath to label a surgeon who might save lives on a routine basis, a lawyer successfully protecting an innocent defendant, or a kindergarten teacher entrusted with the education of our youth as a fool. In an interesting statement, Lee at the very beginning of his book warned, "The greatest error many fly fishermen make is to give trout too much credit."[43] Perhaps professional anglers also give themselves too much credit.

When we think about angling prowess, we must remember that fishing only requires great skill because we make it intentionally hard to catch trout by insisting on the use of flies, rods, and reels. It really is not hard to catch fish. Traditional and modern cultures use nets with great success for most species. A stick of dynamite also works quite well. If someone is a believer in catch-and-release practices, electrofishing will do the job without scarring trout with a hook. The point is, fly fishing is not about catching fish; it is about catching fish in an aesthetically pleasing manner. It is the triumph of form over function.

On the flip side, when fish are too easy to catch, anglers complain. John Merwin, founder of *Fly Rod & Reel* magazine and author of nearly a dozen books, described a fishing trip where cutthroat trout were really biting and he was clearly upset that a less accomplished angler caught multiple fish. He said, "As an experiment, I flipped out a cigarette butt, which was likewise taken immediately by one of the trout."[44] This was obviously not what he had in mind as sport. Merwin continued: "So it was with our brief cutthroat experience that day; there was just no sport in it. It was embarrassing, too, as if we were taking unfair advantage of fish that had become unnaturally vulnerable."[45] The problem in the writer's mind was that fishing for trout was supposed to be a challenge which, when successfully done, highlights angler wisdom. If any fool can catch fish, how can anglers prove their intelligence? Quinnett admitted an analogous reaction: "Many wild trout advocates disdain hatchery fish precisely because they are too stupid to protect themselves and stupid fish do not make good sport."[46] Once again, the angler was trying to pretend fishing is a battle between equals where brainpower triumphs.

Displaying similar sentiments, Lee mentioned "reckless feeding patterns"[47] and stated: "If I had my 'druthers' I'd never catch another hatchery trout."[48] The cynical twist is that hatchery fish are stupid and reckless because we unintentionally trained them to act this way while we raised them in rearing stations. These hatcheries, in turn, exist solely to supply trout for our fishing pleasure. I ask you, who looks foolish now?

~ ~ ~ Although hatcheries fail to educate trout, many sites are hard at work to edify new generations of anglers about the joys of fishing by hosting numerous school fieldtrips and impromptu visits. Some facilities have simple visitor centers that focus mostly on the science of running a hatchery. Others incorporate much more elaborate displays on watersheds as a whole. The New Jersey Department of Environmental Protection runs Pequest Trout Hatchery and Natural Resources Education Center. This is the hatchery that supplies eggs for the state's very successful Trout in the Classroom program.[49] I checked the website for operational times and learned that in addition to many fishing-related learning experiences that include the film *Hooked on Nature*, a film about hatchery practices, the facility operates a butterfly garden and offers displays for backyard wildlife habitat. I planned a visit but stupidly got the operational hours wrong and arrived a bit early. The staff was nice enough to let me poke around while a crew cleaned the floors.

The education center contained a modern set of displays and exhibits in a large room. The center did a nice job of displaying information on a variety of environmental topics with only approximately one-third of displays focused on fish. Still, the importance of trout was hard to miss. A large glass tank held several trout of different species and immediately caught my attention. Water gently bubbled in one end of the tank, but was otherwise fairly calm. A bit of algae grew on the glass and the aquarium colors were drab. Fish sat pathetically in their confines. It was certainly hard to picture these individuals as worthy adversaries in some life and death struggle of line and rod. One particularly sad individual was wedged under a branch in a crevice on the bottom of the tank. I pressed my nose against the glass and looked into the eye of a deity. For a moment, I had a Hollywood-inspired desire to free this trapped soul, but what was the point when it had a better life expectancy in the aquarium? Whether the fish knew what I was thinking or not, it did not say. It just kept peering through the glass with a singular eye on the side of its head. This staring contest ended, predictably, with me blinking in defeat. A bit bored, I backed away and decided to look at the other static displays in the room. One sign explained how seven thousand gallons of water per minute was pumped from the ground for use by the hatchery and then treated before it was released to the Pequest River. Another sign talked about the $12.5 million price tag for the facility. I decided I had better see how the money was spent and headed out on the self-guided tour.

It was a gray day with a light drizzle that was certainly more of a hassle for me than the main inhabitants of the place. The outdoor tour took me past the egg collection and fry rearing building. Signs in windows showed trout being stripped for their sperm and eggs using methods developed centuries earlier. Other signs proudly showed modern automatic feeders and hatchery trucks. A truck-mounted feeding hopper was shown creeping along raceways in another photograph. I quickly pictured the frothy feeding frenzy that would follow the slow passage of this vehicle. According to the sign, this process was repeated four times every day. The next picture showed a mechanical sorting device used to separate fish for stocking. If the sign had stated that this contraption was used to tie live trout pretzels, it would have seemed credible, for the fish in the machine were twisted into incredible angles as they were analyzed automatically to see if they measured up. According to the next sign, the facility operates nine diesel trucks, each capable of carrying four thousand fish. Remembering math skills I originally learned as a grade-schooler, I calculated that it required at least 175 trips each year to dispense the annual production of 700,000 trout.

I pressed on despite the foul weather, passing a sign that helped visitors identify various birds of prey that might be seen in the area. The tour ended on a large wooden platform overlooking the raceways. The hatchery was massive. A huge expanse of pavement, concrete pens and overhead anti-bird wires stretched more than several acres. Each raceway was ten feet wide and five hundred feet long. There were ten or more different trout-filled, concrete canals. I recalled that at least the aquarium trout in the visitor center had a branch to hide under; trout in the raceways had nothing but linear concrete surface to contemplate. It was hard to see the trout because small ripples covered the water surface as rain drifted down. Still, I could tell I was not alone. I slowly began to realize that swimming in front of me, hidden just below the surface, were more than half a million trout — hundreds of thousands of fish reared to entertain the most lethal predators on the planet. I stood alone on the observation platform and pondered this idea as the rain drizzled on. I was armed only with a camera, pencil and paper, so I certainly did not look very menacing. The trout, on the other hand, were one of the most successful invasive species known. Collectively, they could consume my bodyweight in seconds. I began to feel a bit outnumbered and out of place. I was also much less prepared for the wet weather than the creations in front of me, so I retraced my steps back to my car, shed my raincoat and went to find some breakfast.

Earlier on this same trip, I learned that not all government aquaculture centers focus purely on production. I happened across a major federal research center focused on fish while I was on my way to look for an old hatchery site in West Virginia. As I entered the state, a huge sign announced the state was "Wild and Wonderful." As I drove, I figured I was on the right track to the hatchery when I passed a maximum security prison. When I finally arrived in Kearneysville, I found the U.S. Department of Agriculture's brand new research complex called the National Center for Cool and Cold Water Aquaculture. Fisheries biologists here develop improved germplasm, genomics, genetics and physiology. Here fish are genetically mapped and modified. Biologists utilize DNA to improve trout production, study and avoid bacterial diseases and try to produce better fish for consumers. Put simply, they are looking to create Supertrout. The fish of choice is the rainbow, the same fish that interbreeds with several other species of native trout. The lab's first big success came with the publication of an article titled, "Genes May Lead Way to Bigger Rainbow Trout."[50] As the title suggests, bigger is better in this lab. Other work is conducted to improve rainbow trout's tolerance for population crowding and disease resistance in artificial-rearing environments. With these diverse lines of research, the hope is to breed new genetic lines of trout that will be larger, happier with their unnaturally high population densities and less reliant on antibiotics to keep them alive in the crammed pens where diseases spread rapidly. Although the facility does many things, running tours for unannounced visitors is not one of them. As I waited to be turned away inside the reception area, I noticed a picture on the wall that showed the old state-run hatchery; and I learned that a few of the old circular pens were still intact. After I was shown the door, I dejectedly decided to check out the old site.

Just down the road I passed the U.S. Geological Survey Leetown Science Center, home of the National Fish Health Research Laboratory. The facility does research on the physical, chemical and biological impacts on aquatic organisms, especially threatened and endangered species. It turns out that research at the facility in Leetown was instrumental in understanding whirling disease so prevalent in many rainbow trout. The Fish Health Division at the site continues to work on diseases and genetics. They even do research to reduce the environmental impacts of hatcheries on the environment. However, there is a great deal more focus on restoration of imperiled species, including one research branch focused on restoration of anadromous salmon and shad species along the Connecticut River in my home state. Although I worked for the U.S. Geological Survey for many years, I decided not to try and pay this rather bland and boxy-looking building a visit this trip. Across the street sat a few circular hatchery pens with a small swirl of water inside each. Unless the local researchers had managed to invent invisible trout, they were empty. Still I felt my trip to Kearneysville did not end in vain.

The facilities on Leetown Road in West Virginia are just part of a major worldwide research engine with a focus on trout and salmon. A quick Internet search of scientific publications in reputable, peer-reviewed journals yields thousands of articles to read. The search software Science Direct yielded between 3,000 and 10,000 articles on sunfish, minnows, lamprey, and sturgeon. Bowfin had just 625 publications. Catfish were shown a bit more respect with more than 16,000 journal entries. However, when it came to salmon and trout, more than 150,000 articles on the subject have been produced to date. From our elementary school children to our nation's leading scientists, trout capture people's attention and shape our learning.

~ ~ ~ For most youth, fishing lessons are taught by dad or maybe mom. It is a ritual of passage repeated a thousand times in small brooks and lakes. With my own daughter I faced a dilemma: should I impose my own beliefs on her and refuse her the chance to try fishing or let her discover her own feelings? She eventually asked to try out a rod and hook. I suspect she was actually more interested in night crawlers than fish. She talked about rising with the sun and then overturning logs in search of these true earth dwellers. She was eager to bait a hook because she had never seen the writhing body of a worm impaled by a tiny metal spear. I worried about her reaction to this painful dance that experienced anglers no longer notice. But the pragmatist in me argued, why waste emotions on creatures that die by the millions every time rain showers chase them onto the sunbaked pavement of a hundred suburban cul-de-sacs? So I was a bit evasive when she broached the subject of fishing and did my best to hide my conflicted feelings. Ultimately, I knew it was an experience that I could not deny her. After all, I still remember the feel of the first nibbles transmitted through an invisible line to my tiny hands when my dad first took me out. I could sense but not see the sleek shape still hidden below the water. It was an experience that transformed me as it has millions of others.

In the definitive act of cowardice, I ultimately shirked my responsibilities as a parent and let my father-in-law lead my daughter on her first fishing trip. I lurked in the background and adopted the role of scientific spectator. They did not fish for trout; they went for panfish: bluegills, pumpkin seed, yellow perch, and black crappie. The day was a shining success with a fish caught and released with almost every cast. Three cameras blazed in the background as relatives tried to capture the momentous occasion. With cancer looming large, we knew this would be one of the pair's last big adventures.

The event was so much fun for my daughter she asked to repeat it the very next day. This time the fish were a bit harder to catch. The hook suddenly seemed much more dangerous and my daughter was afraid to reel in the line. Neglected cameras hung from shoulder straps. After a short time, her appetite for fishing seemed satisfied and the entourage headed back home. Her grandfather has since died, and it appears my daughter's desire to fish expired with him. However, I am quite sure she will fondly remember her first day of fishing for the rest of her life. One point was clear; fishing can be a very emotional and educational undertaking for young and old alike.

CHAPTER FIVE

The Lucky Charm

*We plant millions and billions of fry and fish to no purpose, because we
do not have exact knowledge as to how to plant, where to plant, when to plant
and whether there will be protection and food for the fry and fish when planted.
We stock the same waters with different species of fish and cannot foresee the
future curse we are inflicting upon these waters. We advise the destruction of
kingfishers and herons on wild waters but do not know whether the good they
do in the destruction of frogs and coarse fish more than counterbalances the
trout they poach.*

~ HENRY INGRAHAM, 1926

*I*f I want to increase my fishing luck, I will purchase a trout pendant crafted out of either sterling silver or, preferably, 24K gold. A chain made by a skilled jeweler would support my adornment. A goldsmith takes precious wire and carefully manipulates it to serve a sole purpose: the chain must support the charm. The necklace itself would be a work of beauty. Each loop a perfect circle that interlinks with other circles to create a continuous series that is both strong and flexible. The trout ornament would be the weight that dominates the necklace and threatens to break the sequence. If any of the links in the progression are weakened or damaged, the whole system will fail and the trout will come crashing down.

When describing predator-prey interactions in an ecosystem, the concept of an interlinking group of separate life cycles also applies. The so-called food chain is comprised of different species all trying to simultaneously survive and reproduce. Smaller species usually are eaten by bigger species all the way up the sequence. Trout are not positioned at the top of the heap and must worry about being just another link in the chain. Ospreys and river otters, for example, rely on fish as a food source. But even an otter might end up in the belly of a coyote or mountain lion if not careful. The food system works as long as there are no weak links. When the cycle is disrupted, species near the top suffer and those at the bottom can run amok.

Strange modifications to this food system have been perpetrated by anglers to create the fishing they desire. New species of trout are introduced, competitive species removed, and new links added to the trout's food chain in an effort to benefit trout growth and the associated growth of anglers' egos. Everyone knows that anglers are not subtle when it comes to their "bling" and the bigger the medallion, the better. Charles Lanman, a famous wandering angler and author, was not above cutting up suckers, perch, and eels to chum Adirondack lakes to attract large trout to catch.[1] Today, bigger fish mean more food delivered to hatcheries. Through this process, marine species find their way into bellies of freshwater trout. As you might guess, it takes skilled hands and a persistent manner to manipulate food chains. Like jewelers, clever individuals tinker to fashion new sequences from separate cycles to support trout. Consequently, the food chain has become distorted and weakened to support the weight of our favorite charming fish. The resulting modifications to the cycle of life are impossible to fully comprehend or calculate. The potential dangers are obvious.

~ ~ ~ Problems with invasive trout highlight negative impacts possible when exotic species outcompete native fauna for food resources in the chain of life. Negative outcomes have often been the result of misguided anglers who wanted to improve fishing for trout and did not realize that new species would simply replace old ones. In practices that continue today, forage and game fish are illegally dumped by anglers even in sensitive waters such as lakes in Acadia National Park. The Park Service posts signs begging people to stop the practice. Although individuals have transferred fish to new waters with little regard for the consequences, and still do, clubs have been historically to blame for many introductions — with occasionally truly bizarre additions occurring on a whim. In one outlandish example, Colonel James Mooney, a prominent member of Wawayanda Club, received a small flock of flamingoes and set them free on a marsh at Fire Island, New York.[2] He subsequently became likely the first recipient of the famed pink flamingo on the lawn gag in 1888 after he expressed disappointment that his birds did not return. As part of a prank, club members constructed faux flamingo out of seaweed, wood and red muslin fabric, and successfully pulled off their ruse, much to the Colonel's chagrin. The incident foretold of a booming industry in plastic pink flamingoes after chemical industries developed sufficiently to mass-produce these ruddy icons.

Clubs and individual anglers soon learned to subtract as well as they could add. Although trout are natural prey for birds and mammals, attempts were made to eliminate these "losses." The losses are, of course, defined entirely from a human perspective. Bird netting at most hatcheries is just one example of modern passive measures taken to defend trout. Many people put fences around vegetable gardens, so it is hard to find fault with nets designed to protect crops in a nonviolent way. However, other historic methods of preventing predation of trout have resembled video games rated M for mature — that is, shooting everything in sight. Famous anglers bragged about figurative notches on their guns that represented everything from crayfish to river otters.

Literary references recommending elimination of species that prey on game fish date back to Izaak Walton's *The Compleat Angler*, which begins with the main character, Piscator, describing himself as "a brother of the angle, and therefore an enemy of the otter."[3] Elsewhere in the book, characters excitedly exclaim, "Look, 'tis a bitch-otter, and she has lately whelped, let's go to the place where she was put down, and not far from it you will find her young ones, I dare warrant you, and kill them all too."[4] Our main hero states, "I am glad these otters were killed: and I am sorry there are no more otter-killers."[5] Walton described other "vermin" that want to "destroy" fish,[6] and he conveniently listed troublesome predators: "But the poor fish have enemies enough besides such unnatural fishermen, as namely, the otters that I spake of, the Cormorant, the Bittern, the Osprey, the Sea-gull, the Heron, the King-fisher, the Gorara, the Puet, the Swan, Goose, Duck, and the Crabber, which some call the Water-rat: against all which any honest man may make a just quarrel."[7] It is a handy list for anglers, and when Walton described killing these "enemies" as "just" and "honest,"[8] he rationalized eradication of predators with a human-centered morality. The importance of Walton on subsequent thinking cannot be overstated. In fact, in a recent poll of local anglers in Great Smoky National Park, 50 percent more people indicated otters were the greatest threat to native populations of brook trout than believed nonnative trout were.[9] Scientific evidence suggests otherwise, so why the lack of acknowledgment of invasive trout? Perhaps it was the use of the word "threat" in the survey. If anglers value trout above other species, how could trout ever be a threat? It is a bit of wordsmithing that would make Walton proud.

Walton's words released an army of armed anglers against otters, and Adirondack fur trappers subsequently supplied support. Many fur trappers in the nineteenth century doubled as guides for wealthy hunters and anglers in the wilds of the Great North Woods. Trappers shot all manner of animals and reveled in opportunities to rid the region of big predators. John Cheney, one of the area's most famous guides, reportedly shot six hundred deer, forty-eight bear, seven bobcat, six wolves, and one mountain lion, in a thirteen-year period and even trapped the last beaver in the Adirondacks.[10] When similar slaughters diminished fur availability, trappers found new ways to make a living. Luckily for Cheney and his colleagues, the Adirondacks were a vogue location for urbanites and their escalating interest in wilderness exploration. Famous guides including Cheney and Alvah Dunning, brought anglers and hunters to the woods and entertained them with their stories of hunting exploits, which were later immortalized in writing.[11] Their tales of great hunts must have impressed anglers; certainly they did little to dissuade them from grabbing a rifle.

The combination of Walton and the lore of the backwoods hunter unleashed a widespread practice of eradication of predatory species in the early twentieth century. According to historic U.S. and British trout-management books, ducks, gulls, herons, red-breasted mergansers, cormorants, goosanders, red-throated divers, kingfishers, sand martins, owls, river otters, mink, muskrats, Norway rats, carp, pickerel, pike, perch, eels, chub, suckers, frogs, water snakes, and turtles near trout waters should all be shot or trapped to save trout.[12] Decades later, the 1998 book, *Ultimate Freshwater Fishing* contained a section titled, "A Life under Threat," where John Bailey stated, "seals, herons, cormorants, otters, mink, bears, martens, and a whole host of other animals and birds have a liking for fish flesh."[13] Even water striders, sticklebacks and minnows were targets early on.[14] Famed Catskill angler Edward Hewitt listed additional trout enemies including dragonfly larvae, crayfish, crows, osprey, screech owls, yellowleg snipe, garter snakes, raccoons, and house cats.[15] All told, that is a long list of species systematically hunted to benefit trout.

Anglers on both sides of the pond took eradication to obscene levels. In a 1927 book, William Carter Platts said herons should be "shot first and given the benefit of the doubt afterwards."[16] He also described a Frankenstein-esque scene to exterminate undesirable fish he called "blazing the barbell," where a mob of torch-carrying men walked down streams at night to corner and trap this aquatic monster.[17] In 1906, a *Forest and Stream* reader from New York bragged about killing 189 kingfishers and using their feathers to make a pillow for his fishing camp. He may have also held onto a few feathers to tie some of the many styles of classic salmon flies that require kingfisher plumage. Using the presumably false name of Wooden Sinker, he described kingfishers as "fish thieves" and completed a long optimistic calculation to illustrate that 111,000 trout were saved.[18] He bragged that he fed kingfisher carcasses to fish — presumably to refashion the food chain in a manner more to his liking. Although it is improbable we will ever discover who Wooden Sinker really was, it sounds a lot like one of Hewitt's anonymous writings.

As we know, Hewitt had a tremendous impact on fisheries management through the publication of his various books and he made very clear his feelings about animals that preyed on trout by adopting Walton's term "vermin." He even published an article in *Outdoor Life* magazine in 1935 titled, "Shall We Let Vermin Steal Our Trout?"[19] which was referenced in scientific articles as late as 1992.[20] One of Hewitt's suggestions was to embed sharpened stakes below the waterline with dead fish on the pointy end to entice diving ospreys to impale themselves.[21] Hewitt also proposed that money spent on hatcheries would be better spent on eradicating species that preyed on trout. He stated, "Destruction of the blue crane, the heron, kingfisher, coons and crows will do more to increase numbers of small trout than any amount of stocking with small fish which is just a waste unless the enemies are kept in check."[22] In fact, Hewitt obsessed about quantifying numbers of trout that various vermin were capable of eating. In Hewitt's 1943 book, another individual described Hewitt's fixation, "his wading is interrupted by dashes to the shore, where Mr. Hewitt captures turtles, frogs, garter snakes, and other foes of the trout, cutting them open or squeezing their throats to see how many fish they have inside them."[23] In 1930, Hewitt mentioned that a kingfisher he caught and killed contained seventeen trout fry in its stomach.[24] He then calculated that 113 kingfishers trapped on his property over a two-year period would have consumed 93,600 trout in 180 days of feeding. That certainly paralleled the calculation of kingfisher carnage performed by mystery author, Wooden Sinker. Hewitt mentioned finding 140 small trout in a great blue heron and 33 in a vaguely defined brown heron.[25] He suggested a group of approximately seven herons ate 3,000 small trout in about two weeks' time. He also experimented to see how many trout a heron could eat at one time, but gave up after the captured bird ate 160 fish.[26] Keep in mind that an adult great blue heron usually weighs around five pounds[27] and 160 small fry weighing half an ounce each would also total five pounds. It is hard to imagine a bird eating its own weight in food in one meal, but that seems to be what Hewitt is suggesting. Conversely, according to a 1997 Department of Agriculture publication, a great blue heron requires three-quarters of a pound or less of food a day.[28] It probably did not matter to Hewitt if it was 160 or just one trout, five pounds or an ounce; if something ate trout, it was a vermin and should be eradicated.

Many of Hewitt's statements cannot be trusted as scientifically valid. He introduced beaver with the hope that their dams would create homes for trout, then decided they created unfavorable conditions and should be removed. He concluded by saying, "I can state without reservation that their effect is bad."[29] In reality beaver are very good for aquatic environments. Beaver ponds provide critical habitat for amphibians and warmer water species of fish and collect organic matter and sediments, which helps to improve water quality downstream. These ponds help to neutralize acidic waters, which is especially important in the Catskills and Adirondacks where acid rain severely impacts trout populations. Beaver ponds provide trout habitat at times, but generally benefit other species more than trout. Today we understand that Hewitt's conclusions were too narrowly focused.

Hewitt made other incorrect assertions. He accused great blue herons and mink of killing just for fun.[30] He claimed one snapping turtle destroyed a thousand pounds of trout in his rearing pond in a single winter.[31] Even Hewitt recognized that this was a tall task for a single adult snapping turtle that might weigh thirty-five pounds at most and he postulated that: "They kill far more than they eat just for the sport of doing it I suppose, as one turtle certainly could not eat 1,000 pounds of trout in a year."[32] He reported five other cases where rearing ponds full of trout in the fall were cleaned out by snapping turtles by spring.[33] Of course, snapping turtles are cold blooded and only survive Northeast winters in ice-covered ponds through hibernation. Hibernating turtles do not pose much danger to fish. It seems much more likely that disease, not a single snapping turtle, killed the half ton of trout. Later, Hewitt discussed problems of furunculosis, which infected his hatchery stock and rapidly killed off trout.[34] In reality, the snapping turtle probably did Hewitt a service in spring by eating carcasses of diseased and decaying trout that probably littered the bottom of Hewitt's rearing pond.

Eventually, Hewitt recognized that his past extermination practices created unintended consequences.[35] Extermination of some predators caused population explosions in other species, which exposed trout to new threats. Thus, he warned to proceed slowly when wiping out vermin. But, there is little evidence he ever truly changed his gun-slinging attitude. Luckily, some anglers were less likely to shoot first and ask questions later, as the quote by Henry Ingraham at the beginning of this chapter and numerous passages in Wilson H. Armistead's 1920 book show.[36] Although Armistead acknowledged that many species occasionally preyed on trout, he wondered about the relative numbers of trout actually taken. Near hatchery ponds he advocated disposal of predators if exclusionary netting was not feasible. On rivers, his approach somewhat softened. On one hand, cormorants reportedly consumed at least their own weight in fish each day and he recommended hunting old and young alike at nesting colonies. On the other hand, he suggested herons prefer frogs to fish and "a few are not of any serious consequence."[37] Armistead countered Walton and admitted he was never convinced that otters do any serious harm on rivers. Likewise, with regard to kingfishers he concluded: "This bird is such a beautiful creature that few people would destroy it for the sake of the few trout it takes from a stream."[38] Apparently, Armistead never met Hewitt. Unfortunately, few American anglers and writers referenced Armistead or Ingraham, but looked instead to Hewitt for guidance.

Eventually scientists developed reliable estimates for losses by various species of wading birds at hatcheries and fish farms. In 1992, researchers from Pennsylvania State University found that only seven of twenty-one potential predatory species successfully and repeatedly captured fish in a study conducted at multiple hatcheries.[39] Furthermore, six of these species spent 72.8 to 83.5 percent of their time in non-foraging activities. Mostly birds perched and watched. Researchers concluded that belted kingfishers and great blue herons accounted for relatively small losses of trout, and green-backed herons and ospreys for almost none. Mallards, common grackles, and crows were the prime poachers. A study produced eleven years later reported that at catfish aquaculture facilities, at least 85 percent of fish captured by great blue herons in fall and winter were diseased, and 76 percent were terminally ill.[40] Therefore, the potential exists that few fish eaten by wading birds at hatcheries would be stocked irrespective of the predation, and the perceived damage they do was historically overestimated. In natural environments with better fish cover, these wading birds are even less likely to significantly impact trout populations.

Sometimes misinformation comes from government agencies, in this case the U.S. Department of Agriculture, Animal and Plant Inspection Service, Wildlife Services branch. According to the agency website, this obscure branch of the federal government exists to "resolve wildlife conflicts to allow people and wildlife to coexist."[41] In a frequently cited study completed in 1999, three Wildlife Services scientists removed the esophagus and stomachs from great blue herons that had been "collected by shotgun" at five different hatcheries in Pennsylvania and New York.[42] Scientists emptied the birds' stomachs to determine what they ate after they had already been carefully observed feeding at hatcheries thirty to sixty minutes before they were shot. According to stomach analysis, the herons ate 1.6 trout per visit. Although the article does not make this point, it is noteworthy that the consumed trout were exotic invasive species, while the herons were native. Researchers also enclosed raceways with netting and compared them to those open to predatory birds to quantify losses of trout. They concluded that the trials "confirm the extreme losses that can result from great blue heron predation," which seemed like a reasonable deduction until I looked at their data and questionable math.[43] In reality, trout mortality was higher in protected raceways at two of the five sites, and trout deaths attributable to herons were only 8 percent at two of the remaining three sites. The researchers lacked adequate data to summarily conclude that herons uniformly cause economic losses at hatcheries, and they offered no explanation why raceways open to predation by herons lowered mortality rates versus pens where birds were excluded. Since the scientists abstained, I will take a crack at a hypothesis. If herons preferentially eat diseased fish — as other studies have suggested — heron predation might be beneficial because it limits exposure of healthy fish to the spread of diseases. In any case, the agency's conclusion that "trout producers should take necessary preventive measures to protect their fish stocks"[44] is unsubstantiated. Ultimately, Wildlife Services decided wildlife conflicts were resolved as long as trout and herons do not coexist.

Today, shooting herons and kingfishers is illegal, unless hatchery owners have U.S. Fish and Wildlife Service depredation permits. With those permission slips it is ready, aim, fire. Federal law amendments proposed in 1997 and later adopted stipulate that, at aquaculture facilities, double-crested cormorants can be lured in with decoys and recordings and shot without any need of permits during daylight hours. Authorized agency employees can even help out by shooting birds at their roosting areas. No permits are required to kill other species that include raccoons, weasels, blackbirds, grackles, and crows. However, in fairness, the government suggests more passive methods to deter predators. For example, a 1997 Department of Agriculture publication, "Control of Bird Predation at Aquaculture Facilities," recommended riding around in vehicles all waking hours of the day, seven days a week, firing live ammunition or pyrotechnics at birds.[45] Alternatively, managers were told to replace scarecrows with human shooters from time to time as a special surprise. The article also suggested "harassing" roosting sites with two-hour light and sound shows within a fifteen-mile radius of rearing facilities. A circle with this radius is an area greater in size than Acadia, Arches, Bryce Canyon, Great Basin, Mesa Verde, and Zion National Parks combined. Crater Lake, Great Sand Dunes, Hawaii Volcanoes, Mount Rainier, Olympic, Redwoods, Rocky Mountain, and Shenandoah National Parks are each significantly smaller in acreage than this zone around a single hatchery. As shooters patrol the roughly seven-hundred-square-mile area surrounding hatcheries, perhaps they might pull out a calculator to determine if they are staying within the $132.42 expense the government computed for the estimated ten hours of labor, one hundred miles of driving and more than three hundred rounds of ammunition needed each day. With fuel prices now more than double those in 1997 and increased concerns about sustainable practices, perhaps shooters should drive hybrids to lower costs and environmental impacts.

Most remaining modern methods of predator control at hatcheries are quieter and involve installations of netting and electrical fences. When I visited Quinebaug Hatchery, it was guarded with fences and bird netting, and displayed educational signs that mentioned predation by great blue herons, ospreys, and kingfishers. A picture of one bald eagle at the hatchery had an adjacent sign explaining the need to "eliminate the losses to these beautiful (but hungry) airborne predators." In Sunderland, Massachusetts, I noticed no such signs and was appreciative when a hatchery employee happily pointed out a pair of distant bald eagles. Nearby, trout swam silently under hemlock and cedar trees draped in a golden glow of a low autumn morning sun. These fish also rested comfortably below a roof of gently arching, anti-aircraft netting. Catskill Hatchery is located in the trout-centric village of Livingston Manor, snuggled between the Beaverkill River and Willowemoc Creek, not far from where Hewitt operated a hatchery on the Neversink. The hatchery is one of ten salmonid facilities in the state. It specializes in the production of brown trout and houses its broodstock in a long raceway enclosed with arched, corrugated-steel covers. Roof sections run on rails and roll open to reveal trout. When closed to protect trout from aerial assault, this covered raceway resembles an undersized aircraft hangar. Only by peeking through small hatches could I see into pens. Staring into the broodstock raceway gave me an adrenaline rush as I watched behemoth hangar queens quickly appear, drift effortlessly past, and rapidly vanish from view. It was here, and with support of the state Conservation Department, that Hewitt began a new stocking campaign to introduce landlocked salmon to the Neversink River.[46]

In the last three years of his life, Hewitt took advantage of an opportunity presented when Neversink Reservoir flooded the downstream portion of his property. As Ed Van Put, a fisheries biologist with the New York Department of Environmental Conservation, explained, Hewitt purchased three batches of salmon eggs from Scotland and convinced the state to raise them in Catskill Hatchery for stocking into the reservoir.[47] Ultimately the effort failed, but an avid fly fisherman and state fisheries biologist figured the problem was a lack of food. Beginning in 1973, the state began to stock nonnative rainbow smelt and then salmon fry in the reservoir.[48] The programs were deemed successful and continue despite the fact that this reservoir is a main water supply to New York City. Even if the state eventually changes its mind, removing these exotics would be almost impossible without the use of fish poisons, known as piscicides — which the citizens of Manhattan might not appreciate.

Because the Neversink salmon project and several other fisheries management ideas can be traced back to Hewitt, it is worth speculating about where he developed his ideas. Hewitt did a great deal of foreign travel and spent time casting flies with English fishing legend G. E. M. Skues on the River Itchen.[49] He was even more heavily influenced by his experience with three trips to the Houghton Club, the second-oldest fishing club in the world, which had just sixteen members who controlled four miles of the River Test in Stockbridge, England. Hewitt stated that, "the Houghton Club is the finest sporting place I ever visited."[50] The club, founded in 1822, was the ultimate embodiment of exclusiveness, with membership reserved for top aristocracy. The club continues today and remains one of the world's most elitist clubs. During Hewitt's day the club employed a head keeper named William James Lunn, who shared many secrets with Hewitt. Lunn learned his trade from his father as part of a family of keepers who managed the club's lands for more than a century. In many ways, Hewitt's various management attempts on the Neversink River seem driven by a desire to try to replicate conditions on the Rivers Test and Itchen.

More than anything, Hewitt was impressed by the growth rates of trout on the Test and experimented with ways to duplicate the processes. He introduced exotic invasive species when he thought they might provide good food for trout. Books by Armistead in 1920, William Carter Platts in 1927, and James Cecil Mottram in 1928 showed that manipulation of plant life and introduction of mollusks and fresh water shrimp were routinely practiced by river keepers in England.[51] English trout management, a labor-intensive undertaking, required three to five hours a day devoted just to manipulating weed growth on river bottoms.[52] Huge time investments were also expected to muck out mud, clean out smaller waterways, trim plants along banks and erect netting to create insect and snail reserves as food for trout. Interestingly, Mottram's primary profession was a medical doctor. He did most of his research on cancer and the impacts of radiation, a source from which, perhaps, Hewitt developed his idea to experiment with radium at his hatchery. Additionally, both Mottram and Hewitt checked growth rates of trout with a microscopic inspection of scales.[53]

Following this English lead, Hewitt introduced various types of freshwater shrimp to the Neversink River and tried twelve varieties of freshwater snail, including African and New Zealand imports.[54] The New Zealand mud snail is currently a major species of concern in this country, inadvertently spread by anglers to new waters.[55] They outcompete native snails, disrupt food chains, and eventually impact fish. Hewitt was mainly impressed with an African variety of snail that expanded in one year from fifty to several hundred thousand individuals in his pond.[56] Although those growth numbers are the modern definition of an exotic-invasive population explosion, Hewitt ambitiously built a small snail hatchery on his property for the rapid production of these glacial-paced creatures. Fascinatingly, the use of snail hatcheries was a subject that both Mottram and Platts devoted entire chapters to in their books.[57] Well, maybe *fascinating* is too strong a word. Hewitt also planted varieties of mayflies as a food source for trout. Like Armistead, he recommended that "every variety of water plant which can be found should be tried in each stream,"[58] which should make any angler familiar with the modern nemesis of milfoil and rock snot cringe. Interestingly, milfoil was a species Armistead specifically recommended planting,[59] but it is now a major problem in this country because no species eat this plant. Consequently, milfoil spreads almost unchecked. Hewitt used a shotgun spray approach to biological introductions, bragging that he successfully established several new species of plants and animals in the Neversink River.[60] Any modern angler who understands warnings about carefully washing off boats and waders to avoid transferring aquatic nuisance species from water body to water body knows all too well not to crow about introducing exotic invasive species. Hewitt and others also shot crows on sight—in case one needs another reason not to imitate these iridescent loudmouths.

When introductions of exotic invasive species failed to replicate growth rates of trout on the River Test, Hewitt opted for directly feeding trout in the Neversink River, developing an early automatic fish feeder in the 1930s.[61] The device was powered by a small water wheel that periodically dispensed food, much like modern automatic hatcheries feeders. He used these feeders directly on the Neversink River, but later removed them because lazy fish simply sat below the water-powered food mills and refused to cooperate with his fly fishing. He then tried hand feeding to encourage trout to spread out. Still, trout accustomed to eating entrails as they sank to the riverbed would not rise to his lures, so he developed floating food to train trout to surface to feed. This eventually became a staple of modern hatchery practices. Hewitt concluded his chapter by stating: "I regard stream feeding skillfully done as the greatest advance so far in the making of really fine trout fishing for great numbers of large fish which everyone wants to catch. I do not know of any way in which this can be done otherwise in our American waters."[62] He recommended weekly feedings and mentioned similar tests he spurred in Michigan. Although Hewitt does not name the Michigan researcher, only one name makes sense, world-renowned fish scientist Carl Leavitt Hubbs.

Prior to the 1930s, isolated individuals and private fishing clubs were responsible for most of the efforts to modify food chains. To increase the scale of the effort required government involvement, but this was unlikely until science paved the way to demonstrate new methods of feeding and eradicating enemies of trout. Enter Hubbs who developed a new school of ichthyology at the University of Michigan. Although Hubbs did many great things, the period from 1930 to 1935, when he was a professor at Michigan, is open to debate. We should start at the beginning because, as Hubbs would probably admit later in life, there is always danger when one gets ahead of himself.

Hubbs was a biologist by training and spent his early years adding to and curating collections of fish.[63] He had dark hair, a high forehead and a rounded face that served as a perfect post to store glasses. His look exuded a quiet confidence and a bit of mild irritation at being interrupted from something more pressing to pose for a photograph. Hubbs, described as a type-A personality and "a steamroller of a man,"[64] was born in Arizona and spent much of his youth in California. Robert J. Behnke, one of the country's foremost experts on trout, suggested that Hubbs was part of an American dynasty of ichthyology that began with David Starr Jordan.[65] Jordan, the president of Stanford University at the time, picked Hubbs to be the next great ichthyologist. Shortly afterward, Hubbs was off to Michigan.

Hubbs was the embodiment of an internationally known, nationally renowned, award-winning scientist. During Hubbs's time at Michigan, the school's fish collection shot from five thousand to nearly two million specimens.[66] By the time Hubbs left Michigan, he had produced more than 300 publications, mostly on fishes of the world; and by the time of his death in 1979, his publications tallied 712 titles.[67] Perhaps Hubbs's greatest honor was his election to the National Academy of Sciences in 1952. Hubbs even discovered a new subspecies of trout, Alvord cutthroat.[68] Unfortunately, that species became extinct sometime after discovery because rainbow trout were stocked into its ecosystem.

When Hubbs first began to get involved in fisheries management, he simply adopted techniques already used within the state and elsewhere on private estates. In 1930, he continued predation studies focused on common terns, as well as other birds, fishes, mammals, and reptiles.[69] Compared to other animals, he warned that "fishes in contrast take part in extremely varied and extensive food chains."[70] Yet he still suggested that biological manipulation of food sources was the wave of the future for fisheries management and promoted introductions of new species of plants and animals. In 1936, Hubbs reported that introductions of freshwater shrimp, more aptly defined as amphipods or scuds, had progressed to a commercial scale with adoption by clubs including the Huron Mountain Club.[71] Overall, he followed an agrarian model and stated fisheries management would soon utilize: "the conception of fish and game as a crop which can be increased by cultivation; with the realization that environmental factors limit the crop, and the environment may be altered to multiply the crop."[72] The similarities to older English styles of trout gardening were clear, but Hubbs now brought the power of a PhD to the field.

In 1930, Hubbs approached management of game species of fish with a new scientific methodology that mirrored Pinchot's forestry practices. In the 1930s, Hubbs used terms including "environmental control" and "aquatic farming,"[73] while then Pennsylvania Governor Pinchot's fish commissioner, Oliver Deibler, discussed "stream farming."[74] This new angler-allied aquatic agriculture was based on a theory that mere protection cannot grow fish and stocking was prohibitively expensive. Although he admitted it might not be practical, Hubbs mentioned using commercial fertilizers, for example superphosphate, to improve stream productivity.[75] That idea and some others probably came directly from Hewitt's books, which Hubbs referenced in his writings. Scientists now recognize fertilizer as a major nonpoint source pollutant that impairs aquatic species, especially pollution-intolerant trout. History shows that farming and trout fisheries are not universally compatible.

The idea of farming creates mixed images. It is possible to envision a small farm run by a family with multigenerational ties to a property they own. We can picture a collection of people who know and care about their land. Alternatively, we might visualize a modern agribusiness where food is manufactured more than it is grown. In this case, slide rule–wielding administrators maximize production with little regard for the long-term health of soil or water. Proponents of trout farming viewed their pursuit as agribusiness. Hubbs stated,

> The ultra-preservationists, as I call them, wish to prevent the sordid hand of man from further despoiling natural conditions; their interest in the natural relations between all forms of life is incompatible with fish management, which strives to modify the natural populations and the environmental conditions so that a few species desired by the sportsman will dominate the waters.[76]

In the battle between preservationists and conservationists like Pinchot and many other anglers, Hubbs was on the side of conservation and called for use of nature's resources. Unlike preservationists, he envisioned intensive management designed to maximize yield. Hubbs would probably have lumped modern environmentalists into the ultra-preservationists group. It was recognized that his approach might negatively impact other species, but that was considered acceptable if game fish prospered. Interestingly, Hubbs apparently had a change of heart later in life and fought to protect native species from a specific practice of eradication he had pioneered and perfected.[77]

During his time in Michigan, Hubbs oversaw programs he later regretted, including introductions of exotic invasive fish and the broad use of poisons to eradicate trash fish.[78] Under Hubbs's direction, his graduate students pioneered use of the piscicide rotenone.[79] Rotenone is an extract that exists in plant leaves, stems, and roots of several different species especially derris root.[80] Rotenone was first used by native peoples throughout the world as a way to catch fish, and scientists adopted it in 1912 as a means to easily gather fish specimens.[81] Hubbs used this sampling method himself.[82] By 1929, rotenone was commercially shipped to the United States for use as an insecticide.[83] Hubbs quickly saw a new use for this fish poison and first began the use of rotenone for fisheries management in 1934.[84] His idea was simple: poison a lake to completely remove all aquatic species and then stock it with game fish.

Hubbs's team of scientific researchers showed that rotenone removed competitors in lakes and greatly increased both survival and angler harvest of stocked fish, including exotic salmon and brook and rainbow trout.[85] R. W. Eschmeyer was a leading researcher with Hubbs and the second of Hubbs's graduate students to complete a PhD at the University of Michigan.[86] He focused his work on lakes and ponds, and was later assisted by another of Hubbs's graduate students, David S. Shetter.[87] Their first application of rotenone was in two small ponds on an estate that held large populations of previously stocked carp and goldfish.[88] Rotenone changed that. By 1942, a total of thirty-two lakes in Michigan were systematically exterminated, mostly to make way for trout and, to a lesser extent, bass.[89] Eventually, rotenone use spread to exterminate undesirable fish species in rivers and streams.

In 1939, Justin W. Leonard, another Hubbs graduate student, determined various lethal doses of rotenone for different kinds of fish and different physical settings. Leonard acknowledged that rotenone was poisonous to humans in large doses and described respiratory difficulties he suffered while handling the substance, but concluded toxicity was mostly directed at fish. In describing physiological impacts of rotenone on fish he stated,

> The first discernible indication that the poison is felt [is] by a wild, erratic, and apparently uncontrolled dashing and plunging. The fish moves at top speed, throws itself blindly against the aquarium walls, and swims on its side or back almost as frequently as in the normal position. This flurry, which may last from five to thirty seconds, usually takes the fish to the surface, where it breaks water repeatedly. The seizure terminates in a convulsive stiffening of the body, accompanied by uncoordinated twitching of the fins and tail. In this condition the fish drifts slowly to the bottom of the tank, where it comes to rest on its side.[90]

The account goes on to describe occasional resurrections of activity as part of the death throes. In essence, rotenone suffocates fish with a slow strangulation that is apparently as terrifying to fish as it is lethal.

People were impressed with this Michigan work, which led to a dramatic spread in rotenone use in a span of only fifteen years in water bodies including drinking water supplies. In 1938, the National Park Service and state agencies in New Hampshire and Illinois used rotenone.[91] By 1948, rotenone treatments were documented in rivers, reservoirs, and lakes of at least twenty-five states and Canadian provinces with at least eighty eradicated lakes and reservoirs in three states alone.[92] Some applications included treating lakes three hundred acres in extent or greater. It was a brutal plan carried out with scientific efficiency to remake food chains and eradicate competitors of trout. Two researchers from the New Hampshire Fish and Game Department reported on resumed experiments in New Hampshire in August 1945 after a period of inactivity in eradication efforts during the war.[93] One month after a B-52 dropped Robert Oppenheimer's atomic bomb on Japan, scientists again dropped Hubbs's rotenone bomb in the Granite State. A New Hampshire study indicated so much rotenone was used that conditions were toxic for brook trout for more than one hundred twenty-five days in two of the seven treated ponds.[94] In New York in the 1950s, ponds remained toxic to trout for at least thirty to fifty days following treatment.[95] Altogether, monocultures of stocked trout were intentionally maintained with toxins until the late 1980s to improve fishing.[96]

Rotenone use has drawbacks, even for wiping out so-called "trash fish" like introduced carp. One researcher in 1963 did a study in Texas and found that rotenone eradication actually benefited some fish the poison was designed to eliminate. The article's title sounded scientific enough, but appeared under a quote with the heading, "Poison, Poison, Who's Got the Poison."[97] Reportedly, "rough fish," especially carp species originally targeted for eradication by Hubbs, are less susceptible to rotenone. They lay so many eggs that their populations recover rapidly if not entirely wiped out. Surviving rough fish then dominate to even a larger extent:

> Not only does the poisoning drastically disturb the more or less stable ecologic interactions, it also tends to be selective in its effect. Other than killing fish it also eliminates or drastically reduces the organisms most likely to provide food for game fishes and on the other hand has little adverse effect on those items most directly in the food chains leading toward carp and suckers.[98]

Essentially, rotenone does more harm than good — creating new ecosystems devoid of carp and suckers and centered on trout: "When one considers other basic ecologic facts, the often reported but undocumented 'benefits' from reducing rough-fish populations become even more absurd."[99] Clearly, eradication of undesirable fish was not well regarded by this well-regarded scientist. The most interesting aspect of this article: it was written by Dr. Clark Hubbs, Carl Hubbs's son. Clark was himself a professor of zoology, an author of hundreds of articles, and an award-winning ichthyologist.[100]

Whatever his feelings for his father, Clark had an axe to grind with rotenone. He said rotenone use was routine and review of project proposals was cursory at best. He noted limited documentation on benefits of piscicide use. In fact, the government agency responsible for one project ignored his expertise and approved federal funding in one day.[101] One massive eradication of undesirable fish project occurred in 1962 on the Green River in Utah. Anders Halverson does a beautiful job setting the scene in his book, *An Entirely Synthetic Fish*, so I will not rehash the details here.[102] Suffice it to say that dumping hundreds of gallons of rotenone along a four-hundred-fifty-mile stretch of river for a period of three days and nights created dramatic results. Biological impacts were already well known by fisheries agencies that successfully eradicated undesirable species along twenty-five hundred miles of streams and two hundred twenty-five thousand acres of lakes. However, in this case, U.S. Fish and Wildlife Service efforts resulted in the death of four hundred fifty tons of fish and countless invertebrates, unintentionally spurring a national firestorm of criticism. In a complete reversal, Carl led the charge to stop the project.[103] Much like Dr. Richard Gatling, inventor of the first machine gun, Alfred Nobel, inventor of dynamite, and Dr. Robert Oppenheimer, who was critical in the development of atomic bombs, Dr. Carl Hubbs became concerned about the weapon of mass destruction he had created. To each pioneer, an invention that initially seemed like a way to save lives, later caused widespread death. In the former cases, scientists and inventors tried to save human lives; in Hubbs's case he initially tried to save lives of game fish. Although Hubbs was unsuccessful at stopping the project on the Green River, the public response he helped stir eventually led to establishment of the Endangered Species Act and completely refocused the mission of the U.S. Fish and Wildlife Service.[104] Of course, he also deserves blame for initially advocating rotenone use to create monocultures of game fish.

Another key driving force in movements that pushed the federal government to adopt new environmental policies, especially the Clean Drinking Water Act of 1972, was Rachel Carson's seminal book, *Silent Spring*. This 1962 book described dangers of pesticides like DDT. *Silent Spring* terrified many and forced all to take notice.[105] To these readers, the massive Green River rotenone project must have been menacing. Perhaps a few began to think differently about trout fishing. Somehow a sport that was supposed to expose people to nature instead spawned management practices that destroyed nature and exposed people to poison.

Although rotenone was temporarily banned in 2006 for further study, the Environmental Protection Agency (EPA) currently considers it a permissible piscicide. In relisting the substance in 2007, they warned of "identified potential risks that, if left unmitigated, may pose unreasonable risks or adverse effects to humans or the environment."[106] According to this report, human exposure to rotenone was possible both when people caught and ate fish that were exposed to poison but lived, and through consumption of drinking water from treated reservoirs. Furthermore, skin exposure occurred when people swam, waded, or fished in poisoned areas. Despite these warnings, continued rotenone use for fish eradication was deemed beneficial to society.

Many future articles that reference rotenone are likely to refer to its use to reestablish native trout in areas previously impacted by stocking of exotic species. However, some government agencies already adopted a switch to the use of gill nets to eradicate invasive trout from lakes.[107] They realized that saving an aquatic environment from impacts of exotic fish is pointless if all other species are wiped out too. But in the Adirondacks, the New York Department of Environmental Conservation now uses rotenone to remove exotic species such as rainbow smelt, which were introduced as a forage fish for trout.[108] The program began in the 1950s. It is worth remembering that this same state agency later intentionally transported and stocked rainbow smelt from the Adirondacks into the Neversink Reservoir as a forage species for introduced salmon in the 1970s. Here is an agency that cannot decide if exotic species of forage fish should die at the ends of government spray nozzles or in the stomachs of nonnative salmonids.

~ ~ ~ Hatchery trout are not part of natural food chains in a traditional sense, but they do need to eat. The Twin Mountain Fish Hatchery and Fish and Wildlife Center in New Hampshire placed coin-operated dispensing machines along a walkway near a round pen of large trout. For a single quarter visitors can receive a handful of trout pellets and become part of the modern trout life cycle. Earlier hatchery feeding practices were less ap-pealing and involved grinding up cattle, sheep, or pig innards for trout. As one New York State Department of Environmental Conservation employee described in a *New York Times* article: "We used to feed them pork mouths, pork spleens, pork livers — parts is parts — which I had to grind up for them. ... That was one messy job."[109] Mottram even talked of using whale meat.[110] Hewitt copied an equally bizarre food source from Mr. Boase of St. An-drews, Scotland. Under Hewitt's direction, Long Island fishermen collected mussels, boiled them for five minutes to remove their shells, pickled them in salt and transported the meat more than forty miles to his Neversink property.[111] Trout do not particularly like mussels pickled in salt, so shell-fish were washed in the river for five hours in a special perforated drum to remove salt, and then fed to trout. Even after all this work, Hewitt admitted the resultant fast-growing trout needed to be caught immediately because they were not hardy enough to survive winter. Furthermore, tests of livers revealed deformities in these trout and other fish fed various investigational foods. Ensuing trout were fat diseased fish with no idea how to survive in a river environment. Despite these problems, Hewitt concluded: "All stocking experience has shown up to the present time that planting fish of catch-able size is the quickest and most economical way to secure good fishing."[112] However, historic accounts of fishing on the Neversink River suggested native trout were historically plentiful but not particularly large.[113] Hewitt essentially manufactured fish for sport that did not resemble those that lived in the Neversink River in previous centuries. Although feeding saltwater mussels to trout seems a bit crazy, it is hauntingly similar to modern food sources for hatchery fish: marine species are caught and heavily processed into food pellets to feed catchable trout. In both cases, trout are feeding on species that were never part of food cycles of freshwater streams.

Hewitt's trout grew big enough on mussels, but he knew that mass production of fish required a more efficient and easily stored food. So, he developed and sold Hewitt Balanced Trout Feed beginning in 1933.[114] Although he was secretive about the formula in 1934, his 1930 book had mentioned a feed made of one-third equal parts sheep innards, white beans, and ground dry shrimp.[115] This dry feed, worked into a paste before oils and fresh meats were added, contained 4.0 to 4.5 percent fats. He reported that a one-pound trout required two to two and a half pounds of this feed. Modern hatcheries greatly improved on this ratio and almost doubled the dry-food-pellet-to-trout conversion. Hewitt also sold iodine additives to enhance growth and provide disease protection. Once again, Hewitt established new hatchery and trout management practices that persist in modified form today.

Few contemporary hatcheries want hassles associated with mixing pastes, shipping mussels, or grinding meat. Many modern trout owners instead rely on Purina Mills, makers of the famous Puppy Chow brand. Purina's Aqua Max Trout Food, formerly called Trout Chow, comes in six different sizes from powdered to one-quarter inch in size. The manufacturer recommends feeding trout up to twelve times a day with two to eight grams of food per day for an eight-inch fish.[116] My experience at Quinebaug Hatchery showed me just how efficiently food is dispersed. It also showed that a good deal of food passes through trout and into local environments.

To know what gets into trout and local environments, it would be helpful to know what is in fish pellets. Feed given to trout generally includes mostly protein and smaller amounts of fat, with some amino acids, vitamins, and minerals thrown in for good health. For example, Nelson's Sterling Silver Cup Fish Feeds used at Quinebaug Hatchery contain 40 percent protein and more than 10 percent fat.[117] Although it is hard to find exact recipes for trout food from commercial manufacturers, we can get a sense of the ingredients by looking at a 2003 Request for Quotation for a three-year supply for fish food for the U.S. Fish and Wildlife Service.[118] The order was for a minimum of 0.5 million and up to 2.5 million pounds of fish food. Protein was required to come primarily from herring, anchovy, or menhaden saltwater fish sources, with wheat, soybean, or cottonseed used as a secondary source, and up to 12 percent ash. Mineral requirements included zinc sulfate, magnesium sulfate, cupric sulfate, and either potassium iodate or ethylenediamine dihydroiodide. Twelve vitamins including vitamins A, B, and D were also specified in the request. Finally, the agency required the addition of Roxantin Red 10 or an equivalent coloring agent. Commercial trout food manufacturers reported that Roxantin Red is added for pigment enhancement in skin and flesh. The resultant "you-are-what-you-eat" trout may not sound yummy, but at least they look good.

Halverson wrote a 2008 article that indicated state and federal hatcheries alone raised more than 130 million trout nationwide with a gross combined weight of more than 28 million pounds of fish in 2004.[119] The average size for these fish was more than one-fifth of a pound. With a conversion of 1.2 pounds of food per pound of trout, feeding these hungry mouths required approximately 34 million pounds of food each year. If we consider fish farms for direct human consumption, the total gross combined weight of trout farmed is closer to 57 million pounds.[120] Menhaden are a primary source of fish meal in the country, and most of these forage fish weigh less than a pound. A big fat herring might weigh 1.5 pounds. Anchovies are closer to an ounce or two. Therefore, I can only imagine how many menhaden, herring, and anchovies are required to help produce 57 million pounds of trout. If we then throw in some antibiotics and other medicines, we have quite a mess. Furthermore, marine fish are transported in ships thousands of miles from fishing grounds. They are trucked in pellet form hundreds or thousands of miles inland to feed trout grown thousands of miles from their native waters. The reared fish themselves will be transported many miles to waiting anglers who then, collectively, drive thousands of miles to catch trout. In the end, some trout probably require more pounds of petroleum to reach anglers' homes than pounds of food to grow. Now consider the fact that many anglers will tell others to throw trout back into rivers for conservation purposes. Here, sooner or later, these fish will die. Thanks to petroleum and fish proteins and oils used in trout pellets, the ocean's nutrients now flow to rivers.

North America currently leads the world in formulated animal diet, much as we do in the formulated human diet we like to call fast food. Use of formulated feed for aquaculture, called "aquafeeds," is the fastest-growing type of formulated feed worldwide, with a 6 to 8 percent increase per year.[121] In 2007, more than one hundred thirty thousand metric tons of fish meal and oil were used mostly for animal feeds in the United States, and we exported an additional ninety-six thousand metric tons. That translates to a total of more than seven hundred million pounds of fish parts and additives consumed by our pets and livestock each year. For marine species that currently make up the bulk of pellets, those numbers are unsustainable and could be devastating. It is no wonder people are getting a little concerned about overharvesting ocean fish stocks.

Although the majority of fish meal and fish oil used worldwide originates from South America, not the United States, both the U.S. Department of Agriculture and National Oceanic and Atmospheric Administration are growing increasingly concerned about the overharvest of marine fishes to supply pellet food for aquaculture.[122] In 2010, the agencies suggested that current marine fisheries are fully utilized. Not surprisingly, costs for fish meal have tripled since 2002. These agencies also warned that marine fisheries may not be capable of even yielding current catches and more strict catch limits or quotas may be on the horizon. Supply might no longer meet demand. Beginning in 2007, in response to those concerns, the agencies set in motion the Alternative Feeds Initiative to look for a different method to feed fish in hatcheries and aquaculture facilities.

As Hewitt's experience demonstrated, it is not easy to find a source of aquafeed that is commercially viable, healthy for both fish and humans, and environmentally sustainable. For the last fifty years, fish meal supplied the primary protein source in trout feeds.[123] Meanwhile, research showed that fish meal is not a required dietary component for trout. One idea is to produce more fish food from plants. A typical salmon diet is already at least half plant materials, so why should hatchery fish be any different? A research panel suggested a 4 percent increase in soybean protein could potentially replace current worldwide demand for fish meal and oil and require virtually no increase in cropland because of historic increases in yield per acre of soybean crops. Trout and salmon could become green in more ways than one. Alternatively, fisheries processing waste from commercial production of fish for human consumption could single-handedly replace harvests of menhaden, anchovies, sardines, and herring for aquaculture pellets. Currently, about half of every two-pound fish that finds its way to local markets ends up as fish trimmings and scraps. Although there are significant challenges to utilization of these waste products for aquafeeds before they spoil, it is mostly a technological not environmental challenge. Even waste products from biofuel and bioplastic production are being considered as feed for aquaculture.[124] Imagine a world where we power cars on ethanol and trout pop out of the tailpipe. Maybe it doesn't sound very tasty, but many anglers just throw fish back in rivers after they catch them anyway, so what is the difference? The more important point is that any of the above models—the vegetarian, table-scrap, or biowaste trout—could help save ocean ecosystems from the overharvesting of marine forage fish. Either that or we could just stop demanding so many trout.

~ ~ ~ Today, consumers are better informed and more demanding when it comes to what we eat, and usually with good reason. Concerns about overharvesting of species and environmental damage from various animal husbandry and farming practices have people thinking about the long-term health of our planet. People are also wondering about their own health. They want to know where their food comes from and how it was produced. A national trend of food scares and environmental concerns prompted a "buy organic" movement. Organic labels are essentially stamps of approval based on standards from the U.S. Department of Agriculture (USDA). Some people suggest these standards are too lax, while others insist on products that display green USDA organic labels. Certainly trout, a national symbol of purity and wholesomeness, must be untainted enough to be labeled as organic. Not so.

Most hatchery trout fail the organic label test partly because they are treated with antibiotics.[125] Historically, trout raised in both state and federal hatcheries are fed antibiotics to affect reproduction, aid growth, control parasites, and treat and prevent disease.[126] These antibiotics include oxytetracycline-HCl, sulfamerazine, and the mixture of ormetoprim and sulfadimethoxine, which are approved for use by a different federal agency, the U.S. Food and Drug Administration (FDA). According to a U.S. Fish and Wildlife Service (USFWS) drug summary and history and accompanying fact sheet for Oxytetracycline Medicated Feed INAD 9332, this antibiotic was "long used in feed to control mortality."[127] The standard treatment for trout and salmon is a ten-day dose and treated fish can be released for stocking or local markets as soon as twenty-one days after treatment ends. That is enough to give me a queasy stomach, but this story does not end there.

Concern over pollution in fish flesh began to rise in 2004 after publication of an article in *Science*.[128] Salmon are high in the food chain, and these fatty carnivores bioaccumulate pollutants from all the little meals they consume over their lifespan. A group of six scientists, concerned about high organic contaminant levels in farm-raised salmon, collected more than seven hundred fish samples for testing. Their article documented high levels of PCBs, dioxins, toxaphene, and dieldrin in farm-raised Atlantic salmon compared to wild salmon.[129] The likely source of contamination was traced to salmon feed obtained from two companies who supply approximately 80 percent of the global market for aquafeed. These feeds are derived from reconstituted small pelagic fishes like menhaden and herring, which themselves bioaccumulate pollutants. Rachel Carson showed this nation that you are what you eat, poisons and all. Because humans are fatty carnivores that like to horde toxins just as much as salmon, the authors of the *Science* article suggested human health advisories. Here the U.S. Environmental Protection Agency enters the picture. The EPA works to protect human health partly by setting standards for consumption of contaminated foods based on exposure levels and potential links to known cancer- and non-cancer-related diseases. EPA guidelines triggered health advisories with a recommended maximum consumption of only six farm-raised salmon a year. Interestingly, the advisory levels the *Science* authors selected were based on EPA guidelines because FDA guidelines "are not strictly health-based, and do not provide guidance for acceptable levels of toxaphene and dioxins in fish."[130] The authors cautioned that adverse neurobehavioral, immune effects, and endocrine disruption were not considered and might prompt even more restrictive consumptive recommendations. The overall message of *caveat emptor*, or "buyer beware," was clear.

Because most hatchery-raised salmon and trout rely on the same commercial food sources as the farm-raised fish studied in the 2004 *Science* article, people began to wonder about pollutant levels in the flesh of hatchery-raised and stocked species. In response to public unease, the USFWS collected tissue samples from Atlantic salmon, lake trout, and rainbow trout from 138 fish raised in five different facilities within the National Fish Hatchery System (NFH).[131] Samples were analyzed at the Northeast Fisheries Center (NEFC) in Lamar, Pennsylvania, not far from the Huntsdale Hatchery, which supplies golden rainbow trout to the state. According to results of the NEFC study, PCB and dioxin levels were high enough in both hatchery-raised lake and rainbow trout to trigger EPA health advisories with a recommended consumption of only 0.5 meals per month for these fish.[132] Atlantic salmon posed slightly less concern, and hungry anglers were encouraged to finish their single fish dinner every month. However, levels of PCBs were actually higher in hatchery broodstock than in some farm-raised salmon tested for the *Science* article. I doubt these were the results USFWS wanted to put the public at ease. Based on daily creel limits for many states supplied by these hatcheries, anglers can catch their maximum recommended yearly supply of PCBs and dioxins in just one day of fishing for federally tainted trout. Somehow, chemicals originally dumped into rivers by human industries subsequently flowed into the ocean and then followed food chains right back up to their maker. Amazingly, preserving and mounting trophy trout on walls not only provides decoration, it also prevents people from getting cancer.

In a seemingly unrelated topic, the EPA is directly involved in classifying and protecting water quality in the country under the auspices of the Clean Water Act of 1972 (CWA). Interestingly, the EPA use trout as one of many indicator species in its Index of Biotic Integrity (IBI) system to help identify healthy bodies of water because trout are intolerant of pollutants and habitat disturbances.[133] Surprisingly, the IBI does not appear to draw any distinction between wild and hatchery-raised trout. The EPA often ignores the fact that no other taxa has been so extensively stocked, introduced, and genetically altered as trout. The agency also often conveniently ignores the fact that the presence of an exotic invasive species of trout is itself an indicator of environmental disturbance, not evidence for a healthy ecosystem as the metric implies. Furthermore, it is truly ironic that the hatchery-raised trout used as an indicator species fails to pass the proposed USDA organic criteria and is a contamination source for PCBs and dioxins. Trout, used as markers of purity to help identify safe waters, are simultaneously shunned by many consumers because they are tainted.

Of course, the story gets even worse. The U.S. Geological Survey (USGS) tests water quality in the nation's waters and recently conducted specific tests for antibiotics in water within thirteen fish hatcheries.[134] They found that 38 percent of hatcheries sampled showed trace quantities of antibiotics in their water. The USGS recommended that hatcheries take actions to limit release of this contaminated water. Unfortunately, many hatcheries discharge waste water directly back into neighboring rivers and streams. You may wonder how hatcheries can legally dump this apparently toxic material into public waters. Although organic and particulate constituents are regulated, there are currently no water quality standards for antibiotics and most other medicines. These various pharmaceutical products often pass through human bodies; feed cattle, chickens, and even trout; exit in our waste; and flow into our nation's water bodies. Hatcheries are not breaking laws, since there are no relevant statutes that apply. Independent researchers have noted how nutrient contamination from hatchery waste impacts stream ecosystems; they warned that hatchery-raised trout are a potential source of contamination for herons and egrets.[135] Trout and hatcheries are true indicators of pollution because they are themselves the source!

It is worth trying a back-of-the-envelope calculation to determine how much waste product might be leaving hatcheries annually. If we assume an optimistic food-to-trout conversion factor of 1.2 to 1.0, as producers of Nelson's Sterling Silver Cup Fish Feeds suggest,[136] and ignore hatchery mortality that contributes nutrient waste from decaying trout, feeding America's thirty-four million pounds of hatchery trout produces approximately seven million pounds of waste. Keep in mind that this is a best-case scenario in terms of conversion of food to fish, and the ratio may be only 1.4 to 1.0 or higher if feeding is not properly managed. If we include the full production of farm trout nationally, we produce eleven million pounds of trout waste as a potential source of nutrient contamination. The primary government organization tasked with permitting this type of nutrient waste circles back to the EPA through the CWA.

The food chain of the typical hatchery trout is complicated to say the least, so let's see if we have the federal alphabetic soup straight. The USFWS raises trout in the NFH system that trigger EPA health advisories based on testing done by the NEFC. However, these trout don't necessarily set off less stringent FDA tolerance levels, for PCBs and dioxins. Furthermore, the EPA uses these same trout in its IBI, which are not pristine enough to be organic according to the USDA because trout are raised by the USFWS using antibiotics approved by the FDA that the USGS and others warn could contaminate aquatic environments. The USGS also raised concerns that nutrient contaminants permitted by the EPA under the CWA emanate from NFH sites and other hatcheries and negatively impact aquatic ecosystems. OMG!

In ending this chapter it is hard to know where to start. When we consider the historic eradication of species, our system of modern production of aquafeed from marine fish for freshwater recreational fisheries, unintended consequences of hatchery production on creatures in aquatic ecosystems, and the bureaucratic entanglements of federal and state oversight agencies, the contemporary food cycles of trout seem as twisted and knotted as necklaces my daughter often begs me to untangle for her. At her request, I painstakingly work to free all the links. Despite my careful efforts, I know that, unless the chain is left untouched, it will once again become entwined and ultimately broken. Given the present state of trout food chains, it is hard not to think about trout and the aquatic ecosystems they will momentarily inhabit as tangled chains. Marine fish are caught with nets to feed freshwater fish in hatcheries protected by netting. In many cases these trout are exotic to rivers where they will be set free and subsequently drive native species to the brink of extinction. Several native species of birds are shot near hatcheries to protect nonnative fish. Bird plumage is used to create flies that mimic macroinvertebrates. The macroinvertebrates and plants they eat may both be exotic species introduced by pioneering river managers to increase food for trout. Skilled anglers use these artificial flies to fool synthetic fish into biting what these trout think are alien macroinvertebrates. After a prized fish is finally reeled in, chances are it will be set free again by an angler citing a moral code known as the ethics of catch-and-release fishing. Keep in mind that, perhaps more than any other species, trout are hunted for fun not food. Somehow, this whole effort is designed to produce fish that are delicacies in restaurants, but are so revered that anglers argue as sacrilege the killing and eating of trout from a river. This is probably for the best anyway, since these fish are probably laced with toxic chemicals that found their way from a river to the ocean back to hatcheries and into trout. My, what a tangled food web we weave!

CHAPTER SIX

To Serve a Higher Soul

*Fishing, and particularly fly fishing for trout and salmon, has solaced
and stimulated the minds of poets, artists, philosophers, professional men and
statesmen beyond that of any other sport; indirectly influencing history, art
and literature through the acts and expressions of men whose minds have been
strengthened and refreshed during the days and nights spent by solitary streams.*

~ HENRY INGRAHAM, 1926

*I*t is worth pondering how humans justify the control of nature in our nation's rivers; religion is a useful place to start. Religions serve many roles in the modern world. Faith can give people hope for the future. Morality and a sense of good are the underpinnings for a healthy society and often display a strong connection to holy writings. Religious leaders provide guidance that helps to enrich lives of many individuals. Places of worship give people a sense of community and belonging that helps to reaffirm their sense of worth. Without religion, the world could be a scary place. With religion, it is often just as frightening.

Throughout history, religions clash in both the true and more symbolic sense. Religious leaders can, on occasion, call for seemingly unethical measures in the name of faith. In the extreme, devout conviction leads to intolerance and war. People become passionate when their ideals are questioned or confronted with contrasting views. A literal interpretation of a sacred text leaves little room for acceptance of outside ideas that run contrary to the doctrine. Scientific discovery is sometimes attacked or discarded when it conflicts with more pious accounts. In these battles, individuals are asked to choose between two sets of experts, with scientific and religious scholars describing opposing accounts of the same events. Belief in creationism by many Christians and the scientific community's assertion of evolution is one good example of a topic that creates great turmoil. For persons looking to find their way in the modern world, difficult decisions need to be made to rectify these contrasting perspectives. It is certainly confusing to be forced to decide between beliefs founded on faith versus those based solely on what can be directly sensed. Ultimately, no one seems to have all the answers to satisfy human nature.

Make no mistake; fishing is a religion to many people, and the generalities above apply just as directly to this specific form of worship. Certainly, some folks fish impassively simply to gather food or to enjoy the sound of water rumbling over rocks. For these individuals, fishing may merely be one of many hobbies that help make life pleasurable. However, ardent anglers find trout fishing more than a mechanical exercise or a search for food. Fervent fisherfolk are more than happy to report that trout fishing is a divine way of life. They recite, "Fishing is a religion." Fly fishing appears to be even godlier as Tom Brokaw averred: "If fishing is a religion, fly-fishing is high church."[1] In a book jacket cover by famous angling author John Gierach, fishing is described as a philosophical pursuit.[2] For anglers who ascribe to the idea that trout fishing is a higher way of thinking, their chosen faith requires devotion. In the religion of rod and reel, trout become a central focus of worship and serve as an iconic symbol. Talk of trout inspires passions in anglers as they describe their favorite breed, fishing spot, or experience with line and hook. The symbolism of trout extends beyond the physical attributes of the fish. Trout are described as majestic and glorious. Authors talk about trout appreciation, angler's serenity, and a connection to nature. Let us not forget, as some well-known angling authors are happy to remind us, the fish is a symbol for Christianity. Trout are needed in heavy supply to recreate heaven on earth. Taken to an extreme, the religion of trout fishing can ultimately lead to an unquestioning belief in any action that helps raise more fish to sustain the sport.

To spread the fishing faith requires hard work from dedicated disciples. In this scenario, hatchery programs and state game agencies assume the role of missionaries setting up churches in numerous rivers and lakes. Few question methods they use as long as the trout are fruitful and multiply. Collection baskets are passed around and donations gathered in the form of annual fishing licenses, fees for club memberships, and contributions for lobbying activities. Expert fly casters serve as evangelists and spread their belief in the sanctity of trout through a myriad of television shows, books, and private fishing lessons. Hosts of various programs stand in front of cameras and carefully spin their philosophies as they patiently wait for fish to make cameos. Because hosts exhibit great skill with a rod, their opinion on the fate of our nation's waters presumably carries more weight than that of novice anglers. Countless converts buy the sanctioned dress of the trout angler and trudge off to their local stream in waders and fishing vest. As they immerse their feet to baptize themselves in the sacred waters of their favorite wild trout stream, they remember the words of angling preachers who instructed them that fishing is a virtuous pursuit. Anglers follow the ritual of cast, catch, and release as they try to become one with their surroundings. They are reminded that people who fish hold claim to moral high ground because as a group they advocate for stewardship of rivers, lakes, and fisheries contained within. Trout caught are immortalized in stories and photographs. Some artisans even specialize in depictions of emblematic trout. These painters often work in watercolors, a medium that certainly makes sense for an American symbol of water purity. Few people see these fish as simply a product of an industry with economic motives. Fewer still see trout as a representation of man's attempt to dominate nature and our failure to appreciate natural beauty in other aquatic and terrestrial species.

To question why we artificially stock rivers and manipulate them to serve trout is to question some people's faith. People do not like to have their faith scrutinized. They are even less pleased when it is criticized. But, we must look carefully at what trout fishing has become. Anglers and fisheries managers do not intentionally advocate destructive ecological practices. These people spend time fishing because of a love for trout and aquatic environments. Without their support, American rivers would surely be in a sad state. However, when trout and other game fish are held in such high esteem, it devalues other organisms in aquatic and terrestrial environments. Consequently, the ascension of trout comes at the expense of other species and of rivers themselves.

Human concepts of religion, morality, lifestyle choice and a wilderness ethic all play roles in constructing a perception of trout angling as an honorable undertaking. Fisheries managers, equipment suppliers, fishing tutors and angling authors all work to sell the fishing way of life to novices and experienced practitioners alike. Carefully crafted images of trout fishing often serve to camouflage the realities of compromises made to support the sport. When it comes to trout, good intelligent people often seem to substitute belief for logic. Seemingly dubious practices are described as ethical and moral. Hypocritical statements are made about respect for a fish that is often objectified. Even concepts of nature and wildness are contorted to better conform to the ideals of the human-centric view of the world of trout. To truly understand the impact of trout management on American rivers, we must first understand the rationalizations used to justify these practices. To ignore the importance of conviction in our own decision making would be foolish. Failure to recognize the role that belief plays in other people's choices would be disastrous. So let's take a careful look and explore anglers' favorite catch phrases used to support a human grand plan for trout, which ultimately serves to hook a nation on fishing.

~ ~ ~ When Americans discuss religion, the conversation often begins with a mention of the Bible. When it comes to fishing for trout, the bible is Izaak Walton's *The Compleat Angler*. At one time, Walton's book was either the second or third bestselling book in the English language.[3] The other candidate for second on the list was *Pilgrim's Progress*, a contemporaneous book about finding the righteous path to Heaven. The number one seller was the Holy Bible itself. *The Compleat Angler* resulted in approximately four hundred editions in three hundred years. One edition alone sold eighty thousand copies in the 1880s.[4] The book was known in the United States in the 1840s, as evidenced by nature purist Henry David Thoreau's references. In addition, subsequent authors produced numerous books and articles reanalyzing both *The Compleat Angler* and its author. It almost appears that writers of books on angling risked excommunication from the fly-fishing caste if they failed to praise Walton or at least mention him in their own text. Walton is described as the patron saint of fly fishermen.[5] Hewitt ends his 1948 book with a quote by Walton. More recently, David James Duncan wrote a hilarious fiction called, *The River Why*, with a pair of chapters beginning with the title "The Great Izaak Walton Controversy."[6] In almost every chapter, Walton's name pops up like a cowlick on a blind date. Eventually, the hero of the story meets the girl of his dreams. Too tongue-tied to speak coherently, he somehow manages to recite multiple lines from Walton as a way to win over her heart. Still other authors love to debate whether Walton was more skilled fishing with an artificial fly or with bait. Biographers try to recreate his ancient fishing equipment to better appreciate his instruction. I would certainly have a hard time finding a book on trout fishing that does not quote the idol Walton.

Walton, born in Stafford, England, in 1593, lived ninety years and was eventually buried in Winchester Cathedral. Although not born well off, Walton made a living as both a merchant and an author, managing to accumulate a good deal of wealth. He died owning or leasing at least four different properties.[7] Walton was a merchant by trade, but religion played a pivotal part in his life. Walton married the daughter of a bishop; his son became the canon of Salisbury Cathedral; and his daughter married the eventual canon of Winchester Cathedral. In addition to his book on fishing, Walton wrote five biographies, collectively known as *Walton's Lives*. These books described theologians, religious poets, church leaders, and a diplomat for the king. With these connections and others, Walton was well versed in the leading religious teachings of the Church of England. One biographer suggested that: "He was saturated with religion and with theology from his youth up, and the man who only knows of him as a fisherman will receive a mighty revelation when he discovers he was a most religious man, as well as a theologian."[8] This religion also spilled over into politics. During Walton's lifetime, the Puritan Revolution movement began to demand reduced rule by nobility and church bishops. However, Walton was sympathetic to both the king and Anglican Church. He was even involved in a plot to smuggle the crown jewels for King Charles II.[9] Considering his opposition to the religious freedom and shared governance movement that motivated the pilgrims' journey to Plymouth Plantation, I am a bit surprised Walton became so popular in the United States. Perhaps he transcends politics because of the hope he supplies to others. From his modest beginnings to his eventual intermingling with religious leaders and nobility, Walton stands as a true symbol of upward mobility.

The Compleat Angler did not hide its attempt to associate fishing with religion. Beginning with the title page, Walton connected fishing and Christianity by quoting biblical passages that mentioned fishing. He claimed that "in the Scripture, angling is always taken in the best sense."[10] Walton pointed out that four of Christ's disciples were simple fishermen, and he suggested that Christ showed preference to these four relative to the other eight. Throughout the book Walton carefully worked to unite fishing and Christianity as compatible pursuits. He wanted readers to believe that fishing enhances a virtuous lifestyle. If I believe as Walton did, a fishing pole must be the first true divining rod. Pick one up and it will immediately point me in the direction of God!

The Compleat Angler represented an instruction manual for the soul of the gentleman angler. In describing Walton's literary style, one expert suggested that "his subjects are often treated as the personified embodiment of ideal qualities or characters."[11] Walton directed readers along a path for lifelong fulfillment that led straight to rivers. Throughout the book words like *virtuous, noble, civil, honest,* and *high esteem* are used to describe fishing and fishermen. Numerous poems, songs, and religious references described the righteous life of anglers. Walton encouraged readers to philosophically consider rivers and the fish they contain. In fact, the full title for the book is *The Compleat Angler: or the Contemplative Man's Recreation.* Perhaps Walton was wise enough to recognize that the book would be less successful if it was just a mundane description of technique. He worked to suggest that proficiency in fishing helps demonstrate human intelligence and wisdom. Walton claimed, "God never did make a more calm, quiet, innocent recreation, than angling."[12] Walton insinuated that fishing is not just a human creation to acquire food, but is an ordained undertaking from the master planner.

The hero of the story, for it is told as a story, is the character Piscator. Piscator meets two other gentlemen, and quickly wins over the heart of one who subsequently becomes his scholar. By book's end, this new disciple of the angle, Venator, is a devoted follower and swears an oath of loyalty to the angling lifestyle:

> And my good Master, I will not forget the doctrine which you told me Socrates taught his Scholars, that they should not think to be honored so much for being Philosophers, as to honor Philosophy by their virtuous lives. You advised me to the like concerning Angling, and I will endeavor to do so, and to live like those many worthy men of which you made mention in the former part of your discourse. This is my firm resolution.[13]

It is clear throughout the book that by developing this character Walton wanted readers to do more than just occasionally enjoy fishing. Readers were encouraged to make fishing a central part of their lives and offer themselves to its pursuit. He wanted people to follow his direction with a literal, not an interpretive, reading of his text. The portrayal of an instructive master and dedicated follower pledging allegiance to the teachings certainly draws some interesting parallels to the life of Christ. Whether this writing style was intentionally used by Walton to mimic the Bible or was simply an effective writing method, it helped to further enhance the religious underpinning for trout fishing that the author tried so hard to establish.

In much the same way that disciples served Christ and Venator followed Piscator, Charles Cotton, a high-born and cultured individual, became a real-life devotee of Walton. Cotton eventually supplied an appendix to Walton's book, a new testimony, if you will, that was included in the fifth edition. In this later section, Cotton became both the writer and a character in the book. He and the resurrected character of Venator sang the praises of Walton. Cotton referred to himself as the son and servant of Walton, whom he called father. Similarly, more recent authors heaped endless praise on Cotton and referred to trips to see Cotton's old house as pilgrimages.

Despite these religious overtones, *The Compleat Angler* did try to be comprehensive in its coverage of angling. Regardless of the tone and approach, the book was still a manual of fishing methods with practical advice on how to fish for a large variety of species, which types of bait to use, and how to make fishing tackle. Methods for adding scents that made bait "irresistibly attractive"[14] are mentioned—a practice that sounds a bit like modern infomercials and magazine ads for miracle products to entice fish to bite. Walton described stocking and rearing fish in man-made ponds. The methods are remarkably similar to those described more than two and a half centuries later in U.S. Bureau of Fisheries publications on hatchery practices.[15] There are gaffes when, for example, Walton claimed that grayling from the River Loire feed on gold and had been found with grains of gold in their stomachs. Yet few people mention flaws in the book or question the master. Instead, the book became a classic, and today newly minted copies are available in libraries and bookstores throughout the country.

The impact of *The Compleat Angler* on modern fishing books is undeniable. Modern books adopt Walton's basic style and continue to intertwine angling and religion in more subtle ways. In many cases, the books describe a nature ethic in fishing, with a stress on wildness, where trout become a symbol of purity. The capture of trout becomes a quest for wholesomeness. For example, Paul Quinnett said: "I have wondered if it is the wildness in fish that somehow renews the wildness in us. . . . It is as if the fighting fish is the longed-for iron key that opens the golden door to our uncensored souls and what might be still wild in us."[16] When I open the golden door and envision the carefully guarded, pearly gates to heaven, I will need to remember that Saint Peter, the angel holding the iron keys, was one of the disciple fishermen whom Walton honored in his book. Quinnett continued: "A day fishing that quiet brook meandering through that unspoiled meadow can, however momentarily, carry even the most befouled modern man back to the natural rhythms of life and death and to that Eden toward which, in our haste to leave it behind, too few of us have bothered to steal a backward glance."[17] It is hard not to connect fishing and religion when references to Eden are included. Here and elsewhere fishing is portrayed as a miracle cure for modern man. Quinnett basically described the angler's version of the laying on of hands. The author wants us to reconnect with an untamed spirit that was somehow lost when we were evicted from Eden.

The concepts of wilderness hold powerful importance in the American psyche. Wildness itself is a virtue worshiped by countless citizens, myself included. Seemingly untouched settings elicit phrases that include "God's country" and "heaven on earth." I certainly understand the value of a nature ethic and I love the notion of wilderness, even if few places I visit truly fit the description. Still, when authors discuss trout, the cynic in me wonders about Quinnett's suggestion that trout have wildness in such abundance that just hauling one in with a carbon fiber fishing pole and a titanium reel can help us forget the modern world and tap our uncorrupted spirit. Are the unspoiled nature and wildness associated with trout still effective remedies for modern man if people are catching hatchery-raised fish in rivers modified by humans to improve fishing? Few authors of angling books ask these types of questions. It is more likely that many anglers carry idyllic images from books with them as they head off with rod and reel. They may not look with a critical eye at the truth of the modern fishing scene. Still, some could argue that it does not matter if trout are more a manufactured product than a part of an ecosystem — so long as participants still feel a connection to nature. However, it is hard to connect fishing, wildness, and wisdom if anglers are driven by delusions. Perhaps, in recognition of this contradiction, numerous anglers disdain hatchery trout and seek only their wild brethren. If we truly believe that wild trout provide the ultimate path to salvation, we are left with one underlying question: what exactly does it mean to be a wild trout?

The idea of wild trout conjures up solitary, sleek water warriors capable of fending for themselves against an onslaught of countless natural dangers. Visions of trout help to ignite our pioneering spirit. We envision fish that evolved to cope with swift currents, extremes of temperature and carefully camouflaged predators. When angling authors talk about wildness in fish, we imagine a connection with raw untamed strength that was lost in humans thousands of years ago. Pragmatic anglers perhaps picture a connection with a thin translucent monofilament line constructed of fluorocarbon. Idealists visualize a more spiritual symbiosis. But most of us were born in human hatcheries called hospitals; we grew up in cities or suburbs where very little of the adventurer remains. We are not wild. How could we possibly share a spiritual bond with the embodiment of unspoiled nature?

So I ask again, what exactly does it mean to be a wild trout? Wild trout advocates place a much greater value on these fish than their hatchery-raised cousins. Nothing is more glorious or majestic than wild trout in these anglers' eyes. Clearly, there must be a major distinction. Are trout in a hatchery wild? Clearly the answer is no. Even if we place them in the most pristine river in the country, the stigma of a hatchery birth will always relegate these fish to a secondary status. Are trout wild if they were born in a river from parents that barely survived long enough outside their hatchery enclosure to deposit a few eggs in a small gravel depression? Unfortunately, these new-born trout still probably carry the genetic imprint of more than 100 years of domesticated rearing in a hatchery under the watchful eye of man. These trout's lineage might run back to a small region of California waters, but later individuals might now find themselves on the other side of a continent in a stream that never saw trout until iron rails connected two distant oceans. Such trout may be direct descendants of multiple generations of fish that never left a hatchery. Is that wild? According to experts, yes!

The definition of wild trout used by state agencies comes down to the ultimate argument of nature versus nurture: As long as a population of trout is perpetuated by reproduction in that river, their offspring are wild, regardless of the original species range or origin of their ancestors. According to that logic, years of selective breeding that favored fish capable of living in overcrowded, monotone hatchery runs that helped program fish to respond to meals dispersed by automatic pellet feeders do not diminish the wild nature of trout just one generation removed from fish factories. DNA and genetics carefully manipulated and unintentionally tweaked for decades in hatcheries do not matter. Despite all the carefully crafted language and imagery of wild trout proponents, the concoction of the words *wild* and *trout* does not mean trout are native species perfectly evolved to survive in this particular aquatic environment. Any trout born in a river is wild, no matter how genetically and ecologically messed-up the fish has become. Even golden rainbow trout are considered wild if their Creamsicle-colored parents avoided herons long enough to deposit a couple of eggs in a stream. In essence, clear waters in streams can carry both befouled modern man and his beloved trout back to the natural rhythms of life and death. We humans must be pretty hopeless cases if one of the most highly domesticated aquatic species on earth has something to teach us about wildness.

Although they are rarely referred to as such, wild trout are often the problem, not the solution. When stocked populations of nonnative trout go wild, they seem to follow few of the normal rules in local ecosystems. Wild rainbow trout are responsible for hybridization with native Californian golden trout that pushed that species close to the brink. Westslope cutthroat trout face extinction from interbreeding with both wild rainbow and wild Yellowstone cutthroat trout.[18] Elsewhere, indigenous Yellowstone cutthroat trout are themselves victims of genetic dilution from populations of wild nonnative trout. Green cutthroat trout, thought to be extinct in 1937, are still listed as threatened due in large part to invasions of rainbow, brook, and brown trout, many of them wild. Rio Grande cutthroat and Colorado River cutthroat trout are both severely limited in their former range because of competition from stocked populations of trout that went wild. Little Colorado spinedace, native fish found in Northern Arizona, experience high predation rates from wild trout.[19] Native bull trout are listed as a threatened species in the Northwestern United States largely because of the impact of wild eastern brook trout. Seventy to 80 percent of high-mountain lakes in the Sierra Nevada Mountains contain introduced populations of wild trout that pushed several species, especially mountain yellow-legged frog, to dangerously low levels.[20] It was this problem that prompted the U.S. Forest Service to try to eradicate wild brook trout from selected lakes in the 1990s. Colorado pikeminow and razorback sucker are two native endangered species on the Colorado River in serious decline from impacts that include predation by wild rainbow and brown trout. Humpback chub is another unique native species in the Colorado River listed under the Endangered Species Act. To help save this species approximately nineteen thousand wild rainbow trout and smaller numbers of wild brown trout were removed from the Colorado River by the Arizona Fish and Game Department from 2003 to 2006 and given to local tribal communities for use as fertilizer.[21] The fact that trout are wild does not mean that they are not responsible for serious ecosystem disturbances. In reality, nonnative wild trout are simply uninhibited and promiscuous tourists reproducing beyond control: the trout edition of gills gone wild!

Most anglers would cringe if I suggested that catching wild brown trout and throwing them on the bank to slowly suffocate and perhaps feed hungry scavengers would do more ecological good than harm. Perhaps it will save an undiscovered macroinvertebrate that was being pushed to its limits by this new predator. If watching a brass-and-cream-colored trout with reddish-brown spots slowly asphyxiate in the sun sounds cruel, just remember it happens to nongame fish all the time. If a sluggish, tasteless, ugly, bottom-feeding species that competes with trout is caught, it frequently ends up in the woods versus the creek when the hook is removed. If it has ever been known to actually eat a trout fry or attack an adult trout the way a lamprey does, it cannot expect a fair trial before sentencing. It might be a native species that descended from generations of fish right in the very stretch of water where it was caught, but to generations of anglers it will never be truly wild. If it cannot be wild, it cannot be worshiped, so into the bushes it goes.

On the other hand, stocked trout have plenty of their own hurdles to overcome. Hence, we come to our first moral challenge. As a pair of Cambridge scholars eloquently observed: "Releasing fish into the wild knowing they are totally unprepared for survival and the majority will die, presents a considerable ethical conundrum that ought to be addressed."[22] Somehow when we talk about trout fishing as a religious experience and we practice catch-and-release fishing to prevent harm to our revered prize, we ignore the plain truth that the entire trout-fishing industry is on ethically shaky ground.

We raise trout by the millions knowing they are genetically programmed to fail in the wild. Fish despised in hatcheries become the ultimate symbol of purity when they successfully invade an ecosystem and drive native populations to the brink of extinction. The few offspring of hatchery trout that do not perish then become canonized as wild objects of desire.

The fact that so many anglers place so much worth on this supposed wildness is completely mystifying and quite comedic. Of course, even anglers sometimes see the farce in the supposed connection between spiritualism and trout. At times Quinnett took a slightly more humorous approach to the religion of trout fishing. He joked about sitting in the pew at church as a young man thinking about angling. He wondered if God went fishing with Adam and Eve and taught them how to fly fish. Later in the book he quipped about Adam and Eve's expulsion from Eden and suggested the loss of access to great fishing was one of the biggest punishments. At one point in the book, Quinnett even seemed to recognize his own hypocrisy when he tried to link religion and fishing. He kidded that the word *angling* also means to manipulate conditions for a desired outcome. I certainly would not disagree with the author that angling is a scheme, a manipulation to get fish. If an angler's ultimate goal is to justify his desire to dominate another species and an entire ecosystem with rod and reel, why not convince others that he is engaged in a virtuous pursuit for the embodiment of wildness? The intentional linkage of fishing to spiritual and ethical aspects of religion is angling in more than one sense.

Human history certainly teaches us that people are capable of incredible destruction when we use religion to justify our actions. The skeptic in me wonders if the religion and ethics of fishing apply only to serve human needs. According to Walton, God practically demands fishing from the faithful, so why would we ever question practices that improve angling success? Is that the point of all these books on angling? If this sounds far-fetched, please remember that generations of anglers altered aquatic species distributions, changed the genetics of trout, manipulated food chains by eradicating predators, and physically modified rivers to improve fishing. Is it incomprehensible that government agencies would downplay ecological concerns and instead promote a hobby that brings in taxes and huge sums of money to local businesses? Is it really that hard to believe that some anglers would intentionally or subconsciously use words and twisted reason to justify fishing practices? Whatever people's beliefs, righteousness clearly serves a very useful purpose for the angling community.

~ ~ ~ Religion is often about devotion. But devotion does not necessarily need to be about religion. For example, love is a pure act of loyalty and marriage is often considered the ultimate commitment. Similarly, parents talk about dedication to their children. Even in sporting stadiums throughout the country, teams talk about their devoted fans. Similarities to a religious life are apparent, and the level of loyalty is admirable. Not surprisingly, writers of angling books do not always rely solely on religious language. Instead of couching fishing directly or subtly in pious terms, they often describe it as a lifestyle that requires strong individual commitment. There is a sense in angling books that we need to dedicate ourselves to fishing, not to simply view angling as a part-time hobby and definitely not as a food-gathering exercise. Writers compare fishing to falling in love: the quintessential act of commitment and the most admirable human emotion. But anyone who has fallen in love knows that passion can lead to fixation. These same writers willingly admit that anglers can become totally obsessed with fishing and lose their perspective. Although authors suggest that to deny a passion for fishing is somehow to deny our humanity,[23] most readers will recognize that millions of people still manage to live completely contented lives without regularly baiting a hook or casting a fly. Fishing might provide a useful outlet for many individuals, but it should not be permitted to obscure our thinking.

Reliance on steadfast devotion rarely leads to sound decision making, and when fishing becomes an obsession, inconsistencies in logic become obvious. John Bailey, an author of at least two dozen fishing books, stated at the outset of his 1998 book that fish are more than simple objects or commodities, and serve more of a purpose than just amusement.[24] He described the majestic qualities and beauty of fish, and the desire to cherish them. He begged readers always to make the welfare of fish their first consideration. These early sections of the book certainly lay the foundations for a strong moral foundation in fishing. However, Bailey blew those ethics right out of the water later in the book. The first clue was a multitude of pictures that show anglers holding trophy fish, which look very much like mere objects of conquest in the photographs. As is the case in many books, each fish was enormous, and proud anglers struggled to support their hefty prizes. Bailey included a whole series of subheadings that described battles and apparent sacrifices by anglers with headings like "Worth It All."[25] Despite author's claims to the contrary, size did matter. For all the earlier talk in his book about connecting to nature and respect for fish, the photographs and captions tell a different story. When anglers held exhausted fish out of water to photo-document the capture, they did not make the welfare of fish their first priority. Deliberately or not, many angling books suggest that it really *is* about the catch, not the process or surroundings.

Speaking of the catch, a basic belief termed the ethics of "catch-and-release fishing" dominates the thinking of many anglers. The aspiration is always to set free the splendor that has been captured. As we heard since our youth, beauty is in the eye of the beholder. If I practice catch-and-release fishing, I will be sure to first carefully wet my hands and avoid touching the gills when I behold the beauty I be holdin'. Like a good Christian, I will perform a revival ceremony before we finally part ways. I simply point the trout into the current to breathe life back into the fish. Hallelujah! Let us see if I can catch him again.

The moral argument for catch-and-release fishing suggests that trout are there for our enjoyment — that killing them after they are caught raises ethical concerns. State agencies jumped on the movement and set aside sections of river for catch-and-release only. Author Joe Brooks pleaded that readers should "admire and release" their catch of steelhead trout.[26] It might be worth keeping in mind that the steelhead trout he talked about were not native to the English stream he fished. Brooks reminded us that "we should bear in mind that fishing is not nearly as much fun for the fish."[27] Does this mean the author was suggesting that fishing provides even a little bit of amusement for the fish? Does Brooks perhaps think of this as an exercise program a bit like walking a dog? I seriously doubt that a trout complains about being bored and so decides to go bite that giant hook to liven things up at the pool party. Rest assured — fishing is not in any way fun for fish!

Catch-and-release ethics are often preached to the young. Allen Say, a Caldecott Medal winner, wrote a children's book on fly fishing where a wise uncle serves as a mentor for a new generation of anglers. The uncle patiently replies to his nephew's question when he lets a trout go. "'Why didn't I kill the fish?' said Uncle. 'I like to leave the river the way I found it.'"[28] The illustration shows Uncle holding a rainbow trout, which is the poster child for the intentional manipulation of rivers with the introduction of nonnative species. The nephew eventually gets his chance to cast and manages to hook an equally large rainbow trout. The book carefully describes how the nephew expertly exhausts the trout before reeling it in. The emotional climax of the book comes when the uncle explains that the boy will need to stab the trout in the head with a knife if he wants to keep the fish. The boy makes the seemingly morally sound choice, dramatically dropping the knife and gently lowering the fish back into the water. The book's message to young readers is that it is better to fish for fun than for food. The boy hero of our story dutifully repeats his uncle's words about leaving the river the way he found it. Luckily for this youth, generations of people had already heavily modified the aquatic environment so that he can find it full of rainbow trout when he arrives. The author of *L.L. Bean's Fly-Fishing Handbook* explained that his parents and grandparents were excellent role models and taught him to both catch and respect fish.[29] The author continues: "Fewer people are killing their fish today. They realize that tempting a fish to the fly and playing it on sensitive fly tackle is often the best part of fishing, and that releasing them provides fish to tempt another day."[30] I understand the pragmatic decision to leave the fish in the river, but how respectful is it to torment an animal just for fun? I wonder if his parents and grandparents forgot to teach him not to play with his food, especially if he does not actually plan to eat it? Respect for living creatures is certainly an admirable trait, but when we worship trout we begin to make strange decisions.

Generally, the more serious the angler author, the more catch-and-release fishing will be a theme in the book. But not all talk about catch-and-release falls into the realm of ethics. Some authors make the simple point that keeping a fish removes a hungry mouth from the river. When people fish, they pretend to provide nourishment to trout. In this case, having more mouths to feed is a good thing because it increases the number of fish caught. Here motivations for catch-and-release fishing are presented in purely sensible terms. Anglers want to catch the same fish multiple times. These individuals conveniently ignore the fact that many fish caught with a rod and hook die regardless of the angler's intention. Art Lee mentions the ugly side of catch-and-release fishing: "Some fish are a tragic sight, snouts torn, (and) maxillaries missing."[31] Coming from a person who catches hundreds of trout a year, it is fair to assume he has seen enough fish to know. And here is another dilemma: if many trout do not survive being caught and released purely for sport, can anglers claim that catch-and-release fishing is ethical? Is killing just for fun justifiable if a fish was artificially raised as a game fish, poorly adapted to live in a river and most likely an exotic invader that terrorized native fauna? I guess the angling authorities are correct when they say trout fishing is equal parts sport and philosophical pursuit.

Still, catch-and-release fishing forges ahead and is now widely adopted. But, if the movement is widely practiced, why are state and federal hatcheries still required to stock millions of trout annually in rivers that mandate catch-and-release fishing? It turns out it is not easy to be dragged to shore against your will by a piece of metal jabbed into your lip. This fact certainly is not a revelation. Pulitzer Prize–winning author John McPhee, an ardent shad fisherman, wrote that "there is no such thing as humane torture, and striking steel into a fish and pulling it into submission is torture."[32] Consequently, science shows that many fish die due to catch-and-release practices. In Alaska, 62 percent of fish caught received a hooking injury, and 28 percent had already been damaged by fishing hooks that put these fish at greater risk for disease and infections.[33] Lee described a much sought-after brown trout in Pennsylvania that "had collected a veritable beard of flies" over the years by breaking off the same angler's fishing lines.[34] Eventually, the Captain Ahab of this story got his great fish, but I am curious how healthy this poor creature was with so many possible sources of infection. Did the fisherman eventually outwit the fish as suggested in the book, or simply wear it down with the so-called death by a thousand cuts? Unfortunately, many of these types of injuries occur even with barbless hooks. And, as it turns out, hooks are only half the problem.

A study in Yellowstone National Park estimated the average cutthroat trout was caught 9.7 times. The study warned that the stress on fish due to what was termed "severe muscular exertion" could be cumulative.[35] Imagine using all your energy to fight for your very existence. At the moment you are most exhausted and fighting for breath, some aquatic monster grabs you and holds you underwater to get a good look at you before they snap a picture. Eventually, you will be tossed back on land in a semiconscious state due to oxygen deprivation. As you lie on shore, you must now defend yourself from grizzly bears hiding in the bushes. All told, you will need to repeat this procedure ten times during your life. Now imagine you are a wild trout and only have a life expectancy of seven or eight years at best, and you probably will not be targeted by an angler your first year. That means you can look forward to completely exhausting yourself in your survival struggle twice a year for five years just to amuse someone. The final time you are caught someone will probably nail you to a board so they can show you off and brag about outwitting you. Does that sound like an ethical activity to you? Moral anglers might want to think they are leaving rivers as they found them, but fish know this is not true.

Anglers usually view a fish's extreme efforts from a slightly different perspective, focusing on how much fun it is to reel in a fish struggling for its life. Many angling books describe severe muscular exertion, using terms that attempt to honor trout with accolades that include *defiant, resistant, spunky,* and *pugnacious.* Quinnett summed it up nicely and stated that "in the relationship between fisherman and fish, we measure a fish's spirit by how well, once hooked, it struggles to free itself."[36] Nobody respects a fish that raises the white flag when it is on the line. We want fish that resist being pulled to shore with reckless abandon. Rainbow trout are renowned as fabulous aerial performers because they tend to jump out of the water when hooked. In reality, these fish are not trying to be theatrical. Leaping rainbow trout are in an all-out panic, a desperate struggle for continued existence. These fish don't understand this is just a temporary game that will end as soon as a digital camera records the catch. The toil of the depleted fish supplies the thrills anglers seek; unfortunately, the effort can easily kill the fish.

The death toll for fish is not just an unexpected and unavoidable consequence of fishing; it is inherent in procedures used to catch trout. Standard fishing practice calls for anglers to wear down a fish before they try to land it, to prevent a trout from breaking the fishing line. This is called "playing the fish" and is the best part of fishing according to many authors. Playing a fish is really the ultimate embodiment of the human subjugation of nature, carefully drawn out as excruciatingly long as the fish can endure. Lee instructed his readers about proper technique and stated that:

> The intent of playing the trout is to wear them down, to drain their energy until they become manageable. Taking the fight out of a fish is a function of applying relentless pressure to tire it out. A trout must be alternatively spurred and reined into sapping its own reserves of strength, a goal attainable only if the fish is persistently denied rest.[37]

Keep in mind that Lee planned to immediately let this fish go to fend for itself once caught. Perhaps, like some trout admirers, he puckered up and gave the trout a little peck on the head for good luck. This action of apparent esteem for trout, in reality, is the angler's kiss of death. Bailey preached catch-and-release, writing, "after two deep dives and three spirited runs, the fish was on the surface, taking in oxygen, and I knew it was mine."[38] Presumably, the battered object of conquest was left to care for itself again when the encounter was over. Even my favorite author, McPhee, talked about battling an American shad for more than two hours before finally reeling in the fish.[39] He is a meat fisherman who loves the taste of shad roe and was humane enough to keep that fish instead of dumping it back in the river. If fish are reeled in again, anglers claim catch-and-release causes no harm.

Alternatively, if fish die hours later and are silently swept away downstream, anglers remain happily oblivious.

The German people and their government do not think very highly of catch-and-release fishing and have, in fact, made it illegal. In order to obtain a necessary permit to use rod and reel, anglers need to state a sensible reason for fishing. Fishing for food is considered a legitimate intention, while fishing for fun is not. What anglers catch they must keep and should plan on eating. Overall, individual anglers will catch fewer fish because they will need to stop when they reach their creel limit. Fewer fish are injured, and those that are hurt mostly get consumed by people. Maybe individuals do not need to fish in the pure sense, but we all need to eat and fishing provides necessary nutrients. It is a very practical argument made in a country known for pragmatism. This sentiment is almost diametrically opposed when it comes to trout in the United States and England. Although catching and eating a trout is perfectly legal, numerous anglers in these places still consider it a crime. In some of our rivers, federal and state law supports this viewpoint; legally mandating that anglers can only torture fish for fun. Pennsylvania established regulations for "catch-and-release" fishing as of 1935.[40] Now governments levy stiff penalties for those who do not comply. Anglers in restrictive catch-and-release waters might end up wounding and killing many more fish than German counterparts, but none of the American trout will be eaten by humans. How different countries fishing for the same species of brown and rainbow trout have come to such different conclusions about angling is hard to understand.

Some writers acknowledge the moral predicament in the sport. They recognize the problem of exhausting fish and specifically point to the very fine tippets used to catch big trout. The tippet is essentially the small line leading to the hook, and most experts have a fascination with using the lightest possible line. But light line breaks easily, so anglers cannot pull very hard to reel in fish. Consequently, they must almost completely drain each fish to the point where it can barely swim; otherwise the fishing line will break, leaving the trout with a hook stuck in its mouth. An angler's options are to either snap the line, leaving the hook lodged in the mouth of the fish, which must then find a way to eat with its new ornament, or weaken the fish with a major physical struggle and then let it try to recover before it dies. This highlights yet another major hypocrisy in catch-and-release fishing. People love to make fishing challenging by using light tackle while simultaneously touting an ethical requirement to release fish they catch. Yet, anglers show little regard for the trout's health with this method of catching fish. When anglers talk about the thrill of playing a fish, they are describing the fun of watching a fish slowly suffer and potentially die. Meanwhile, they call for others to consider the welfare of fish foremost. Anglers might have a clear conscience when they liberate a fish just caught, but that doesn't mean the fish has survived. Even from a purely practical sense, that sounds pretty dumb. Much like the fine tippet itself, their suggestion that catch-and-release fishing is morally sound is a weak line of reasoning that is sure to fail if relied on too heavily.

One review article estimated the stress on trout and salmon following capture with hooks resulted in mortality rates of at least 9 percent and as high as 86 percent in five different studies.[41] Other studies suggested that mortality is much lower, in the 3 to 5 percent range.[42] Perhaps the most comprehensive study, a single analysis of fifty-three different scientific studies, found an average mortality rate of 18 percent.[43] I am not sure which study to believe, but I would not be happy with any of those survival odds if it were my doctor giving me those chances for a nonessential surgical procedure. If I had to face that same procedure ten times in my life, I would be justifiably petrified. If we select the number from the most comprehensive study and assume 82 percent of fish survive each time they are released, then calculate the survival rate for being caught a total of ten times, like trout in Yellowstone National Park, the overall chance of surviving drops to less than 14 percent. With a corresponding mortality rate of more than 86 percent from multiple catches, it is easy to see why heavy stocking is needed. Catch-and-release mortality is compounded by the fact that hatchery trout are poorly adapted to life in a river from the outset. Catch-and-release preachers ask us to ignore these numbers and believe in the spiritual value of injuring a fish. Describing the overall approach as the "ethics" of catch-and-release fishing is so ludicrous that even a kindergartener could see the holes in the logic. Perhaps that is why the movement needs children's books on the subject — so that proponents can obscure logic with flowery tales of stewardship of nature and reverence for trout. If I sound bitter, I apologize, but it is hard to wax poetic with a mouth full of barbs. Please remember that as a child I was hooked on trout fishing too!

I have played the hypocrite many times in my life, so I certainly recognize this flaw in the writing of others. This leads to some questions: If trout fishing really is about having a religious experience or connecting with nature, why do they call them "game fish"? Why are large trout referred to as "trophies"? Why is reeling in a fish termed "playing" a trout? Obviously, recreational fishing is a game. In this game the rewards and consequences are unequal. Fishing pits an individual interested in having some light amusement against an animal fighting for its existence. To increase our own enjoyment, it is often best to imagine we risk something ourselves in the sport. Books describe struggles between anglers and trout. Words like *battle, fight,* and *contest* are tossed in to remind us how seriously we need to approach fishing. But how much do anglers really risk in these hostilities? What will be lost with defeat except a few dollars in artificial flies and lures? Even with victory, the catch-and-release edict requires us to throw away the spoils of war. Triumphant anglers then can retell their story of the skirmish to honor their own superiority over a hatchery product that was delivered to the battlefield specifically to lose the war.

As with many games where one-upmanship plays a role, most anglers want trophy fish big enough to impress their friends. A fishing toolbox comes standard with a ruler and a scale. Many anglers catch-and-release until they get that keeper they are looking for. The result: many casualties and one prize. Other anglers rely on tallies of fish caught. Historic pictures show pioneer fishermen with huge hauls of fish at their feet. Anglers and game agencies even like to calculate the number of fish caught per hour as a means of determining if a river holds enough trout in their estimation. State fishing agencies and private fishing derbies hold competitions for the largest fish caught or largest cumulative weight of fish reeled in. The theme of bigger is better and more is marvelous is repeated in almost every fishing book. The book *Trout Fishing in the Catskills* seems to record every large trout ever caught and each big haul of fish in the region.[44] In these publications, it is nearly impossible to find a picture of an angler holding a trout under the legal limit. As a result of these inherent pressures, anglers are infamous for exaggerating the sizes and numbers of the fish they catch or let get away. This trend underscores a basic mentality in the sport: the amount of fun is measured in inches, pounds, or total number caught. I am certainly used to making judgments based on inches, pounds, centimeters, and kilograms. I also know that it takes many more measurements of different features and inhabitants to begin to piece together the picture of a complex habitat.

A river environment is about as complex a system as there is in nature. Trout are just one of many species of fish that happen to inhabit our rivers. Although many anglers judge trout to be more worthy than other aquatic inhabitants, trout cannot be separated from the ecosystem within which they live. Even in hatcheries, trout impact food chains and the world outside the fence. Trout are no more majestic or glorious than other fish; they are just more sought after. Attempts at religious overtones, claims of ethical underpinnings, and false imagery of the wildness of trout simply serve the human aspiration to justify the subjugation of nature to promote a species of desire. Ultimately, it is the human hunger and reverence for trout that needs to be principally managed, not the species itself.

CHAPTER SEVEN

Building a Dream Home

Just as the rings made by a rising fish in still water travel in ever-widening circles till they finally disappear, so any tampering with Nature's methods sets influences to work whose effects will be felt by a circle of living creatures in a way perhaps unguessed at. Before attempting the improvement of conditions in any water, it is necessary to know the chain of circumstances which has led to the conditions which exist.

~ WINSTON ARMISTEAD, 1920

*T*he first hatchery I remember was a trout facility in Massachusetts on the Swift River below Quabbin Reservoir. I do not remember many details of my visit because I was just a cub scout at the time, traveling to the hatchery with my dad. Like most distant memories, what I recall is a series of mental snapshots that I now strain to recall and link together. My first remembrance is of brushing elbows with adults as we peeked through a chain-link fence and stared down at a reservoir spillway where the Swift River now begins. We saw scores of large trout undulating in the current far below. Undoubtedly, the adjacent scout leaders were silently cursing the No Fishing signs, their lips breathlessly expressing the frustrations, lest the cub scouts hear. The next psychological photograph is of a round hatchery pen filled with enormous trout to awe young visitors. Finally, I remember walking along the edge of a river that was wide enough to be intimidating. But, there was something very strange about this landscape. The river contained several large triangles that jutted out from the banks almost to the middle of the channel. They were obviously built by humans. I was ecstatic about the opportunity to walk out and stand in a place where my feet should have been wet. I had no idea what these geometric figures were designed to do, and nobody would have predicted that these devices would later play an important role in my career.

As it turns out, I was standing on a deflector. Deflectors represent one of four classes of structures constructed to serve trout. Deflectors are one of the more interesting designs of so-called "stream-improvement structures" and are used to narrow down a channel, much like a nozzle on a hose, to increase the erosive force of flow. The enhanced current then scours out sediments to excavate a deep area for fish. Deflectors come in many different shapes and sizes, but all work in essentially this same manner. A similar effect is achieved with several types of dams. Most dams, regardless of their intended purpose, create an impoundment upstream of the barrier and plunging flow that scours out a second deep pool just below the lip. When dams are used to create pool habitat, they are usually low in height to permit at least some fish passage. Together, dams and deflectors are utilized to increase the number of pools in a river to create the deep-water habitat utilized by trout. These pools are necessary for fish survival during periods of warm low flow in late summer as well as ice-covered winter days. Anglers are particularly interested in pools because the largest trout are often found there and, in many cases, the larger the pool the larger the trout. Early American angling clubs showed a preference for pool habitat when they purchased rivers with milldams or even constructed their own impoundments. In 1927, Platts said, "if the mountain trout want pools—and they do indeed—give them pools."[1] He subsequently provided details on exactly how to dam rivers to satisfy the trout's cravings.

Designers of stream-improvement projects have two other groups of structures in their tool box. Cover structures, which include the lunkers on the Salmon River, take on the most variety in form and are placed near the water surface with a gap to the channel bed below providing space where fish can swim. They are intended to supply a place for trout to hide from predators and the sun. As the name implies, they offer overhead cover that mimics habitat normally provided by logs and undercut channel banks. The final style of structures is so controversial that some would argue that it does not belong in this cluster of marvels; but it is undeniable that they are all often linked in time and place. Revetments are placed on the sides of channels and used to arrest erosion of sediment and soil that line the banks of most rivers. The infamous riprap wall is just one commonly found style, and the Salmon River's root wad revetments are another. Revetments do not often provide habitat for fish, but are used to combat erosion that many river managers consider public enemy number one for trout. Altogether, these four classes of structures create a technological approach to enhance habitat and limit channel adjustments both laterally and vertically. Over the last eighty years, structures were lauded for their alleged ability to improve conditions for game fish, especially trout. A great deal of research that directly contradicts those claims now exists. Regardless of whether these structures benefit trout or not, it is worth looking at the mind-set of the proponents of this new architectural approach to river management. The question arises: "What were they thinking?"

~ ~ ~ If at first you don't succeed, try and try again. If that still doesn't work, maybe you should try something else. This was the lesson learned from early fish stocking experiments in the nineteenth century. As the 1800s came to a close, trout populations continued their decline. The number of private hatcheries increased, but even at the time there was a realization that stocking alone could not overcome problems associated with poor fishing practices, especially the crisis of overfishing. More and more people were leaving their homes for the countryside as expansion of rail service and the introduction of automobiles allowed for better access to remote locations.

Problems in the homes of trout also became apparent, and concerned anglers reported great loss of fish from pollution sources, including sewage, ash, sawdust, coal dust, oil, and starch. Land-use impacts from deforestation, log drives, removal of wood in rivers, swamp draining, river straightening, dam construction and flow reduction from canals and irrigation also were serious threats to trout near the end of the nineteenth and beginning of the twentieth century. In response to the failure of stocking to improve fish populations, wealthy landowners and clubs — groups that included some of the individuals directly responsible for the ills of the land — soon experimented with physical modifications of rivers. Anglers were out to build a new dream home for trout.

As early as the 1870s, the Willowemoc Club in the Catskills of New York constructed artificial spawning beds and cleaned streams of siltation, debris, and barriers from local streams.[2] Members were beginning to recognize that conditions in streams were not always ideal because of human impacts in watersheds. They also were starting a trend of treating the effect rather than the cause of trouble. A founding member of the club soon published a suggestion to begin physically changing the appearance of aquatic habitat to better suit trout.[3] The 1885 article was inspired by a combination of brilliant scientific observation and snobbery. James Spencer Van Cleef, a prominent lawyer from Poughkeepsie — born along the Hudson River, educated at Rutgers University — became involved in public policy and eventually wrote the general fish and game laws for New York State.[4] But before that time, he was destined to help kick-start an important trend that still continues today: he used the magic word, "restore," to describe his plans.[5]

Van Cleef was under no illusions about the problems of his day and acknowledged the limitations in fisheries-management practices of the time: their overreliance on stocking, the problems of introduced exotic species, the possible adverse effects of eradicating predatory species, and the failures of fishways to provide passage at industrial dams. He also noted that deforestation dramatically reduced the number of logs and root wads in local streams. He suggested replanting streamside vegetation and restrictions on logging. He also recommended placement of dead wood back in pools to provide good cover habitat for trout. Van Cleef thought that trout restocking was pointless until lost physical habitat was restored. Remarkably, scientists now concur that the loss of logs, snags, and stumps, or large woody debris as it was later called, is a primary problem limiting physical habitat in our nation's rivers. Van Cleef referred to wood as *snags*, a common term in those days, which correlated nicely with a second motivation he had in mind. As leader of a club with large private land holdings, he considered public fishing an act of poaching and complained that the historic use of nets for food harvest was a major cause of overfishing. He reasoned that a few carefully placed logs and root wads would ensnare nets and prevent this practice. The snags could provide habitat and ensure only angling with fly rods.

Van Cleef's overall philosophy to save trout in 1885 can probably be best summed up by his concluding words: "Let the home of the trout be regarded as his castle. Entice him from it if you can, but do not invade it."[6] Perhaps if Van Cleef's inspired idea to mimic nature had ended there, aquatic habitats would be much healthier now. However, he also wanted to fortify the castle with humanly conceived architectural and engineering marvels. First, Van Cleef helped install artificial spawning beds on Sandy Pond as early as 1878.[7] In 1884, he convinced another club he founded, the Sundown Fishing Club, to install structures on Rondout Creek. It was the start of a new way of doing business in the Catskill Mountains.

It seems likely that some of the first stream-improvement structures were designed to replicate and replace milldams lost when water-powered industries disappeared. Whatever the initial motivation, shortly after Van Cleef's work on the Rondout, a local sawmill operator was hired to install stream-improvement structures on the Beaverkill River using oxen in 1892.[8] The dam was designed with a log positioned across the channel and large flat boulders propped up on the upstream side of the log to make a continuous impoundment. The hope was that pools formed both upstream and downstream of the dam would house trout. Upstream, water would back up and create cool, deep water. Downstream flow would plunge down, aerate the water and excavate a second pool. The design was so well constructed and conceived that many of the original structures survived more than a hundred years.[9] Another more important Catskill angler mesmerized by the use of stream structures was Edward Hewitt. His legacy of stream-improvement designs is likely to outlive even the century-old rock and wood monuments built by his fellow Catskill anglers.

It is first worth attempting a characterization of Hewitt's views on the environment before we look at his structure crusade. Nothing in my reading of Hewitt's six books revealed the sense that there was even a primitive nature ethic motivating his actions. His violent attitude toward vermin certainly does not mesh well with modern environmental ideals. His father had not seemed concerned with pollution when he served as the director of the

Federal Reclamation Service and vehemently defended the use of streams as a legitimate and proper way to dispose of waste.[10] This attitude is not surprising in a family of industrialists who ran massive glue, mining, and iron companies. Edward heavily fertilized his farms along the Neversink to improve hay production for cattle;[11] a practice now known as a major cause of nonpoint source pollution. His very last book entry included mention of an ongoing patent with his grandson for a new process with a mysterious chemical additive to soils that was intended to force soil bacteria to release ammonia.[12] Hewitt even talked about the issue of human sewage in one book and concluded that in some cases it was detrimental, but in other situations did no harm to fish.[13] Reading his books, I could clearly see that Edward was an industrialist at heart. His autobiographies focus more on his family's manufacturing history than being outdoors. Most people mentioned were known more for industrial and business exploits than early environmental thinking. Hewitt personally prevented development of land along the Neversink River, but he was so singularly focused on the production of a flawless world for trout that he ignored environmental consequences. He adopted a reach-scale solution to watershed deforestation where all the effort was concentrated along a short stretch of river on a specific property. Hewitt's "all-for-trout-and-trout-for-one" attitude was best exemplified in his call for a massive building campaign on the Neversink River.

As a child when he wasn't terrorizing local police, Hewitt played with pieces of wood and made small dams on trickles of water running along the gutters of New York City.[14] Perhaps these early games inspired him as much as his later exposure to English rivers and books. In any case, Hewitt first constructed structures in New Jersey as a young man, probably near his family's estate at Ringwood Manor and at his first summer estate, Wewappo Farm.[15] However, it was really on the Neversink River that he made a lasting mark. He probably rode the New York Ontario and Western Railroad out of New York City on his way to his Catskill getaway. As Hewitt made his way toward his retreat, he passed within a few miles of a dwelling that housed Stephen Crane while Crane was writing the Civil War classic, *The Red Badge of Courage*: a story about the soldiers that Hewitt's father helped to arm with rifles.[16] Hewitt later became an ambitious writer and advertised a fishing philosophy with his series of books and articles. Instead of artificial stocking, he advocated for a system of habitat-improvement structures to modify physical environments in rivers.

Hewitt thought that placement of trees cabled to riverbanks was one of the best things that could be done to physically improve habitat on rivers.[17] Tree placement was a fairly unobtrusive method that mirrored natural processes that delivered this type of large woody debris to channels. Hewitt was not afraid to try more aggressive modifications that involved the use of power shovels to excavate artificial pools where springs entered rivers.[18] His idea was to provide trout with spring-fed, warmer-water residences for winter. Hewitt had proclaimed that winter habitat was the most critical limit on trout survival.[19] He recognized these refuges made trout easy prey, so he recommended guarding the trout with game wardens, brush, and barbed wire to keep out predators and poachers alike. His basic belief: that with enough money and effort, good fishing was possible anywhere.[20] It is interesting to note that Franklin Roosevelt was the governor of New York from 1928 until 1932 and was destined to play a more national role in both politics and river modification in a few years. Roosevelt and Hewitt shared an earlier connection through the South Side Sportsmen's Club where both their fathers were members. By the early 1930s, Edward Hewitt's work was extensively known and had likely caught the eye of the future president.

Although Hewitt's many ideas and books made a splash, his true fame in stream modification involved the design of a low-head dam that eventually bore his name. Referenced for decades to come, it remains in use today.[21] Members of both the Suffolk and South Side Sportsmen's Clubs gravitated to sites with milldams and moderate-size reservoirs, where deep water provided habitat for trout during winter and warmer summer months. These Long Island reservoirs might have been the bane of free-flowing rivers, but clubs focused more on fish and waterfowl than rivers. Many anglers still flock to reservoirs and tailwaters because trout often congregate in these areas, becoming easy targets for rod and reel. Perhaps inspired by the Long Island clubs, other milldams of old, and designs he saw in Europe, Hewitt argued that dams were cheap, permanent structures that provided cover, greater water depth, and slower velocities.[22] He recommended placing dams approximately every two to three widths of the river. Modern studies of rivers suggest that pools naturally average between four and eight channel widths apart, so Hewitt's spacing greatly modified the normal distribution of habitat along rivers. In particular, it would reduce riffle habitat preferred by macroinvertebrates and other food sources for fish, and favor more the habitats for large trout. On a big wide river like the Neversink, shallow water in riffles with limited overhanging branches provides good light penetration to the channel bed and increased plant and macroinvertebrate productivity. Perhaps a reduction of riffle habitat and biological production was one reason Hewitt resorted to directly feeding trout in the river.

Hewitt liked dams. He thought that the continuous changes usually characterizing rivers were the demise, not the cause, of good habitat creation. He was wrong. He essentially wanted to use dams to stop rivers from moving bedload.[23] Bedload includes large gravel and cobble sediment naturally transported by a river as a rolling and bouncing parade of stones. At times a river resembles a full marching band of rallying rock. Processions of particles stretch from one side of a river to the next. When currents are particularly strong, large thuds are audible as boulders smack against each other. At other times, single pebbles slowly roll along while the remaining rock musicians wait to resume their play. The impact of a single spring freshet may be hard to discern, but the overall impact of decades of the slow progress of particles is an onslaught of sediment headed down river. Nature usually makes room for new arrivals by moving a similar busload of material down and out. Withdrawals from the hypothetical riverbank accounts are replaced by new deposits. People are happy enough economically if transfers leave their bank balances steady. We do not have attachments to individual bills or coins; it is the sum that matters. Similarly, if everything is in balance in a river and the population of particles remains roughly equal, then even if all the stone inhabitants are new, nothing as a whole really changes. This process is referred to as dynamic equilibrium, a key concept in geomorphology; an idea not yet appreciated in the 1930s when Hewitt promoted his dam ideas.

Hewitt believed that a rowdy ruckus of rock was a very destructive force. His opinion was based on an incident when several trout were buried by sediment during a flood.[24] Hewitt was not particularly friendly to anything that hurt trout. He could not kill rocks that had crushed his beloved fish, but he could try and force them to cease and desist. The dam was his primary weapon. The first two styles Hewitt tried were similar to designs mentioned by Mottram, but were not successful due to erosion and undermining.[25] The third design is the now-standard plank design, made from a combination of sawed timber and round logs. First a large log or series of logs was placed across a channel with both ends carefully embedded into the banks. Several longitudinal support logs were then placed higher on each side of the river to limit the undermining of cross-logs. Finally, the downstream ends of planks were nailed to the cross-logs with the upstream ends buried in the bed of the channel. To install these dams involves plenty of localized reshuffling of the riverbed, but produces a structure that was strong and long-lived. Hewitt erected numerous examples of the structure that would bear his name as a wall to uninvited stony visitors. Much like public poachers, Hewitt would ban particle passage on his property. His optimistic vision was quickly put to the test. Although it failed in many ways, it was never fully discarded as impractical. In fact, visitors to the region can expect to see more recent versions approved and constructed by the New York Department of Environmental Conservation in nearby trout streams. Hewitt's dream lives on.

Only three years after his first book touting the use of dams was published, Hewitt warned against the overuse of these structures due to problems he encountered with both bedload transport and warming waters.[26] It seemed that the river had a nasty habit of filling up pools on the upstream side of dams and thus wiping out the nice deepwater habitat he had planned. In 1930, he echoed an earlier claim made by Platts[27] that widening rivers at dams benefited insect life.[28] Four years later, Hewitt recognized that wide, shallow areas upstream of dams were perfect places for the sun to warm water to the point of negatively influencing trout.[29] Hewitt also realized that the supply of sediment from upstream was endless — and intentionally barring its movement was apt to create more problems than it solved. Erosion around early versions of his structures added to the problem. Hewitt was beginning to realize that dynamic equilibrium is a tough balance to maintain. He warned: "This experience goes to show that one or two seasons is not enough to make certain of anything in a trout brook."[30] History shows that this warning to monitor projects over longer timescales fell on deaf ears.

Hewitt was never one to leave things understated, and with dams it appears he thought big. The family property is in the area now partially occupied by the Neversink Reservoir — ironically, a main source of public water supply for New York City, where his dad and uncle were mayors. Hewitt's first Neversink purchase occurred just one year before rumors began to circulate that the city was looking for a reservoir site in the region. The final selection of the site was being decided throughout the 1920s when Hewitt amassed his estate.[31] In 1939, New York City filed maps in the Sullivan County Clerk's Office showing which properties would be taken through condemnation. People were then notified to be out of their homes by July 7, 1940. In 1940, construction began on new roads and bridges around the proposed site, a route that took motorists on the far shore of the river and away from Hewitt's estate. However, World War II caused a long delay in construction of the reservoir itself and it was not until 1950, seven years before his death, that 1,315 acres were appropriated from Hewitt. Hewitt lost this land including concrete ponds he used to raise trout. Amazingly, this was the second time Hewitt lost land to eminent domain for a public water supply. His six-hundred-acre Wewappo farm in New Jersey had been taken earlier for the site of Newark Reservoir.[32] He either had rotten luck, or it was a trend.

In 1930, Hewitt made it clear that he wanted a reservoir below his property. He stated that: "It is, therefore, a tremendous advantage on any trout stream to have a large reservoir for fish below the fishing area."[33] He eventually got his wish. It is worth noting that the final dam location and reservoir elevation do not seem like they could have worked out any better for Hewitt. His property was the last one upstream of the impoundment. The final Neversink reservoir level flooded approximately half the miles of river he owned and his trout hatchery ponds, but ended up leaving the camp he built unaffected. Lucky for him, even a small change in location or elevation of the dam would have had much bigger impacts on the remainder of his estate. Furthermore, the loss of the rearing ponds was of little concern because World War II had already forced him to cease operation of his private hatchery and it seems unlikely that the seventy-plus-year-old Hewitt wanted to reestablish the facility. Instead, the reservoir served as a low-cost hatchery for trout in his section of river and created excellent lake fishing. Mirroring comments by Platts,[34] Hewitt noted that large trout grew in local reservoirs and then moved into the river to spawn much like salmon, with wondrous results for trout anglers.[35] And speaking of salmon, the 1,461-acre reservoir gave Hewitt a chance to try to establish his beloved salmon in Neversink Reservoir, something he had previously tried on the river itself without success.[36]

Perhaps the most important benefit to Hewitt from the dam resulted in an elimination of competing anglers. The reservoir actually further limited public access to his property, partially because small roads heading north from the town of Neversink were severed. The town of Neversink, located downstream of Hewitt's property, was a hub of trout-fishing activity complete with guides, boardinghouses, and various equipment suppliers.[37] It was probably also the center of much resentment over Hewitt's privatization of prime trout waters. The eventual dam location was immediately downstream of Neversink and destroyed both the town and the famous fishing spot called Black Hole.[38] Meanwhile, the area upstream of the town was much more sparsely settled. When the dam was finally completed and filled, Hewitt was left with much of his property, as well as with new lakeside access to a reservoir that promised to have excellent fishing with limited public access. The numerous residents of Neversink were left with a government check and old postcards showing the place they used to love. Hewitt was either tremendously lucky or very good at using the multitude of political connections at his disposal.

If we consider Hewitt's general approach to rivers, his fundamental notion that a utopian society of trout can be manufactured at each New York industrialist's retreat comes with fundamental flaws. One underlying problem with the localized mentality adopted by Hewitt and other prosperous practitioners he inspired stems from competing agendas of various landowners. Inevitably, each landowner along a river adopts a narrow-sightedness in how they run their operation. We know Hewitt was not well liked by less fortunate members of the local community. People complained that he monopolized the river's natural resources by excluding the public. Not only was this true, but Hewitt's downright selfishness included using his wealth to build structures for surreptitiously poaching trout from his neighbors. He basically installed dams that served the same function as the turnstiles of the New York City subway system. The first dam was screened to allow trout to move downstream but not upstream.[39] As you might guess, he placed the new technological spectacle on the upstream end of his property. He later developed another marvel that prevented trout from moving downstream and built that on the lower end of his river.[40] He now had a way to funnel as many trout as possible into his own multi-mile stretch of water. I cannot imagine this endearing Hewitt to his immediate neighbors. All this occurred while Hewitt criticized the state fish commission for stocking efforts geared toward fee-paying sportsmen. This, he said, stemmed from the underlying problem that the state did not control enough land to manage resources effectively.[41] Hewitt argued that stocking was a waste and instead pushed his idea to manipulate the rivers themselves. Somehow, despite early problems, controversies, and fundamental flaws in rationale, stream-improvement work would expand in less than five years from a private effort in a small region of New York to a massive nationwide effort spurred by government funding.

~ ~ ~ I first began to research the history of the nineteenth- and early twentieth-century stream-improvement movement at the turn of the most recent century. I was astonished to discover that century-old structures persisted on the Beaverkill River.[42] To me, the fact that adventuresome anglers devised devices that could impact trout habitat for that time span was both astounding and ominous. I immediately headed to the Catskills to uncover some examples. When I arrived, I was greeted by a wall of No Trespassing signs. Despite the difficulties in actually getting anywhere near the river, I did manage to sneak some glimpses of several sections. I was amazed at how much of the vertical drop in elevation along sections of the river was controlled by various styles of habitat dams. The slightly sinuous Beaverkill River had been turned into a grand sweeping staircase of sorts. As early as 1927, writers were suggesting the placement of dams close together to convert mountain rivers into a series of flat pools.[43] The Catskill landowners clearly heeded the call. By my crude estimation, the multitude of dams easily controlled more than half, and maybe as much as 90 percent of the elevation drop along portions of the channel. I longed to grab some survey equipment and find out for sure, but I was faced with those pesky signs that warned me violators would be prosecuted to the fullest extent of the law. I was powerless to proceed.

To a stream interested in moving sediment, changes in elevation provide power. In fact, it is referred to as "stream power" and is symbolized by the Greek symbol omega. When stream power exerts its force on the bed of a channel and starts to get things moving, it is referred to as doing "work." With the Beaverkill carefully corralled by dams, the river's work and the associated bedload movement would be highly curtailed. It might prevent burial of trout as Hewitt initially hoped, but it also limited the process of dynamic equilibrium. Furthermore, it probably encouraged a much more menacing geomorphic process for trout called embeddedness. Embeddedness entails the slow accumulation of fine-sediment grains between larger pebbles and cobbles. It is currently a major concern for many coldwater fisheries managers and is often evaluated in stream-habitat assessments. Normally, the small spaces around larger stones provide perfect refuge for fish eggs and the macroinvertebrates that help feed juvenile and adult trout outside the hatchery. As anyone with a fly rod could inform you, most wet and dry flies tied by angling artisans are designed to mimic these macroinvertebrate inhabitants. But when a river bottom becomes embedded with fine sediments, especially in the impoundment behind a dam, the homes for these aquatic insects are destroyed. That does not sound like a good thing for one of America's most famous trout rivers. Of course, the government's historic efforts to clean out and channelize the region's rivers with bulldozers following flood events do not help matters either.[44] Obviously, the embeddedness problem could not be too bad or the Beaverkill would be unpopular with anglers. Then again, heavy stocking of trout destined to survive but a short while could help to conceal the problem.

Nature's normal solution for embeddedness is to flush the channel bed with periodic floods that carry fine sediments away downstream. Every few years, small floods create a slight commotion, do their work and then fade away. In one of the real ironies of misunderstanding, the erosive power of floods helps to save trout, not harm them as Hewitt initially postulated. As long as the supply of sediment from upstream is not too great, these periodic flushing events help rejuvenate the river. But with much of the elevation drop of the Beaverkill confined to short drops over the lips of dams, localized stream power would be much lower than in pre-Colonial times. Rocks would not move under all but the most extreme flood events, and a sort of pavement of pebble and stone would begin to form. In rivers where this process is most dramatic, the bed of a channel begins to resemble a cobblestone street. Between these larger stones, sand filters in like mortar and remains in place as long as it is sheltered from strong currents by the larger rocks. If the bed is rarely disrupted, the amount of sand begins to increase. Soon, these small changes generate big impacts on aquatic organisms that rely on this habitat. Although I could not cross the multitude of fences and warning signs to lend my expertise to the situation, I suspected that this was the case on portions of the Beaverkill. Much like the stereotypical omega male, here was a river that had lost most of its power to the structural mechanism of wealthy landowners and could no longer do the work it historically performed.

As I looked upstream and downstream from bridge crossings and places where the river flowed near roads, I noticed that both the style of No Trespassing signs and the structures themselves changed at each property line. Here was a river that was compartmentalized by a multitude of special-interest fishing groups. Each club and owner had a slightly different concept of the dream home for trout. Directors of some parcels leaned more toward log structures while some firmly preferred rock. Many used both in designs that mirrored the region's first devices. The river began to take on an appearance of a poorly devised patchwork quilt. Generations of individual lovers of trout had invested enormous sums of money to separately stitch the perfect stretch of habitat. Each square was carefully sewn together in a reasonably aesthetic manner, but together the assemblage just did not work.

Although I might not want someone like Hewitt as my adjacent property owner for fear he would slowly siphon away my fish, perhaps it does not seem to be a major environmental problem when a single property owner tinkers around with a short section of river. If we consider that adjacent property owners are probably doing the same thing, we might become a little more anxious, but probably not alarmed. The real problem is that rivers are connected systems. If we remember our tricky friend, dynamic equilibrium, we are reminded that erosion from one spot is often replaced by deposition from further upstream. This balance keeps the river in check and forms the ever-shifting form of stability that characterizes many rivers. If people start to play around with this balance, the equilibrium part goes away and we are just left with a dynamic system that likes to rapidly move, erode, or deposit.

On one hand, a lack of sediment transportation by the river can spell disaster as embeddedness creeps in. Alternatively, construction of and erosion around dams enhances sediment mobility, especially if the structure fails, as is often the case. I photographed several dams and deflectors in the Catskill region that had been destroyed, probably by the localized erosion they had helped generate. Erosion and the so-called destructive nature of floods were a major concern to Hewitt, and it is interesting to think that his solution may have made matters worse for those poor souls who lived below. To solve the issue, property owners might try to arrest some bank erosion here, deepen a pool over there with a dam and create a new riffle with spawning gravel somewhere in the middle. These little projects might then create the need for downstream neighbors to do the same as new piles of sediment arrive on their doorstep. The overall impact of this hodgepodge style of management is to create a complex series of band-aid fixes with increased sediment recruitment that never gets at the underlying problem in the watershed. If the underlying problem in the watershed is a lack of channel stability resulting from decades of deforestation, agriculture, and milldams, then initiating a series of construction projects in the river only exacerbates the situation.

It is possible that individual property owners along the Beaverkill River were reacting to changes wrought by their neighbors' stream-improvement activities as much as any basin-wide land-use impacts. These folks collectively imposed a tremendous impact on the way the entire river functioned. Worse still, they were now all forced to follow this path because retreating from the approach could spell doom for their company of anglers. For example, if one club decides that they are tired of staring at geometric structures while fishing, removing a dam kicks in dynamic equilibrium. The construction activity itself will upset the riverbed, and the steeper channel will now be free to resume the work it has longed to do for nearly a century. Sediment will move and might fill in the downstream neighbors' pools. Meanwhile, the newly freed segment of river will begin to lose sediment faster than it is replaced because upstream clubs are still stodgily hoarding rocks behind dams on their properties. If erosion and vertical incision of the river gets bad enough here in the middle, it can even begin to work its way upstream and start to undermine habitat dams up there. When that happens, sediment will now storm downstream and overwhelm sections of river where dams were initially removed. This cacophony of changes and impacts is referred to as "complex response" by geomorphologists and is actually not as farfetched as it might sound.

One important scientific article describing complex response was titled "Implications of Complex Response of Drainage Systems for Quaternary Alluvial Stratigraphy," coauthored by Stanley Schumm and Randy Parker.[45] Schumm was already a legend when he cowrote the paper. He was one of several prominent fluvial geomorphologists that began to make a name for themselves in the 1950s and 1960s. His contemporaries included M. Gordon "Reds" Wolman, William Emmett, Garnett Williams, and Luna Leopold among others. Wolman was instrumental in developing techniques to estimate sediment size that would later play a role in evaluating embeddedness. Emmett, the guru of bedload, understood stream power and dynamic equilibrium as well as anyone. Williams worked on understanding controls on the width of channels that would later play a critical role in channel-restoration work. Leopold worked on a myriad of topics that include the spacing of pools. The son of Aldo Leopold, he helped finish his father's classic book, A Sand County Almanac.[46] Meanwhile, Schumm understood channel change as no one else did. At the time, Parker was Schumm's graduate student at Colorado State University. He eventually went to work for the U.S. Geological Survey in Denver, which is where I eventually met him. Parker may also be the most laughed-at father in America. He is the real-life inspiration for the father/geologist character, Randy Marsh, in the popular South Park animated sitcom. But in the early 1970s, he was still an unknown graduate student working with one of the nation's greatest geological minds.

Schumm and Parker set out to understand a strange phenomenon observed in the Southwest. Channels in this region went through apparent cycles of erosion and deposition. The simplest explanation was that rapid shifts in climate created interconnected adjustments in channel behavior. But Schumm had studied the phenomenon for years and was convinced there was more to the story. In particular, rivers appeared to display multiple personalities with simultaneous erosion and deposition occurring short distances apart. Local variations in climate could not explain that behavior. Schumm worked with a series of graduate students both in small canyons spread throughout the Great Plains and the Southwest and in a modest, sheet-metal warehouse-like structure surrounded by discarded experimental equipment. The structure was called the REF, or Rainfall Erosion Facility. The name was more impressive than the building deserved. It still sits in a forgotten spot along the last few westward feet of the Great Plains just before they run into the Rockies. It is situated on a satellite campus of Colorado State University behind the much more impressive ERC, or Engineering Research Center. Piles of Plexiglas and metal fabrications litter the ground and are the remains of decades of experiments conducted by engineers at the ERC. The much smaller geoscience facility is partially pieced together by parts scavenged out of the prairie grasses. It was here that the idea for complex response began to formulate in the scientists' minds.

The basic story of complex response is in reality fairly simple. Erosion begets deposition, which leads to more erosion, followed by deposition and so on down the line. If something perturbs a channel and pushes it past some breaking point, a so-called threshold, a chain reaction of changes is likely to result. The initial impetus for the alteration might be a regional change in climate or a human-induced impact, for example, overgrazing of prairie grasses on the Great Plains. Although the scientific debate is still active on this particular mechanism, at least some gully erosion in the great prairie region resulted from human overexploitation of the area in the late nineteenth and early twentieth centuries. Too many grazers and not enough grass. As a graduate student, I visited some of the deep gullies, called arroyos, that had formed in Colorado in the not too distant past. I saw for myself how different segments of the same channel could be undergoing completely opposite responses to the same triggering mechanism. I learned that a watershed could only be pushed so far before it reacted dramatically.

This yin-yang response of channels was on my mind as I sat staring at the Beaverkill River. Engineers, fisheries biologists and local anglers, armed with an army of dams, initiated what will be a constant battle to stabilize each pebble and stone. In a century-long endeavor to create the ideal home for trout, they turned one of the region's most beloved rivers into a furniture showroom for every design of instream structure imaginable. Would-be improvement aficionados eager to equip their own streams, could stop by and pick out what they liked. Landowners turned the living, moving entity of the river into an artistic endeavor, frozen in time. The Beaverkill was no longer a river; it was a museum of modern art for stream-improvement artifacts. I wondered if the constant effort to achieve stability of the system with dam after dam would eventually help to unravel the river. Could the tangled network of stream-improvement structures spell the eventual undoing of the Beaverkill River? Sooner or later, the river will give us its answer.

CHAPTER EIGHT

Stream Improvement Plows Ahead

*In view of the fact that our lakes and streams were formed by natural
processes and were not created or especially designed for the species of fish
which we desire, it is logical to believe that with adequate knowledge and a
definite design or purpose in mind, we can improve on nature and make
some of our waters more favorable for the desired species.*

~ CLARENCE TARZWELL, 1935

*A*lthough techniques for modifying river habitat predate the 1930s, stream improvement became a product of the depression. When I think of the Great Depression, stories jump to mind of the stock market crash that directly impacted many wealthy anglers. Perhaps some sold Long Island, Catskill, and Adirondack properties at great financial loss. However, this depression was not just an economic collapse on Wall Street; it also involved an agricultural nightmare of our own making. The Great Depression intensified because of a failure of science when settlers tried to turn the Great American Desert into the quintessential American Dream.

In 2006, Timothy Egan penned *The Worst Hard Times*, twenty years after Mark Reisner wrote his classic book, *Cadillac Desert*.[1] Both books beautifully summarize problems with agriculture and the allocation of water in the central and western United States. As they explained, the biggest myth that plagued the Great Plains at the end of the nineteenth century was the utopian belief that "rain follows the plow." People commonly believed they could convert prairies into a new agricultural paradise by simply turning over sod and planting crops. A scientific idealism developed that purported plows would slowly crack open dense roots of tall- and short-grass prairies and release moisture trapped within the soil to rise up to form new clouds. Trees planted by settlers would further add to the ascension of water molecules. Then, the new workings of man would help them fall back down again. Smoke from passing trains dissecting the landscape would be one impetus. Commotion from these iron-railed and steaming marvels, spinning windmills at each homestead, and new human ants dotting the region would help vibrate the air and shake water drops from the sky like almonds harvested from a tree. Quick-talking peddlers even promised settlers that dynamiting the air could strip the heavens of its precious cargo of moisture. The semiarid landscape would be magically transformed by new rains created by these countless acts of human endurance and perseverance. The only problem: the theory was wrong.

Flaws in this idealistic notion surfaced in the form of localized droughts from 1893 through 1894 in Kansas and a more sustained period from 1917 to 1921 in Montana.[2] Multiple events culminated in the Great Dust Bowl from 1930 to 1936. Lack of precipitation doomed crops to brown shriveled remains. Hot winds blew away dried stalks and picked up soil on exposed fields. Topsoil layers of entire counties simply up and blew away. Homesteaders stuffed rags in windowsills to prevent the onslaught of silt from invading their homes. Water supplies turned to muddy sludge in open tanks below the giant steel pinwheels erected to mine the clear liquid from the ground. An unpleasant feel of grit in food was a daily reality.

People seriously underestimated how effectively evolution had constructed a complexly intertwined ecosystem. Prairie grasses had evolved to thrive in a landscape that cruelly alternated between abundant rains and severe droughts. Change one component, in this case the prairie sod, and the whole landscape gets blown away. The myth that American ingenuity could succeed where Mother Nature failed was shattered in one giant dark and dusty cloud that was slowly billowing east. Franklin Roosevelt took notice from the White House and was forced into action including assistance by federal workers implementing new sweeping conservation projects.[3]

The Dust Bowl created problems for local rivers and streams as massive loads of silt and mud began to inundate aquatic environments. Despite the fact that many midwestern systems were directly impacted by the calamities of nature, the real lesson of the disaster was apparently lost on many river managers. Rain may not follow the plow, and disaster may follow human efforts to remake the natural landscape of the Great Plains, but that did not mean that clever fisheries proponents would fail with their stream-improvement technologies to turn every stretch of river into a paradise for trout.

~ ~ ~ The underlying rationale for stream improvement is firmly entrenched in the notion that humans can improve on nature. This belief was spurred by a change in attitude and rapid growth in engineering. In the 1880s there were approximately seven thousand engineers working in the United States. That grew to one hundred thirty-six thousand engineers by 1920 and two hundred twenty-six thousand by 1930.[4] Not inconsequentially, this period also experienced important influences from industry including mass production and standardization. The Model T helped to transport New York anglers to distant streams and perhaps served as an inspiration. If Henry Ford could revolutionize the manufacture of cars, his fellow anglers and industrialists could do the same for trout production. They would take lessons learned from their manufacturing lines in a new movement to modernize the trout stream. The focus was to eliminate waste and inefficiency through intensive manipulation of the system. The principles of scientific management were beginning to take hold. It was during this period that stream improvement matured under the leadership of a University of Michigan research group. A new scientific revolution for the manufacture of trout was about to take place in Ann Arbor, less than fifty miles from Ford's original conveyor belt–driven assembly line at Highland Park.

In 1927, Dr. Jan Metzelaar carried out experiments for the Michigan Department of Conservation reintroducing wood to rivers, a process he called "resnagging."[5] The work involved cutting down trees and reassembling this downed timber into intricate log jams.[6] Today, this is a common restoration technique. Metzelaar was born in the Netherlands and was likely influenced by European methods before his arrival in the United States in 1922. He also may have been familiar with work done by Van Cleef in New York. Metzelaar became a U.S. citizen in 1929 but died two days later while conducting lake research for the Department of Conservation. The Institute for Fisheries Research, located on the University of Michigan campus, was formed in response to his death to formalize the relationship between the state agency and the University of Michigan.[7] Funding was supplied by the state and a substantial subsidy from the Michigan Division of the Izaak Walton League of America.[8] The Izaak Walton League, a conservation group formed in 1922 in response to deteriorating conditions in top U.S. fishing streams, obviously took its name from the famous author. President Hoover served as president of the Izaak Walton League before he led the nation from 1929 to 1933.[9] To get the new research institute going in Michigan would require a comparable dynamic leader. It would require Dr. Rotenone himself, Carl Hubbs.

The Institute for Fisheries Research was the first scientific organization to research stream improvement.[10] In 1930, Hubbs wrote a glowing account of his predecessor and called him a hero and "martyr to his science."[11] Six years later the tone was very different. Despite Metzelaar's earlier work, Hubbs claimed independent development of the idea to add wood to rivers. He called Metzelaar "impetuous," said the pioneering work was "not well done" and was "hardly stream improvement of any consequence."[12] He mocked his predecessor for an inability to convince the state to support the work. At the time these statements were made, Hubbs was the most influential figure in stream improvement in the country and was kicking off an important academic session in Washington on a massive nationwide effort he had helped inspire. The session was part of a high-profile wildlife conference requested by then president Franklin D. Roosevelt. Hubbs was clearly in the spotlight in 1936, but how had he flipped on the switch?

Food chains, collecting specimens, and cataloging fish were all part of Hubbs's professional training as a biologist. The dynamics of rivers and construction of devices to modify the forces within were not. But despite the holes in Hubbs's training, he decided to experiment with civil engineering and fluvial geomorphology all the same. The move exhibits both hubris and a lack of appreciation for the physical complexity of rivers. Even Albert Einstein's son struggled when he tried to develop equations to predict sediment transport by rivers, because turbulence, the inspiration behind the mathematical concept of chaos, plays such a major role in the process. Hubbs's overconfidence would be repeated by others. He was still a young professor and new director of the institute at the time, intent on churning out publications with incredible rapidity. Interestingly, despite his eventual importance to the movement, this chapter of his life has been largely forgotten and is almost entirely missing from his official National Academy of Science biography.[13] However, it was undeniably Hubbs who supplied the scientific stamp of validity to the haphazard practices of Hewitt and other contemporaneous trout tinkerers.

Right from the start, Hubbs was a full-blown supporter of scientific management. Echoing Hewitt's comments, Hubbs suggested that stream improvement provided the only means to meet the demands from very heavy fishing pressures. His Michigan group believed that "the stream can be modified almost to any degree desired."[14] Clarence M. Tarzwell was Hubbs's first graduate student to receive a PhD and was in charge of stream improvement for the institute.[15] His quote at the top of the chapter shows that much of the rationale for the extensive installation of instream structures sprang from a desire to eliminate supposed inefficiencies in natural channels. Scientific management pushed this new generation of fisheries biologists to a more intensive utilization of aquatic resources. They hoped that trout follow the project.

Remarkably, stream improvement in the 1930s was partially motivated to placate apparently lazy anglers. Hubbs declared that stream improvement could "shorten the time between bites" and reduce the long walks between successive pools so "fishing would bear less resemblance to golf."[16] He suggested that long stretches of troutless water could be modified to yield good catches in a few months. Clearly, Hubbs, a highly trained ichthyologist, knew it was impossible to grow mature trout that quickly. Maybe he expected fish to relocate from other parts of the river, but that is not in keeping with his stated focus to improve production. It is more likely Hubbs expected new populations would be supplied by hatcheries. However, the Hubbs contingent also claimed stocking was prohibitively expensive and legal restrictions on catch limits did not grow fish. They used this logic to argue that physical changes to streams provided the only means to meet demands from very heavy fishing pressures. By accepting the condition of overfishing, the doctors were treating the symptoms, not diagnosing the causes.

In the institute's first official publication, *Methods for the Improvement of Michigan Trout Streams*, Hubbs and his colleagues recommended the placement of fifty stream-improvement structures per mile of river for a typical twenty- to forty-foot wide channel.[17] That level of construction would yield three structures for every football-field length of river. Essentially, the more houses built for trout, the higher the population concentration. With this Michigan blueprint, river managers became a reverse form of slum lord, with individual trout supplied by hatchery fish factories to the high-density housing complexes they built.

Hubbs's group began their stream-improvement careers in 1930 with a project in the Little Manistee River, which historically held no native trout. They used funds from the Michigan Department of Conservation and the Izaak Walton League of America to construct all manner of dams, deflectors, and cover structures with additional streamside plantings to shade the water.[18] Thinking stream modification would be easy and any installation worthwhile, they declared that most people familiar with fishing and rivers could determine which improvements were desirable.[19] They were soon to learn that experience is the best teacher of all.

Hubbs's key assistant, John R. Greeley, came from the New York Biological Survey after he completed a PhD at Cornell University.[20] He previously worked under Dr. Emmeline Moore, a pioneering female biologist who also obtained her PhD from Cornell and worked for the New York Conservation Commission starting in 1926. Hubbs attracted other key individuals from New York, including Albert S. Hazzard. This contingent was probably intimately familiar with early stream-improvement projects carried out in the Catskills. The first institute publication in 1932 included an annotated bibliography with reference to Ingraham's 1926 book and it indicated that Hewitt's 1931 book was the best American work on trout stream management methods at the time.[21] Although Hewitt and Hubbs would seem an unlikely pair, they were linked by the same desire to control nature.

Hubbs and his cohorts completed their first project in the Little Manistee River and, by 1932, forged ahead with a total installation of almost 1,000 structures statewide.[22] Strange designs of dams, deflectors, and fixed and floating cover structures were manufactured en mass. Any conceivable design was fair game. Cover structures and deflectors often were combined to direct flow under the covers to keep these areas free from siltation. Deflectors also were used in pairs to improve their effectiveness. Structures utilized low profiles to avoid damage by floods, ice, and rotting. The authors even recommended the installation of structures in summer and early fall to take advantage of low water. It all sounded like a very precise and well-planned experiment in local rivers and streams.

By 1933, Hubbs was lead author on four articles touting his methods. These were pretty much the only research articles that existed in the United States on stream improvement to that date.[23] However, as Hewitt's experience with dams showed, three years is not long enough to understand how a complex river ecosystem responds to change wrought by large floods that occur only every decade or so. Not surprisingly, less than five years after the first project was started and after four publications already hyped the techniques, almost one-third of the structures on the Little Manistee were destroyed.[24] Floods and the natural dynamics of river systems were to blame. Two decades later, one U.S. Forest Service biologist characterized the 1930s work as overreliant on a large variety of structures, full of mistakes, and ineffective at making desirable stream habitat if problems existed in the watershed.[25] Hubbs's assertion that all projects are worthwhile was wrong.

In 1930, Hubbs prophesied that fisheries research "has no political boundaries."[26] As predicted, his work first expanded from Michigan to Iowa and Wisconsin.[27] This occurred just a few years before these areas experienced the full effects of the Dust Bowl. In response to the institute's 1932 publication, work spread to other regions within a year. Hubbs counted on strong backing from Fred Westerman, chief of the Michigan Department of Conservation and Fisheries Division from 1925 until 1959, who also served as the president of the American Fisheries Society in 1933 and 1934.[28] Still, the overall scale of the work was small. Structures cost anywhere from $1 to $4 each and labor constituted a major expense.[29] For their isolated experiments to turn into a nationwide industrial movement, they needed cheap labor, and lots of it.

Stream improvement remained an occupation supervised by wealthy landowners and studied by a small group of academics until the federal government stepped in to provide a lending hand; or actually thousands of them. Federal involvement in river management was part of a growing trend, in part precipitated by the government's role during the flood of 1927 on the Mississippi River, which created a disaster too big for individual states to handle.[30] Eventually, the government became an overseer of rivers and the hazards they posed. However, there is a big difference between flood control to protect human lives and stream improvement for trout. In 1932, federal aid first became available for stream improvement, but on a limited scale. Enter the Dust Bowl, the Great Depression, and unemployment rates that are still the benchmark for bad times. Throw in a new American president with a strong interest in fishing and a plan to deal with economic bad times, and we have the necessary conditions to bring the full force of the federal government to bear on the scientific management of rivers.

In 1933, Franklin Roosevelt took over the presidency from Hoover. During his first one hundred days in office, Roosevelt introduced the New Deal, including Emergency Conservation Work, commonly called the Civilian Conservation Corps or simply the ccc. The ccc did not initially tackle stream-improvement work, but after what was described by Hubbs's key assistant Hazzard as "considerable persuasion and a little pressure, perhaps," the methods were adopted.[31] If we remember Roosevelt's passion for fishing, his connection to the South Side Sportsmen's Club and his governorship of New York when Hewitt published a book on stream improvement, it seems likely that it was Roosevelt who applied political pressure. Nor should we forget that Pinchot could also persuade the Forest Service, an agency that played a major role in stream-improvement work. Perhaps it does not matter who pulled the strings; the important point was that project planners finally had the cheap labor they needed to plow ahead with stream improvement.

Although Hubbs's projects were only evaluated for four years, his group supplied the sole scientifically tested techniques, so naturally their methods were immediately adopted nationwide by the ccc and Forest Service. As part of this process, Hubbs's assistants dispersed to pursue ccc work in various parts of the country. Tarzwell joined the Forest Service in Hubbs's home state of Arizona and Greeley headed back to New York.[32] Yet there were not enough Michigan devotees to supervise all the new projects, a problem compounded by the fact that many ccc workers came from urban areas and had never seen trout streams before. Clearly, this new generation of practitioners needed guidance, so Hubbs's team set up brief training workshops to teach their methods. Hubbs's group worked with U.S. Forest Service and U.S. Soil Conservation Service personnel, who then oversaw technical aspects of the projects. One of these two-week "intensive-training sessions" was held in Cache National Forest near Logan, Utah.[33] According to a 1936 account by Paul Needham, a graduate of Moore's program and former coworker with Greeley and Hazzard, the school trained Forest Service supervisors who later worked in California, Oregon, Washington, and elsewhere. A group of twenty-five men discussed the latest methods and practiced installing structures in the local area. After two weeks, they were considered experts and dispersed throughout the region to supervise crews of untrained CCC workers. It was a method of rapid knowledge dissemination that would be repeated later by Dave Rosgen, a former Forest Service employee and founder of Wildland Hydrology. Both generations would test the assumption that stream modification was simple.

By 1934, CCC stream-improvement projects were initiated on public land in at least twenty-two states. The CCC established more than fifteen hundred camps of two hundred men each, and hastily erected 31,084 structures on 406 mountain streams between 1933 and 1935.[34] Stream-improvement advocates were so eager to modify rivers with CCC help that most work was carried out before detailed design criteria were widely available. Finally, the U.S. Bureau of Fisheries and Forest Service worked together to publish a memorandum in 1935 called, *Methods for the Improvement of Streams*.[35] The author was the chief of the Bureau of Fisheries, Dr. Herbert Spencer Davis, but he was assisted by Hazzard and a third scientist. Interestingly, that very same year, Hazzard would become the Institute for Fisheries Research's second director, serving until 1955.[36] The three authors cautioned that a thorough study of the whole stream was needed before work commenced. They suggested projects should be done in moderation, keeping the motto "leave well enough alone" in mind when in doubt.[37] Clearly, concerns existed following the first two years of CCC projects. The publication outlined a plan to conduct improvements where a newly minted supervisor picked a structure from the manual, drove a stake into a site with a letter designating the style of device and then allowed construction crews to proceed without further instruction or supervision beyond the ultimate design goal to "build for permanency."[38] The array of designs included Hewitt's basic plank dam and other structures including K-dams, V-dams, log-and-wood triangular deflectors, cover structures, and wire cribbing rock-filled devices. Despite the overall cookbook approach to river modification, the publication did at least warn that structures should not mar the natural beauty of National Forests or make fish easier to catch. Most interestingly, lead author Davis was a little leery of the whole idea of stream improvement.

In another 1935 publication, Davis suggested that there was an overreliance on stream-improvement techniques and made a plea for a more natural appearance to structures.[39] He argued that the professed benefit of stream improvement had grown beyond its value as a management tool and was erroneously viewed as a miracle cure to ensure larger catches in the mind of the average angler. The next year during an address, he even took what appear to be potshots at Hubbs by suggesting that the wide use of structures advocated by some authors was unwise. Davis stated: "No greater fallacy was ever promulgated than the not uncommon idea that any man equipped with an ax, pick, and shovel, can qualify for stream improvement."[40] Davis was directly attacking Hubbs's assertion that stream-improvement work was easy. Davis also questioned the claimed benefit for food organisms and bemoaned the lack of "authentic information" to demonstrate the value of stream improvement.[41] Finally, Davis suggested that experiments were desperately needed before stream improvement could be considered scientific. It would have been interesting to watch Hubbs's reaction to these comments as he sat chairing this conference session in Washington.

The U.S. Forest Service produced its own handbook on the use of structures in 1936. Designs drew heavily from works by Michigan's Conservation Department, Davis's 1935 joint agency publication, and the Board of Fish Commissioners of Pennsylvania, represented by Oliver Deibler.[42] Commissioner Deibler's boss at the time was Governor Pinchot,[43] so perhaps it is not surprising that the Forest Service looked to Deibler for direction on stream improvement. From the outset, the Forest Service manual included passages that suggested caution because previous projects had done more harm than good. However, the authors also recited the old scientific management philosophy that "the forces of nature, if skillfully directed, may be made to work far more efficiently and produce more beneficial results than if left to their own devices."[44] Instead, the publication ensured that public streams would be left to Forest Service devices, including dams, deflectors and shelter structures. Even streams that "have never been subject to man's destructive uses," were fair game.[45] The structures were intended to safely handle maximum flood conditions expected in a ten-year interval and included several designs not seen in earlier publications. The Forest Service manual adopted language employed by Hubbs opposed to the more cautious tones Davis preferred. Perhaps this was in deference to the increasingly public and political prominence Hubbs attained in 1936.

A picture of the political power and national importance of stream improvement becomes clear in 1936 when President Roosevelt reorganized the twenty-second annual American Game Conference into the five-day North American Wildlife Conference and moved it from New York to the nation's capital.[46] The conference was broadcast via radio by NBC. Although Roosevelt was not able to attend, he had the Secretary of Agriculture read a letter to the audience that stated the social and economic importance of wildlife to the nation. Similar statements were presented in abstention by the president of Mexico, General Lazaro Cardenas, and Hewitt's friend, Prime Minister Mackenzie King of Canada. The conference was a who's who of wildlife management attended by the secretaries of the interior, commerce, and agriculture, and directors of the Forest Service, Bureau of Fisheries, National Park Service, and Biological Survey. Even Aldo Leopold, the pioneering environmentalist, was asked to make a speech. Interestingly, Leopold was an early opponent to stocking of nonnative trout in New Mexico because of its adverse impacts on native cutthroat trout.[47] Hubbs was not only in attendance; he was asked to chair one of twelve special sessions held during the conference. It was here that he had to sit through Davis's verbal barbs. But Hubbs chaired the planning committee and—with Hazzard's and Greeley's help as committee members and Davis as the sole remaining member—stacked the deck. In the "Stream and Lake Improvement" session, Hubbs gave one talk and assembled a total of seven other speakers including separate talks by his former underlings Tarzwell and Greeley, stream-improvement manual author Deibler, and Hazzard's and Greeley's former coworker Needham.[48] Davis appeared to be the only dissenting voice. The preceding morning, another session titled "Fish Management" competed for crowds against two other special sessions. In subsequent years, the national meeting was repeated and many individuals returned. Clearly, scientific management and stream improvement in particular were seen as both important national initiatives and political tools for an administration that was desperately trying to improve conditions in an economically depressed nation.

Until the economy improved, the CCC would continue to do its improvement work. By 1936, an official press memorandum reported that the CCC had modified approximately 5,000 miles of stream, built more than 3,800 rearing ponds and introduced nearly 200 million fish in streams and lakes.[49] However, these numbers may be a gross underestimate because Hazzard and Tarzwell reported more than 4,000 miles of stream development and 2,235 structures in Michigan alone.[50] Furthermore, Greeley reported 75 miles of stream work with more than 2,000 structures in New York as early as 1934.[51] By 1936, Tarzwell reported 352 miles of stream-improvement work had been conducted in Arizona and New Mexico.[52] Deibler announced almost

1,000 miles of "improved stream" in Pennsylvania by 1936.[53] If we tally projects in just these five states, more than 5,400 miles were modified. Two years later, approximately 1,600 structures were placed by the CCC in New Mexico and at least 245 miles of work was done in Colorado.[54] Whatever the final score nationwide, the miles of newly completed projects piled up almost as fast as miles of hatchery trout do today. Even this scale of change was not enough for Davis's replacement, and the new chief of the Bureau of Fisheries recommended that all public lands should be brought under the auspices of scientific management.[55] With most states involved in the countrywide initiative by the late 1930s, it is certain that our nation's rivers were not the same as they were a decade earlier.

When Hubbs initially developed stream-improvement techniques, he stated that methods must be adopted from other locales only after those methods were tested in new areas.[56] However, CCC crews offered a unique opportunity for expansion of the program, so attempts at more multiyear studies in Michigan were temporarily abandoned. As could be expected, this urgency led to problems and, as early as 1935, Hubbs's own graduate students suggested some techniques developed in Michigan were unsuitable in other regions.[57] Davis joined the fray and suggested there was a big difference between meadow channels in Michigan and mountain channels in most National Forests.[58] Furthermore, in at least some regions, instream structures were placed without preliminary surveys of the channels being improved. Tarzwell described an "emergency character of the work" and mentioned a lack of planning for projects.[59] Crews would show up and begin to install structures without ever bothering to find out if the stream actually needed improving. The warning to "leave well enough alone" was totally ignored.

Perhaps it is not surprising to learn that experimental and trial-and-error approaches to CCC projects were planned. But the haphazard nature of the work sounded like a try-to-err approach more than anything resembling a true experiment. Today, restoration efforts are still described as experimental or are alternatively called demonstration projects. About the only thing demonstrated by 1930s projects was a complete inability to abide by the basic tenets of the scientific method at the core of scientific management. True experiments require careful observation of results. The words *experiment* and *trial* are essentially synonyms for investigation. If we look at a nonscience example, it becomes clear just how problematic it is to suggest an approach is more methodical than it is in reality. Imagine two detectives tasked with solving a murder who show little enthusiasm for a case; they eventually show up to the crime scene, make a couple of casual observations, but collect no hard evidence. They then take a few educated guesses and point a finger at a suspect. Few people would be comfortable calling that a proper investigation. At the trial, their arguments are based solely on conjecture. The judge rightly dismisses the case and a murderer is freed to walk the streets. Most people would call that trial an error. No one would consider that a sound way to get to the bottom of a crime.

When it comes to stream improvement, a truly experimental approach means people need to monitor projects and make observations. We might imagine with a labor force of hundreds of thousands of men that a lack of manpower would be the last complaint voiced. Nevertheless, this excuse by project managers was used to explain why they had not bothered to conduct scientific inquiries to see if money was well spent. Essentially, ccc supervisors started experiments they did not intend to finish. As a result, almost no assessment work was undertaken and even fewer results were published. It was instigation without investigation. Amazingly, Tarzwell reported in 1935 that more than a million dollars were spent on installations, but only a few thousand on study.[60] The national trial to transform rivers into a heavenly home for salmonids had gone awry. Untested experiments littered the countryside. Science and scientific management were no longer part of the equation. We had instigated a headlong hunt to remake a nation's aquatic ecosystem based on the unsubstantiated belief in the perfect trout stream. It was about as unscientific an approach to the problem as imaginable, done under the intellectual direction of a renowned scientist.

There are beliefs and then there are realities. In reality, projects were not holding up as well as some people suggested. Even Hubbs admitted that many installations were lost in his first projects.[61] He countered that fewer losses occurred in subsequent years.[62] That situation does not sound ideal, but at least he implied things were moving in the right direction. However, if I want an objective review of the food at a restaurant, it is probably not a good idea to ask the chef. Likewise, to really know if stream improvement has improved streams, it is a bad idea to rely on the opinions of the people who designed, built, and then promoted it. Although this would seem to be self-evident, many of the first evaluations were written by the same people who had to justify the economic expenses. Not surprisingly, mostly positive conclusions were produced by researchers directly connected to the pioneering work in Michigan. Conversely, more critical findings began to surface from more distant practitioners. It was a case of whom to believe.

It is not a surprise that the first study to provide a scientific test of the impact of stream-improvement structures on trout was conducted by one of the original Institute for Fisheries Research fellows. Unexpectedly, the study was not conducted in Michigan, but perhaps more appropriately in Hubbs's home state of Arizona.[63] In 1938, Tarzwell decided it was time to investigate CCC work done in that state from 1933 to 1935. He eventually concluded the project a success and stream improvement a worthwhile investment. To support his claim, he used a creel census to estimate the number of fish caught on a modified channel, Horton Creek, and an unmodified channel, Tonto Creek. This creel census relied on voluntary reporting of the number of fish caught by anglers. This type of investigation was not ideal in Tarzwell's mind, but was cheaper and faster than the more thorough before-and-after study of stream biology he deemed more appropriate. Basically, the study assumed that the more fish caught, the better the project. For this study to be truly scientific, the two streams should be as "near identical as possible."[64] That condition included the amount of fishing conducted, which is where a problem arose.

Two years before Tarzwell's study was published, a researcher from Vermont suggested in comments at the end of a talk that Tarzwell attended, "If stream improvement does nothing more than to make more places to fish and relieve the intensity of fishing spots, it will allow trout to spread out."[65] But it doesn't. In 1935, Deibler indicated at the end of a talk by Tarzwell that Pennsylvania's first project drew large numbers of anglers.[66] One of Hubbs's graduates also reported in 1945 that the placement of instream structures resulted in a concentration of the fishing where improvements were made.[67] A look at Tarzwell's Arizona data showed the same result. Furthermore, a previous study in New York showed that "it is interesting to note that fish quickly moved into the area which had been cleared of fish."[68] Consequently, data on the number of fish caught in a particular location could be more of a function of where people fished throughout a season than where trout are at the beginning of the season. The article was written by a team of scientists led by Moore. Tarzwell should have been familiar with this publication and the problem it posed for his study because his former colleague, Greeley, was a coauthor.

As it turns out, Horton Creek and Tonto Creek join where the study was conducted, so fish from the heavily stocked Tonto could easily migrate to replace fish caught on Horton Creek. Tarzwell noted a marked increase in the number of undersized trout in the two streams and suggested that the larger number of undersized fish on Horton Creek was a result of better natural reproduction. But four years before, it was noted that small trout dominated a New York stream because "poor growth rate by long-term exposure to angling, which removes only the larger fish" created competition of many smaller trout.[69] In essence, intense fishing pressure removed large trout and simultaneously increased the total number of smaller fish because they were no longer eaten by big fish. More ruinous to Tarzwell's claim for project success was the decreased size and number of trout caught per hour on the creek he modified. Anglers essentially needed to spend more time fishing to catch the same number of fish because many people flocked to structures and, the fish they caught were smaller. Today, we can use computers and modern statistical methods to reanalyze Tarzwell's data. I did in 2006; it turned out that the structures had nothing to do with the increased catch on Horton Creek.[70] It was simply a matter of more people fishing at that site. Unbeknownst to decades of river managers who read and quoted Tarzwell and his study, the Michigan group's first major trial for stream improvement contained major scientific errors and subsequently reached the wrong conclusion.

To most anglers, the details of the design of a scientific study or statistical test are much less important than firsthand experience. If after years of fishing, an angler suddenly witnesses an increase in the number of catchable trout immediately after the completion of a stream-improvement project, it would be easy to conclude that instream structures were the elixir of life for streams. State fish and game agencies made sure that was exactly the reaction anglers experienced. Deibler explained how Pennsylvania created "trout fishing de luxe."[71] The state's first stream improvement project, located in Bellefonte near an important hatchery, was aptly named Fisherman's Paradise. I visited "paradise" many years ago and noted a state hatchery just upstream from a treeless section of stream littered with deflectors. According to Deibler, the state purchased 1.25 miles of channel and placed several devices to improve fishing after he first visited Hewitt's Neversink property in 1933 for inspiration and borrowed other ideas from Michigan.[72] Instead of just relying on luck at this point, the state "then, in order to attract fishermen to this place so they could see what we had done" stocked the stream very heavily with nine thousand ten- to seventeen-inch brown, brook, and rainbow trout.[73] This equated to more miles of nose-to-nose trout than miles of modified stream. In 1934, more than five thousand anglers, including five hundred women and girls, used barbless hooks and artificial lures to catch and release eleven thousand trout and capture and remove two thousand five hundred.[74] In 1936, almost seven thousand anglers showed up. Deibler reported that the project spurred a major public response and "in almost every county in the state the sportsmen themselves were carrying on the work, or were successful in setting up federal-aid projects."[75] In 1935 alone, the Works Progress Administration committed more than $500,000 to projects in fifty Pennsylvania counties. With reports such as these, it is hard not to be skeptical about early claims of stream-improvement success.

Even in the 1930s, not everyone involved in CCC projects was impressed. Nature has a way of making fools of those who try to tame her or improve upon her design. The managers of early projects soon learned this lesson. For example, after only two years in Iowa, cover structures were completely destroyed in a supposedly improved channel.[76] Based on the project failure, the designer suggested that management efforts in the watershed should first center on reforestation and erosion control before money was expended on instream structures. Keep in mind that at this time the failure of scientific management to remake the Great Plains was evident in the form of large piles of dust and silt blowing eastwardly across the state. In 1938, just three years after Iowa's disappointment, engineering defects were found in a large percentage of structures installed in Idaho, Nevada, Utah, and Wyoming.[77] Fish failed to spawn in gravels behind structures, and fish were frightened by and avoided cover structures that swayed in the current. Erosion around devices was so bad, in fact, that it proved destructive to macroinvertebrates. The project manager concluded that stream-improvement was not economically sound in high-mountain streams. These people understood that, in fact, channels could not be easily engineered to solve the problem of overfishing.

The single biggest problem with stream improvement was a failure of project designers to appreciate the dynamic nature of rivers. Several key geomorphic processes including bedload transport, lateral migration, and riparian and channel interactions were largely overlooked. When deflectors or dams washed away in floods, proponents of instream structures simply concluded that a better design was needed. That conclusion is easy to reach if a project is looked at in isolation. Unfortunately, in the 1930s there were a multitude of projects but a dearth of reliable evidence on the value of investments. Because techniques were not systematically evaluated and results not disseminated, the national trend of underperforming projects was easy to miss. So, individual designers just set out to build a better trout trap. Engineering difficulties suffered by early projects encouraged a focus on structure stability, and success was soon measured in engineering terms with little concern for long-term biological impacts. Somehow, river managers started to care more about the survival of structures than trout.

Hubbs predicted that scientific fish management would "develop enormously in the coming decade,"[78] but World War II changed everything. Or more accurately, it created a case of national amnesia. Suddenly, concerns over trout angling seemed insignificant in comparison to the growing national emergency posed by war. The United States needed to turn itself into an industrial giant and build an enormous armed force. The multitude of hands working to emplace rocks and logs along rivers and streams was now needed to man machinery, grab rifles and build true fortifications. CCC camps were abandoned and Congress closed the program in 1942. The complete shift of national attention also ended most hopes that we could learn something from the grand experiment to improve streams. Hubbs's dream for a scientific solution to trout management suddenly turned to dust.

~ ~ ~ Although little research or project implementation continued during the war years, a very important study was completed by Hubbs's old group and published in 1949.[79] The research team was under the direction of former graduate student David S. Shetter, accompanied by Hazzard and O. H. Clark. Additional planning was provided by Justin Leonard, the former graduate student who investigated the lethality of rotenone. Leonard was now in charge of Hunt Creek Fisheries Experimental Station, where the new study was conducted. This group of scientists pointed to Hubbs's early work and the need for "experiments to measure the actual result of such work."[80] A decade and a half after the first project and years after thousands of miles of streams were reconfigured, Hubbs's old associates admitted stream improvement was of unproven worth.

Their plan was to collect data before instream structures were installed and compare the numbers to those collected after the project was complete. Decades later, scientists would point to this seminal work as the first comprehensive before-and-after evaluation of stream improvement to be published.[81] In reality, the group's study was not a true before-and-after experiment as advertised because earlier CCC structures existed at the site prior to the study, albeit in a damaged state. The authors mention the "remains of nine log wing deflectors installed by the CCC."[82] Perhaps this fact alone is the most damning evidence for the entire CCC grand experiment. Here was a site that was improved by the CCC under the ultimate direction of their mentor

Hubbs, right in Michigan where his techniques were developed, but this site was still viewed as deficient enough to warrant another major stream-improvement project less than ten years later. Apparently, this CCC project failed to fix problems even in the state where Hubbs's methods were most heavily studied.

For the 1940s study, the Michigan team installed twenty-three new deflectors in 1941, one deflector in 1943, and five deflectors in 1944 to replace newly damaged ones.[83] The fact that they were able to do any non-war-related construction during that period highlights some political power. The numbers they used to subsequently evaluate these structures were based on surveys of the number of trout in angler's creels, caught with nets and by electrically shocking fish, a process called electrofishing. The study reported lower trout populations from 1941 to 1942, followed by an increase from 1942 to 1944.[84] A simple conclusion to draw would be that structures benefited fish, and that is just what the authors suggested. However, there were other factors in the watershed to consider, most notably the underlying issue of fishing pressure.

Although the authors attributed increased fish population to the existence of structures, they also noted that fishing pressure decreased because of wartime travel restrictions. Nationwide, the number of people fishing dropped when unemployed workers looking for food during the Great Depression and others later enlisted in military efforts in factories and platoons during World War II. The Michigan group's own data showed that total angling hours at the research site dropped almost 19 percent during the war, but they argued this did not impact their experiment.[85] The location of fishing also changed as anglers flocked to the newly modified reach with hopes of improved fishing. Not surprisingly, more anglers tended to catch more fish and those fish ended up in creels and then the creel census. A more careful review of their data showed that the number of fish caught per hour increased more in one of the two unmodified sections of the river than in the "improved" section. Obviously, conditions were uniformly getting better for trout if a reach untouched by instream structures showed improvement. According to some ugly statistical tests I performed in 2006, the presence of instream structures did not explain the increased number of fish caught in the modified reach, but changes in fishing pressure did.[86] Shetter and his colleagues were apparently wrong; structures did not increase trout numbers. But it was too late for retractions; the damage was already done. Regardless of the limitations of the investigation, for decades this publication was viewed as evidence that stream improvement effectively increased trout populations.

More importantly, this publication and the 1938 article by Tarzwell showed that anglers found instream structures irresistible even if trout did not.

During the remainder of the 1940s and 1950s, few innovations in the design or use of instream structures developed. The new ideas were often far from ecologically sound. Concrete blocks were used to construct instream structures, and pools were artificially scoured using fire hoses.[87] Forest Service manuals produced to replace the 1936 publication relied on the same basic classes of structures and many identical designs.[88] Experienced foremen were still encouraged to devise their own types of instream structures.[89] Despite warnings by Davis in 1936, the Pennsylvania Fish Commission produced a stream-improvement guide for "use by 'do-it-yourself' citizens" as late as 1969.[90] Even now, the commission provides structure drawings in a handy digital form on its website.[91] Similarly, a 1974 publication on stream improvement authored by the executive assistant to the director of the New York Division of Fish and Wildlife recommended that "a couple of fishing buddies" should spend time randomly rolling boulders into the middle of channels to form shelter even if it is only effective for one year.[92] Today, the National Park Service must warn anglers that it is illegal to move rocks in this way because it harms fish and aquatic insects.[93] Amazingly, a 1950s Forest Service handbook suggested using dynamite to blast out pools and fishways in natural bedrock channels, although the author admitted the success of these attempts was not established at the time.[94] Pennsylvania provided the ultimate sign of how little had changed from the 1930s to the 1990s when it used pictures of the same dam design, a modified version of Hewitt's dams that Commissioner Deibler originally saw in 1933, on the cover of publications from 1961 until 1999.[95]

In 1992, the prestigious National Research Council noted that published recommendations in the 1980s and early 1990s often followed a rule-of-thumb nature where experience was substituted for scientific understanding.[96] They warned that this intuitive approach could cause more unexpected harm than good. Despite these warnings, only about 10 percent of restoration ventures included monitoring to evaluate project success by 2005.[97] Project designers continued to use the terms *experimental, demonstration,* and *trial-and-error,* continually failing to adhere to the scientific method that requires data collection critical to unbiased project evaluation.

The small number of projects studied over the last fifty years, often suffered from a lack of objectivity, and results were ambiguous at best.[98] In one of the most bizarre scientific studies on instream structures, a scientist from the South Dakota Department of Game, Fish and Parks somehow convinced the neighboring state of Montana to let him modify Trout Creek in the early 1950s.[99] He then destroyed natural habitat and replaced it with instream structures to see if exotic invasive trout would adopt the artificial barracks as their new home. The fish did and, evidently, the experiment was a success. But what exactly does this prove and what is the underlying motivation? Why would any angler prefer deflectors and dams to root wads and logs? Perhaps it is the artificial simplicity of the system itself that is appealing.

When we consider the typical design of deflectors, it is not hard to understand how easy they would be to fish. If water levels are low you could stand right on the device and give yourself plenty of room to cast without concern that you would snag a bush. The structure is designed to create pool habitat for trout, and it occurs in roughly the same place relative to the apparatus at each site. With triangular-shaped deflectors, it is almost as if a giant arrowhead points to the river and advertises, "fish here." Similarly, cover structures are generally straight with no random protruding parts that typify tree branches. There is little risk that a poorly placed fly will tangle itself around a twig and ruin the chances of catching a fish. Unlike naturally undercut sections of banks where overhanging roots may obscure the view, anglers also know just how far back lunker structures extend. They are just big enough to hold a lunker of a trout.

In a 2006 comprehensive study of instream structures, I reviewed seventy-nine publications produced prior to 1980 and found only 2 reliable statistical tests out of a total of 215 analyses that indicated instream structures benefited fish populations.[100] Less than 1 percent of the tests showed positive results. In 2003, a group of British scientists completed the largest-scale evaluation of instream structures ever conducted and found "there is little evidence of any general benefit to fish of small-scale instream structures" to improve fish abundance, species richness, diversity or equitability.[101] Other studies in 2003 and 2004 found no verifiable increase in fish populations in response to channel modifications.[102] A 2008 literature review of 345 studies was more positively inclined toward the use of instream structures, but the authors cautioned that results were often highly variable or inconclusive.[103] Furthermore, there was little documented evidence that instream structures benefit species other than trout and salmon. This study also cited the basic problem that project designers were more likely to report data from successful versus unsuccessful efforts. Perhaps this explains why results are only available from a small fraction of projects undertaken. As various comprehensive studies show, instream structures often do not work, and if they fail, project managers are unlikely to advertise that fact. Overall, there is little proof that a century-long investment in stream improvement with static structures restored anything to our nation's rivers and streams.

~ ~ ~   Back in Connecticut at Veteran's Fishing Area, the legacy of the CCC undertaking is still written in rock and wood. Collapsed cover structures destroyed habitat types they were designed to create. A collection of other structure styles inspired by Hewitt and Hubbs also stands as a solemn tribute to the army of CCC workers that remade the landscape. There are a series of deflectors that were designed to narrow flow and erode out deep pools for fish. As is typical of most deflectors, these Veteran's Fishing Area winged warriors were low-elevation, triangular obstructions protruding as much as 75 percent across the channel.[104] Originally, large logs were pinned together with steel rods and scattered boulders filled in the central portions of the apparatus. In a reversal of fortunes with the bank revetments, the logs largely remained while internal boulders were forced from their wooden fortifications. Now, large angular boulders stand in contrast to the more rounded stones that made up much of the bed of the river. Riprap boulders even filled in pools they were supposed to create, thus destroying the specific habitat they were intended to produce.

A few examples of 1930s-era habitat dams also persist. Dams fared better in some cases, but in other places flow eroded around the ends of logs and outflanked the structures. It was not the first time this outcome has been observed in a CCC project. A decades-old study investigating an eighteen-year-old Forest Service and CCC restoration project in California found that 76 percent of the original forty-one structures were washed out or rendered ineffective.[105] Every one of the rock deflectors, earth dams, arched dams, straight dams, and plank dams was outflanked by flow. As in Connecticut, many of the destroyed structures persisted to create an aesthetic detriment and some structures did more ecosystem harm than good. The author concluded that even when structures were well built, constant maintenance was required if the structures were to perform their intended duty. But in California and other documented sites in New Mexico and West Virginia, CCC structures never received any care and were slowly destroyed over time.[106] Even after the war, maintenance was skipped and most anglers largely forgot about the wood and stone campaign perpetrated in our nation's waterways. As World War II showed and Sir Winston Churchill warned: "Those who fail to learn from history are doomed to repeat it."

CHAPTER NINE

Structural Failures in the System

It is, however, unfortunate in many ways that stream improvement should have made such rapid strides in popular favor before we have the factual foundation on which this work must be based if it is to become a permanent and essential feature of fisheries management. . . . We must recognize that it is still in the experimental stage and that we are sorely in need of authentic information as to its true value.

~ HERBERT DAVIS, 1936

$\mathcal{M}$ount Washington and the surrounding peaks of the Presidential Range provide a backdrop for the most rugged and gorgeous region in New England. New Hampshire's whitish-gray granite pokes above timberline while white birches blanket lower slopes of these balding peaks. High points offer spectacular vistas for anyone hardy enough to climb the rock-strewn hiking paths along the flanks of the mountains. Rivers that include the Ammonoosuc, Saco, Wild, and Swift line their beds with huge stones stolen from ancient summits worn away millennia before. These rounded boulders brightly reflect sunlight on cloudless days as they jut above clear cool water. They provide the best rock-hopping opportunities you can find anywhere. Several times I ventured north to collect data on these rivers that rival any I have seen in terms of beauty. Although survey work can be laborious, my heart rate always quickens with excitement when I see New Hampshire's steep rivers. Luckily, swimming holes abound and provide welcome respites during hot days spent slogging around in sweaty waders. It was on one such expedition when two students and I visited a river with a twisted, tangled past. Hidden along a forested valley, the Zealand River provides a lesser-known gateway into the Pemigewasset Wilderness area in the heart of the region. When people imagine a gateway, it is possible to envision either a picturesque entry route or a chain-link fence. I discovered that in the case of the Zealand River, both definitions apply equally well.

Although the Zealand River does not actually contain a fence in the traditional sense, it does have hundreds of rock-filled metal baskets constructed from wire mesh similar to that found along any chain-link barrier. These wire and rock contrivances, called gabions by the restoration community, are basically an engineer's version of a large boulder. The students and I stumbled upon them as we surveyed up and down what would otherwise have been a beautiful river. Decades before, engineers figured if they could not find big rocks to build stream-improvement structures for trout, they could build cheap facsimile boulders by tying several smaller stones together. String obviously would not work, so they used wire mesh. Today, you can find gabions lining portions of interstates, in retaining walls on public property, and in streams. They were the last things we expected, or hoped, to find in a remote Forest Service river, but find them we did.

Gabions were first used in rivers within the United States beginning in 1957 on the North River in George Washington National Forest, Virginia.[1] Years ago I was actually on my way south to visit these gabions when I detoured to hatcheries in Pennsylvania and Maryland to hunt for golden rainbow trout. I felt the same conflicted set of emotions as I wondered what I would find when I arrived at the North River. A giant rock-filled wire basket does not just get up and walk away; nor do they decay very rapidly. One day after I saw my first golden Frankenstein fish, I visited the first gabion installed in a U.S. river. It was put there by the Forest Service as a way to control erosion and provide fish habitat. Before the Virginia project was completed, both the Forest Service and the company that supplied materials and construction services looked north to New Hampshire. Shortly after the flood of 1959, the Zealand River became the second riverine site in the United States where gabions were extensively used. By 1965, more than one hundred fifty bank-protection and grade-control structures, each comprised of ten to thirty wire-gabion baskets, were placed along ten-plus miles of combined river length at the North and Zealand Rivers. These gabions were arranged in different configurations to produce a series of designs. All told, they tossed in seven dams, sixty-nine retaining walls and seventeen deflectors in Virginia and thirty-seven dams, twenty-four retaining walls and three deflectors in New Hampshire. Afterward, the construction company looked elsewhere to sell its basket weirs and wares and local forest rangers were left to assess the damage.

Although floods naturally undermine banks and create erosion that helps establish aquatic habitats used by trout, Forest Service gabions were officially installed "to arrest this cycle of erosion" and keep banks from "unraveling."[2] As two Forest Service experts explained at the time, "the connection between gabions and trout, while not apparent at first, is an obvious one once the implications of floods on trout are grasped."[3] The Forest Service stance was part of Hewitt's continuing trend of overreaction to large natural floods, typified by a fear of channel migration and attempts to prevent perceived damage to trout. Although floods are normal, the Forest Service also knew that their forestry practices along the surrounding hillsides exacerbated erosion and channel change. As early as 1885, anglers recognized that reductions of trout populations in the Catskills were at least partially the result of the loss of physical habitat accompanying deforestation from extensive logging activities.[4] Even the Johnstown Flood might have been made worse by deforestation.[5] Ultimately, the Forest Service decided that gabion-lined rivers were the answer to protecting trout from logging-related erosion throughout the watersheds.

One of the original concepts behind gabion use was the seemingly ingenious idea that vegetation growth on top of rock-filled baskets would eventually provide the perfect camouflage to hide the contraptions. In theory, soil and decayed leaves would fill crevices among stones and wire, and tiny roots would grow to reinforce gabions and provide an almost impenetrable wall against floods. However, in Virginia even after more than six decades of vegetation encroachment, gabions remain more visible than hidden. In New Hampshire, a more insidious problem occurred. A quick scan of the granite state landscape confirms that birch trees are especially adept at growing in rocky conditions with little soil. Gabions provided a welcoming rooting place for one of New Hampshire's most abundant residents. Many birch trees grow directly atop these structures. Although tree colonization was what project designers hoped for, nature has a funny way of laying waste to the best-intended plans.

Trees naturally grow toward the sunniest places they can find. Along the Zealand River, the sunniest place was not toward the woods, but toward the water. Here and along almost any river, it is not at all surprising to see trees grow a bit cockeyed, with branches nicely shading the water below. If roots are firmly wedged into a complex network of rock nooks and soil crannies, most trees can handle being a little bit off-kilter. The trees shade water and prevent daily warming that could otherwise damage coldwater fisheries. Biologists recognize these advantages and often look for this appealing attribute when they evaluate habitat quality, knowing that trout will use these branches for cover. Unfortunately, some of the young birch trees that hung over the Zealand River did not have their roots firmly planted in the ground. The white-barked umbrellas had their roots entwined in gabion revetments — and nature used these trees to teach designers a little lesson about leverage!

When I walked the length of the Zealand project site, I noted numerous places where rows of gabion retaining walls pitched forward and fell into the channel. I saw these twisted revetments holding dead and waterlogged birch trees that had grown on top of gabions like overgrown birthday candles. Although it took me some time to make the connection, I finally realized that as these trees grew and extended branches over the river, they eventually pried the whole structure loose. These gabions mainly relied on gravity to keep them in place. Without large forces to push them around, engineers expected them to stay put. But, as colonial farmers discovered long ago when they pried loose countless boulders from their hopelessly stony fields, a long wooden pole provides lots of leverage to fight the force of gravity for even the biggest rock. In fact, along the Zealand River, the length of the paper-barked crowbars annually grew longer, and more leafy candles were added every year. The tranquility of more than one snowy day was probably rudely disrupted by the wrenching sound of tangled metal and rock crashing through river ice as white-frosted gabions were yanked from their perches by snow-laden birches. Like mischievous kids caught standing next to ruined birthday cakes with frosting still on their hands, birch trees remained at the scene of the crime with their roots still linked to their misdeeds.

The projects in Virginia and New Hampshire revealed other sad flaws. To stop the river from undermining structures, gabions were placed below the waterline along channel banks where bedload and floating logs could hammer away at support wires. Abrasion of metal strands already compromised by the chemically corrosive combination of iron, oxygen and water left long gashes in the base of baskets. Small rocks poured from slashed gabions like rice grains from a leaky bag. As wire baskets lost their rectangular shape and their structural integrity, entire retaining walls collapsed and dams failed. Long walls of metal and rock remained strewn at odd angles in the water, looking more like some type of military installation than an environmental solution. In other places the rivers simply meandered away from structures that now sit abandoned in the woods. Once I learned what to look for, it was easy to foretell a cycle of future problems. I saw trees doomed to turn wire into water when they pried loose another gabion. Gabions sat badly worn, ready to spill their contents into the river and create more fatal weaknesses in the parent structure. These basket-case rivers are worse disasters than any flood could have created.

The Forest Service faced an unpleasant dilemma with three equally unattractive choices. It could let the process continue with predictably negative consequences for the stream. The lack of activity could lead to more channel narrowing as rows of gabions crash down. The resulting narrower and deeper water would be more erosive, leading to more down-cutting, increasing failure of gabions, enhancing the exact problem the retaining walls and dams were intended to solve. Alternatively, federal foresters could fell saplings as a temporary solution and then plan for continual pruning and maintenance. Unfortunately, cutting down trees on structures would expose the nightmarish gabions for all to see. Furthermore, loss of forest cover along these streams could doom trout by increasing water temperatures and destroying valuable cover habitat. Finally, the Forest Service could decide to pay an exorbitant price to private engineering firms to remove structures. Sadly, gabions are extremely difficult and costly to remove because, by design, the wire mesh becomes entangled in roots and partially buried by sediment and soil. Limited removal of gabions was already attempted at both sites, but portions of baskets remained as a tangled mess of wires. Complete removal of gabions would disrupt vegetation, soil, and sediments along channel banks and expose the river's flanks to even greater degrees of erosion.

The Forest Service ultimately decided to use its meager funds to search for a long-term solution following the removal option at both sites. The rivers are being slowly restored from the damage done by stream improvement. As part of this new phase of stream improvement, the agency insists that large sections of channel be protected from the supposedly destructive forces of floods in Virginia by a new breed of structures. Although I am pretty sure that you've heard this story before, in the last decade the Forest Service opted to restore the North River with instream structures installed by workers trained through a series of short courses. This new generation of restorers uses a newly named approach relying on old ideas carefully repackaged for a modern group of river managers by a man with a personality as big as his cowboy hat.

~ ~ ~ Dave Rosgen is the single most important person in channel-restoration work in the country today. In 1993 he received the Outstanding Achievement Award from the U.S. Environmental Protection Agency. In 2004, *Time* included him in a list of the world's most innovative minds.[6] He is a dynamic speaker who gathers devoted fans and restoration converts while he teaches them his philosophy of river modification. He is described as

> an honest-to-god Westerner from ranching stock with a lifetime's practice training cutting horses, who sports a rodeo belt buckle he won, western shirts, and a white cowboy hat. He is energetic, opinionated and extremely self-confident, and expresses himself in practiced folksy phrases: idiots have, "a terminal case of the dumbshits," well-meaning idiots have, "their heart to cranium ratio out of whack," and following the advice of either is like, "'crapping your chaps and sitting in the saddle."[7]

The authors who provided this colorful description reported that his enticing persona spawns look-alikes who proudly adorn themselves with Rosgen's characteristic white cowboy hat for photo opportunities in front of their newly completed restoration projects. When he is not teaching certification classes, fly fishing for trout, or remodeling rivers with a bulldozer, the main man in the cowboy hat rides horses on his ranch north of Fort Collins, Colorado. He has alternatively been called "The River Doctor," "The River Saver," and a slew of less attractive four-letter words by his detractors. He is presently at the center of a controversy called "The Rosgen Wars." Without his input, the national stream restoration effort might be moving at a snail's pace. With his involvement, the science of river habitat manipulation is rocketing toward an uncertain and potentially dangerous future.

River restoration work is unlike design work for buildings, bridges, and aeronautical craft in that no national licensing certification or qualification standards currently exist. Now, as in the past, there is no way to prove anybody knows what they are doing. As the history of stream improvement shows, individuals frequently underestimate river complexity and install doomed structures to the detriment of aquatic species. To help ensure some level of proficiency in an otherwise wide-open field, many federal and state agencies currently require anyone bidding on restoration projects to first receive training in a series of specified courses. The classes are almost exclusively offered by Rosgen through his company, Wildland Hydrology Consultants. Amazingly, Rosgen has very limited formal training himself. Rosgen's pupils learn the ways of an approach he calls Natural Channel Design (NCD) that is, at the very least, a brilliant marketing scheme.

Rosgen courses attract mostly engineers and fisheries biologists who are trying to develop their knowledge of river mechanics and geomorphology. Approximately 85 percent of attendees come from agency staffs or consulting firms.[8] For someone interested in taking the basic two-day class, the tuition runs just $400.[9] However, practitioners usually need additional certifications. Many take a five-level sequence of classes that involves seven weeks of meetings and an outlay of more than $10,000 per person. Approximately 14,000 students have already completed classes under Rosgen's tutelage,[10] earning his company millions of dollars and irking university professors to no end.

Rosgen was born in northern Idaho during World War II and spent time fishing for trout as a youth. He received a BS in forest industries from California State University at Humboldt in 1965, then went on to work for the U.S. Forest Service in his home state but grew frustrated by the agency's mismanagement of lands and apparent lack of concern for trout streams he had fished years before. As he surveyed public lands in his new role as a forest hydrologist, he was disgusted to see sand-filled streams that previously held good trout-fishing pools. About the same time the Forest Service was installing gabions in Virginia and New Hampshire to deal with floods and disastrous forestry practices back East, Rosgen tracked down Luna Leopold, who was already making a name for himself as one of the nation's leading geomorphologists.[11] Rosgen worked with Leopold to develop ideas on how to modify rivers to benefit trout, but he failed to convince his superiors in the Forest Service to change their destructive ways in Idaho. Finally, he quit the agency in 1985 because of a dispute over a dam he opposed. Next, he founded a consulting company and looked to solve river problems himself. He first obtained a certification in hydrology from the American Institute of Hydrologists.[12] He even managed in 2003 to convince Dr. Richard Hey from the University of East Anglia to grant him a PhD that required no coursework.[13]

Critics question the validity of the doctoral degree because of Rosgen's cozy relationship with Hey, who teaches courses for Rosgen's company.[14] Whether Rosgen deserves the title of doctor or not, there is little doubt that he spent very little actual time in the classroom learning about fluvial geomorphology, civil engineering, or physics. It is perhaps for this very reason that fisheries bureaucrats tasked with the job of managing restoration programs in their states, look to Rosgen to cut through red tape and simplify the process of training fisheries biologists and engineers. Despite his almost complete lack of formal training in the physical sciences and engineering, Rosgen is now the primary teacher of stream restoration in the United States. According to current government policies, even a PhD in watershed science is worth less than a few days spent listening to Rosgen and his team of instructors. Rosgen managed to borrow published ideas from several esteemed river scientists, including icon Stan Schumm, and reprinted, re-branded, and resold these concepts for a fee. Under new agency guidelines often embedded in government requests for proposals, the original creators of the scientific knowledge that NCD is based on are prohibited from supervising projects because they have not completed Rosgen's courses and are therefore considered unqualified. Before his death, even Schumm was shunned.

Today, more people recognize Rosgen's name than Schumm, Garnet Williams, or William Emmett. Rosgen's rise to prominence received a major boost in 1992 when a team of mostly biologists and engineers working for the National Research Council produced a book titled, *Restoration of Aquatic Ecosystems*, designed to lay out the future course for remaking the nation's waterways.[15] Despite the fact that Rosgen had yet to publish any of his ideas in peer-reviewed scientific journals, this group of some of the nation's most prominent biologists and engineers endorsed Rosgen's methods by highlighting his restoration efforts on the San Juan River in Colorado. It is worth noting that the project was only five years old when it was praised by the council—not much time to determine if the new design could handle years of sediment transport and channel change any better than older designs. The committee also published a nice table of habitat structures approved by Rosgen. As a simple measure of success, Rosgen bragged about a seventeen-inch brown trout he caught on a dry fly at the site two years after construction.[16] In hindsight, it seems highly unlikely that this nonnative fish reached that impressive length in just two years. Two years after this committee backing, Rosgen published a short article in a lesser-known scientific journal, followed by a privately produced textbook. With these small literary contributions and the strong backing of the powerful National Research Council, he has become the only show in town. Federal organizations including the Environmental Protection Agency, Fish and Wildlife Service, Natural Resources Conservation Service, and even the Forest Service, endorse or even require NCD methods for projects under their supervision. State agencies also jumped on the NCD bandwagon, sending fisheries biologists to Rosgen's courses and requiring engineering firms to conform to NCD principles when they submit restoration plans. Despite warnings and outcries of concern from the geologic community and their subset of fluvial geomorphologists, Dave Rosgen and river restoration have become synonymous in the United States.

The heart of the NCD approach is a forty-step procedure designed to provide all the details needed to understand a problematic river. In theory, portions of the idea have merit, and many of the same steps are followed by ardent opponents of NCD. However, following the rough outline of a forty-step, eight-phase list of procedures certainly is no guarantee of success. Just as it is easy to envision a teenager crashing the family car hours after attending a driver's education class with a list of forty instructions on what to do and not do behind the wheel, many Rosgen-inspired restoration projects come to a fateful end despite their supposed adherence to NCD principles.

A key decision within the NCD multistep process is the selection of one or several reaches of river that will serve as templates for newly reconfigured waterways. Templates are referred to as "reference reaches" and, in theory, their use is reasonable as long as everything is known about the history and characteristics of these supposedly ideal stretches of water. Unfortunately, reference reaches are rarely studied with the type of historical detail that most geomorphologists deem necessary. In the worst cases, reference reaches have as many problems as project rivers, and these faulty templates produce even worse facsimiles. In other scenarios, reference reaches are appealing to fisheries managers simply because they provide good fishing irrespective of other ecological problems that might persist. Because the goal of many NCD projects is simply to improve angling opportunities, good fishing is sometimes considered good enough.

Geologists have a favorite phrase that sums up their approach to science: "the present is the key to the past." The point is that by studying current processes and the features they create, geologists can piece together what created the ancient landscapes preserved in sediment and stone. Geomorphologists apply the same principle to try to decipher underlying problems in rivers. However, in a move that causes great concern and consternation for these earthy scientists, Rosgen has turned geologic logic on its ear and developed an approach suggesting that "the present is the key to the future." Rosgen is more than happy to judge a book by its cover and has claimed his classification system can "predict a river's behavior from its appearance."[17] Geologists, thoroughly unconvinced, argue that rivers are more dynamic than Rosgen would have his pupils believe.

Geologists were generally caught off guard by Rosgen's rapid ascendance and grew deeply concerned about flawed logic and the lack of emphasis on natural history in the NCD system. In 2004, a committee of geomorphologists from the Geological Society of America produced a position statement in an ineffectual attempt to articulate their concerns over NCD.[18] They expressed their conceptual and theoretical objections to NCD and simply asked to be part of the team of decision makers involved in restoration design. Although the Environmental Protection Agency later stated that "it is essential that predictions and other analyses be conducted by individuals with experience in geomorphology, hydrology, engineering, and other scientific disciplines specifically trained in hillslope [e.g., land use/cover and soil properties], hydrologic processes, and channel processes specifically related to sediment erosion and deposition,"[19] they then slapped geologists in the face by turning to Rosgen to develop the EPA's new Watershed Assessment of River Stability and Sediment Supply (WARSSS) tool. Despite his lack of training in the mechanics of sediment transport and fluvial geomorphology, the EPA felt that Rosgen offered the best chance to provide a national method that would be used to predict erosion problems in channels and calculate the total amount of sediment carried by rivers. This agency move further isolated geologists from policy-making decisions clearly within geomorphologists' realm of expertise. The implementation of WARSSS as a planning tool also greatly expanded Rosgen's influence on the management of U.S. waterways.[20]

Rosgen's WARSSS methods rely heavily on reference reaches and assumptions about channel stability that geomorphologists continue to question. Much like followers of NCD, practitioners of WARSSS use simple diagrams and limited educational background taught in short courses to evaluate geomorphic processes and erosive potential. When it comes to NCD and WARSSS, geologists continue to argue that seven weeks is not much time to learn the intricacies of fluvial geomorphology and subjects like sediment transport. The science of sediment transport is not rocket science, as the saying goes, but it is pretty darn close, relying on similar underlying knowledge of mechanics, fluid dynamics, and turbulence. A true appreciation of sediment transport also relies on hydrologic principles that include the frequency and magnitude of flood events. To correctly apply these theoretical principles, scientists need to measure physical forces and quantities in an outdoor flood setting that can be arduous or even life threatening. It is a major scientific challenge. In fact, coming up with an equation to predict sediment movement continues to be an elusive goal, difficult enough to give even Albert Einstein's son, Hans Albert, a lifetime of challenges. Hans eventually developed complicated formulas to predict the movement of sediment along the bed of channels. They are still regarded as some of the best ever developed. However, even his carefully constructed computations fail much of the time to accurately predict how river sediments move.

It would seem logical that a certain flow level should produce a predictable amount of sediment bouncing, rolling, and swirling in the current. However, this is not the case even for a specific spot in a river because rivers tend to carry more sediments as the flood waters are waning than when they are rising. In this case, history matters. Many geomorphologists continue to devote entire careers to explaining rivers' strange behavior when it comes to sediment and its movement. Unfortunately, the Environmental Protection Agency knew that geomorphologists would want to make sediment transport complex, and the agency wanted easy answers. They turned to Rosgen, knowing that expensive NCD and WARSSS short courses do not make their money by providing endless warnings about river complexity and sowing the seeds of doubt in their graduates. The courses by Wildland Hydrology are popular because they provide simple sets of steps for implementing restoration projects and encourage people to put their education into action. If we turn the tables, I wonder how comfortable EPA staff would be flying in rocket ships designed by geologists with only seven weeks of short-course training in aeronautical engineering.

In the end, outcries from the geologic community have been mostly ignored. Perhaps it is because, unlike many of these scientists, Rosgen is a great communicator who manages to accomplish what scores of renowned researchers before him refused or failed to do. He boils down river science, simplifying it for newcomers. In classes and interviews, Rosgen explains that he tries "to copy what works in nature"[21] and teaches "how to think like a river."[22] It sounds impressive, but few of Rosgen's ideas, methodologies, or structural designs are truly novel. Most of the core concepts come from geomorphic and engineering principles developed by others decades before. He tweaks standard techniques and repackages systems designed to classify rivers by their shape into a seemingly straightforward system that has huge appeal to life scientists accustomed to categorizing organisms. Engineers also appreciate the reliance on traditional methods of construction. According to Rosgen, his system is capable of capturing the characteristics of any river in the world.[23] Now it is almost impossible to have a conversation with a fisheries biologist or river engineer without the terms C4c, B3 or E6b tossed in to describe a local channel.

In contrast, the geomorphological research community directly opposes the concept of universally applicable methods to restore streams because its discipline views rivers as inherently complex systems that must be individually studied and understood. When asked for similar blanket statements and generalities, most scientists shrink from offering widely applicable summaries. They tend to rely on favorite phrases that include "it depends," "under normal conditions," and best of all, "more study is needed." It is not hard to see why river managers looking for definitive answers and reassurances grew tired of geomorphologists and gravitated toward NCD practitioners. Frustrated practitioners even made public requests for better information from geomorphologists and ecologists to aid them in project design.[24] In many ways, geomorphologists did research that helped convince people rivers needed saving, but when asked how to proceed, they were unprepared to provide good answers.

Rosgen is controversial, but he is not the devil that some people would make him out to be. He has helped restoration designers think more about natural processes, has argued against many older stream modifications, and has tried to incorporate more geomorphology in channel design. The NCD approach is certainly better than CCC projects that failed even to survey streams in advance. Therefore, it is worth asking if the current outcry from geologists about the inadequacies of NCD is simply a case of sour grapes from frustration over missing the billion-dollar boat that river restoration became. It seems more involved than that.

Although the foundations for understanding river form and function were clearly developed by a group of fluvial geomorphologists beginning in the 1960s, few if any current fluvial geomorphologists are involved in the NCD movement. One factor that prevents geologists from becoming more directly involved in river restoration science is a fundamental difference in the view toward applied science. Engineers are, by definition, people who build things. They were largely responsible for construction of many of the dams, channelized rivers, riprap revetments, and concrete canals that have killed aquatic ecosystems in the past. Newer generations of engineers seek to fix these earlier digressions by using hands-on approaches that still focus on physical modifications of rivers. Similarly, fisheries biologists have manipulated species distributions since the time when brown and rainbow trout were sprinkled across the landscape like crop seeds. In an effort to create the perfect trout stream, biologists like Carl Hubbs later tossed in instream structures to change the appearance of streams. For engineers and biologists, Rosgen's NCD approach is a natural progression for two disciplines already comfortable rearranging rivers to benefit trout.

Geology is mostly an observational science where geologists rarely manipulate the world around them for experimental purposes. Many older fluvial geomorphologists cut their teeth documenting damage done to American waterways from a myriad of human activities. In the 1960s, geomorphologists first researched problems associated with urbanization and associated changes in flood levels and channel erosion. Some of these same studies later served as a foundation for NCD. In the 1960s, 1970s, and 1980s, geomorphologists played critical roles in documenting physical changes to rivers wrought by dams, channelization, and removal of large woody debris. These battles often pitted earth scientists against civil engineers, foresters, or river managers. In each case, the underlying messages from geomorphologists were warnings that river modifications created consequences that were much more complicated and lasted decades longer than many people initially suspected. To the aggravation of many, they often concluded that more study was needed. Geomorphologists felt poorly prepared, even reluctant, to begin aiding a restorative movement that still primarily relied on physical modifications to rivers as a way to produce desirable ecosystems. Not surprisingly, many geomorphologists were downright skeptical and quick to point out problems in NCD projects when they arose. What began as a series of low rumblings from scientists that had spent decades documenting anthropogenic damage became a public battle raging in the last decade. It makes me wonder: Who truly deserves the hero's proverbial white cowboy hat for saving rivers?

Geomorphologists continue to sound the charge in their war against Rosgen. A recent shot was fired in an article in *Science* by Dorothy Merritts and Robert Walter. The study highlighted a major problem in NCD-style restoration when projects proceed without true geologic expertise. These two scientists essentially found that many of the channels in the Mid-Atlantic States were much more severely impacted by human change than anyone previously imagined. This geologic ignorance helped explain poor results of many NCD restoration efforts in the region. NCD architects failed to recognize that the streams they were restoring or using as reference reaches were in fact relatively recent channels cut through a series of sediment-filled reservoirs from much older dams. The original streams were not naturally meandering channels preferred by anglers and restoration designers. The precolonial streams were previously shallow, swampy places. The article caused such a stir in the restoration arena that the *New York Times* decided to write about the issue in 2008 and quoted numerous geomorphologists with reservations about NCD. Rebecca Lave added to the fray with a dissertation completed at the University of California at Berkley with the enticing title, "The Rosgen Wars and the Shifting Political Economy of Expertise."[25] As Lave explained, one of the biggest concerns from geomorphologists stems from what they see as NCD projects with an insistence on rivers that are stable with a capital S.

Stability can result from a dynamic or static situation. For example, professional bike riders can be balanced and remain stable while tooling along at 30 mph. They can push off other riders, ride across bumpy terrain and still have perfect control of their two-wheeled machines. As any mischievous kid knows, a bike rolling down a hill does not even need a rider to remain temporarily upright. Alternatively, a bike is stable when it is chained to a rack. Heavy metal links prevent wheels from creating forward motion and the bike from tipping. Rosgen appears to prefer the heavy-chain approach. He advocates for boulder barriers and root wad revetments to keep rivers from changing course. The NCD view of river dynamism and its recommended engineering approach can best be summed up using an old utterance with a new interpretation. Stop moving: dam it!

Despite the planning focus on natural attributes of rivers, physical modifications called for in the NCD focus on static, immobile rivers. They are fixed in place with four basic ingredients: check dams, cover devices, revetments, and deflectors.[26] Rosgen certainly offered up some criticisms and warnings of past practices that relied heavily on instream structures. However, in 1986 he also provided guidelines that encourage the use of old designs.[27] He pointed to commonly cited reference manuals including a U.S. Forest Service design handbook from Monte Seehorn.[28] Seehorn's handbook is just a redrawing of old designs from decades before.[29] Consequently, various dams and deflector designs in Rosgen's book are directly descended—in many cases unchanged—from log and wooden wonders installed in National Forests in the 1930s. Interestingly, Seehorn did not bother to reference Rosgen when he updated his Forest Service manual seven years later.[30] Rosgen even promoted a design of devices built from gabion baskets.[31] Except for the recommendation to use his classification scheme to test whether a particular design of structure is appropriate, very little change in the historic structural approach is evident.

Rosgen's designs did evolve a bit with time, which suggests the first structures he recommended fared no better than they did decades before. But his new designs still closely resemble devices used many times before. When it comes to grade control, Rosgen now advocates for a series of low check dams that are still decades old in basic function but now hide under fancy new names. Principal among these is the boulder cross-vane, which is essentially just a curved version of boulder weirs in use by the CCC and Forest Service under the Roosevelt administration. Rosgen's log version is a new take on the 1930s K-dams and wedge dams. These cross-vanes are an integral part of almost any NCD design because, in this system, a dam is the best way to fix, or more appropriately affix, a river. Rosgen's J-hook vane is essentially a cross between depression-age peninsular deflectors and check dams. In wider channels, Rosgen plunks two cross-vanes together to create W-weirs. The W-weir could be viewed as the older V-shaped gabion dam Rosgen borrowed in 1986, but with the ends bent downstream.[32] Naming his designs after letters of the alphabet is a 1930s-era practice that places Rosgen's J-hook and W-weir structures in alphabetical order among more ancient A-deflectors, I-deflectors, K-dams, V-deflectors, V-dams, and Y-deflectors.

There is little evidence that Rosgen's designs are novel, innovative or natural. They certainly are not what normally work in nature, as he claimed. Although the new tweaks on outdated ideas might have corrected some engineering flaws in the old designs, these devices are still used to prevent a channel from undergoing natural lateral migration and downcutting that is environmentally beneficial in most cases. In fact, one of the best-known consultants in the country, who relies on the NCD approach, offers a guarantee that their structures will not move.[33] Obviously, if a structure in the middle of a stream stays put, that implies that the river is chained up and isn't going anywhere either.

Perhaps the idea of a project guarantee for NCD structures sounds impressive. However, in many ways it is really just about playing the odds to impress clients. For a project with a design life of ten years, built to withstand the corresponding ten-year flood, designers have a good chance of never having to see their designs tested before the project officially exceeds the design life and all bets are off. As strange as it may seem, there is a greater than one-in-three chance that flows at a restoration site will not reach or exceed the ten-year discharge level in the span of a decade. Toss in a one-in-three chance of seeing a flood that greatly exceeds the ten-year flood—let's say a twenty-five-year event or greater, which will void the warranty because it greatly exceeded project design capacities. That leaves a pretty low probability that a restoration project will actually be tested by a flood near the maximum design flow. There is a good chance engineering firms will never learn whether their designs met expectations. Once the decade-long life of the project is reached, all parties are off the hook—except the river! As the history of the CCC showed, rivers could be J-hooked into extended visits from decaying structures that harm ecosystems.

When it comes down to the critical question, "What is natural about Natural Channel Design structures?" the devil is in the details. Cross-vanes, W-weirs, and J-hooks are pretty hard to find in an unmodified pool-riffle stream. Although rounded boulders do form natural dam-like steps with plunge pools in steeper channels, these haphazard amalgamations almost never develop in the type of lower-gradient rivers where most NCD projects take place. Similarly, logs can align themselves across channels, but never with the architectural precision and convenient synthetic fabrics adopted in NCD designs. Rosgen's root wad revetments, like those installed on the Blackledge River, are novel inventions in that logs are now planted stump side out, despite the fact that this almost never occurs in nature—rarely do trees decide to yank out their roots and bury their heads in the sand. It is much more common for a tree to fall into a river while the last remaining roots desperately cling to the banks, but that is not the NCD way. Despite these inconsistencies, NCD still rules the roost. One reason NCD structures are appealing to designers is because Rosgen figured out a way to camouflage decade-old structures by using more rounded boulders and logs with branches and roots. The other benefit is that when a device suffers a structural failure, the more natural appearance of the construction materials helps to hide engineering flaws. But no matter how you sell it, grade-control structures and revetments are not features you will find in any channel designed by nature.

Unlike Rosgen and his army of NCD converts, fluvial geomorphologists view river dynamics and associated shifts in channel location brought on by erosion and deposition as incredibly important attributes of healthy aquatic ecosystems. Many specific habitats are created by river motion. Undercut banks provide cover. Meander cutoffs create abandoned sections of channel that serve as backwater nurseries. Many shade-providing vegetation species, including the all-important cottonwood trees that dominate floodplains of the West, colonize riparian zones in freshly deposited flood sediments. Take away the floods and deposition and you take away the trees. In addition to flood impacts on vegetation, gravels must be periodically scoured and redeposited to wash away silt from salmonid spawning sites. Otherwise, fine sediment will smother the tiny pink translucent orbs and minute fry that pop out, which ultimately increases the reliance on hatcheries to supply trout. If Rosgen managed to impose his view of static stability on rivers throughout the country, it would be an ecological disaster. Unfortunately, thanks to new policies used to compensate for construction projects, NCD use is expanding for primarily economic reasons.

Streams always had banks, and now they also have bankers. Stream mitigation banking, or SMB, the latest brainchild of government agencies, is designed to provide a market-based solution to environmental issues. In many states, the system simply requires developers responsible for destruction of a specified length of stream to replace it with a similar length and type of restored channel. The restored channels are provided by mitigation bankers. Although ecosystems are complex cooperative assemblages with many interconnected characteristics, the quality of habitat in some states is simply designated by Rosgen's classification scheme for ease of use. This simple method is a gross overuse of Rosgen's classification because it suggests that the entire ecological value of an aquatic bionetwork can be neatly encapsulated in a simple B2, F5 or A1a+ designation. Even Rosgen admitted that was not his initial intention.[34] Furthermore, construction companies and consultants make out economically on both ends because they get paid to destroy one stream and then supposedly fix another. As part of the SMB scheme, bankers actively search out and restore segments of channels that can later be sold to developers for compensatory requirements. The assumption about aquatic organisms is that "if you build it they will come," but few SMB projects successfully reestablish ecosystem functional integrity.[35] Firms that restore channels and supply mitigation credits to this commercial market look for easy-to-complete projects, not rivers in dire need of saving.[36] Therefore, a trend of restoring many small upland streams replaces working on the more challenging larger channels. Developers look for the lowest-priced credits, which places a premium on cost over quality. Everyone involved seems to benefit from the system except for the aquatic species used as bartering chips. It is the most egregious example of how Rosgen's NCD methods ignore complexity in natural river environments in favor of an approach that is easy to apply. Ultimately, SMB threatens aquatic ecosystems with NCD projects that have a limited lifespan and potential long-term negative impacts. In the future, who will pay for the second-generation restoration projects that will eventually be needed to fix decayed NCD root wad revetments, failed cross-vanes, and botched J-hooks? For now, aquatic ecosystems are being sold down the river by SMB.

Other serious objections to NCD projects cite the continued focus on restoration of short stretches of river to improve fishing in place of investments in solving more basin-wide problems. Funding agencies spend thousands of dollars to toss in a few fish-habitat-improvement structures in place of initiatives that might reduce nonpoint source pollution farther upstream in the watershed before it even enters streams, or encouraging systems that would infiltrate rainwater and limit excess runoff from impervious areas. These critiques are nothing new and are not specific to NCD methods, but Rosgen's stream solutions still refocus restoration efforts on projects with very limited areal extent. NCD sites are usually measured in feet of river modified, not square miles of watershed protected. The value of these projects remains largely unknown because the problem of limited monitoring continues to plague the field.

Despite the fact that the same National Research Council book that launched Rosgen's career also called for more monitoring of projects to evaluate success, the level of post-project evaluation remains small. Only about one in ten sites witness any data collection looking at habitat, biological populations, or ecological processes.[37] Projects are usually evaluated by the same fisheries biologists or engineers who supervised the projects, and few peer-reviewed reports ever surface. Published accounts reveal a mixed bag of results with some effective and some disastrous projects.[38] Although I am very interested in the impact of old restoration projects, I stopped bothering to apply for many grants because most requests for proposals from private foundations want something tangible for their funds. Apparently, pictures of brand new cross-vanes, root wad revetments and J-hooks look good to sponsors. Follow-up reports explaining that the project actually did not work are much less desirable. Grant organizations demonstrate time and again, via their proposal guidelines and funding decisions, that they would rather place rock and stone in rivers than spend money for scientific research on restoration. The true impact of NCD remains largely unknown and the supposed benefits of the approach are based more on anecdotal impressions than scientific evidence. Perhaps for this reason, restored sites still carry the titles "experimental," "demonstration," and "trial," a sad ploy to mask approaches that, in reality, completely ignore the steps necessary to run a true experiment or trial.

Despite the overwhelming appeal of Rosgen's system to most government agencies and consulting firms, not all fisheries biologists, river managers, and civil engineers are impressed with the simplicity of NCD. I became involved in salmon restoration work in Maine only after Jed Wright, a biologist from the U.S. Fish and Wildlife Service, took an NCD class and decided that maybe things were more geomorphologically complex than he was being led to believe. So he contacted a few regional geomorphologists and got them involved. Dan Cenderelli, a member of the Stream Team staff at the U.S. Forest Service office in Fort Collins, Colorado, works with others to improve fish passage at roads by making culverts larger and less disruptive. Mike Kline and other scientists at the Vermont Agency of Natural Resources work to include more geomorphology in stream assessment and restoration work. Professors that include Peggy Johnson from Pennsylvania State University, Cully Hession at Virginia Tech, and Mathias Kondolf at the University of California at Berkley are just a few examples of a new generation of engineers and applied scientists that research rivers, evaluate restoration projects, and teach about the importance of natural channel processes.[39] James MacBroom, a consulting engineer from one of Connecticut's premier river-restoration firms, utilizes a river-classification system developed and endorsed by fluvial geomorphologists. He generally places little faith in the NCD system. Although some of his projects rely more on instream structures than I might prefer, he seems to understand the value of river dynamics much better than Rosgen. These people represent just a few of the individuals who work hard to improve restoration practices in this country. However, more often than not, private consultants and fisheries managers in government agencies turn to NCD to solve problems they perceive in rivers.

Government agencies like checklists when it comes to managing restoration projects, so why not use one to evaluate the whole NCD methodology? In particular, let's compare the 1930s stream-improvement schemes to the new NCD approach to look for similarities. First off, in both cases individuals with little previous background in fluvial geomorphology, especially the natural sedimentary processes that occur in rivers, are trained by a select group of "experts" through short workshops and taught to follow a cookbook approach to restoration. Check. Federal agencies that include the Forest Service are major promoters of the methodologies taught. Check. Trout and fishing considerations usually reign supreme in the design of projects. Check. Projects rely heavily on static structures to contend with ever-changing fluid conditions in hopes of preventing natural channel change. Check. Grade-control structures, deflectors, and revetments are the tools of choice to affix rivers in place and provide fish habitat. Check. Blueprints for a very limited number of structures are provided in handy design manuals for easy replication in streams nationwide. Check. Projects focus on small reaches of river and localized modifications in place of basin-wide solutions to environmental problems. Check. Organizations and agencies funding the projects care more about completing the next series of modifications than spending funds to study the results of past projects. Check. The term *experimental* is used to mask the failure to collect scientific data to verify the success or failure of projects. Check. Because of this lack of monitoring it is impossible to evaluate if money was well spent. Check. Well, it looks like NCD projects are all checked out.

It certainly seems that despite eighty years of experience, we continue to follow trial-and-error methods, ignore the scientific method in the management of streams, and rely on human-designed devices to improve upon nature. Rosgen appears to be the second coming of Carl Hubbs or the third coming of Edward Hewitt. They all share similar stubborn and overconfident personality traits used to monopolize the field of stream improvement during their eras. They developed methods in their local regions that were then rapidly spread into vastly different environments countrywide. With regard to physical modifications of aquatic habitat, they were more promoters than scientists. While Hewitt used his political pull more for his own benefit, Hubbs and Rosgen convinced government agencies to back nationwide efforts to install structures they promoted. Hubbs's call to action inspired CCC projects that still negatively impact some rivers. Rosgen's restoration products may ultimately prove to be the worst environmental disaster perpetrated on rivers in the last few decades. In the meantime, Rosgen and the host of engineering firms his techniques have enabled really appreciate all the business and thank you for your tax dollars.

To me the saddest outcome from the avalanche of NCD projects is the growing list of rivers and streams that might appear natural to the casual eye, but are just another suite of channels that carry the anthropogenic stamp. Project sites are often selected primarily on ease of equipment access more than highest need. I often find band-aid projects taped to a river adjacent to some gateway road along a section of river that was previously no different than other places upstream or downstream. Most of the projects are well under one mile long, which hardly impacts watershed health.[40] People follow entry roads and unknowingly fish in and among structures and devices that are no more natural than the high-modulus graphite fishing rods they hold. Natural river processes critical to the evolution and continued survival of countless species, including the trout that anglers seek, are replaced by camouflaged engineering devices that unwittingly change people's perceptions of rivers and may damage the ecosystem. If river restoration continues at the current pace, old NCD restoration projects threaten to become the reference reaches of tomorrow. Designs will replace nature on most channels. Our sense of a real river, where change is normal and expected, will be replaced by an artificial belief that rivers can be reconfigured to better meet angler's needs. That approach did not work in the 1930s and it won't work in the future. For a river to be truly restored it must resemble the place it was before humans mucked it up. Rivers will be healthier if the processes of lateral migration, vertical erosion, and wholesale change in river location reestablish their normal ways. To understand rivers, scientists must study their past and try to decipher the old messages written on a landscape that has been subsequently erased and unwittingly written over by humans. Now more than ever, rivers need us to pay attention to what they are trying to teach us about their nature.

~ ~ ~ During spring break of my sophomore year in college, I took my first commercial flight, accompanying Jack Schmidt, a professor and well-known fluvial geomorphologist, on a research project to Oregon. My nose was plastered against the plane window as I took in the landscape below. The Great Plains, Rocky Mountains, and Basin and Range province each intrigued me with interesting patterns that begged to be understood and explained. But my exploration of those regions would have to wait half a decade because I had work to do in the Pacific Northwest. We arrived in Oregon, went straight to the U.S. Geological Survey's Cascade Volcano Observatory, grabbed a giant orange suburban and drove south to an area near the famed Rogue River. We quickly went to work surveying, measuring the size of stones, and cataloging damage done to a small mountain stream by massive sediment inputs from a large Forest Service clear-cut that had subsequently burned over in a wildfire. Like Rosgen, Hewitt, and gabion-backers back East, I was disturbed and saddened by the destruction. I was also overwhelmed by both the size of the landscape and experience. I simultaneously tried to master new scientific techniques and find a sense of scale in this strange new place. Perhaps the thing that most amazed and intimidated me was the height and girth of trees in sections of forest that remained. Old-growth Douglas fir trees towered over both the small stream in this steep mountain valley and my skinny frame.

That summer I managed to finagle a return trip with Schmidt and two other students to assist in the collection of additional data. On this venture our mentor asked us to scout downstream of our study site. It was an incredible opportunity to explore an area previously untouched by logging and we jumped at the offer. We had little sense of the physical challenges that lay ahead. The conifers' trunks were gigantic. In places, fallen trees lay perpendicular to the creek and created wooden walls down the sides of the valley. Even on their sides, trees were taller than us, and crossing over these bark-covered barriers was a major test. I felt a bit like Gulliver in his travels to the giant lands of Brobdingnag as we fought to make progress over and around logs that dwarfed us in every way. Despite the difficulty, we happily pushed along to reconnoiter the creek. We saw how collections of huge logs, or large woody debris as I later learned, created deep pools and trapped sediment scoured from the wasted hillsides farther upstream. In places, saplings grew directly on top of trees that had clearly been lying in the water for decades. Bright zones of sand and dark patches of fine organic material tucked themselves behind logs away from stronger currents. The water was clear, cold and deep in places. Trout dashed around and ducked under branches as we splashed along. The creek was the most complex and beautiful stretch of water I had ever seen. This experience helped convince me and another of the field hands to later pursue our doctorates in fluvial geomorphology. I began to understand that streams present a lifetime of challenges and provide an endless supply of learning opportunities.

While I was poking around the streams of Oregon, I began to wonder how the diminutive trees of New England compared to the West Coast giants with regard to habitat creation. Even after more than a year the question still tempted my thoughts, so I decided to write an honors thesis studying the impact of Vermont's trees on a tiny brook a short drive from campus. Surprisingly, almost none of the professional scientists had looked at the role of large woody debris on channel habitats in New England. I found a wealth of sources that described how downed timber impacted streams in Washington, Oregon, Idaho, and California, but only a single study in nearby New Hampshire. I immersed myself in the Western literature on large woody debris and logged methodologies used by river experts to catalog morphologic adjustments wrought by rotting logs. I devised a simple study, borrowed my roommate's car more times than he probably wanted, and occasionally dragged classmates, including my future wife, out to my study site to hold a tape measure. Eventually it became clear that even smaller trees in New England played an important role storing sediments that could otherwise clog spawning gravels. Large woody debris also created deep pool habitats. I discovered that the history of logging activities on adjacent lands directly impacted the ability of wood to perform these functions. I even managed to publish a short article about the project.[41] The trip to Oregon changed my whole perception of what a small stream should look like. Subsequent thoughts of trees, tributaries, and trout always remained connected in my mind.

The function of wood in rivers is remarkable. To understand all the roles it plays requires both a short and long view of rivers. On a daily basis, logs help steady streams by storing pockets of fine sediment and preventing erosion into the bed of the channel. Aquatic organisms find stable habitats within which to function. Brooks cascade down a series of short drops over log steps. Logs deepen the course of streams, store fine sediment and nutrients upstream of their position and scour out clean gravel-lined pools below. At times, logs control the entire vertical drop along a steep forest channel. In some ways, these various woody steps resemble small dams tossed in by instream-structure proponents, but there is an important difference.

From year to year, natural logs occasionally give way and are replaced by newly fallen trees. For a check dam that would be a disaster, but for streams these wood dynamics are critical on a decadal basis because the bed is scoured in short stretches, preventing siltation of spawning gravels and embeddedness. In other places, large jams of wood alter the course of streams. Sizable wedges of exposed sands and silts soon become colonization grounds for terrestrial plants. These vegetated surfaces develop into sections of floodplain where fine sediments are entwined in root systems and protected by a layer of forest litter. In this way, rivers sweep sediments from their beds and lock them up in stable banks. As long as those changes are not too dramatic, nature will cover over her wounds with a log here and there, a new pool or two and slight migrations in the flow path. Trout, salmon and their aquatic accomplices evolved in this watery world where moderate change is normal and expected.

Although the cumulative results of small yearly adjustments in log positions and stability might be critical for healthy ecosystems, localized changes can also be potentially disastrous for macroinvertebrates or fish fry. However, these environmental stresses are exactly the impetus for genetic change that help organisms create more viable populations on a longer-term basis. On time scales that humans can only imagine, rivers wear away mountains, carve new canyons, and change slowly and predictably. As millennia pass, cutthroat trout become specialized and unique in each major watershed. Different species and independent runs of salmon evolve to overcome the specific challenges they have faced in each river. Unfortunately, the history of stocking has reshuffled the deck and threatens to waste millions of years of careful preparation by nature. As James Van Cleef, Henry Ingraham, Dave Rosgen, and I all have observed, a legacy of logging removes the tools that rivers need to perpetuate the habitats that always await the arrival of new generations of organisms.

Decades after my first study in Vermont I reached the same conclusion other scientists independently arrived at: the loss of large old-growth trees and the massive streamside logs they leave behind is perhaps the most serious threat to physical aquatic habitat. In Maine, these logs can remain in channels for hundreds of years,[42] but centuries of logging have reduced both the size and number of logs found in Down East channels. Amazingly, the state even removed some large woody debris in rivers to aid their salmon stocking efforts by boat. In the study I performed for the U.S. Fish and Wildlife Service on the few rivers in Maine that still hold salmon, a computer simulation

I developed showed how loss of wood negatively impacted distributions of habitat types. It is likely that increased sedimentation of spawning gravels, reduced cover and changed channel depth are some of the factors driving Atlantic salmon to the edge of extinction.

In an ideal world, rivers would be left with wide forested floodplains where the channel can migrate back and forth to recruit wood by undercutting trees as needed. In recognition of this ideal, some groups argue that forested riverbanks provide both environmentally and economically sustainable management. The Connecticut Fund for the Environment proposed new legislation in 2010 for Connecticut that would require a vegetated region or buffer zone along waterways to help ensure streams remain shaded and trees continually supply the habitat needed by fish.[43] The idea is simply to prevent manicured lawns from running right up to the edge of rivers and streams. Providing rivers living space would help limit pollution from lawn fertilizers and pesticides, and allow vegetation to provide the habitat aquatic organisms need. I helped provide some expertise to support the legal push, but political hurtles in the state have prevented passage to date. Although opponents argue that legal restrictions on logging step on private property rights, rivers are a common resource; polluting them corrupts everyone's rights. It is really in everyone's best interest to maintain rivers in the healthiest condition possible. Buffer zones and large woody debris accumulations are certainly much more economical and environmentally friendly than handling sedimentation problems and habitat loss with the temporary band-aid fixes and structural approaches currently attempted.

Buffer zones are critical to greenway initiatives along rivers. These projects set aside floodplain zones for various human and natural activities that appropriately enough include flooding. Local, state, and federal governments now appreciate that it is much less expensive to acquire and set aside lands frequently inundated by floodwaters than to constantly rebuild homes and compensate landowners every time it rains. The hope is to keep corridors near rivers in a vegetated state, although parks and playing fields often replace forests and meadows in urban settings. These floodplains continue to provide a productive, but less intensive, use for humans. If the nation's floodplains can be increasingly seen as places for rivers and riparian trees — not humans — to inhabit, then rivers will take care of restoration themselves and at a fraction of the cost of establishing and maintaining complex bank protection and habitat-improvement structures.

If we take time to listen to the things that rivers are trying to teach us, there may finally be a lesson we can learn from the experimental approaches of the past. Humans need do nothing to a naturally functioning ecosystem for it to thrive and refurbish itself. As I think back to the newly fallen tree I saw years ago in Connecticut's Veteran's Fishing Area in the Salmon River watershed, I realize it is unlikely to last as long as the CCC structures that surrounded it. However, the ecosystem will eventually find a new recruit if the forest is left to regenerate and the river is free to find its own course. The deep pool it created will be replaced by a new scoured section. River dynamism and riparian trees will provide all the raw materials and labor force needed to perpetually restore the river. It is time to retreat and let rivers reestablish command. The environment's haphazard use of trees to supply wood needed for self-restoration is efficiency in its purest form, the true definition of natural channel design.

CHAPTER TEN

The Economy of Scales

Every country house with a water supply should have its fish ponds,
for the purpose of supplying the kitchen as well as for angling.
~ J. J. ARMISTEAD, 1895

*H*istory shows that trout somehow create their own economic system, where people spend money to buy equipment, raise fish, eradicate competing species, and modify rivers. The interplay of economic drivers that includes individual, industry, state, and federal involvement raises questions about who is buying, who is selling, and who is reaping rewards? It is even worth pondering what is the product? People buy and sell trout fillets, while others buy and sell trout fishing. In an odd twist of efficiency, trout can be bought at a grocery store for a fraction of the price it would cost to haul one in at the end of a fly rod. Economic considerations also inevitably entail a discussion of supply and demand. In 2006, demand for angling in the United States was supplied by 25 million people who purchased recreational fishing licenses, including a subset of more than 6.8 million trout anglers.[1] They spent a cumulative total of more than seventy-five million days trolling for trout. An additional almost 1.4 million anglers fished for salmon and steelhead, which added approximately thirteen million more days of fishing to the national totals. High fishing pressures witnessed in modern times resulted in a fourfold rise from the 1940s to the 1990s in the number of days people spent trout fishing.[2] With a customer base in the millions and a disproportionately high percentage of affluent patrons, it is not surprising that commercial entities work to lure current and future anglers to the sport and their products. As with many industries, environmental considerations sometimes take on less importance compared to profit margins. Normally, state and federal agencies titled "environmental protection," "natural resources," "fish and wildlife," or some similarly reassuring names would act as watchdogs to guard the state's ecosystems from industry. However, when it comes to trout fishing, these same agencies usually supply the nonindigenous species that cause ecosystem harm. Somehow, government environmental agencies seem to pay as much attention to dollar signs as endangered species. It raises the question, "What is the true cost of trout fishing?"

For governors, legislators, treasury departments and state agencies overseeing fisheries, the benefit of sport fishing to a region is easily plotted in economic terms. In 2001, the total expenditure by anglers in Arkansas was almost $446 million with 17 percent related to trout fishing.[3] Wisconsin valued its sport fishery at $2.75 billion in 2009 with trout and salmon fishing supplying the key component.[4] Missouri estimated that close to one-quarter of its citizens fished, and trout angling-related activities contributed $382 million annually to the economy with 14 percent related to trout fishing on just 145 miles of streams.[5] That works out to roughly $370,000 per mile of trout angling. Ohio claimed 1.2 million anglers contributed $1.8 billion to the economy and supported seventeen thousand jobs in the state.[6] Countrywide, states use dollar signs to convince citizens of the value of their fisheries.

The main player in the trout fishing numbers game is the U.S. Fish and Wildlife Service. The Agency's Division of Policy and Programs works with economists and others to conduct nationwide surveys of trout angling every five years. If we use their most recent nationwide estimates, trout anglers alone spent $4.8 billion in 2006, which reportedly produced 109,379 jobs and $13.6 billion of total economic impact.[7] In this fishy form of trickle-down economics, every $1 spent by the population of trout anglers reportedly generated almost $3 in economic benefit through a multiplier effect, since spending on equipment, food, and lodging produced more spending by store owners and others. More importantly to federal and state governments, expenditures by anglers generated $1.8 billion in taxes nationwide. Ohio alone claimed that anglers generated $1.1 billion in retail sales with an associated $90 million in tax income.[8] For many states, angling offers a tantalizing investment if they can convince enough people to fish.

The U.S. Fish and Wildlife Service actually contains an entire branch called the Division of Economics that helps spit out report after report on the economic benefit of fish supplied by each of the Agency's National Fish Hatchery (NFH) facilities. In the most recent numbers, Norfork NFH generated $5.86 in tax revenue for every $1 of budget expenditure.[9] Wolf Creek NFH spawned $53 in tax returns for every dollar spent and paid out $10 million in yearly wages. This reportedly generated nearly $18 million in retail sales with almost $34 million in economic output and $2.3 million in taxes.[10] Dale Hollow NFH employed 826 people, paid out $21.5 million in wages, and approached the century mark with $94 of total economic return for every dollar spent at the hatchery.[11] The hatchery claimed they stimulated $39.7 million in retail sales, an overall economic output of $75.1 million and $6 million in taxes as a result of stocking activities. Chattahoochee NFH claimed a more efficient operation with a 100-to-1 return on investment and a total economic impact of more than $32 million annually.[12] Greers Ferry NFH registered even better cash register ding for the dollar with their $588,323 budget providing an annual economic impact from trout production of more than $113 for every dollar spent.[13]

To come up with various estimates of economic activity resulting from trout stocking, the Division of Economics determined the number of trout anglers and total number of hours spent fishing for hatchery fish. Unfortunately, this information was not known with any accuracy, so estimates used assumptions and extrapolations based on very limited data, for example, calculations needed to predict the number of fish caught versus those that died. Economists also estimated the number of anglers per stocked fish based on survey data from small samples of places. In 2004, the Division of Economics estimated a total of about four million days of rainbow trout fishing, then multiplied the angler days times an estimate of expenditures by average anglers in various parts of the country for food, lodging, equipment, supplies, and rentals. Then the economic impact of spending for the people who sold groceries, fishing equipment, hotel rooms, and other sundry items to the anglers was tossed in.

The Fish and Wildlife Service recognized different spending habits for residents and visitors. For example, a survey for Great Smoky Mountains National Park found that locals spent, on average, just $31 per trip, but visiting anglers expended as much as $1,500 annually to fish, with an average of $188 per trip.[14] Therefore, the Division of Economics calculations assumed less benefit for residents, following the assumption that much of the money would be retained in local economies regardless and that money spent by visitors was entirely economic activity attributable to trout fishing. Although the Division of Economics admitted that much of the spending benefited only local businesses, the economic benefits reported suggested more than simple reshuffling of funds when it calculated its multiplier effect. According to this logic, if visitors were not fishing for stocked trout, they would be spending no money doing anything else outside their home town. Anglers would not drive anywhere or eat out at restaurants, boats would not be purchased and sailed on reservoirs, and money would sit in savings accounts instead of being used for other online purchases. The analysis also did not consider shuffled income from people traveling from one area to another. In a simple case, two people could trade locations and each spend $1,000 to fish in each other's locale. This might seem like a wash economically, but the Division of Economics considered that a total of $2,000 of retail expenditures.

With the nation's current economic woes spawning dwindling tax revenues and sagging state government spending on everything from law enforcement to education, any source of tax income would seem to provide a potential benefit to the population as a whole. However, fishing proponents are careful to put strict limitations on how money collected from fishing tackle and pleasure boat and motorboat fuel sales can be spent. The Federal Dingell-Johnson Act, also known as the Sport Fish Restoration Act, was sponsored by a senator from angling hotspot Colorado and a congressman from fish-friendly Michigan. It stipulates that federal tax money collected from various boating- and fishing-related expenditures is placed in a fund that supports boating enhancement programs and fisheries and wildlife conservation. Additional money is set aside for, among other things, aquatic education and a national outreach program to promote boating and fishing. Passed in 1950, it has been amended many times, often to increase the amount of money spent on boat launches. For a state to be eligible to receive funding, it must first pass legislation that ensures that all state money collected from fishing licenses is reinvested in the state's fish department. The Dingell-Johnson Act essentially ensures that tax money collected from these angler and boater expenditures is used almost exclusively to perpetuate fishing and boating activities. If you are not an angler, most of this economic spending and reinvestment of funds will have little positive benefit on your life unless you already live in a fishing nirvana that attracts visitors. The eventual legacy of the act comes down to the true impact of trout angling on river ecosystems. If conservation activities supported by trout angling result in net improvement to aquatic environments and the associated native species, the act could be one of the most important environmental legislative initiatives in the last century. Conversely, if the national fascination with trout fishing ultimately degrades ecosystems and harms indigenous organisms, the Dingell-Johnson Act ensures a nasty spiral of investment that places the nation's waterways in continuously renewed peril.

Because of its role in rearing nonnative trout, the U.S. Fish and Wildlife Service finds itself on opposing sides of the same problem when it comes to aquatic species management. Should the agency stock invasive trout or protect species? Although the Fish and Wildlife Service is largely responsible for ensuring the safety of threatened and endangered species under the Endangered Species Act, its 2006 report on trout fishing made no mention of the multitude of issues related to the negative impacts of exotic invasive trout on native species.[15] Similarly, websites for each of the National Fish Hatcheries that rear trout justify stocking with economic rationalizations despite the agency's own research that shows many of these exotic invasive trout cause ecosystem disruption. Furthermore, costs associated with research on endangered species loss, spending on habitat protection and lost productivity of natural ecosystems did not appear to be included in any of the economic cost-benefit calculations. The agency's current attitude toward angling appears to be best revealed in their 2006 report on the national demographics concerning trout anglers: "A bad day of fishing is better than a good day of work."[16]

The Fish and Wildlife Service stocked almost 85 million trout and salmon in 2004, with rainbow trout dominating the effort in regard to the total weight of fish reared.[17] An analysis by the Division of Economics considered just the agency's top eleven rainbow trout hatcheries and reported that they spent $5.4 million to stock 9.4 million fish weighing 1.9 million pounds. About two-thirds of these trout were provided to the U.S. Army Corps of Engineers, U.S. Bureau of Reclamation, and Tennessee Valley Authority to stock reservoirs in compensation for damage done when these federal agencies built dams, even if these dams never impacted native trout habitats. More than one-quarter of the agency fish were given directly to states to stock. All these trout then reportedly produced a total economic output of more than $325 million due to the multiplier effect. According to those numbers, almost $35 of income is generated for each fish, or $171 per pound of trout reared. Imagine trying to sell a one-pound trout at the local fish market for almost $200. At least half the money was related to retail sales with the state and federal governments taking just less than $10 million in sales and fuel taxes. The hatcheries employed approximately 3,500 workers in 2004 for at least a day and doled out $80 million in wages. The states later reclaimed almost $3 million in income tax, while the federal government's income tax take topped $10 million. These numbers provide a strong economic justification for people who want to promote trout fishing. It is not hard to understand why politicians, state treasurers, business bureaus, and local chambers of commerce would want a hatchery nearby.

When considering cost-benefit analyses for trout at federal reservoirs, it is critical to understand that many federal dams were economically justified using questionable economic calculations. Beginning with the passage of the Flood Control Act of 1936, the federal government stipulated that water resource developments needed benefits to exceed costs of projects.[18] The Army Corps of Engineers, Bureau of Reclamation, and other government agencies assumed monetary equivalents for certain activities, including swimming and fishing, but ignored or devalued environmental costs associated with lost ecosystems and their related activities.[19] Often, large recreational benefits were tossed into calculations to skew the cost-benefit analyses by civil engineers eager to build the next Hoover Dam. The importance of recreation in federal cost-benefit estimates explains the strange variation in the level of protection that surrounds public water supplies in the East versus the West. Many eastern reservoirs built by municipalities are surrounded by chain-link fences and No Trespassing signs, while reservoirs constructed by the federal government invite motor boaters, swimmers, and anglers as part of the core function of reservoirs despite the risk of pollution. National Fish Hatcheries supply many of the fish used to satisfy recreational benefits. Despite decades of criticism by environmentalists, the Fish and Wildlife Service continues the trend of calculating the economic benefits of angling while simultaneously ignoring the environmental costs associated with the loss of species that stem from stocking of strange new species of fish.

State governments are also deeply entwined in the finances of fishing because they too sit squarely on the supply side of the economic equation with their hatcheries manufacturing objects of desire. When fishing pressure increased and anglers asked for more trout than private hatcheries could supply, government hatcheries responded. For one twenty-five-year period beginning in 1959, the production of catchable trout by state and federal hatcheries increased 55 percent.[20] Stocking programs for albino and golden trout highlight profit-driven motivations. Utah took a lead in establishing the profitability of stocking pigmentless rainbows in 1973 when the state began an experimental planting program and associated creel survey.[21] The original results were a bit ambiguous, but a 1983 study by two university professors used economic models of "angler utility" to better understand anglers' preference with regard to albino versus "typical stocked rainbows," referred to simply as TSR in the article. Utility, defined as the satisfaction gained from consuming a commodity, demonstrated that anglers wanted to catch both TSR and albino trout. Basically, if they caught only TSR, then albino trout started to look more appealing and vice versa. The recommendation was that albino trout should be provided somewhere between a one-to-one or one-to-three ratio. The authors reasoned that because albino trout cost no more to rear than TSR, Utah fisheries managers should consider a full stocking program to satisfy angler demand. The state followed the recommendation and later added albino brook trout. Unfortunately, the economic calculations performed by the professors did not factor in the cost to the environment of tossing in these pallid trout. No consideration was given to fish survival in rivers or the potential negative consequences of albinism spreading to native cutthroat populations. Albino and gold-tinted trout are still stocked in many places to increase dollars spent by anglers even when it makes no sense from an ecologic perspective.

States run hatcheries and promote fishing to fill government coffers and keep local economies rolling. Michigan provided a good example of what is reportedly at stake for treasury departments because the Department of Natural Resources estimated that 40 percent of the economic value of all Michigan's fisheries and 70 percent of the economic value derived from Great Lakes fisheries in the state depended on propagated fish.[22] Nearby Pennsylvania contains 10,406 miles defined as wild trout streams, which generated slightly more than $7 million in economic revenue.[23] In comparison, the state stocked 4,712 miles of rivers with trout and these areas generated more than $65 million in economic contributions. These stocked rivers were reportedly twenty times more profitable than wild trout streams. This was just a portion of the total spending for the roughly half million license holders in the state, and it highlights the role hatcheries play in income creation. Here and elsewhere, states lose hatcheries and they lose income.

High demand necessitates lopsided investments in hatcheries and heavy stocking to satisfy anglers. Consequently, in the last few years many states devoted a high percentage of their annual budgets to stock trout. In Georgia, hatchery production and stocking budgets accounted for approximately 26 percent of the section's annual expenditures.[24] Pennsylvania devoted 36 percent of the Fish Fund annual budget to trout production, which totaled $12.4 million in 2009 to rear and stock trout.[25] This money did not include $25.4 million to renovate hatcheries embedded in the recent voter-approved Growing Greener II program. In 1991, Connecticut spent $1.8 million, 44 percent of the Inland Fisheries budget, on hatchery and stocking operations.[26] Nevada spent about half of its total fisheries program budget on trout stocking.[27] Although many anglers call for more wild trout and fewer hatchery products, spending on trout rearing continues to be a major investment for most states.

For states working to maximize their returns on investments, the expense of raising each trout is a primary concern. Hatcheries are analyzed to determine if trout can be produced cheaper, which usually means they need to be grown faster with fewer losses to natural predators and diseases. From a production standpoint, if a hatchery can decrease the time it takes to grow a trout to stocking size, then those fish can be pulled out of the concrete pens sooner to make room for a new batch of fry. The hatchery increases annual output and the cost per fish generally decreases because fixed expenses related to hatchery staff, electrical power supply for pumps and facility maintenance can be distributed across the growing population of products. Hybrid trout that grow fast because they are sterile increase profit margins. Genetically modified fish from federal science labs that are more disease resistant and grow faster to catchable size are even more appealing to the bottom line. This type of reasoning also explains a trend where states build bigger mass-production hatcheries that rear a larger percentage of a region's trout.

The hatcheries themselves are not cheap. The cost to build Connecticut's Quinebaug Hatchery in 1971 was $2.5 million.[28] Pequest Trout Hatchery in New Jersey required $12.5 million in spending in 1981. Michigan rebuilt the Ogden State Fish Hatchery a decade ago for $11 million.[29] Ohio spent $7 million to renovate the state's steelhead production facility at Castalia.[30] Beginning in 2006, Wisconsin renovated the Wild Rose State Fish Hatchery, originally built by the CCC in the 1930s, at a total cost of $33.6 million for the first two phases of a three-phase project with $1.5 million devoted to a visitor and education center.[31] Six million dollars of the renovations were paid as part of an environmental restoration legal agreement with paper companies that created historic pollution problems in the state. To help compensate for damage to native species, paper companies funded a hatchery that will annually stock millions of fish, including four exotic invasive trout and salmon species, but no native brook trout.

Remarkably, per-unit outlays for rearing trout have not changed dramatically over time. Maryland spent approximately $0.59 per trout in 1958.[32] The basic cost of raising legal-sized fish to creel was $1.00 each in Michigan in 1963 dollars.[33] In 1988, Colorado spent $0.57 per trout for production costs or $1.47 if administrative and equipment replacement costs were included.[34] Rhode Island spent about $5.00 to raise each fish to stocking size in recent years.[35] In 2002, South Dakota invested between $1.05 and $4.23 per fish for catchable rainbow, brown, and lake trout.[36] Production costs were also very much size dependent. South Dakota spent just $0.24 per fish for fingerling rainbow trout, but $18.56 for large catchable rainbows. The price to eventually place a fish on an angler's hook includes expenses not captured in just the expenditure of rearing fish at a hatchery. Between 1987 and 1992, the price of producing each trout in Colorado was between $0.57 and $1.11 when only hatchery operating expenses and fish distribution were considered.[37] But costs increased to $1.47 to $1.85 per catchable trout and $2.45 to $2.68 for creel returns when additional costs for administrative overhead, law enforcement, vehicles, hatchery construction and replacement, and the opportunity cost of the hatchery lands were added. From 2006 to 2008,

Pennsylvania estimated the expense to rear one eleven-inch trout was $1.67 with a total cost of $2.73 when all the stocking, administrative overhead and other indirect costs were considered.[38] Most expenses for raising trout were related to personnel expenditures, which tapped two-thirds of the Division of Fish Production's annual budget.[39] The other direct expenses were mostly related to food purchases, although utilities, fuel, motor fleet maintenances, and liquid oxygen supply purchases also grabbed their share of funds. The state's various other divisions and bureaus, including Fisheries Administration, Fish Management, Habitat Management, Environmental Services, Law Enforcement, and Engineering and Property Services, each played a role in the trout program and added to the expenses. However, environmental costs of stocking exotic invasive fish were again ignored in these complex calculations.

Knowing the exact cost per fish produced by hatcheries does not deal with the important question: what is a reasonable price for trout? A 1995 Colorado study attempted an answer by comparing anglers' willingness to pay for trout caught versus hatchery production costs.[40] Four scientists in charge of the study found that the economic value of a trout decreased based on the number of fish caught. By the time anglers caught a fish or two, few were willing to spend more than a dollar to reel in the next hypothetical trout. When scientists next calculated hatchery expenses to deliver these fish, they not only included all the financial outlays at the hatchery and management agency, they also recognized that many fish were lost to other factors after stocking and thus never caught. In response, they recommended multiplying the price per fish leaving a hatchery by 1.67 to estimate true delivery costs. They came up with a price tag of $2.45 per fish. The group then looked at the number of fish caught and concluded that Colorado was overstocking trout on the streams analyzed. Essentially, the state spent more per trout than anglers said they were willing to pay to catch fish. The researchers then suggested the state should rethink the idea of investing in new hatcheries designed to increase overall trout production, which currently totals more than three million trout each year.[41]

Although energy expenditures at hatcheries are rapidly growing and threaten some operations, a considerable expense of rearing trout is related to food costs. South Dakota spent 5 percent of its production costs on fish feed in 2002.[42] In 2009, Pennsylvania's eight trout hatcheries spent more than $1 million on fish food.[43] Here and elsewhere, pellets are stored in giant silos and funneled into truck-mounted hoppers that drive along lines of concrete troughs to dump out food as they pass. Despite the economic efficiency of dispersing dry pellets from trucks, the process has drawbacks as reported by a former New Jersey hatchery worker:

> Slinging dry feed for eight hours a day, every day ... was a dirtier job than pond washing. The feed dust got everywhere — on clothing, skin and in every little crevice on the truck. At least once a week, usually more, Harold Gruver, West Hatchery feeder, would hose down his truck to flush out maggots from wherever they were hiding. When things got really bad, Gruver would joke that he had an easy day because the maggots would carry the bucket of feed to the pond for him.[44]

To keep costs down, other hatcheries replaced staff with automated methods of dispensing pellets at rearing facilities. Computer-controlled dispensers sow reconstituted fish parts and additives to fish that will be planted months later. Some facilities even utilize demand feeders where trout push little levers hanging in the water to get food.[45] It would be interesting to see if trout exhibit any more self-control than typical kids at self-serve soda fountains.

Supplying hatcheries with fish food is an industry in itself, and some clever entrepreneurs decided there is even commercial profit in small-scale sale of trout pellets. They figured that trout trained to eat pellets in a hatchery might also like to eat pellets when they are released to streams. For less than $5, Cabela's or Bass Pro Shops sell *Berkley's PowerBait, Hatchery Formula Trout Nuggets*. According to the product description, it is "in a size and shape that perfectly mimics the food that hatchery fish were raised on."[46] If Pennsylvania is willing to spend $1 million on pellets every year, $5 is a pretty small personal investment to catch their fish. Maybe someday someone will design a fishing lure that looks just like the little pendulum levers used in the demand feeders at hatcheries. They would perhaps seem natural to a stocked trout, probably sell like hotcakes, and help the hatcheries both fund and justify the costs of their stocking programs.

Despite the high costs of running hatcheries, trout fishing is still a very profitable business because of anglers' loose spending habits. Whatever the real numbers are for the economic impact of trout fishing, equipment manufacturers, outfitters, guide services, and fishing stores all recognize the revenue opportunities and reach out to potential customers using a myriad of advertising media. Print provides a tried-and-true method for commercial enterprises to search for clientele. Magazines that include *Field and Stream, Trout, Fly Rod & Reel, Fly Fisherman, Gray's Sporting Journal*, and *American Angler* compete for readers and advertisers. There is often a relationship between magazine publishers and advertisers because editorial staffs must cater the theme and style of content to attract advertising dollars. If an advertiser does not like something in print, the editors often hear about it. Interestingly, many state fishing guides and magazines are supported by revenue received from selling ads to equipment suppliers and guide services. Some of the biggest outfitters and fishing supply sellers in the country buy advertising space in the publications state agencies produce to educate anglers about fishing regulations and safety issues. Commercial interests and government management functions coexist in pages of state publications, much the way their agendas intermingle in streams. What seems unclear is how these interactions influence state agencies as they work to balance fish production and environmental protection.

Fishing reaches into many homes on widescreen TVs where television and cable networks broadcast fishing shows on sporting channels. The World Fishing Network provides full-time coverage, while the Sportsman's Channel, Outdoor Channel, Untamed Sports, Wild TV, Outside Television, Tuff TV, and Pursuit Channel mix several fishing shows in with a range of other programming. The shows themselves are often independently produced and distributed with an affable host purportedly revealing his most prized fishing secrets to national audiences. L.L. Bean and Orvis both host their own fishing shows. It is not hard to guess their underlying motivations. The host's nuggets of wisdom are carefully segmented by commercial breaks filled with new angling products and far-off opportunities for fishing adventures. Thanks to the miracle of modern digital cable, anglers can now spend hours surfing the television waves to catch fishing shows and deals on fishing equipment instead of catching real fish. When angling becomes less about being outside and more about spending on advertised products, the justification for manipulating rivers with hatchery fish grows stronger.

The United States is a country of consumers, but trout fishing can become less about consuming fish and more about spending money on cool equipment and impressive vacation getaways. At the end of the nineteenth century, purchase of equipment was viewed as a way to demonstrate personal wealth.[47] When you calculate the true cost to catch fish in a stream today, the continuing trend becomes clear. Fresh trout fillets cost about $10 to $15 per pound at local stores. Computing the average value of a fish caught on a fly rod takes more guesswork. Anglers first need to invest in equipment. A moderately priced fly rod runs approximately $200. Be advised that according to Joe Brooks, "an angler perfectly equipped to fish for all species of trout dealt within [his] book would need a minimum of six rods."[48] Furthermore, readers of *Gray's Sporting Journal* have amassed, on average, twenty-one fishing rods.[49] If that is the mean, it certainly would be interesting to learn how many rods the magazine's true collectors owned. A reel and fishing line add $150. A single fly costs a couple of dollars, so figure $50 in total for a good selection and some spares. In fact, Art Lee warned that the purchase of flies and lures is often the angler's biggest long-term equipment expense.[50] The customary fishing uniform, comprised of a vest and waders, can easily run $250 or more. Rose-colored glasses sell for $50 or so. With luck you can piece together the rest of your ensemble from scraps at home. That comes to a total of $700. If this estimate sounds a bit high, just consider that a *New York Times* article suggested the equipment necessary to fish for both trout and bass ran approximately $250 in 1907, equaling in excess of $5,000 in today's inflation-corrected currency.[51]

Even after laying down a week's worth of $100 bills, newbie fly casters will rub elbows with anglers who have outspent them by a $1,000 or more. Like a less dominant trout, they can always swim away to a smaller pool if the big fish scare them. And, be advised that pressure to spend more exists. As a case in point, John Bailey warned: "It is a foolish angler who takes no interest in the tools of the trade, and nothing is worse than being let down by equipment at the end of a battle with the fish of a lifetime. Believe me, you don't get over that, ever."[52] If you follow his advice, it may be cheaper to spend money on fishing equipment than the therapy needed to overcome the trauma of losing the big one. Therefore, anglers might want to follow the *L.L. Bean Fly-Fishing Handbook* suggestion to accessorize like the Swiss Army knife of fly fishing.[53] They will want to purchase a wading staff, small knife, clippers, hook sharpener, scissors, compass, folding cup, thermometer, small whistle and eighteen other necessities. Knowing that L.L. Bean makes its money equipping people, we should ignore their advice and just stick to the essentials. If we assume that anglers take good care of their bare-bones $700 equipment, and it lasts for a decade, our yield will be an annual subtotal of $70. A resident fishing license in most states will add at least $20 per year. Ignoring travel, food, and other miscellaneous expenses, our total is approximately $90 a year. The sum of expenditures will be equivalent to about six to nine pounds of store-bought trout fillet each year for a total of ten years.

Now we need to figure out how many fish to catch to accumulate all that meat. A trout of ten inches might weigh about 0.45 pounds or so. Gutting and beheading the fish removes about one-third of the weight. If we are lucky, that leaves about five ounces of fillet and skin for every ten-inch trout caught. To yield six to nine pounds of fillet will require the capture of twenty to thirty ten-inch trout a year. In 1995, the Illinois Department of Natural Resources managed the state's waters to maintain salmonid catch rates of fifteen to twenty fish per one hundred hours.[54] They wanted to see that anyone willing to put in five to seven hours fishing would go home happy. In that state, it would take one hundred to two hundred hours of fishing a year to reach a break-even point. That is a maximum hourly pay rate of $0.90 per hour, incredibly below the federal minimum wage. Theoretically, you could not legally pay anybody enough to fly fish for trout and get a price close to market value!

Trout anglers are usually more concerned about the fish caught than the money spent, so these calculations will do little to dissuade them. It is certainly everybody's legal right to overpay for trout if they want. However, the existing federal and state legislation ensures that a portion of money anglers spend becomes trapped in a tax system that reinvests money in fisheries that primarily benefit wealthier individuals. State and local governments then run programs in public schools that purport to have educational missions, but ultimately serve as recruiting tools to attract more wealthy anglers. As an example, the Trout in the Classroom program in Pennsylvania includes almost one hundred schools, but only three locations in Philadelphia County,[55] where 12 percent of the state's population resides, the percentage of people below the poverty level is twice the state average, and whites are a minority.[56] Yet, in nearby Chester County, which contains one-third the population of Philadelphia County, enjoys more than twice the median income, and is 88 percent white,[57] the program is active in three schools with 50 percent more students in total. This one example suggests that median income, not population density, is a better predictor of where the program's environmental education funds will be directed. This type of inequitable situation should raise concerns about social injustices perpetuated by government educational outreach programs and the taxation systems that support them.

The connection between wealth and angling is as true today as it was in the past. Although it seems impossible to fully characterize the financial assets of all trout anglers, a 2006 national survey by the U.S. Fish and Wildlife Service provides one snapshot. Nationally, 63 percent of trout anglers earned more than the median household income, and almost one-quarter earned more than double the national average. In 2008, the marketing department for Trout Unlimited's *Trout* magazine provided useful demographic data for its publication and its competitors, *Fly Rod & Reel, Fly Fisherman, Gray's Sporting Journal,* and *American Angler.*[58] The five magazines combine for a circulation of more than 400,000 readers. The data was intended to attract advertisers, but it is just as useful to pigeonhole trout anglers. For baseline purposes, the 2010 median household income for the country was just under $50,000.[59] In comparison, the average household income for readers of these five magazines ranged from a respectable $112,600 to a haughty $252,900, or between two and five times the national income average. Remember, this is not the maximum income for those readers. For *Trout* magazine readers in particular, 40 percent had household incomes between $100,000 and $250,000, and 9 percent had household incomes more than five times the national average. At *Gray's Sporting Journal* almost 15 percent of its readers had median incomes in excess of $500,000.

Between 59 percent and 75 percent of readers at three of the five magazines worked in professional or managerial positions, and four magazines reported that between 85 to more than 95 percent of their readers attended college.[60] The demographic results are partially explained by the fact that income and educational background are often correlated. Because the numbers show that trout anglers tend to receive more years of education, the U.S. Fish and Wildlife Service concluded: "It's safe to say that trout anglers are among the most educated anglers."[61] But, that does not prove trout fishing is a smart thing to do. For the prestigious *Gray's Sporting Journal*, almost 40 percent of its readers hold graduate degrees. Meanwhile, the national average is only about 10 percent.[62]

Wealthy trout anglers are good spenders. Together, the 135,000 readers of *Trout* magazine annually spent $57 million on fishing supplies and almost $15 million on fly-tying tools.[63] Their online and catalog purchases equaled $95 million, with almost $33 million of that directed toward fishing-related products. Readers from all five angling magazines averaged between fifteen and thirty-seven days of fishing a year.[64] The national average was closer to eleven days for those participating in the sport in 2006.[65] *Trout* magazine readers alone spent more than $170 million on fishing trips, one-third used fishing guides, and more than half took a fishing trip of more than five hundred miles.[66] The average expenditure worked out to $1,766 on travel, with a mean expense of $869 per trip. Every dollar spent helped governments buy items including more food pellets for hatcheries, more gasoline for stocking trucks, or new agency brochures for school kids.

Throughout the book I have carefully avoided use of the term *fisherman* except in specific instances when it was clear the person was male. I really did not need to bother. Today, as in the past, trout angling is a male-dominated sport. According to marketing material from Trout Unlimited, 96 to 99 percent of readers for the five magazines were male.[67] These lopsided numbers mirror trends reported throughout the country. A National Park Service study indicated that 95 percent of anglers were male at Great Smoky National Park.[68] Pennsylvania estimated that 91 percent of the state's trout anglers are men.[69] The best current national estimate suggested that women comprised 52 percent of the U.S. population but only 21 percent of all trout anglers in 2006.[70] Trout anglers also bucked national averages for age. Three-quarters of all trout anglers were over the age of 35, and this population became more skewed toward the older generations in the last decade. Similarly, readers of the trout magazines had median ages ranging from 47 to 53.3 years old.[71] When people picture a typical trout angler, it certainly would not be unfair to envision an older man holding a rod. The combination of extreme wealth and male domination in fishing today mirrors the famous "old boy network" that is always hard to identify in certain terms.

It certainly seems that trout anglers are not your average Joe. If you are wondering who Trout Unlimited did consider Mr. Joe Q. Angler, the organization website reported that "the average reader of *Trout* magazine is a college-educated, fifty-one-year-old, married man with an annual income of $97,115 and a household income of $122,957."[72] Not bad, Joe. Not bad at all.

Trout angling clearly benefits a subgroup of Americans that would not look out of place in most corporate boardrooms. With wealth comes power and political connections. Members of Trout Unlimited contribute to the organization's lobbying activities, which help to guarantee that politicians understand and value the economic power represented by the group. Over the years, trout angling proponents have used the legislative system to put into practice government laws, including the Dingell-Johnson Act, to ensure tax revenues generated from angling expenditures were reinvested in sports fisheries. Subsequent spending by government fish and game agencies eventually benefited mostly older, wealthy, male citizens. Anglers reinvested in the sport, some privatized good stretches of water; their demand for equipment and travel helped drive up prices. States enacted laws to prevent fishing for food on some rivers and other areas were set aside for fishing with flies only. The high cost for trout angling equipment and the inaccessibility of many trout streams now makes it more difficult for less privileged individuals to have financial and physical access to the sport. Meanwhile, wealthy anglers know that every dollar they spend on fishing equipment puts pennies in state fish and game agency piggy banks to fund band-aid restoration projects and keep trout rolling out of hatchery gates. The most revered rivers often get more reared fish because state surveys ensure trout are supplied where demand is highest. America's most famous fishing waters attract both hatchery trucks and wealthy anglers. Here, the history of wealth and privatization is clearly written on the landscape.

The Catskills are full of symbols of wealth. When I first visited the Beaverkill River, I was astounded at the number of No Trespassing signs. Signs were posted with incredible regularity to bar anybody foolish enough to think that they had a right to fish these waters. Most postings had a club name or property owner scribbled along the bottom. It was as if local landowners held stock in companies that made these signs. Near a prominent bridge, I noticed that signs were even hung by wire across the river facing toward the bridge. Maybe the signs held a warning to kingfishers flying down along the river, or perhaps landowners were worried that eager anglers might leap from the bridge in their over exuberance to fish the region's sacred waters. The situation is much the same in the Rocky Mountains as famed angling author John Gierach reported: "A sign saying 'Come See the Real West' means this is one place where the real West no longer exists. Signs in the real West say 'No Trespassing.'"[73] Today as in the past, many of the best places on rivers are reserved for affluent anglers. Concerns over poaching persist. A 1994 book designed to introduce children to fly fishing discussed the state of Connecticut's Turn in Poachers Program and suggested direct confrontation may be "necessary" in some circumstances to prevent poaching.[74] The doctor and author stated: "There are some sour truths that children must learn on the path to adulthood. These include all the awful 'p' words: pain, pestilence, plague, and poachers."[75] The author certainly did choose an interesting cluster of evils for our nation's youth to consider. Perhaps if I provide a plea that poaching is not a principal pandemic and pursuing open opposition to prowlers presents the problem of potentially putting petite pupils in peril, this published physician would perceive my point. On second thought, maybe I am just p'ing into the wind.

Exclusive fishing clubs continue to surface elsewhere today. According to a website for the now defunct Spring Ridge Club, they established one of the most exclusive groups in central Pennsylvania just nineteen miles west of Pennsylvania State University.[76] Donny Beaver started the club in 2001, establishing a cluster of cabins, cottages, and lodges on 125 acres at the confluence of the Little Juniata River and Spruce Creek. The club leased almost ten miles of land on five channels. The membership fee was around $75,000 with annual dues a bit more than $4,000. The club got into a lawsuit with a local river guide and the state when it posted No Trespassing signs and erected cables across the waterway to keep out nonmember anglers on what the state insisted was a publicly navigable waterway. In the United States, landowners own land as the name implies, but have no legal right to bar access to people traveling by boat along navigable rivers. Although the definition of a navigable waterway is not always that easy to put into practice, streams suitable for canoe passage can fit the description. The club eventually lost its case in court in 2006 and dropped its appeal in 2008.[77] Meanwhile, the commercial endeavor went through a number of name changes and currently hides under the label Homewaters Club, which is perhaps a bit ironic considering the lost lawsuit. The latest website claimed more than thirty-five miles of water under their control in Pennsylvania, with a reciprocal agreement with the Alpine River Club of Colorado and their private holdings in the Vail and Steamboat Springs areas.[78] Both clubs advertised opportunities to fish away from the general public for those who can afford the experience. In 2012, Homewaters Club membership was just $50,000 for the top tier package and as low as $475 for a single day. As fairly recent publications pointed out: "Fishing was part of a gentleman's training in Walton's time."[79] If $50,000 seems like a bargain to establish your credentials, Homewaters will open its doors after you open your checkbook.

Unlike the Homewaters Club, which seems desperate for recruits and income, the Anglers' Club of New York currently does not maintain a public website. Membership is by introduction only.[80] In fact, getting any details about the club is very difficult. Since 1940, the club has been housed in a twenty-five-hundred-square-foot space within a modest, landmarked building on Broad Street adjacent to Fraunces Tavern.[81] The tavern is a building of historic importance in the American Revolution and was acquired in 1904 by the Sons of the Revolution. According to the Anglers' Club of New York director, the club has a private restaurant, open Monday to Friday from 11:00 AM to 5:00 PM, where some of the six hundred members enjoy each other's company and trade stories about their fishing experiences.[82] However, few members enjoyed their dinner on January 24, 1975, when a bomb planted by the Fuerzas Armadas de Liberación Nacional, or FALN, detonated at Fraunces Tavern, killing four and wounding more than fifty others. FALN was a Puerto Rican separatist group that used terrorist tactics in a fight for independence. Both buildings were probably logical targets as symbols of capitalism and elitism in America; the official FALN communiqué from the day of the bombing referenced the "reactionary corporate executives inside."[83] It is perhaps the most bizarre example of the incredible wealth, political power, and notoriety associated with American trout anglers.

~ ~ ~ Economic spending by federal and state governments extends beyond budgets used to grow fish in hatcheries. States spend thousands of dollars each year to physically modify rivers and streams for various purposes, usually with NCD methods. These expenditures include money spent to train restoration experts at courses taught by Rosgen and others. From one standpoint, state and federal money spent on restoration courses would be wasted if people who received training did not themselves design and manage restoration projects. One the other hand, projects primarily designed to create better trout fishing with physical modifications and no monitoring could be equally wasteful. Either way, river restoration itself recently became big business with more than $1 billion a year spent on projects in the United States alone.[84] As long as fishing continues to be a major driver of these projects, underlying economic motivations of government agencies and environmental concerns for nongame species will surface. I recently went on a small excursion in Connecticut to visit one restoration site that represents just a sliver of the national spending to create new habitats for trout. The design was inspired by lessons learned in one of Rosgen's courses and now serves as a bit of an exhibition for the state inland fisheries agency.

The Hop River Trail occupies the former rail bed of the Hartford, Providence, and Fishkill Railroad, which began operations in 1849. The old cinder-covered rail bed is one of many in the region recently reclaimed as a transportation route in an initiative to convert rails to trails. My family and I love to seek out new bike trails and this route along the Hop River was a favorite. From Willimantic we began a slow steady northwest bicycle climb along a path that was at times wide and smooth, but narrowed to gravelly single-track sections in places. Early on we caught glimpses of the Hop River where it was deep and dark. Just a mile or two upstream the sun penetrated a few feet of water to reveal a boulder bed that was covered with a chocolate brown layer of growth. The trail continued alongside wetlands with black nutrient and ion-filled waters, their nearly stagnant flows connecting to the river under small bridges. Further along, the old rail line traversed higher along the sides of the valley in search of elevation to cross a distant drainage divide.

As the miles tallied on, the Hop River decreased in size and was eventually lost to the distant valley bottom. Small tributaries tumbled over rocks and down steeper slopes in search of the waiting river below. Other channels contained only dry rocky beds, but showed evidence of recent rain-filled flows. The gradient of the trail slowly increased and after ten miles of travel we all downshifted, resigning ourselves to a new slower pace. As the trail began to turn more northerly, tall walls of bedrock — still stained black from years of sooty steam locomotive passage — emerged to warn of the final push toward Bolton Notch. These rock cutouts bookended old drainage ditches on both sides of the trail that were once excavated to keep railroad ties from rotting. Water trickled back downgrade and eventually found its way to the Hop River, then the Willimantic River, Shetucket River, Quinebaug River, Thames River, and finally Long Island Sound. After a few more pedal strokes, shadows of a dark tunnel under a modern highway appeared along the old commuter rail route. The sound of our huffing and puffing replaced the noise of steam exhaust emanating from the portal.

A short distance north, the old route passed between another set of black-smeared rocky walls where the railroad blasted through hillsides to provide a faster, more direct route to Hartford. Rusty water ran on both side of the trail but flowed north toward a small drainage that in due course emptied into the Connecticut River. Less than a quarter of a mile later another fairly inconspicuous stream appeared, emanating from a small pond adjacent to the interstate. This stream ran into a pile of riprap, juked left and then wound a bit back and forth through knee-high plants in a garden-sized opening below tall trees. The brook eventually entered a corrugated metal culvert and crossed under the rail trail. Here water followed the old drainage channel and flowed for nine hundred feet immediately adjacent to the old railway embankment. Except for a slightly increased flow, the channel appeared similar to other drainage canals cut along the old railway, but it wasn't.

The history of the stream is revealed by the name itself. Railroad Brook did not exist in this section before engineers and dynamite reconfigured the landscape and moved a length of stream.[85] Although the stream flows for almost three miles, it was the quarter-mile-long section of brook immediately adjacent to the trail that caught the state's attention. During railway construction, this length of waterway was relocated to make way for the right-of-way. As a result, it looked nothing like a natural Connecticut stream two decades ago. The state was particularly concerned about nonpoint source pollution. The problem of siltation was of special interest because the brook often flooded and robbed the rail bed of its sediment. Luckily, bedrock lined sections of the channel and prevented erosion from stirring up too much trouble. Because the gravel rail bed offered few places for roots to take hold, the brook contained few streamside plants. Despite all these problems, the stream still maintained a small population of brook trout, albeit with poor growth and survival rates, and some blacknose dace. Because less than 2 percent of Connecticut's fourteen thousand miles of streams currently contain healthy populations of brook trout, any pocket of promise is of interest to the state.[86] The inland fisheries folks figured a cleverly devised project could solve issues in the stream and benefit resident populations of fish.

In 2000, the state spent one month and $122,100 to remake the brook. The upstream 300 feet of channel was relocated to a new Rosgenesque course, trained to follow a meandering path and lined with lunkers and riprap to ensure it stayed there. Downstream the rail bed was raised 1.5 feet to prevent flooding of the trail, and deflectors and grade control structures were sprinkled in at nicely spaced intervals. Gravel was imported to the site and placed along the bed of the channel to provide a more natural substrate for fish. Large blocks of stone were set along the side of the channel to prevent bank erosion and provide a clear separation of trail and trout. Shrubs were arranged here and there to add foliage along the trail edge. The state then made sure to plant a series of signs to explain the project. Photographs show before and after shots with short titles that help introduce trail users to terminology adopted by Rosgen devotees. Adult bikers stop to look at signs while kids play in the stream and look for fish, frogs, and other signs of life.

Railroad Brook was not much to look at even in its restored state. It reminded me of many of the neighborhood streams I explored as a kid. Most elementary-age visitors could easily hop back and forth across the waterway without wetting their sneakers. Even if they did stumble in, water depths were mostly less than a foot deep. The brook was a perfect place to race toy boats with young friends, skipping along the cinder trail to cheer the entries in the little flotilla. The elfin carved kayaks might scare fish but few people would care. No self-respecting fly angler would consider casting into the stream—even if they did manage to place their favorite Eastern green drake on the water surface, the majority of their floating line would land on dry ground! They would probably have more luck catching trout with their bare hands. It seems like a very unlikely place for the state to build a demonstration project to highlight the value of channel restoration. For the cost of roughly $100 per foot of restored channel, one-third the cost of many projects in New York and one-seventh those in urban areas,[87] the state completed a project that seemed more at home on a model railroad layout than a natural landscape.

The upstream section generally looked like a natural channel and fallen branches augmented the habitat artificially created by lunkers. A sign explained that LUNKERS are "Little Underwater Neighborhood Keepers Encompassing Reotactic Salmonids." Unfortunately, *rheotactic* is misspelled on the sign and few people understand that this scientific jargon refers only to fish that swim in place in strong currents. Downstream along the brook, things did not fare well. The stream decided to do some of its own remodeling in the last few years and eroded away much of the stone-lined artificial bank that was created for it. The rail trail again slowly sloped toward the stream in places and readily surrendered its silt. Some of the fancy log revetments were missing and the remaining deflectors created few deep areas. The few plants on the edge of the trail were short leafy weeds and grasses that added only a splash of green. Without signs placed by the state to explain the restoration process, few people would suspect the state knew the place existed.

The state made sure that people knew about their efforts by placing signs and posting webpages on the project. Three months after the restoration was completed, the state produced an online document titled "Success Stories," which touted the venture.[88] They also promised to conduct a four-year population study to determine the effectiveness of the reconfiguration and instream structures. Population results eventually appeared on a second webpage and showed that brook trout populations increased by 178 percent the fourth year compared to before the state modified the stream.[89] Of course 2004, the year selected for comparison, was a bit of a post-project anomaly since its population was more than two times any of the previous three years and more than three times the following four years.[90] The 2004 population increase was largely due to big numbers of newborn trout, though few of those fish seemed to survive the following year. This suggests the project failed to improve survival rates as hoped. Furthermore, the state's website failed to mention that blacknose dace, the other target of the project, experienced a 39 percent population decrease. Although population numbers were collected until 2008, the agency did not update the website to report the 17 percent decrease in the number of brook trout and 65 percent decrease in blacknose dace populations from 2005 to 2008. Perhaps most interesting, the agency's use of percentages camouflaged the fact that even at the height of project success in 2004, the entire $122,100 outlay increased the total number of brook trout in the restored reach from a preproject average of just more than nineteen trout to a temporary high of sixty-seven brookies. That worked out to $2,557 per extra fish even if we ignore blacknose dace data like the state did.

One place where things improved was in the new meandering portion of the channel where five additional trout and almost nine hundred blacknose dace were spotted in 2002 and 2003. Obviously, any new section of water provided more aquatic habitat than the soil it replaced, but nine hundred dace seemed pretty good for a three-hundred-foot section. In the restored drainage ditch, the number of trout over the age of one also increased from the low preproject average of 0.5 trout in the two-year-old or older class to an average of 2.6 and a maximum of 5 older trout after completion. Elsewhere there was little evidence of ecological benefits from the educational endeavor.

Because of the state's preoccupation with problems of sedimentation, one goal of the project was to reduce erosion, a presumed problem for populations of fish below the restored reach. However, the population downstream averaged 14 fewer trout and only 2 more blacknose dace per year by project end. In the ultimate test of the enterprise, comparing the four years before the project was undertaken versus the last four years the State bothered to collect data, the annual average of just less than 317 of all types of fish found before the state fixed things dropped to only 264 fish after they were done. The restoration effort was probably not the direct cause of fish population declines, but it certainly did not help. State fisheries biologists and private project engineers had good intentions, but either their NCD methods were flawed or Railroad Brook was not the right place to restore a trout fishery. In Rosgen's words, they had "their heart-to-cranium ratio out of whack."

Restoring ecological health to a waterway with native species is obviously a good thing. I give credit to the state for caring about a place that is of little interest to anglers. But Railroad Brook is a place that still gets me a bit steamed up. Turning a drainage ditch along a railway right-of-way into a miniature demonstration project of deflectors and lunkers to house tiny trout seems a waste of valuable restoration dollars. Advertising the project as a success and hiding the project's deficiencies from the public perpetuates misconceptions and bad ideas about river restoration using manufactured devices. Providing misleading advertising information sounds more like the profit-driven tactics of a commercial enterprise than government attempts at environmental protection ruled by good science. For some reason, the state picked an old earthen gutter called Railroad Brook to highlight what was learned in restoration class. The project ultimately teaches us much more than the agency perhaps wanted to reveal.

CHAPTER ELEVEN

Reel Retreats Restored to Real Places

Man who is changing the surface of this earth and its fauna and flora more rapidly than any process of nature heretofore. Man the prodigal destroyer, but who must become the restorer, or his very existence will become as much a chapter of past history as is the chapter of the Ichthyosaur.

— HENRY INGRAHAM, 1926

*I*n 2011, I decided to go back to Massachusetts to find the deflectors on the Swift River I had stumbled upon as a kid. Part of me wondered if my Swift childhood recollections accurately reflected the realities of the river or were influenced by more recent experiences. These deflectors subconsciously started a spark that did not fully ignite until I finally staggered across similar CCC deflectors at Veteran's Fishing Area. I was heartened but melancholy when I returned more than thirty years after my first visit and found triangular shapes that looked pretty much as I remembered. A week after my return trip, I was amazed to learn that Clark Hubbs, Carl's son, served as a CCC stream survey leader for the western Massachusetts region in 1942 only three years after Quabbin Reservoir was completed on the Swift River.[1] I immediately recognized the possibility that Clark might have installed these same deflectors, but I decided to leave that question alone. At this stage of my life, I understand the complex history of these strange devices of deflection better, and I now appreciate how a pile of wood and rock can change the direction of a person's life.

I now realize that rivers bursting with restoration devices, streams full of structures and waterways overloaded with exotic hatchery products are not real places. Practices that utilized fence material, concrete blocks, tar paper, steel rods, plastic sheeting and even worn tires to create aquatic habitat for trout have trashed these streams, highlighting the lack of respect paid to waterways by anglers in the past.[2] Maybe fishing is fine, thanks to heavy stocking, but any sense of wildness is an illusion. The environment is just a shadow of a healthy ecosystem. Natural channel complexity is reduced. Biodiversity is diminished. Perhaps the most disturbing fact is that with newer habitat-improvement methods it is often difficult to identify alterations and reconfigurations. Despite professional training, it took me years to comfortably distinguish what is natural and what is manmade in some places. I fear that repeated efforts to restore rivers for trout will result in such a cacophony of changes that people will forget what a real river looks like. If we lose real rivers, we lose healthy ecosystems.

Luckily, not all is doom and gloom in the world of river restoration. One of the most exciting and important developments began in the last two decades and is barreling ahead with growing speed. States, with strong support by many environmental and fishing groups, are ending the damnation of rivers by removing hydropower impoundments. What started as localized efforts in small watersheds with low dams, later expanded into a major undertaking with large barriers coming down in the Penobscot and Kennebec Rivers in Maine and the Elwah and White Salmon Rivers in Washington. Trout Unlimited, American Rivers, The Nature Conservancy, state and federal fisheries biologists, civil engineers and geomorphologists often work in successful collaborations to bring down dams that long prevented sediments from descending and salmon and trout from ascending rivers. For the first time in my life, the number of big dams in the United States is decreasing. Although dam removal is not without some pitfalls, largely because of a legacy of contaminated sediments behind many impoundments, the long-term benefits of dam removal outweigh the costs in most places. Obviously, because of the massive scale of disturbance with dam removal something will need to be done to reestablish healthy ecosystems in the sediment laden wastelands that were once reservoirs. The challenge is to develop better ways to enhance aquatic ecosystems through natural means that help to reinstate rivers of old.

At this point in a book it is customary to point the direction forward. But instead of pointing to the future, I will look to the past for inspiration on how to save rivers from ourselves. Henry Ingraham's quote at the beginning of the chapter is as accurate now as it was then. He invoked a call to action that still has not been answered to any great satisfaction. Saving our nation's waters is important. Waters need to be protected and rivers revived. However, I am not in favor of many of the activities termed "conservation" or "restoration" in the past stipulations that measure success solely with regard to trout angling. Restoration was often about creation of the angler's vision of an aquatic Eden, where perception trumps reality. I suggest that the term *restoration* needs to be carefully reserved for the loftiest of goals. Tinkering with trout streams to yield more fish to catch does not give birth to a restorer. Maybe even the words *restore* and *restoration* are not strong enough anymore. They have been diluted by countless one-sided projects benefiting trout at the expense of ecosystems as a whole. Someday our faith in the word might be reestablished, but right now it is a political hornet's nest. A stronger ideal is needed to represent true rehabilitation, and I will borrow from Carl Hubbs and suggest we must try for *ultra-preservation*. We need to create and vigorously protect at least a few places where nature, not man, determines the future course of rivers and the trout they contain.

In 1885, before local rivers were damaged by massive stocking efforts and genetic manipulation, bituminous highways, and mass-produced automobiles were mostly science fiction, Van Cleef wrote,

I have become satisfied that the destruction of the trees bordering on these streams and the changed condition of the banks produced thereby, has resulted in the destruction of the natural harbors or hiding places of the trout, that this is the main cause of the depletion, and that until these harbors are restored, it will be useless to hope for any practical benefit from restocking them.[3]

At the time, stream improvement was still an experiment yet to be tried. Our understanding and appreciation for the complexity of aquatic ecosystems and river processes was infantile, but Van Cleef clearly exhibited a scientific mind and a love for trout unrivaled by most anglers that followed him. He saw a fairly simple problem and recommended a simple solution. So maybe after more than 125 years, it is finally time to listen and take his advice. We should not invade the home of trout and instead try to put back what we took from rivers. It is time to abide by the true meaning of the word *restore*, and bring back our nation's rivers by providing nature with the tools, space and time needed to act like real rivers. Reestablishing vegetated corridors along rivers is a good start.

Although past trout restoration projects inspired by Hewitt, Hubbs, and Rosgen tended to copy methods from other regions and homogenize the look of waterways, ideal rivers will look very different in Nebraska versus New York. In prairies, natural rivers will migrate through sections of tall blowing grasses to create undercut banks that provide cover habitat for fish. Blocks of sod will slump into streams and provide new sources of nourishment and greater impetus for sinuous changes. Perhaps a New York creek will require addition of wood and snags as Van Cleef suggested. Wood will provide structure and habitat for a myriad of organisms while protecting brook trout from predators that include anglers. Back in 1870, fishing legend John Burroughs described the difficulty of fly casting on several famous Catskill trout rivers because he was constantly snagging trees.[4] He found trout were small but plentiful. Modern angling has lost its historical perspective; today trout streams are revered when they hold a few large fish that can be easily seen and targeted with a fly. This vision of the perfect trout stream does not fit the realities of a natural river, one historically chocked with large woody debris. Few people seem to call for rivers that contain fewer large fish and more obstacles to casting. But if trout anglers want to really connect with nature, they must accept the good with the bad and seek out the authentic rivers of the past.

In medicine, increasing numbers of health care providers treat the whole body instead of merely treating symptoms. They now help patients understand the root of problems in their combined search for long-term well-being. Watersheds need holistic medicine too, not reach-scale restoration. Patching up a reach of river here and there does not solve the problems aquatic ecosystems face. Almost one hundred years ago, Wilson Armistead laid out the basic problem with reach-scale river management when he said,

> Whilst a trout stream should be treated as a whole, it is usually divided
> into sections over which different owners have control. This is a very seri-
> ous handicap, because it is practically impossible to deal with any section
> of a stream without having regard to the waters above and those below.[5]

It was a clear a call for watershed-scale management. It is time to follow his advice. The establishment of the Connecticut River Blueway is an excellent example of large-scale thinking that needs to be embraced to solve local problems. Cooperation of various government agencies needs support from countless contributions by landowners who will use fewer fertilizers, herbicides, and pesticides. Construction workers and farmers need to care about erosion problems and constantly work to limit impacts associated with their professions, not simply throw up hastily devised silt fences and hay bales to avoid fines. Driveways and parking lots should be reconstructed to encourage infiltration of rainwater instead of shuffling flooding problems through a culvert to downstream neighbors. These types of "best management practices" are widely acknowledged, but it takes money, political will and individual responsibility to put these ideas into action. Inviting a few trout into the classroom and recruiting young anglers, as Trout Unlimited does, might be one way to encourage the next generation to care. Alternatively, more diverse educational programs and opportunities to explore local brooks could prove even more successful. However it is to be achieved, we need people to deeply care about the water they drink and the streams that flow through their towns: the genuine landscape of our nation's native trout.

It is with a good deal of frustration that I must admit I do not have all the answers to fix rivers in this country. Dumping logs in rivers might improve some habitats, but will not solve all problems. In limited cases, instream structures might be needed to save a building or even a stream. In places where species are endangered, hatcheries might continue to be part of the solution. Maybe a heron or cormorant will need to be shot to protect the last of a dying breed of cutthroat trout swimming in a concrete pen. Because nobody has yet figured out a foolproof way to restore aquatic habitat, future projects must still be considered experimental. But I hope that people will pay attention this time and take careful notes so that we can learn from our past mistakes and forge a better future.

Sadly, as I conclude this book, I am unable to paint a picture of the perfect wild river because, despite my travels, I am not sure I have ever really seen one. Perhaps it is the uncertainty itself that is most disheartening. New England lost its wildness long ago when it lost its old-growth forests, historic salmon runs, and rivers dominated by brook trout. When I traveled cross-country headed west, the Black Hills of South Dakota provided a welcome relief after miles of flatter landscape, but the streams also contained exotic trout. In Utah, cinnamon-colored sandstone is carved into amazing shapes and contours at a scale that dwarfs human sculptures. Even the time-less tortured canyons I saw in the Escalante region endured the wrath of exotic invasive species of plants. Rivers I explored ended in bathtub rings that still frame Lake Powell and its collection of introduced game fish. In Alaska I stood along small creeks choked with red salmon preparing salmon redds. I spotted their fins from a highway headed to Valdez. I overlooked both salmon and silhouettes of distant buildings. The fish waved goodbye with their tails as they swam away from the oily harbor city that threatens to assault their offspring with another ill-fated tanker. In the United States, most rivers display scars left by humans. Perhaps a few spots still hold hints of a wilder past, but these special places are much too hard to uncover.

The wildest river I know well is North Saint Vrain Creek in the aptly named Wild Basin region of Rocky Mountain National Park. It is a land of clear cold water and a backdrop of snow-capped mountains. I spent years investigating this river as a graduate student. Interestingly, North Saint Vrain Creek eventually flowed past the home of famous fishing writer, John Gierach. Perhaps we saw each other one day, but never met. Maybe our attention was intent on our own view of the river, and we both somehow missed the big picture. North Saint Vrain Creek was part of Gierach's frequent pursuit of trout. The creek was part of my quest to become a scientist. It was also the last place that I ever fished. I was fly fishing for trout, but somehow I just did not feel good about what I was doing. I knew this river and knew these trout, but catching them as a hunter did not seem to fit with my main occupation as an observer of nature. I was not interested in modifying the landscape or even capturing it. I wanted to understand the place I'd come to love, and leave only footprints. Unlike the folks who stocked the river with rainbow trout, I wanted to keep North Saint Vrain Creek as I found it.

When I think about rainbows and North Saint Vrain Creek, I always remember the trout I saw that almost caught a hummingbird. Part of me was happy for both the bird and trout. Both were strong healthy creatures fighting for survival in a somewhat wild place. This fish went for broke, driven by the promise of a huge reward. I often think about that event and remind myself that sometimes it is good to take a chance on a long shot. Perhaps the idea of a river that shows no sign of human influence is a long shot, but isn't it worth the chance? As parents, environmentalists, or lovers of rivers, we all should be inspired to beat the odds and fight for purity of nature. We should fight for truly wild rivers. Not all rivers, perhaps, but at least a few more scattered through the country. I do not pretend to have all the answers on how to achieve this goal. I am not capable of painting what is desired. Nor do I have a blueprint for the ideal river. But, I do have a vision in my head. That is, at least, a place to start.

Picture a river just visible in the emerging light of a sunrise vibrantly painting it with the colors of nature. The day's first rays escape over distant snow-covered peaks to illuminate the water. A steady gurgling beat emanates from below as thousands of tiny bubbles inflate, then implode in the flow. Sunlight flickers on the rippled surface creating a visually pulsing sensation that is both stimulating and mesmerizing. Seconds or perhaps minutes indiscernibly tick by as you search in vain for signs of earlier travelers. The water is in constant motion, but the sense of change is marked only as occasional leaves gently twist past on their voyage downstream. In a peaceful reverie your mind gently takes you below the ripples. Down here life abounds and the feel of oxygen surrounds you in the clear cold water. Native trout, just discernible in your periphery, interact seamlessly with the environment. They sway just above the rocks as they dance to the rhythm of the flow. You rock gently back and forth on your feet as you imagine the strong steady current tickling your sides. This is the river of your dreams, and the place where you have always wanted to visit. It certainly is beautiful, but how can you get there from here?

Finding nature in our nation's streams will not result from aimless wanderings. It will take thoughtful action and careful choices. We must decide if the angler fishing for golden rainbow trout is wise or foolish. We can devise and construct rock and wood castles to safeguard hatchery fish, or we can admit that nature has a better way of doing things. We need to choose the best way to respect and value a species as beautiful as trout. Maybe one person will simply decide to play the childhood game of tag with a fish, casting only flies that have hooks carefully covered. Fish will be lost, but more might be gained as a new appreciation for rivers emerges. Other anglers might advocate for change while they continue to catch and release. Perhaps if you are like me, your fishing rod will begin to collect dust. Although fishing is not necessarily the problem, management and industry efforts designed to encourage fishing for economic gain are partly to blame. I chose to stop funding a system that perpetuates the introduction of nonnative species, releases stream pollution from hormones and antibiotics used at hatcheries and encourages massive reconfigurations of river systems to benefit a single species — especially since that species is me! I refuse to be an economic driver of these destructive environmental practices. However, I fully understand people's continued fascination with fishing and find it hard to detest what seemed so pure and innocent during my childhood. Fishing led me to the rivers I love. The sight of a trout still creates an adolescent enthusiasm and a reverence for the splendor of nature. In the future, I will continue to scan each brook I visit for signs of salmon and trout.

If you and I bump into each other on the water, let's both remember to take off our rose-colored glasses. Let's look at the river in a new light. When we do, we should ask ourselves the question, what footprints do we leave behind in our quest for trout?

Notes

INTRODUCTION. IN SEARCH OF GOLD

The epigraph is from J. Gierach, *Still Life with Brook Trout* (New York: Simon and Schuster, 2005), 192.

ONE. CONTROVERSY OVER THE SALMON'S MIGRATION

The epigraph is from J. Bailey, *Ultimate Freshwater Fishing* (New York: DK Publishing, 1998), 88.

1. "Blackledge River Habitat Restoration Project," Connecticut Department of Energy and Environmental Protection, www.ct.gov/dep/lib/dep/fishing/restoration/blackledge .pdf (accessed May 20, 2012).

2. A. M. Tuthill, "Breakup Ice Control Structures," *U.S. Army Corps of Engineers ERDC/CRREL* TN-05–5, November (2005): 1–21.

3. "Appendix D: History of Atlantic Salmon in the Connecticut River and Status of the Connecticut River Atlantic Salmon Restoration Program," U.S. Fish and Wildlife Service, last modified September 13, 2010, www.fws.gov/r5crc/Stuff/appd.html.

4. F. W. Kircheis, L.L.C., "Sea Lamprey: *Petromyzon marinus* Linnaeus 1758," U.S. Fish and Wildlife Service, last modified January 2004, www.fws.gov/GOMCP/pdfs/ lampreyreport.pdf.

5. R. J. Behnke, *Trout and Salmon of North America* (New York: Free Press, 2002).

6. "U.S. Fish and Wildlife Service Will No Longer Produce Salmon for Connecticut River Restoration Program," U.S. Fish and Wildlife Service, Connecticut River Coordinator's Office, www.fws.gov/r5crc/index.html (accessed November 30, 2012).

7. G. Rahr and X. Augerot, "A Proactive Sanctuary Strategy to Anchor and Restore High-Priority Wild Salmon Ecosystems," Wild Salmon Center, last modified 2005, www.wildsalmoncenter.org/pdf/salmon_2100_Rahr_Augerot.pdf.

8. Behnke, *Trout and Salmon of North America.*

9. Behnke, *Trout and Salmon of North America.*

10. J. B. Dunham, D. S. Pilliod, and M. K. Young, "Assessing the Consequences of Nonnative Trout in Headwater Ecosystems in Western North America," *Fisheries* 29 (2004): 18.

11. J. Bailey, *Ultimate Freshwater Fishing* (New York: DK Publishing, 1998), 100.

12. M. A. Halverson, "Stocking Trends: A Quantitative Review of Governmental Fish Stocking in the United States, 1931–2004," *Fisheries* 33 (2008): 69–75.

13. M. Goodwin, *Trout Streams of Eastern Connecticut* (Ledyard, CT: Trout Unlimited, Thames Valley Chapter, 2004).

14. G. W. Hunter III, L. M. Thorpe, and D. E. Grosvenor, "An Attempt to Evaluate the Effects of Stream Improvement in Connecticut," in *Transactions of the Fifth North American Wildlife Conference* (Washington, DC: *American Wildlife Institute*, 1941), 276–91.

15. Hunter et al., "An Attempt to Evaluate the Effects of Stream Improvement in Connecticut," 276.

16. M. E. Seehorn, *Stream Habitat Improvement Handbook* Technical Publication R8-TP 16 (Atlanta, GA: U.S. Forest Service, Southern Region, 1992).

17. E. P. Cliff, *Wildlife Habitat Improvement Handbook* (Washington, DC: U.S. Forest Service, 1969); M. A. Gee, *Stream Improvement Handbook* (Washington, DC: U.S. Forest Service, 1952); M. B. Arthur, *Fish Stream Improvement Handbook* (Washington, DC: U.S. Forest Service, 1936); H. S. Davis, *Methods for the Improvement of Streams* (Washington, DC: U.S. Department of Commerce, Bureau of Fisheries, 1935).

18. D. M. Thompson, "Long-Term Effect of Instream Habitat-Improvement Structures on Channel Morphology along the Blackledge and Salmon Rivers, Connecticut, USA," *Environmental Management* 29 (2002): 250–65.

19. D. M. Thompson, "A Geomorphic Explanation for a Meander Cutoff Following Channel Relocation of a Coarse-Bedded Channel," *Environmental Management* 31 (2003): 385–400.

20. Goodwin, *Trout Streams of Eastern Connecticut.*

21. "Department of Environmental Conservation Announces Trophy Fish Award Ceremony," Connecticut Department of Environmental Conservation News Release, February 13, 2009, http://ct.gov/dep/cwp/view.asp?A=3605&Q=433956 (accessed May 1, 2012).

TWO. FIRST-CLASS ENTERTAINMENT

The epigraph is from W. C. Platts, *Trout Streams* (London: Harmsworth, 1977), 142.

1. N. Karas, *Brook Trout* (Guilford, CT: Lyons, 2002).

2. R. B. MacKay, introduction to *Long Island Country Homes and Their Architects, 1860–1940*, ed. R. B. MacKay, A. K. Baker, and C. A. Traynor (New York: Palace, 1997), 19–23.

3. Karas, *Brook Trout.*

4. Karas, *Brook Trout.*

5. MacKay, introduction to *Long Island Country Homes and Their Architects, 1860–1940.*

6. A. Walker, "The Family Behind the Popular Phrase," *Keeping Up with the Joneses*, last modified 2009, www.jonesnyhistory.com/.

7. South Side Sportsmen's Club, *Officers, Members, Constitution and Rules of the South Side Sportsmen's Club of Long Island, Oakdale* (New York: C. C. Burnett and Company, 1907).

8. Karas, *Brook Trout.*

9. "Cultivation of Trout," *New York Times*, March 15, 1885.

10. Karas, *Brook Trout.*

11. Karas, *Brook Trout*, 167.

12. Karas, *Brook Trout*, 173.

13. Karas, *Brook Trout*, 184.

14. E. Van Put, *Trout Fishing in the Catskills* (New York: Skyhorse, 2007); Karas, *Brook Trout.*

15. E. Van Put, *The Beaverkill* (New York: Lyons & Burford, 1996).

16. Van Put, *Trout Fishing in the Catskills*.

17. Karas, *Brook Trout*.

18. L. Squeri, *Better in the Poconos* (University Park: Pennsylvania State University Press, 2002).

19. Squeri, *Better in the Poconos*.

20. Squeri, *Better in the Poconos*.

21. Squeri, *Better in the Poconos*.

22. Van Put, *Trout Fishing in the Catskills*.

23. Van Put, *Trout Fishing in the Catskills*.

24. D. McCullough, *The Johnstown Flood* (New York: Simon and Schuster, 1968).

25. McCullough, *The Johnstown Flood*, 57.

26. McCullough, *The Johnstown Flood*, 258, 262.

27. P. Schneider, *The Adirondacks* (New York: Henry Holt, 1997).

28. "Fishing Rights," *Forest and Stream*, 61 (1903): 22, 28–29.

29. "Rockefeller Beats Guides," *New York Times*, November 14, 1906.

30. "The Anglers' Club of New York," *Forest and Stream* 65 (1905): 474.

31. "The Anglers' Club of New York," *Forest and Stream* 65 (1905): 517–18.

32. J. Gierach, *Still Life with Brook Trout* (New York: Simon and Schuster, 2005), 140.

33. J. M. Thoms, "A Place Called Pennask," *The British Columbian Quarterly* 133 (2002): 69–98.

34. Thoms, "A Place Called Pennask."

35. Thoms, "A Place Called Pennask."

36. O. M. Deibler, "Stream Improvement in Pennsylvania and Its Results," in *Proceedings of the North American Wildlife Conference* (Washington, DC: U.S. Government Printing Office, 1936), 439–40.

37. M. B. Otis, "Stream Improvement," in *The Stream Conservation Handbook*, ed. J. M. Migel (New York: Crown, 1974), 99–122.

38. Van Put, *Trout Fishing in the Catskills*.

39. Karas, *Brook Trout*.

40. Schneider, *The Adirondacks*.

41. McCullough, *The Johnstown Flood*.

42. S. Sora, *Secret Societies of America's Elite* (Rochester, VT: Destiny Books, 2003).

43. Deibler, "Stream Improvement in Pennsylvania and Its Results."

44. A. Nevins, *Abram S. Hewitt with Some Account of Peter Cooper* (New York: Harper & Brothers, 1935); "History of Long Pond Ironworks," Friends of Long Pond Ironworks, Inc., www.longpondironworks.org/history.htm (accessed May 9, 2012).

45. Schneider, *The Adirondacks*.

46. Schneider, *The Adirondacks*.

47. Schneider, *The Adirondacks*.

48. E. E. Wohl, *Virtual Rivers* (New Haven, CT: Yale University, 2001).

49. C. Miller, "All in the Family: The Pinchot's of Milford," *Pennsylvania History* 66 (1999): 117–42.

50. Miller, "All in the Family: The Pinchot's of Milford."

51. Van Put, *Trout Fishing in the Catskills*.

52. Miller, "All in the Family: The Pinchot's of Milford."

53. G. Pinchot, "The Relation of Forests to Stream Control," *Annals of the American Academy of Political and Social Science* 31 (1908): 219–27.

54. Pinchot, "The Relation of Forests to Stream Control," 222.

55. Pinchot, "The Relation of Forests to Stream Control," 225.

56. D. R. Montgomery, *Dirt* (Berkeley: University of California Press, 2007).

57. G. Pinchot, *Fishing Talk* (Harrisburg, PA: Stackpole Books, 1936).

58. Pinchot, *Fishing Talk*, 212.

59. E. R. Hewitt, *A Trout and Salmon Fisherman for Seventy-Five Years* (New York: Charles Scribner's Sons, 1948).

60. Hewitt, *A Trout and Salmon Fisherman for Seventy-Five Years*, 188.

61. L. Wulff, "Edward Hewitt," *Rod & Reel*, November/December (1983): 59–60.

62. E. R. Hewitt, *Those Were the Days* (New York: Duell, Sloan and Pearce, 1943).

63. Nevins, *Abram S. Hewitt with Some Account of Peter Cooper*.

64. H. K. Steen, ed., *The Conservation Diaries of Gifford Pinchot* (Durhamn, NC: The Forest History Society, 2001).

65. Various accounts are included from the book, Hewitt, *Those Were the Days*.

66. E. R. Hewitt, *Days from Seventy-Five to Ninety* (New York: Duell, Sloan and Pearce, 1957).

67. Hewitt, *Those Were the Days*, vii.

68. Hewitt, *Days from Seventy-Five to Ninety*, 6.

69. Various accounts are included from the book, Hewitt, *Those Were the Days*.

70. Hewitt, *Those Were the Days*.

71. Hewitt, *Days from Seventy-Five to Ninety*.

72. Hewitt, *Those Were the Days*, 140.

73. Hewitt, *Those Were the Days*.

74. Van Put, *Trout Fishing in the Catskills*; Wulff, "Edward Hewitt."

75. Various accounts are included from the book, Hewitt, *Those Were the Days*.

76. Hewitt, *Days from Seventy-Five to Ninety*.

77. E. R. Hewitt, *Telling on the Trout* (New York: Charles Scribner's Sons, 1930), 213.

78. Wulff, "Edward Hewitt," 59.

79. Hewitt, *Telling on the Trout*, 150.

80. Wulff, "Edward Hewitt," 59.

81. Hewitt, *Those Were the Days*.

82. Hewitt, *Days from Seventy-Five to Ninety*, 36–37.

83. Hewitt, *Days from Seventy-Five to Ninety*.

84. Van Put, *Trout Fishing in the Catskills*.

85. Van Put, *Trout Fishing in the Catskills*.

86. Van Put, *Trout Fishing in the Catskills*.

87. Van Put, *Trout Fishing in the Catskills*.

88. Van Put, *The Beaverkill*.

89. E. R. Hewitt, *Better Trout Streams* (New York: Charles Scribner's Sons, 1931).

90. E. R. Hewitt, *A Trout and Salmon Fisherman for Seventy-Five Years* (New York: Charles Scribner's Sons, 1948).

91. Van Put, *Trout Fishing in the Catskills*.

92. M. Orlando, "Passion, Dynamism and a 'Heart of Gold,'" *Times Beacon Record Media*, last modified December 30, 2005, www.northshoreoflongisland.com/Articles -i-2005-12-29-55141.112114_Passion_dynamism_and_a_heart_of_gold.html.

93. E. M. Yaffe, *Ingraham Bunting* (Savannah, GA: Frederic C. Beil Publisher, 2005).

94. Yaffe, *Ingraham Bunting*.

95. Orlando, "Passion, Dynamism and a 'Heart of Gold.'"

96. H. A. Ingraham, *American Trout Streams* (New York: The Anglers' Club of New York, 1926).

97. B. Mares, *Fishing with the Presidents* (Mechanicsburg, PA: Stackpole, 1999).

98. Karas, *Brook Trout*.

99. Schneider, *The Adirondacks*.

100. J. E. Carter, *An Outdoor Journal* (Fayetteville: University of Arkansas Press, 1994).

101. Mares, *Fishing with the Presidents*.

102. "The Museum Exhibit Galleries," Herbert Hoover Presidential Library and Museum, accessed December 2, 2012, http://hoover.archives.gov/exhibits/Hooverstory/gallery09/index.html.

103. W. C. Platt, *Trout Streams* (London: Harmsworth, 1977), 146.

104. Mares, *Fishing with the Presidents*.

105. Mares, *Fishing with the Presidents*, 207.

106. E. Rickstad, "Former President Clinton Visits Orvis Store at Ocean Reef Club," *Orvis News*, posted April 18, 2011, www.orvisnews.com/FlyFishing/President-Clinton -Visits-Orvis-at-Ocean-Reef-Club.aspx.

107. M. D., "Obama Approves New Obama Caddis Pupa," *DS Flyfishing*, www .dsflyfishing.com/fishing-blog/obama-approves-new-obama-caddis-pupa.html (accessed May 9, 2012).

108. Various accounts from the book, Mares, *Fishing with the Presidents*.

109. Mares, *Fishing with the Presidents*.

110. E. G. D., "Cleveland's Summer Home," *New York Times*, July 13, 1891.

111. M. Algeo, *The President Is a Sick Man* (Chicago: Chicago Review, 2011).

112. Various accounts from the book, Mares, *Fishing with the Presidents*.

113. Various accounts from the book, Mares, *Fishing with the Presidents*.

114. Mares, *Fishing with the Presidents*.

115. Various accounts from the book, Mares, *Fishing with the Presidents*.

THREE. FISH FACTORIES FEED LOTS

The epigraph is from C. Brown and R. L. Day, "The Future of Stock Enhancements: Lessons from Hatchery Practices from Conservation Biology," *Fish and Fishes* 3 (2002): 81.

1. C. Brown and R. L. Day, "The Future of Stock Enhancements: Lessons from Hatchery Practices from Conservation Biology," *Fish and Fisheries* (2002): 84.

2. S. A. Forbes, "The Investigation of a River System in the Interest of Its Fisheries," *Transactions of the American Fisheries Society* 40 (1910): 179–93.

3. H. S. Davis, *Culture and Diseases of Game Fish* (Los Angeles: University of California Press, 1967).

4. G. E. Whelan, "A Historical Perspective on the Philosophy behind the Use of Propagated Fish in Fisheries Management: Michigan's 130-Year Experience," *American Fisheries Society Symposium* 44 (2004): 307–15.

5. E. R. Hewitt, *A Trout and Salmon Fisherman for Seventy-Five Years* (New York: Charles Scribner's Sons, 1948).

6. "Fish Stocking Lists (2011)," New York State Department of Environmental Conservation, www.dec.ny.gov/outdoor/30467.html (accessed May 14, 2012).

7. Stocking numbers and mileage calculations were determined from various state websites: "Connecticut Fish Distribution Report 2011," State Of Connecticut Department Of Energy & Environmental Protection, www.ct.gov/dep/lib/dep/fishing/general _information/fishdistributionreport.pdf (accessed May 14, 2012); "2011 Year to Date Stocking Report," State of Maine Department of Inland Fisheries and Wildlife, www .maine.gov/ifw/fishing/reports/pdfs/2011AnnualStockingReport.pdf (accessed May 14, 2012); "MassWildlife News Release: Spring into Trout Stocking," Massachusetts Division of Fisheries and Wildlife, March 31, 2011, www.mass.gov/dfwele/dfw/mwnews/2011/ mwnews_1011.htm#item4; "MassWildlife News Release: 2011 Fall Trout Stocking," Massachusetts Division of Fisheries and Wildlife, September 29, 2011, www.mass.gov/ dfwele/dfw/mwnews/2011/mwnews_1011.htm#item4; "New Hampshire Fish Stocking Report for 2011," New Hampshire Fish and Game, www.wildlife.state.nh.us/Fishing/ Stocking/2011/full.html (accessed May 14, 2012); G. Mastrati, "News Release: DEM Currently Stocking Rainbow Trout and Salmon for Winter Ice Fishing Season," Rhode Island Department of Environmental Management, December 19, 2011, www.dem.ri .gov/news/2011/pr/1219111.htm; G. Mastrati, "News Release: DEM Currently Stocking Rainbow Trout and Salmon for Winter Ice Fishing Season, Rhode Island Department of Environmental Management, February 17, 2011, www.dem.ri.gov/news/2011/pr/0217112 .htm; G. Mastrati, "DEM Begins Stocking 80,000 Trout in Advance of April 9th Opening of Freshwater Fishing Season," Rhode Island Department of Environmental Management, March 31, 2011, www.dem.ri.gov/news/2011/pr/0331111.htm; "Stocking Schedule for 2011," Vermont Fish & Wildlife Department, www.anr.state.vt.us/fwd/stockingschedule.aspx (accessed May 14, 2012).

8. Stocking numbers and mileage calculations were determined from various state websites: "Spring 2012 Trout Stocking Schedule," Maryland Department of Natural Resources, www.dnr.state.md.us/fisheries/stocking/printversion.pdf (accessed May 14, 2012); "Pequest Trout Hatchery Stocking Summaries — 2011," New Jersey Department of Environmental Protection, www.state.nj.us/dep/fgw/peqsum11.htm (accessed May 14, 2012); "Trout Stocking 2012," Pennsylvania Fish and Boat Commission, http://fishandboat .com/stock.htm (accessed May 14, 2012).

9. "Delaware State Trout Stamp Program and Results of the 2013 Contest," Delaware Department of Natural Resources and Environmental Control, www.dnrec.delaware.gov/ fw/Fisheries/Pages/TroutStamp.aspx (accessed May 14, 2012).

10. "Fisheries Resources and Species Management: California Golden Trout (native)," California Department of Fish and Game, www.dfg.ca.gov/fish/REsources/WildTrout/ WT_CaGoldenDesc.asp (accessed May 9, 2012).

11. F. H. Clark, "Pleiotropic Effect of the Gene for Golden Color in Rainbow Trout,"

The Journal of Heredity 61 (1970): 8–10; S. Dobosz, K. Kohlman, K. Gorykczo, and H. Kuzminski, "Growth and Vitality in the Yellow Forms of Rainbow Trout," *Journal of Applied Ichthyology* 16 (2000): 117–20.

12. G. H. Thorgaard, "Incidence of Albinos as a Monitor for Induced Triploidy in Rainbow Trout," *Aquaculture* 137 (1995): 121–30; "2011 Fish Stocking Information," Utah Division of Wildlife Resources, http://wildlife.utah.gov/dwr/fishing/stocking.html?year =2011(accessed May 15, 2012).

13. "PFBC Chronology," Pennsylvania Fish and Boat Commission, http://fishandboat. com/chrono.htm (accessed May 16, 2012); "2011 Fish Stocking Information," Utah Division of Wildlife; G. H. Thorgaard, "Incidence of Albinos as a Monitor for Induced Triploidy in Rainbow Trout."

14. "Frequently Asked Questions," U.S. Fish and Wildlife Service, www.fws.gov/ midwest/JordanRiver/FAQ.htm (accessed May 16, 2012).

15. Clark, "Pleiotropic Effect of the Gene for Golden Color in Rainbow Trout," 8.

16. Clark, "Pleiotropic Effect of the Gene for Golden Color in Rainbow Trout."

17. J. E. Wright, "The Palomino Rainbow Trout," *Pennsylvania Angler* 41 (1972): 8–9.

18. Clark, "Pleiotropic Effect of the Gene for Golden Color in Rainbow Trout."

19. B. Schweit, "Lighting Trout, Trophy Rainbows Show in Good Numbers at Santa Ana River Lakes," *Western Outdoor News*, February 25, 2011, www.wonews .com/t-SCFreshReport_sarl_022511.aspx.

20. J. M. Blanc, H. Poisson, and E. Quillet, "A blue variant in the rainbow trout, *Oncorhynchus mykiss* Walbaum," *Journal of Heredity* 97 (2006): 89–93; Dobosz et al., "Growth and Vitality in the Yellow Forms of Rainbow Trout."

21. W. R. Bridges and B. von Limbach, "Inheritance of Albinism in Rainbow Trout," *Journal of Heredity* 63 (1972): 152–53; Clark, "Pleiotropic Effect of the Gene for Golden Color in Rainbow Trout."

22. Wright, "The Palomino Rainbow Trout."

23. Dobosz et al., "Growth and Vitality in the Yellow Forms of Rainbow Trout."

24. Blanc et al., "A Blue Variant in the Rainbow Trout, *Oncorhynchus mykiss* Walbaum."

25. "2011 Fish Stocking Information," Utah Division of Wildlife.

26. Stocking numbers and mileage calculations were determined from various state websites: "Fisheries Management in Public Waters," Georgia Wildlife Resources Division, www.georgiawildlife.com/node/931 (accessed May 14, 2012); "Coldwater Stocking by County," North Carolina Wildlife Resources Commission, www.ncwildlife.org/Fishing/ HatcheriesStocking/NCWRCStocking/ColdwaterStockingbyCounty.aspx (accessed May 14, 2012); "Walhalla State Fish Hatcheries," South Carolina Department of Natural Resources, http://hatcheries.dnr.sc.gov/walhalla/index.html (accessed May 14, 2012); "Coldwater Fish Production and Stocking," Virginia Department of Game and Inland Fisheries, www.dgif.virginia.gov/fishing/stocking/coldwater.asp (accessed May 14, 2012).

27. J. H. Gray, "Who We Are: Our Mission, Goals and Geographic Area," U.S. Fish and Wildlife Service Wolf Creek National Fish Hatchery, www.fws.gov/wolfcreek/ aboutus.html (accessed May 14, 2012).

28. "Streams and Small Lakes (March to September)," Tennessee Wildlife Resources Agency, www.tn.gov/twra/fish/StreamRiver/stockedtrout/stockedtrout.html (accessed

May 14, 2012); J. Caudill, *Economic Effects of Rainbow Trout Production by the National Fisheries Program* (Arlington, VA: U.S. Fish and Wildlife Service, Division of Economics, 2005).

29. Stocking numbers were compiled from various state websites: "Illinois' 2011 Spring Trout Season Opens April 2, Rainbow Trout Stocked at 43 Locations," Illinois Department of Natural Resources, March 9, 2011, www.illinois.gov/pressreleases/ ShowPressRelease.cfm?SubjectID=1&RecNum=9268; "2012 Trout Stocking Plan," Indiana Division Of Fish And Wildlife, www.in.gov/dnr/fishwild/files/fw-2012_TROUT _STOCKING_PLAN.pdf (accessed May 14, 2012); "2011 Fall Catchable Trout Releases in Ohio," Ohio Department of Natural Resources, Division of Wildlife, http://ohiodnr .com/tabid/6135/Default.aspx (accessed May 14, 2012).

30. Stocking numbers were compiled from various state websites: "Harrietta State Fish Hatchery," Michigan Department of Natural Resources, www.michigan.gov/dnr/0,4570,7 -153-10364_28277-22495 — ,00.html (accessed May 14, 2012); "Oden State Fish Hatchery," Michigan Department of Natural Resources, www.michigan.gov/dnr/0,4570,7-153-10364 _28277-22423 — ,00.html (accessed May 14, 2012); "Marquette State Fish Hatchery," Michigan Department of Natural Resources, www.michigan.gov/dnr/0,4570,7-153-10364 _28277-22460 — ,00.html (accessed May 14, 2012); "Platte River State Fish Hatchery," Michigan Department of Natural Resources, www.michigan.gov/dnr/0,4570,7-153-10364 _28277-22491 — ,00.html (accessed May 14, 2012); "Thompson State Fish Hatchery," Michigan Department of Natural Resources, www.michigan.gov/dnr/0,4570,7-153-10364 _28277-22486 — ,00.html (accessed May 14, 2012); "Wolf Lake State Fish Hatchery," Michigan Department of Natural Resources, www.michigan.gov/dnr/0,4570,7-153-10364 _28277-22498 — ,00.html (accessed May 14, 2012); "Fish Stocking Summaries," Wisconsin Department Of Natural Resources, Bureau Of Fisheries Management, http://infotrek.er .usgs.gov/doc/wdnr_biology/Public_Stocking/StateMapHotspotsAllYears.htm (accessed May 14, 2012); "Coldwater Hatchery Management," Minnesota Department of Natural Resources, www.dnr.state.mn.us/fish/trout/coldwater.html (accessed May 15, 2012).

31. Stocking numbers were compiled from various state websites: "Scheduled Trout Stockings for 2011," Arkansas Game and Fish Commission, www.agfc.com/ fishing/Documents/TP_TroutStocking2011.pdf (accessed May 15, 2012); "Manchester Fish Hatchery," Iowa Department of Conservation, www.iowadnr.gov/InsideDNR/ DNRStaffOffices/FishHatcheries/ManchesterFishHatchery.aspx (accessed May 15, 2012); "Bennett Spring Fish Hatchery," Missouri Department of Conservation, http:// mdc.mo.gov/regions/southwest/bennett-spring-fish-hatchery (accessed May 15), 2012,; "Maramec Spring Hatchery," Missouri Department of Conservation, http://mdc.mo.gov/ regions/ozark/maramec-spring-park-and-hatchery (accessed May 15, 2012); "Montauk Fish Hatchery," Missouri Department of Conservation, http://mdc.mo.gov/regions/ozark/ montauk-fish-hatchery (accessed May 15, 2012); "Roaring River Hatchery and Trout Park," Missouri Department of Conservation, http://mdc.mo.gov/regions/southwest/roaring -river-hatchery-and-trout-park (accessed May 15, 2012); "Shepherd of the Hills Fish Hatchery," Missouri Department of Conservation, http://mdc.mo.gov/regions/southwest/ shepherd-hills-fish-hatchery (accessed May 15, 2012).

32. Stocking numbers were compiled from various state websites: "Trout Stocking

Schedule," Kansas Department of Wildlife, Parks and Tourism, www.kdwpt.state
.ks.us/news/Fishing/Special-Fishing-Programs-for-You/Trout-Fishing-Program/
Stocking-Schedule (accessed May 15, 2012); "Fish Stocking Reports," Nebraska Game
and Parks Commission, http://outdoornebraska.ne.gov/fishing/guides/fishguide/
FGstocking.asp (accessed May 15, 2012); North Dakota Game and Fish Department,
"Fish Stocking List: Major Waters by County Name," updated April 14, 2012, http://gf
.nd.gov/gnfapps/reports/fisheries/FishStockingMajorWaters.pdf; North Dakota Game
and Fish Department, "Fish Stocking List: Small Waters by County Name," updated
April 14, 2012, http://gf.nd.gov/gnfapps/reports/fisheries/FishStockingSmallwaters
.pdf; "Trout Stocking Schedule," Oklahoma Department of Wildlife Conservation, www
.wildlifedepartment.com/fishing/trout_stock_schedule.htm (accessed May 15, 2012); "2011
Fish Stocking Report," South Dakota Fish, Game and Parks, http://gfp.sd.gov/fishing
-boating/tacklebox/lake-surveys/fish-stocking.aspx (accessed May 15, 2012); "2011–2012
Trout Stocking Schedule," Texas Parks and Wildlife Department, www.tpwd.state.tx.us/
fishboat/fish/management/stocking/trout_2012.phtml (accessed May 15, 2012).

33. "The Fish Hatchery Game — An Interactive Math and Science Resource," Colorado
Department of Natural Resources, last modified December 27, 2011, http://wildlife.state.
co.us/Education/TeacherResources/FishHatcheryGame/Pages/HatcheryManager.aspx.

34. "What Are Aquatic Invasive Species?" Wyoming Game and Fish Department,
http://wgfd.wyo.gov/web2011/fishing-1000216.aspx (accessed May 16, 2012).

35. Stocking numbers were compiled from various state websites: "Auburn Hatchery,"
Wyoming Game and Fish Department, http://wgfd.wyo.gov/web2011/wgfd-1000347
.aspx (accessed May 16, 2012); "Boulder Fish Rearing Station," Wyoming Game and Fish
Department, http://wgfd.wyo.gov/web2011/wgfd-1000348.aspx (accessed May 16, 2012);
"Clarks Fork Hatchery," Wyoming Game and Fish Department, http://wgfd.wyo.gov/
web2011/wgfd-1000349.aspx (accessed May 16, 2012); "Dan Speas Fish Rearing Station,"
Wyoming Game and Fish Department, http://wgfd.wyo.gov/web2011/wgfd-1000351.aspx
(accessed May 16, 2012); "Daniel Hatchery," Wyoming Game and Fish Department, http://
wgfd.wyo.gov/web2011/wgfd-1000352.aspx (accessed May 16, 2012); "Dubois Hatchery,"
Wyoming Game and Fish Department, http://wgfd.wyo.gov/web2011/wgfd-1000353.aspx
(accessed May 16, 2012); "Story Hatchery and Visitor Center," Wyoming Game and Fish
Department, http://wgfd.wyo.gov/web2011/wgfd-1000354.aspx (accessed May 16, 2012);
"Ten Sleep Hatchery," Wyoming Game and Fish Department, , http://wgfd.wyo.gov/
web2011/wgfd-1000355.aspx (accessed May 16, 2012); "Tillet Springs Rearing Station,"
Wyoming Game and Fish Department, http://wgfd.wyo.gov/web2011/wgfd-1000356
.aspx (accessed May 16, 2012); "Wigwam Rearing Station," Wyoming Game and Fish
Department, http://wgfd.wyo.gov/web2011/wgfd-1000357.aspx (accessed May 16, 2012).

36. P. Fuller, "*Salmo letnica*," USGS Nonindigenous Aquatic Species Database, last
modified March 30, 2012, http://nas.er.usgs.gov/queries/factsheet.aspx?SpeciesID=925.

37. "2011 Fish stocking information," Utah Division of Wildlife.

38. "Lees Ferry Trout Fishery," Glen Canyon Dam Adaptive Management Program,
www.gcdamp.gov/fs/LeesFTF.pdf (accessed May 16, 2012).

39. M. E. Anderson, M. W. Ackerman, K. D. Hilwig, A. E. Fuller, and P. D. Alley,
"Evidence of Young Humpback Chub Overwintering in the Mainstream Colorado River,

Marble Canyon, Arizona, USA," *The Open Fish Science Journal* 3 (2010): 42–50; "Bright Angel Creek Trout Reduction Project," National Park Service, www.nps.gov/grca/naturescience/trout-reduction.htm (accessed May 16, 2012).

40. "NDOW Finalizes Fish Stocking Plans for Next Two Years," Nevada Department of Wildlife, www.ndow.org/about/news/pr/2011/jan/fish_stocking.shtm (accessed May 15, 2012).

41. A. J. Benson, M. M. Richerson, E. Maynard, J. Larson and A. Fusaro, "*Dreissena bugensis*," USGS Nonindigenous Aquatic Species Database, last modified March 19, 2012, http://nas.er.usgs.gov/queries/factsheet.aspx?speciesid=95.

42. R. J. Behnke, *Trout and Salmon of North America* (New York: Free Press, 2002).

43. Behnke, *Trout and Salmon of North America*.

44. "Hatcheries," Arizona State Game and Fish, www.azgfd.gov/h_f/hatcheries.shtml (accessed May 15, 2012); "NDOW Finalizes Fish Stocking Plans for Next Two Years."

45. "2010 Stocking Plan," Montana Fish, Wildlife and Parks, last modified March 22, 2010, http://fwp.mt.gov/fwpDoc.html?id=42515.

46. Stocking numbers were compiled from state websites: "2012 Trout Stocking Schedules," Oregon Department of Fish and Wildlife, www.dfw.state.or.us/resources/fishing/trout_stocking_schedules/ (accessed May 16, 2012); "Statewide Trout Stocking Plan," Washington Department of Fish and Wildlife, http://wdfw.wa.gov/fishing/plants/statewide/ (accessed May 16, 2012).

47. Pacific Rivers Council, "The Need for Stocking Reform in California: Preserving the Golden State's Freshwater Heritage," Pacific Rivers Council, last modified 2006, www.biologicaldiversity.org/campaigns/fish-stocking_reform/pdfs/CA-Fish-Stocking-Reform.pdf.

48. "Statewide Stocking Plan Introduction," Alaska Department of Fish and Game, www.adfg.alaska.gov/Static/fishing/pdfs/hatcheries/12intro.pdf (accessed May 16, 2012).

49. "Welcome to Trout Unlimited—Hawaiian Style!" Trout Unlimited Hawaii (Waikahe'olu) Chapter, www.tuhi.org/ (accessed May 15, 2012).

50. E. M. Thurman, J. E. Dietze, and E. A. Scribner, "Occurrence of Antibiotics in Water from Fish Hatcheries," *U.S. Geological Survey Fact Sheet* 120-02 (2002): 1–5; M. A. Halverson, "Stocking Trends: A Quantitative Review of Governmental Fish Stocking in the United States, 1931–2004," *Fisheries* 33 (2008): 69–75; M. B. Rust et al., *The Future of Aquafeeds* (Silver Spring, MD: NOAA/USDA Alternative Feeds Initiative, 2010).

51. Thurman et al., "Occurrence of Antibiotics in Water from Fish Hatcheries."

52. M. A. Halverson, *An Entirely Synthetic Fish* (New Haven, CT: Yale University, 2010).

53. Rust et al., *The Future of Aquafeeds*.

54. Halverson, *An Entirely Synthetic Fish*.

55. Whelan, "A Historical Perspective," 311.

56. Brown and Day, "The Future of Stock Enhancements."

57. "Hatcheries," Colorado Division of Wildlife, last modified March 15, 2011, http://wildlife.state.co.us/Fishing/Management/Hatcheries/Pages/Hatcheries.aspx.

58. "Weekly Fishing Report, May 12, 2009," Colorado Division of Wildlife, last modified May 12, 2009, www.colorado.com/ai/COLORADODIVISIONOFWILDLIFE 5_12_09.pdf.

59. "Coldwater Hatcheries," North Carolina Wildlife Resources Commission, www .ncwildlife.org/Fishing/HatcheriesStocking/NCWRCHatcheries/ColdwaterHatcheries .aspx (accessed May 14, 2012).

60. "Clarks Fork Hatchery," Wyoming Game and Fish Department, http://wgfd.wyo .gov/web2011/wgfd-1000349.aspx (accessed May 16, 2012).

61. "Stocked Trout Program: Cost Report," Pennsylvania Fish and Boat Commission, last modified March 2009, http://fishandboat.com/pafish/trout/stocked_cost_study2009 .pdf.

62. "DEC Fish Hatcheries FAQs," New York Department of Environmental Conservation, www.dec.ny.gov/outdoor/21668.html (accessed June 20, 2012).

63. "Daniel Hatchery," Wyoming Game and Fish Department, http://wgfd.wyo.gov/ web2011/wgfd-1000352.aspx (accessed May 16, 2012).

64. "Weekly Fishing Report, May 12, 2009," Colorado Division of Wildlife.

65. J. Bailey, *Ultimate Freshwater Fishing* (New York: DK Publishing, 1998), 100.

66. M. Freeman, "It's Raining Trout, Hallelujah," *Mail Tribune* (Southern Oregon), August 2, 2007, www.mailtribune.com/apps/pbcs.dll/article?AID=/20070802/ SPORTS/708020319&cid=sitesearch.

67. Freeman, "It's Raining Trout, Hallelujah," 2.

68. T. Hallows, "Stocking Fish from the Sky: Airplanes Drop Fish into High Mountain Lakes," *Utah Division of Wildlife Resources, Wildlife Review*, http://wildlife.utah.gov/wr/ (accessed May 9, 2012).

69. Hallows, "Stocking Fish from the Sky," 5.

70. Hallows, "Stocking Fish from the Sky," 10.

71. Hewitt, *A Trout and Salmon Fisherman for Seventy-Five Years*.

72. S. Halpern, "Fish Rain from the Sky in a Twice-Annual Rite," *New York Times*, June 11, 1989, 38.

73. "Trout Stocking 2012," Pennsylvania Fish and Boat Commission, http:// fishandboat.com/stock.htm (accessed May 14, 2012).

74. "2011–2012 Trout Stocking Schedule," Texas Parks and Wildlife Department.

75. "Trout Stocking Maps," Delaware Department of Natural Resources and Environmental Control, www.dnrec.state.de.us/fw/Trout/TroutMaps.htm (accessed May 14, 2012); "Trout Fishing," Maryland Department of Natural Resources, www.dnr.state.md .us/fisheries/stocking/index.asp (accessed May 14, 2012); "2012 Trout Stocking Schedules," Oregon Department of Fish and Wildlife; "2011–2012 Trout Stocking Schedule," Texas Parks and Wildlife.

76. J. Brooks, *Trout Fishing* (New York: Sedgewood, 1985), 25.

77. "Trout Season Begins," WNPR radio broadcast, April 17, 2009.

78. M. Goodwin, *Trout Streams of Eastern Connecticut* (Ledyard, CT: Trout Unlimited, Thames Valley Chapter, 2004).

79. "West Virginia Division of Natural Resources Wildlife Resources Section Trout Tagging Study," West Virginia Division of Natural Resources, www.wvdnr.gov/fishing/ PDFFiles/Trout%20Tagging%20Study.pdf (accessed May 24, 2012).

80. "New Hampshire Fish Stocking Report for 2011"; "Trout Stocking 2012," Pennsylvania Fish and Boat Commission.

81. "2011–2012 Trout Stocking Schedule," Texas Parks and Wildlife Department.

82. "2012 Summer Trout Stocking Schedule," Arizona Game and Fish Department, last modified April 3, 2012, www.azgfd.gov/pdfs/h_f/fishing/stocking/2012SumTrout StockSchedule.pdf; "2012 Spring Trout Allocations and In-Season Stocking Days," New Jersey Department of Environmental Protection, last modified April 2, 2012, www.nj.gov/dep/fgw/trt_allocation12_dates.htm; "Daily Trout Stockings," West Virginia Division of Natural Resources, www.wvdnr.gov/fishing/stocking/dailystock.shtm (accessed May 15, 2012).

83. "2011 Fish Stocking Information," Utah Division of Wildlife.

84. "2012 Trout Stocking Schedules," Oregon Department of Fish and Wildlife.

FOUR. EDUCATING THE MASSES

The epigraph is from I. Walton, *The Compleat Angler*, ed. J. Major (New York: T.Y. Crowell, 1898), 26.

1. R. B. Miller, "Survival of Hatchery-Reared Cutthroat Trout in an Alberta Stream," *Transactions of American Fisheries Society* 81 (1952): 35–42; E. R. Vincent, "Effects of Stocking Catchable-Size Rainbow Trout on Two Wild Trout Species in Madison River and O'Dell Creek, Montana," *North American Journal of Fisheries Management* 7 (1987): 91–105.

2. A. Lee, *Fishing Dry Flies for Trout on Rivers and Streams* (Champaign, IL: Human Kinetics, 1988), 8.

3. C. Brown and R. L. Day, "The Future of Stock Enhancements: Lessons from Hatchery Practices from Conservation Biology," *Fish and Fishes* 3 (2002): 79–94; C. Brown and K. Laland, "Social Learning and Life Skills Training for Hatchery Reared Fish," *Journal of Fish Biology* 59 (2005): 471–93.

4. Brown and Day, "The Future of Stock Enhancements," 82.

5. E. R. Hewitt, *Hewitt's Handbook of Stream Improvement* (New York: Marchbanks, 1934), 48.

6. E. Jönsson, J. I. Johnsson, and B. T. Björnsson "Growth Hormone Increase Predation Exposure of Rainbow Trout," *Proceedings: Biological Sciences* 263 (1996): 647–51.

7. D. Álvarez and A. G. Nicieza, "Predator Avoidance Behavior in Wild and Hatchery-Reared Brown Trout: The Role of Experience and Domestication," *Journal of Fish Biology* 63 (2003): 1565–677.

8. J. Brooks, *Trout Fishing* (New York: Sedgewood, 1985), 31.

9. W. A. Donnelly and F. G. Whoriskey, "Background-Color Acclimation of Brook Trout for Crypsis Reduces Risk of Predation by Hooded Mergansers *Lophodytes cucullatus*," *North American Journal of Fisheries Management* 11 (1991): 206–11.

10. G. E. Brown and R. J. F. Smith, "Acquired Predatory Recognition in Juvenile Rainbow Trout (*Oncorhynchus mykiss*): Conditioning Hatchery-Reared Fish to Recognize Cues of a Predator," *Canadian Journal of Fisheries and Aquatic Sciences* 55 (1998): 611–17.

11. R. S. Mirza and D. P. Chivers, "Predator-Recognition Training Enhances Survival of Brook Trout: Evidence from Laboratory and Field-Enclosure Studies," *Canadian Journal of Zoology* 78 (2000): 2198–208.

12. "Trout in the Classroom: Goals," Trout Unlimited,www.troutintheclassroom.org/about/overview/goals (accessed May 22, 2012).

13. "TIC Brochure," PowerPoint presentation found on "Trout in the Classroom: Volunteers," Trout Unlimited, www.troutintheclassroom.org/volunteers (accessed May 22, 2012).

14. "Trout in the Classroom," Trout Unlimited, www.troutintheclassroom.org/teachers/state-specific-resources#NJ (accessed May 22, 2012).

15. "Trout in the Classroom," Potomac-Patuxent Chapter Trout Unlimited, www.bluegrasstu.org/trout_in_the_classroom_11.html (accessed May 22, 2012); "Trout in the Classroom," Bluegrass Chapter Trout Unlimited, www.pptu.org/TIC.shtml (accessed May 22, 2012).

16. "Learn & Participate," Nevada Department of Fish and Game, http://ndow.org/learn/tic/ (accessed May 23, 2012); "Trout in the Classroom: History," Trout Unlimited, www.troutintheclassroom.org/about/history (accessed May 23, 2012).

17. "Welcome to NJ Trout in the Classroom," New Jersey Trout Unlimited, www.njtroutintheclassroom.org/index.php/articles/detail/welcome_to_nj_trout_in_the_classroom/ (accessed May 22, 2012).

18. "In the Spotlight," ConneCT Kids, last modified May 11, 2012, www.kids.ct.gov/kids/cwp/view.asp?a=2577&Q=447856.

19. "TIC School Directory," Pennsylvania Trout in the Classroom, http://patroutintheclassroom.org/MapofTICSchools.aspx (accessed May 24, 2012); E. Rotman, "Hatching Stewardship," *Outdoor California*, March–April (2008): 33–35.

20. "Trout in the Classroom," Idaho Department of Fish and Game, http://fishandgame.idaho.gov/public/education/?getPage=220 (accessed May 22, 2012).

21. "Trout in the Classroom: Lesson Plans," Trout Unlimited, www.troutintheclassroom.org/teachers/lesson-plans (accessed May 22, 2012).

22. "Trout in the Classroom: Dream Stream," Trout Unlimited, www.troutintheclassroom.org/teachers/library/dream-stream (accessed May 22, 2012).

23. "Gift Center," World Wildlife Federation, www.worldwildlife.org/gift-center/gifts/Species-Adoptions.aspx?tc=slo2&sc=AWY1200WCM00&searchen=bing (accessed May 22, 2012).

24. "Trout in the Classroom: Program Sponsors," Trout Unlimited, www.troutintheclassroom.org/about/program-sponsors (accessed May 22, 2012).

25. "Future Fisherman Foundation Partners," Future Fisherman Foundation, www.futurefisherman.org/future-fisherman-foundation-partners/ (accessed July 5, 2012).

26. Rotman, "Hatching Stewardship."

27. "Mission Peak Fly Anglers Club," Mission Peak Fly Anglers Club, last modified May 14, 2012, www.missionpeakflyanglers.org/.

28. "Cold, Clean, Fishable Water," Trout Unlimited, www.tu.org/sites/www.tu.org/files/documents/tu_generalbrochure.pdf (accessed May 22, 2012).

29. "Lobbying Report: Trout Unlimited Q1," U.S. Congress Lobbying Disclosure Act Database, http://soprweb.senate.gov/index.cfm?event=getFilingDetails&filingID=e11782b0-88c4-4a0b-b562-838b867eacb0 (accessed May 22, 2012); "Lobbying Report: Trout Unlimited Q2," U.S. Congress Lobbying Disclosure Act Database, http://soprweb.senate.gov/index.cfm?event=getFilingDetails&filingID=312A61E1-8FD8-4B60-815D-3DCCC74A8527 (accessed May 22, 2012); "Lobbying Report: Trout Unlimited Q3," U.S.

Congress Lobbying Disclosure Act Database, http://soprweb.senate.gov/index.cfm?event
=getFilingDetails&filingID=093a50b5-d736-4493-8289-5dfa58524cc6 (accessed May
22, 2012); "Lobbying Report: Trout Unlimited Q4," U.S. Congress Lobbying Disclosure
Act Database, http://soprweb.senate.gov/index.cfm?event=getFilingDetails&filingID
=ff93b331-a354-412b-8230-1179951f2345 (accessed May 22, 2012).

30. "About Us," Trout Unlimited, www.tu.org/about-us (accessed May 22, 2012).

31. "Action Center," Trout Unlimited, www.tu.org/conservation/action-center (accessed
May 22, 2012).

32. Cover image accompanying the article: "It's Elementary," *Trout* 51 (2009): 44–48.

33. "Trout Unlimited: Stream Explorers," Trout Unlimited, www.streamexplorers.org/
(accessed May 22, 2012).

34. "Trout in the Classroom: eNewsletter, May 1, 2010," Trout Unlimited www
.troutintheclassroom.org/sites/www.troutintheclassroom.org/files/documents/TiC
_eNews_May2010.pdf.

35. J. DiPietro, "Third Annual Trout in The Classroom Release Day a Success," Blue
Ridge Trout Unlimited Chapter, http://blueridgetu.com/Troutin_the_Classroom.html
(accessed May 22, 2012).

36. "The Fish Hatchery Game—An Interactive Math & Science Resource," Colorado
Department of Natural Resources, last modified December 27, 2011, http://wildlife.state.
co.us/Education/TeacherResources/FishHatcheryGame/Pages/HatcheryManager.aspx.

37. G. W. Harvey, *Techniques of Trout Fishing and Fly Tying* (Belleville, PA: Metz
Hatchery, 1985).

38. Harvey, *Techniques of Trout Fishing and Fly Tying.*

39. P. G. Quinnett, *Pavlov's Trout* (Kansas City: Andrews McMeel, 1998), 26.

40. Lee, *Fishing Dry Flies for Trout on Rivers and Streams*, 288.

41. Lee, *Fishing Dry Flies for Trout on Rivers and Streams.*

42. "Reader Demographics Trout Magazine," Trout Unlimited, www.tu.org/sites/www
.tu.org/files/documents/TroutMagDemographics_0.pdf (accessed April 4, 2008).

43. Lee, *Fishing Dry Flies for Trout on Rivers and Streams*, 1.

44. J. Merwin, *The New American Trout Fishing* (New York: MacMillan, 1994), 74.

45. Merwin, *The New American Trout Fishing*, 75.

46. Quinnett, *Pavlov's Trout*, 32.

47. Lee, *Fishing Dry Flies for Trout on Rivers and Streams*, 235.

48. Lee, *Fishing Dry Flies for Trout on Rivers and Streams*, 4.

49. "Welcome to NJ Trout in the Classroom."

50. S. Gahr and C. Rexroad III, "Genes May Lead Way to Bigger Rainbow Trout,"
Agricultural Research 54 (2006): 10.

FIVE. THE LUCKY CHARM

The epigraph is from H. A. Ingraham, *American Trout Streams* (New York: The Anglers'
Club of New York, 1926), vii.

1. P. Schneider, *The Adirondacks* (New York: Henry Holt, 1997).

2. W. C. Harris, "Col. Mooney Finds His Flamingos," *American Angler* 14 (September
29, 1888): 198–99.

3. I. Walton, *The Compleat Angler*, ed. J. Major (New York: T.Y. Crowell, 1898), 3.

4. Walton, *The Compleat Angler*, 50.

5. Walton, *The Compleat Angler*, 50.

6. Walton, *The Compleat Angler*, 15.

7. Walton, *The Compleat Angler*, 52–53.

8. Walton, *The Compleat Angler*, 52.

9. "Brook Trout Fishing Study Summary: Great Smoky Mountains National Park," National Park Service, accessed May 23, 2012, www.nps.gov/grsm/naturescience/upload/fishing-study.pdf.

10. Schneider, *The Adirondacks*.

11. Schneider, *The Adirondacks*.

12. Ingraham, *American Trout Streams*; E. R. Hewitt, *Better Trout Streams* (New York: Charles Scribner's Sons, 1931); J. C. Mottram, *Trout Fisheries* (London: Herbert Jenkins, 1928); W. C. Platt, *Trout Streams* (London: Harmsworth, 1977).

13. J. Bailey, *Ultimate Freshwater Fishing* (New York: DK Publishing, 1998), 23.

14. Platt, *Trout Streams*.

15. Hewitt, *Better Trout Streams*; E. R. Hewitt, "Shall We Let Vermin Steal Our Trout?" *Outdoor Life* 76 (1935): 22–23, 64.

16. Platt, *Trout Streams*, 60.

17. Platt, *Trout Streams*, 90.

18. W. Sinker [E. R. Hewitt?], "About Kingfishers," *Forest and Stream* 67 (1906): 338.

19. Hewitt, "Shall We Let Vermin Steal Our Trout?" 64.

20. J. A. Parkhurst, R. P. Brooks, and D. E. Arnold, "Assessment of Predation at Trout Hatcheries in Central Pennsylvania," *Wildlife Society Bulletin* 20 (1992): 411–19.

21. Hewitt, "Shall We Let Vermin Steal Our Trout?"

22. E. R. Hewitt, *Hewitt's Handbook of Stream Improvement* (New York: Marchbanks, 1934), 39.

23. E. R. Hewitt, *Those Were the Days* (New York: Duell, Sloan and Pearce, 1943), 285.

24. E. R. Hewitt, *Telling on the Trout* (New York: Charles Scribner's Sons, 1930).

25. Hewitt, *Telling on the Trout*.

26. Hewitt, *Telling on the Trout*.

27. D. A. Silbey, *The Sibley Guide to Birds* (New York: Alfred A. Knopf, 2000).

28. G. A. Littauer et al., "Control of Bird Predation at Aquaculture Facilities: Strategies and Cost Estimates," *Southern Regional Aquaculture Center Publication* 402 (1997): 1–4.

29. Hewitt, *Hewitt's Handbook of Stream Improvement*, 41.

30. Hewitt, *Hewitt's Handbook of Stream Improvement*.

31. Hewitt, *Hewitt's Handbook of Stream Improvement*, 64.

32. Hewitt, *Hewitt's Handbook of Stream Improvement*, 64.

33. Hewitt, *Hewitt's Handbook of Stream Improvement*.

34. Hewitt, *Hewitt's Handbook of Stream Improvement*.

35. Hewitt, "Shall We Let Vermin Steal Our Trout?"

36. W. H. Armistead, *Trout Waters Management and Angling* (London: A&C Black, 1920).

37. Armistead, *Trout Waters Management and Angling*, 78.

38. Armistead, *Trout Waters Management and Angling*, 75.

39. Parkhurst et al., "Assessment of predation at trout hatcheries in central Pennsylvania."

40. B. Dorr and J. D. Taylor, "Wading Bird Management and Research on North American Aquaculture Facilities," in *Proceedings of the 10th Wildlife Damage Management Conference*, ed. K. A. Fagerstone and G. W. Witmer (Lincoln, NE: USDA National Wildlife Research Center, Staff Publications, 2003), 52–61.

41. "Wildlife Damage Management," Department of Agriculture, Animal and Plant Inspection Service, Wildlife Services, last modified March 27, 2012, www.aphis.usda.gov/wildlife_damage/.

42. J. F. Glahn, T. Tomsa, and K. J. Preusser, "Impact of Great Blue Heron Predation at Trout-Rearing Facilities in the Northeastern United States," *North American Journal of Aquaculture* 61 (1999): 350.

43. Glahn et al., "Impact of Great Blue Heron Predation," 350.

44. Glahn et al., "Impact of Great Blue Heron Predation," 350.

45. Littauer et al., "Control of Bird Predation at Aquaculture Facilities."

46. E. Van Put, *Trout Fishing in the Catskills* (New York: Skyhorse, 2007).

47. Van Put, *Trout Fishing in the Catskills*.

48. Van Put, *Trout Fishing in the Catskills*.

49. Hewitt, *Telling on the Trout*, 198.

50. Hewitt, *Telling on the Trout*, 198.

51. Armistead, *Trout Waters Management and Angling*; Platt, *Trout Streams*; Mottram, *Trout Fisheries*.

52. Mottram, *Trout Fisheries*.

53. Mottram, *Trout Fisheries*; E. R. Hewitt, *A Trout and Salmon Fisherman for Seventy-Five Years* (New York: Charles Scribner's Sons, 1948).

54. Hewitt, *A Trout and Salmon Fisherman for Seventy-Five Years*.

55. J. B. Dunham, D. S. Pilliod, and M. K. Young, "Assessing the Consequences of Nonnative Trout in Headwater Ecosystems in Western North America," *Fisheries* 29 (2004): 18–26.

56. Hewitt, *A Trout and Salmon Fisherman for Seventy-Five Years*.

57. Platt, *Trout Streams*; Mottram, *Trout Fisheries*.

58. Hewitt, *Telling on the Trout*, 147.

59. Armistead, *Trout Waters Management and Angling*.

60. Hewitt, *A Trout and Salmon Fisherman for Seventy-Five Years*.

61. Hewitt, *Hewitt's Handbook of Stream Improvement*.

62. Hewitt, *Hewitt's Handbook of Stream Improvement*, 74.

63. E. N. Shor, R. H. Rosenblatt, and J. D. Isaacs, *Carl Leavitt Hubbs, 1894–1979* (Washington, DC: National Academy of Sciences, 1987).

64. Halverson, *An Entirely Synthetic Fish*, 100.

65. R. J. Behnke, *Trout and Salmon of North America* (New York: Free Press, 2002).

66. Shor et al., *Carl Leavitt Hubbs, 1894–1979*.

67. Shor et al., *Carl Leavitt Hubbs, 1894–1979*.

68. Behnke, *Trout and Salmon of North America*.

69. C. L. Hubbs, "Fisheries Research in Michigan," *Transactions of the American Fisheries Society* 60 (1930): 182–86.

70. C. L. Hubbs, "Planting Food for Fish," in *Proceedings of the North American Wildlife Conference* (Washington, DC: U.S. Government Publishing Office, 1936), 463.

71. Hubbs, "Planting Food for Fish," 460–64.

72. Hubbs, "Planting Food for Fish," 460.

73. C. L. Hubbs, J. R. Greeley, and C. M. Tarzwell, *Methods for the Improvement of Michigan Trout Streams* (Ann Arbor: Bulletin of the Institute for Fisheries Research 1, University of Michigan, 1932), 2; C. L. Hubbs, "Fish Management: Looking Forward," *Transactions of the American Fisheries Society* 66 (1937): 55.

74. C. M. Tarzwell, "Progress in Lake and Stream Improvement," in *Transactions of the Twenty-First American Games Conference* (New York: American Game Association, 1935), 133.

75. Hubbs, "Planting Food for Fish."

76. Hubbs, "Fish Management: Looking Forward," 52–53.

77. Halverson, *An Entirely Synthetic Fish*.

78. Shor et al., *Carl Leavitt Hubbs, 1894–1979*.

79. R. C. Ball, "A Summary of Experiments in Michigan Lakes on the Elimination of Fish Populations with Rotenone 1934–1942," *Transactions of the American Fisheries Society* 75 (1948): 139–146.

80. L. A. Krumholz, "The Use of Rotenone in Fisheries Research," *Journal of Wildlife Management* 12 (1948): 305–17.

81. Krumholz, "The Use of Rotenone in Fisheries Research."

82. Ball, "A Summary of Experiments."

83. Krumholz, "The Use of Rotenone in Fisheries Research."

84. Ball, "A Summary of Experiments."

85. G. E. Whelan, "A Historical Perspective on the Philosophy behind the Use of Propagated Fish in Fisheries Management: Michigan's 130-Year Experience," *American Fisheries Society Symposium* 44 (2004): 307–15.

86. W. C. Latta, "The Early History of Fisheries Management in Michigan," *Fisheries* 31 (2006): 230–34.

87. Krumholz, "The Use of Rotenone in Fisheries Research."

88. Ball, "A Summary of Experiments."

89. Ball, "A Summary of Experiments."

90. J. W. Leonard, "Notes on the Use of Derris as a Fish Poison," *Transactions of the American Fisheries Society* 68 (1939): 272.

91. Krumholz, "The Use of Rotenone in Fisheries Research."

92. Krumholz, "The Use of Rotenone in Fisheries Research."

93. H. R. Siegler and H. W. Pillsbury, "Use of Derris to Reclaim Ponds for Game Fish," *Journal of Wildlife Management* 10 (1946): 308–16.

94. Siegler and Pillsbury, "Use of Derris to Reclaim Ponds for Game Fish."

95. R. G. Zilliox and M. Pfeiffer, "Restoration of Brook Trout Fishing in a Chain of Connected Waters," *New York Fish and Game Journal* 3 (1956): 167–90.

96. Whelan, "A Historical Perspective on the Philosophy."

97. C. Hubbs, "An Evaluation of the Use of Rotenone as a Means of 'Improving' Sports Fishing in the Concho River, Texas," *Copeia* 1963 (1963): 199–203.

98. Hubbs, "An Evaluation of the Use of Rotenone," 201.

99. Hubbs, "An Evaluation of the Use of Rotenone," 201.

100. D. A. Hendrickson and M. M. Stewart, "Clark Hubbs," *Copeia* 2000 (2000): 619–22.

101. Hubbs, "An Evaluation of the Use of Rotenone."

102. Halverson, *An Entirely Synthetic Fish.*

103. Halverson, *An Entirely Synthetic Fish.*

104. Halverson, *An Entirely Synthetic Fish.*

105. R. Carson, *Silent Spring* (Boston: Houghton Mifflin, 1962).

106. Environmental Protection Agency, "Reregistration Eligibility Decision for Rotenone: List A Case No. 0255," *EPA* 738-R-07-005 (2007): 32.

107. R. A. Knapp and K. R. Matthews, "Eradication of Nonnative Fish by Gill Netting from a Small Mountain Lake in California," *Restoration Ecology* 6 (1998): 207–13.

108. "Protecting Adirondack Fish," New York Department of Environmental Conservation, accessed December 19, 2012, www.dec.ny.gov/outdoor/31920.html.

109. S. Halpern, "Fish Rain from the Sky in a Twice-Annual Rite," *New York Times,* June 11, 1989, 38.

110. Mottram, *Trout Fisheries.*

111. Hewitt, *Hewitt's Handbook of Stream Improvement.*

112. Hewitt, *Hewitt's Handbook of Stream Improvement,* 50.

113. Van Put, *Trout Fishing in the Catskills.*

114. Hewitt, *Hewitt's Handbook of Stream Improvement.*

115. Hewitt, *Telling on the Trout.*

116. Purina Mills, "Trout Feeding Recommendations," www.fishchow.com/trout_chart .html (accessed May 9, 2012).

117. S. M. Henderson, B. Shrable and T. A. Pruitt, "Affect of Five Diets on Growth, Feed Conversion, Fin Quality and Reproductive Efficiency of Erwin Strain Rainbow Trout (*Oncorhynchus mykiss*)," U.S. Fish and Wildlife Service, www.fws.gov/ennis/ investigations/5_diet_study.pdf (accessed May 9, 2012).

118. "87 — Fish Food — Various Locations, Region 3, USFWS," Solicitation 301814Q002, Federal Business Opportunities, last modified August 25, 2003, www.fbo .gov/index?s=opportunity&mode=form&id=06b924e35ea273bbf346c30dcf98c61d&tab =core&_cview=0.

119. M. A. Halverson, "Stocking Trends: A Quantitative Review of Governmental Fish Stocking in the United States, 1931–2004," *Fisheries* 33 (2008): 69–75.

120. M. B. Rust et al., *The Future of Aquafeeds* (Silver Spring, MD: NOAA/USDA Alternative Feeds Initiative, 2010).

121. Rust et al., *The Future of Aquafeeds.*

122. Rust et al., *The Future of Aquafeeds.*

123. Rust et al., *The Future of Aquafeeds.*

124. Rust et al., *The Future of Aquafeeds.*

125. E. M. Thurman, J. E. Dietze, and E. A. Scribner, "Occurrence of Antibiotics in Water from Fish Hatcheries," *USGS Fact Sheet* 120-02 (2002): 1–5.

126. Thurman et al., "Occurrence of Antibiotics."

127. "Drug Summary and History, (USFWS) Oxytetracycline Medicated Feed INAD 9332," U.S. Fish and Wildlife Service, www.fws.gov/fisheries/aadap/summaryHistory9332 .htm (accessed May 9, 2012).

128. R. A. Hites et al., "Global Assessment of Organic Contaminants in Farmed Salmon," *Science* 303 (2004): 226–29.

129. Hites et al., "Global Assessment of Organic Contaminants."

130. Hites et al., "Global Assessment of Organic Contaminants," 228.

131. M. J. Millard et al., "Contaminant Loads in Broodstock Fish in the Region 5 National Fish Hatchery System," U.S. Fish and Wildlife Service, Northeast Region, last modified May, 2004, www.fws.gov/r5crc/pdf/contaminants_broodstock_fish.pdf.

132. Millard et al., "Contaminant Loads in Broodstock Fish."

133. J. D. Grabarkiewicz and W. S. Davis, *An Introduction to Freshwater Fishes as Biological Indicators* (Washington, DC: U.S. Environmental Protection Agency, 2008).

134. Thurman et al., "Occurrence of Antibiotics."

135. T. M. Hurd et al., "Stable Isotope Tracing of Trout Hatchery Carbon to Sediments and Foodwebs of Limestone Springs Creek," *Science of the Total Environment* 405 (2008): 161–72.

136. G. W. Klontz, *A Manual for Rainbow Trout Production on the Family-Owned Farm* (South Murray, UT: Nelson and Sons, 1991).

SIX. TO SERVE A HIGHER SOUL

The epigraph is from H. A. Ingraham, *American Trout Streams* (New York: The Anglers' Club of New York, 1926), xv.

1. "Welcome to Fly Fishing: The Lifetime Sport," Perigee Learning, www .flyfishingthelifetimesport.com/ (accessed May 9, 2012).

2. J. Gierach, *Still Life with Brook Trout* (New York: Simon and Schuster, 2005).

3. J. Brooks, *Trout Fishing* (New York: Sedgewood, 1985); J. Merwin, *The New American Trout Fishing* (New York: MacMillan, 1994).

4. L. Pool and A. J. Pool, *Izaak Walton* (Lunenburg, VT: Stinehour, 1976).

5. Brooks, *Trout Fishing*, 4.

6. D. J. Duncan, *The River Why* (New York: Bantam, 1984).

7. Pool and Pool, *Izaak Walton*.

8. S. Martin, *Izaak Walton and His Friends* (London: Chapman and Hall, 1903), 16.

9. Martin, *Izaak Walton and His Friends*.

10. I. Walton, *The Compleat Angler*, ed. J. Major (New York: T.Y. Crowell, 1898), 39.

11. R. Wendorf, "Visible Rhetorick: Izaak Walton and Iconic Biography," *Modern Philology* 82 (1985): 270.

12. Walton, *The Compleat Angler*, 118.

13. Walton, *The Compleat Angler*, 261.

14. Walton, *The Compleat Angler*, 140.

15. G. C. Leach, "Culture of Rainbow Trout and Brook Trout in Ponds," *Department of Commerce, Bureau of Fisheries, Economic Circular* 41 (1919): 1–19.

16. P. G. Quinnett, *Pavlov's Trout* (Kansas City: Andrews McMeel, 1998), 34.

17. Quinnett, *Pavlov's Trout*, 69.

18. F. W. Allendorf et al., "Intercrosses and the U.S. Endangered Species Act: Should Hybridized Populations Be Included as Westslope Cutthroat Trout?" *Conservation Biology* 18 (2004): 1203–13.

19. D. W. Blinn et al., "Notes: Effects of Rainbow Trout Predation on Little Colorado Spinedace," *Transactions of the American Fisheries Society* 122 (1993): 139–43.

20. R. A. Knapp and K. R. Matthews, "Eradication of Nonnative Fish by Gill Netting from a Small Mountain Lake in California," *Restoration Ecology* 6 (1998): 207–13.

21. M. E. Anderson et al., "Evidence of Young Humpback Chub Overwintering in the Mainstream Colorado River, Marble Canyon, Arizona, USA," *The Open Fish Science Journal* 3 (2010): 42–50.

22. C. Brown and R. L. Day, "The Future of Stock Enhancements: Lessons from Hatchery Practices from Conservation Biology," *Fish and Fishes* 3 (2002): 82.

23. Quinnett, *Pavlov's Trout*.

24. J. Bailey, *Ultimate Freshwater Fishing* (New York: DK Publishing, 1998).

25. Bailey, *Ultimate Freshwater Fishing*, 99.

26. Brooks, *Trout Fishing*, 105.

27. Brooks, *Trout Fishing*, 186.

28. A. Say, *A River Dream* (Boston: Houghton Mifflin, 1988), 14.

29. D. Whitlock, *L.L. Bean Fly-Fishing Handbook* (New York: Lyons, 1996).

30. Whitlock, *L.L. Bean Fly-Fishing Handbook*, 167.

31. A. Lee, *Fishing Dry Flies for Trout on Rivers and Streams* (Champaign, IL: Human Kinetics, 1988), 288.

32. J. McPhee, *The Founding Fish* (New York: Farrar, Straus and Giroux, 2002), 325.

33. J. M. Meka, "The Influence of Hook Type, Angler Experience, and Fish Size on Injury Rates and the Duration of Capture in an Alaskan Catch-and-Release Rainbow Trout Fishery," *North American Journal of Fisheries Management* 24 (2004): 1309–21.

34. Lee, *Fishing Dry Flies for Trout on Rivers and Streams*, 266.

35. D. J. Schill, R. S. Griffith, and R. E. Gresswell, "Hooking Mortality of Cutthroat Trout in a Catch-and-Release Segment of the Yellowstone River, Yellowstone National Park," *North American Journal of Fisheries Management* 6 (1986): 231.

36. Quinnett, *Pavlov's Trout*, 33.

37. Lee, *Fishing Dry Flies for Trout on Rivers and Streams*, 268.

38. Bailey, *Ultimate Freshwater Fishing*, 103.

39. McPhee, *The Founding Fish*.

40. O. M. Deibler, "Stream Improvement in Pennsylvania and Its Results," in *Proceedings of the North American Wildlife Conference* (Washington, DC: U.S. Government Printing Office, 1936), 442.

41. F. S. Chopin and T. Arimoto, "The Condition of Fish Escaping from Fishing Gears—a Review," *Fisheries Research* 21 (1995): 315–27.

42. D. J. Schill and R. L. Scarpella, "Barbed Hook Restrictions in Catch-and-Release Trout Fisheries: A Social Issue," *North American Journal of Fisheries Management* 17 (1997): 873–81; Schill et al., "Hooking Mortality of Cutthroat Trout"; Chopin and Arimoto, "The Condition of Fish Escaping from Fishing Gears."

43. A. Bartholomew and J. A. Bohnsack, "A Review of Catch-and-Release Angling Mortality with Implications for No-Take Reserves," *Reviews in Fish Biology and Fisheries* 15 (2005): 129–54.

44. E. Van Put, *Trout Fishing in the Catskills* (New York: Skyhorse, 2007).

SEVEN. BUILDING A DREAM HOME

The epigraph is from W. H. Armistead, *Trout Waters Management and Angling* (London: A&C Black, 1920), 3.

1. W. C. Platts, *Trout Streams* (London: Field, 1927), 9.

2. E. Van Put, *The Beaverkill* (New York: Lyons & Burford, 1996).

3. J. S. Van Cleef, "How to Restore Our Trout Streams," *Transactions of the American Fisheries Society* 14 (1885): 50–55.

4. E. Van Put, *Trout Fishing in the Catskills* (New York: Skyhorse Publishing, 2007).

5. Van Cleef, "How to Restore Our Trout Streams," 51.

6. Van Cleef, "How to Restore Our Trout Streams," 55.

7. Van Put, *Trout Fishing in the Catskills*.

8. Van Put, *The Beaverkill*.

9. Van Put, *The Beaverkill*.

10. H. A. Ingraham, *American Trout Streams* (New York: The Anglers' Club of New York, 1926).

11. E. R. Hewitt, *Those Were the Days* (New York: Duell, Sloan and Pearce, 1943).

12. E. R. Hewitt, *Days from Seventy-Five to Ninety* (New York: Duell, Sloan and Pearce, 1957).

13. E. R. Hewitt, *A Trout and Salmon Fisherman for Seventy-Five Years* (New York: Charles Scribner's Sons, 1948).

14. Hewitt, *Those Were the Days*.

15. E. R. Hewitt, *Hewitt's Handbook of Stream Improvement* (New York: Marchbanks, 1934); Hewitt, *A Trout and Salmon Fisherman for Seventy-Five Years*.

16. S. Crane, *The Red Badge of Courage* (New York: D. Appleton, 1895).

17. Hewitt, *Hewitt's Handbook of Stream Improvement*.

18. Hewitt, *Hewitt's Handbook of Stream Improvement*.

19. Hewitt, *A Trout and Salmon Fisherman for Seventy-Five Years*.

20. E. R. Hewitt, *Better Trout Streams* (New York: Charles Scribner's Sons, 1931).

21. D. M. Thompson and G. N. Stull, "The Development and Historic Use of Habitat Structures in Channel Restoration in the United States: The Grand Experiment in Fisheries Management," *Géographie Physique et Quaternaire* 56 (2002): 45–60.

22. Hewitt, *Better Trout Streams*.

23. Hewitt, *Better Trout Streams*.

24. Hewitt, *Better Trout Streams*.

25. Hewitt, *Better Trout Streams*.

26. Hewitt, *Hewitt's Handbook of Stream Improvement*.

27. W. C. Platts, *Trout Streams* (London: Field, 1927).

28. E. R. Hewitt, *Telling on the Trout* (New York: Charles Scribner's Sons, 1930).

29. Hewitt, *Hewitt's Handbook of Stream Improvement*.

30. Hewitt, *Hewitt's Handbook of Stream Improvement*, 27.

31. Van Put, *Trout Fishing in the Catskills*.

32. Hewitt, *Those Were the Days*.

33. Hewitt, *Telling on the Trout*, 125.

34. Platts, *Trout Streams*.

35. Hewitt, *Telling on the Trout*.

36. Van Put, *Trout Fishing in the Catskills*.

37. Van Put, *Trout Fishing in the Catskills*.

38. Van Put, *Trout Fishing in the Catskills*.

39. Hewitt, *Better Trout Streams*.

40. Hewitt, *Hewitt's Handbook of Stream Improvement*.

41. Hewitt, *Better Trout Streams*.

42. Van Put, *The Beaverkill*.

43. Platts, *Trout Streams*.

44. Van Put, *Trout Fishing in the Catskills*.

45. S. A. Schumm and R. S. Parker, "Implications of Complex Response of Drainage Systems for Quaternary Alluvial Stratigraphy," *Nature Physical Science* 243 (1973): 99–100.

46. A. Leopold, *A Sand County Almanac* (New York: Ballantine, 1970).

EIGHT. STREAM IMPROVEMENT PLOWS AHEAD

The epigraph is from C. M. Tarzwell, "Progress in Lake and Stream Improvement," in *Transactions of the Twenty-First American Games Conference* (New York: American Game Association, 1935), 124.

1. T. Egan, *The Worst Hard Times* (New York: Houghton Mifflin Harcourt Publishing, 2006); M. Reisner, *Cadillac Desert* (New York, Penguin, 1986).

2. G. D. Libecap and Z. K. Hansen, "'Rain Follows the Plow' and Dryfarming Doctrine: The Climate Information Problem and Homestead Failure in the Upper Great Plains, 1890–1925," *The Journal of Economic History* 62 (2000): 86–120.

3. Egan, *The Worst Hard Times*.

4. J. M. Barry, *Rising Tide* (New York: Simon and Schuster, 1998).

5. C. M. Tarzwell, "Progress in Lake and Stream Improvement," in *Transactions of the Twenty-First American Games Conference* (New York: American Game Association, 1935), 120.

6. Tarzwell, "Progress in Lake and Stream Improvement."

7. E. N. Shor, R. H. Rosenblatt, and J. D. Isaacs, *Carl Leavitt Hubbs, 1894–1979* (Washington, DC: National Academy of Sciences, 1987).

8. C. L. Hubbs, "Fisheries Research in Michigan," *Transactions of the American Fisheries Society* 60 (1930): 182–86.

9. H. E. Went, *Hoover the Fishing President* (Mechanicsburg, PA: Stackpole, 2005).

10. C. L. Hubbs, J. R. Greeley, and C. M. Tarzwell, *Methods for the Improvement of Michigan Trout Streams* (Ann Arbor: Bulletin of the Institute for Fisheries Research 1, University of Michigan, 1932).

11. Hubbs, "Fisheries Research in Michigan," 183.

12. C. L. Hubbs, "Opening Remarks: Stream and Lake Improvement," in *Proceedings*

of the North American Wildlife Conference (Washington, DC: U.S. Government Printing Office, 1936), 428.

13. Shor et al., *Carl Leavitt Hubbs, 1894–1979*.

14. Hubbs et al., *Methods for the Improvement of Michigan Trout Streams*, 3.

15. W. C. Latta, "The Early History of Fisheries Management in Michigan," *Fisheries* 31 (2006): 230–34.

16. C. L. Hubbs, "The Improvement of Trout Streams," *American Forests* 38 (1932): 394.

17. Hubbs et al., *Methods for the Improvement of Michigan Trout Streams*.

18. C. L. Hubbs, "Fisheries Research in Michigan," *Transactions of the American Fisheries Society* 60 (1931): 182–86.

19. Hubbs et al., *Methods for the Improvement of Michigan Trout Streams*.

20. Latta, "The Early History of Fisheries Management in Michigan."

21. Hubbs, "The Improvement of Trout Streams."

22. Hubbs, "The Improvement of Trout Streams."

23. Latta, "The Early History of Fisheries Management in Michigan."

24. C. M. Tarzwell, "Experimental Evidence of the Value of Trout Stream Improvements," *Transactions of the American Fisheries Society* 66 (1936): 177–87.

25. M. A. Gee, *Stream Improvement Handbook* (Washington, DC: U.S. Forest Service, 1952).

26. Hubbs, "Fisheries Research in Michigan," 182.

27. Tarzwell, "Progress in Lake and Stream Improvement."

28. Latta, "The Early History of Fisheries Management in Michigan."

29. J. R. Greeley and C. M. Tarzwell, "How Michigan Is Making Better Trout Streams," *American Forests* 38 (1932): 460–80.

30. Barry, *Rising Tide*.

31. A. S. Hazzard, "Results of Stream Improvement Work in Michigan," in *Transactions of the Second North American Wildlife Conference* (Washington, DC: U.S. Government Printing Office, 1937), 620.

32. Tarzwell, "Experimental Evidence of the Value of Trout Stream Improvements."

33. P. R. Needham, "Stream Improvement in Arid Regions," in *Proceedings of the North American Wildlife Conference* (Washington, DC: U.S. Government Printing Office, 1936), 453.

34. C. J. Hunter, *Better Trout Habitat* (Washington, DC: Island Press, 1991).

35. Hubbs et al., *Methods for the Improvement of Michigan Trout Streams*.

36. Latta, "The Early History of Fisheries Management in Michigan."

37. H. S. Davis, *Methods for the Improvement of Streams* (Washington, DC: U.S. Department of Commerce, Bureau of Fisheries, 1935), 3.

38. Davis, *Methods for the Improvement of Streams*, 6.

39. H. S. Davis, "The Purpose and Value of Stream Improvement," *Transactions of the American Fisheries Society* 64 (1935): 63–67.

40. H. S. Davis, "Stream Improvement in National Forests," in *Proceedings of the North American Wildlife Conference* (Washington, DC: U.S. Government Printing Office, 1936), 450.

41. Davis, "Stream Improvement in National Forests," 447.

42. M. B. Arthur, *Fish Stream Improvement Handbook* (Washington, DC: U.S. Forest Service, 1936).

43. A. P. Sweigart, "Pennsylvania Angler," *Commonwealth of Pennsylvania, Board of Fish Commissioners, News Bulletin for Fisherman*, March, 1932, 1–11.

44. Arthur, *Fish Stream Improvement Handbook*, 1.

45. Arthur, *Fish Stream Improvement Handbook*, 1.

46. "The Conference Background," in *Proceedings of the North American Wildlife Conference* (Washington, DC: U.S. Government Publishing Office, 1936), xvi.

47. R. J. Behnke, *Trout and Salmon of North America* (New York: Free Press, 2002).

48. J. R. Greeley, "Lake and Stream Improvement in New York," in *Proceedings of the North American Wildlife Conference* (Washington, DC: U.S. Government Printing Office, 1936), 434–39; Tarzwell, "Lake and Stream Improvement in Michigan," in *Proceedings of the North American Wildlife Conference* (Washington, DC: U.S. Government Printing Office, 1936), 429–34; O. M. Deibler, "Stream Improvement in Pennsylvania and Its Results," in *Proceedings of the North American Wildlife Conference* (Washington, DC: U.S. Government Printing Office, 1936), 439–43; Needham, "Stream Improvement in Arid Regions."

49. R. Fechner, "Emergency Conservation Work" Memorandum for the press, E.C.W. 127211, November 29, 1936, 1–8.

50. Hazzard, "Results of Stream Improvement Work in Michigan"; Tarzwell, "Experimental Evidence of the Value of Trout Stream Improvements."

51. J. R. Greeley, "Progress of Stream Improvement in New York State," *Transactions of the American Fisheries Society* 65 (1935): 316–22; Tarzwell, "Progress in Lake and Stream Improvement."

52. Tarzwell, "Progress in Lake and Stream Improvement"; Tarzwell, "Experimental Evidence of the Value of Trout Stream Improvements."

53. Deibler, "Stream Improvement in Pennsylvania and Its Results," 443.

54. C. M. Tarzwell, "An Evaluation of the Methods and Results of Stream Improvement in the Southwest," in *Transactions of the Third North American Wildlife Conference* (Washington, DC: American Wildlife Institute, 1938), 339–64; C. N. Feast Jr., "Stream Improvement and Fish Planting Plans in the National Forests of the Central Rocky Mountain Region," in *Transactions of the Third North American Wildlife Conference* (Washington, DC: American Wildlife Institute, 1938), 428–32.

55. F. T. Bell, "Address of Mr. Frank T. Bell, Chief, U.S. Bureau of Fisheries," in *Proceedings of the North American Wildlife Conference* (Washington, DC: U.S. Government Printing Office, 1936), 201–9.

56. C. L. Hubbs, "The Improvement of Trout Streams," *American Forests* 38 (1932): 394–431.

57. Tarzwell, "Progress in Lake and Stream Improvement."

58. Davis, "Stream Improvement in National Forests."

59. Tarzwell, "Experimental Evidence of the Value of Trout Stream Improvements," 339.

60. Tarzwell, "Progress in Lake and Stream Improvement."

61. C. L. Hubbs, C. M. Tarzwell, and R. W. Eschmeyer, "C.C.C. Stream Improvement Work in Michigan," *Transactions of the American Fisheries Society* 63 (1933): 404–14.

62. Hubbs et al., "C.C.C. Stream Improvement Work in Michigan."

63. Tarzwell, "An Evaluation of the Methods and Results of Stream Improvement in the Southwest."

64. Tarzwell, "An Evaluation of the Methods and Results of Stream Improvement in the Southwest," 348.

65. R. Ritzler, "Stream Improvement as Related to Erosion," in *Proceedings of the North American Wildlife Conference* (Washington, DC: U.S. Government Printing Office, 1936), 468.

66. Comment section at the end of: Tarzwell, "Progress in Lake and Stream Improvement."

67. O. H. Clark, "Stream Improvement in Michigan," *Transactions of the American Fisheries Society* 75 (1945): 270–80.

68. E. Moore et al., "A Problem in Trout Stream Management," *Transactions of the American Fisheries Society* 64 (1934): 70.

69. Moore et al., "A Problem in Trout Stream Management," 77.

70. D. M. Thompson, "Did the Pre-1980 Use of Instream Structures Improve Streams? A Reanalysis of Historic Data," *Ecological Applications*, 16 (2006): 784–96.

71. Deibler, "Stream Improvement in Pennsylvania and Its Results," 441.

72. Comment section at the end of Tarzwell, "Progress in Lake and Stream Improvement"; Deibler, "Stream Improvement in Pennsylvania and Its Results."

73. Tarzwell, "Progress in Lake and Stream Improvement," 133; Deibler, "Stream Improvement in Pennsylvania and Its Results."

74. Comment section at the end of Tarzwell, "Progress in Lake and Stream Improvement."

75. Deibler, "Stream Improvement in Pennsylvania and Its Results," 443.

76. W. W. Aitken, "Iowa Stream Improvement Work," *Transactions of the American Fisheries Society* 65 (1935): 322–33.

77. M. J. Madsen, "A Preliminary Investigation into the Results of Stream Improvement in the Intermountain Forest Region," in *Transactions of the Third North American Wildlife Conference* (Washington, DC: American Wildlife Institute, 1938), 497–503.

78. C. L. Hubbs, "Fish Management: Looking Forward," *Transactions of the American Fisheries Society* 66 (1937): 54.

79. D. S. Shetter, O. H. Clark, and A. S. Hazzard, "The Effects of Deflectors in a Section of a Michigan Trout Stream," *Transactions of the American Fisheries Society* 76 (1949): 248–78.

80. Shetter et al., "The Effects of Deflectors in a Section of a Michigan Trout Stream," 248–49.

81. S. Swales and K. O'Hara, "Instream Habitat Devices and Their Use in Freshwater Fisheries Management," *Journal of Environmental Management* 10 (1980): 167–79.

82. Shetter et al., "The Effects of Deflectors in a Section of a Michigan Trout Stream," 250.

83. Shetter et al., "The Effects of Deflectors in a Section of a Michigan Trout Stream."

84. Shetter et al., "The Effects of Deflectors in a Section of a Michigan Trout Stream."

85. Shetter et al., "The Effects of Deflectors in a Section of a Michigan Trout Stream."

86. Thompson, "Did the Pre-1980 Use of Instream Structures Improve Streams?"

87. J. W. Mueller, "Wyoming Stream Improvement," *Wyoming Wild Life* 18 (1954): 30–32; B. H. Unruh and P. E. Giguere, "Living Room for Trout: Deflector Dams Prove Worth on Southern California Streams," *Outdoor California* 16 (1955): 4–5.

88. D. M. Thompson, "The Long-Term Stability and Morphologic Influence of the Use of Instream Structures in Channel Restoration Design," in *Managing Watersheds for Human and Natural Impacts*, ed. G. E. Moglen (Williamsburg, VA: American Society of Civil Engineers, 2005), 1–9.

89. M. A. Gee, *Stream Improvement Handbook* (Washington, DC: U.S. Forest Service, 1952).

90. Pennsylvania Fish Commission, Engineering Division, *Stream Improvement Guide* (Harrisburg, PA: Conservation Education Division, 1968), 1.

91. "Habitat Improvement," Pennsylvania Fish and Boat Commission, http://fishandboat.com/habitat.htm (accessed May 9, 2012).

92. M. B. Otis, "Stream Improvement," in *The Stream Conservation Handbook*, ed. J. M. Migel (New York: Crown, 1974), 99–122.

93. "Fishing," Great Smokey Mountains, National Park Service, www.nps.gov/grsm/planyourvisit/fishing.htm (accessed December 2, 2012).

94. M. A. Gee, *Stream Improvement Handbook*.

95. Pennsylvania Fish Commission, Engineering Division, *Stream Improvement Guide* (Harrisburg, PA: Conservation Education Division, 1961); J. G. Miller and R. Tibbott, *Fish Habitat Improvement for Trout Streams* (Harrisburg: Pennsylvania Fish and Boat Commission, 1984); J. G. Miller and R. Tibbott, *Fish Habitat Improvement for Trout Streams* (Harrisburg: Pennsylvania Fish and Boat Commission, 1992); D. F. Houser and K. J. Lutz, *Fish Habitat Improvement for Trout Streams* (Harrisburg: Pennsylvania Fish and Boat Commission, 1999).

96. National Research Council, *Restoration of Aquatic Ecosystems* (Washington, DC: National Academy, 1992).

97. E. S. Bernhardt et al., "Synthesizing U.S. River Restoration Efforts," *Science* 308 (2005): 636–37.

98. Thompson, "Did the Pre-1980 Use of Instream Structures Improve Streams?"

99. M. F. Boussu, "Relationship between Trout Populations and Cover on a Small Stream," *Journal of Wildlife Management* 18 (1954): 229–39.

100. Thompson, "Did the Pre-1980 Use of Instream Structures Improve Streams?"

101. J. L. Pretty et al., "River Rehabilitation and Fish Populations: Assessing the Benefit of Instream Structures," *Journal of Applied Ecology* 40 (2003): 251.

102. A. H. Moerke and G. A. Lamberti, "Responses in Fish Community Structure to Restoration of Two Indiana Streams," *North American Journal of Fisheries Management* 23 (2003):748–59; N. E. Jones and W. M. Tonn, "Enhancing Productive Capacity in the Canadian Arctic: Assessing the Effectiveness of Instream Habitat Structures in Habitat Compensation," *Transactions of the American Fisheries Society* 133 (2004): 1356–65.

103. P. Roni, K. Hanson, and T. Beechie, "Global Review of the Physical and Biological Effectiveness of Stream Rehabilitation Techniques," *North American Journal of Fisheries Management* 28 (2008.): 856–90.

104. D. M. Thompson, "Long-Term Effect of Instream Habitat-Improvement

Structures on Channel Morphology along the Blackledge and Salmon Rivers, Connecticut, USA," *Environmental Management*, 29 (2002): 250–65.

105. R. Ehlers, "An Evaluation of Stream Improvement Devices Constructed Eighteen Years Ago," *California Fish and Game* 42 (1956): 203–17.

106. D. Robinson, "Devices for Better Fishing," *West Virginia Conservation* 26 (1962): 16–21; D. B. Jester and H. J. McKirdy, "Evaluation of Trout Stream Improvement in New Mexico," *Proceedings of the Annual Conference of Western Association of State Game and Fish Commissioners* 46 (1966): 316–33.

NINE. STRUCTURAL FAILURES IN THE SYSTEM
The epigraph is from H. S. Davis, "Stream Improvement in National Forests," in *Proceedings of the North American Wildlife Conference* (Washington, DC: U.S. Government Printing Office, 1936), 447.

1. R. A. Toblaski and N. K. Tripp, "Gabions for Stream and Erosion Control," *Journal of Soil and Water Conservation* 16 (1961): 284–85; J. Mullan and H. Barrett, "Trout, Floods and Gabions," *Virginia Wildlife* 23 (1962): 18–19.

2. Mullan and Barrett, "Trout, Floods and Gabions," 19.

3. Mullan and Barrett, "Trout, Floods and Gabions," 18.

4. J. S. Van Cleef, "How to Restore Our Trout Streams," *Transactions of the American Fisheries Society* 14 (1885): 50–55.

5. D. McCullough, *The Johnstown Flood* (New York: Simon and Schuster, 1968).

6. P. Dawson, "The Stream Saver," *Time*, June 8, 2004, www.time.com/time/specials/packages/article/0,28804,1995235_1995382_1995447,00.html.

7. R. A. Lave, M. W. Doyle, and M. Robertson, "Privatizing Stream Restoration in the US," *Social Studies of Science* 40 (2010): 684.

8. Lave et al., "Privatizing Stream Restoration in the US."

9. "River Short Courses — Registration Form," Wildland Hydrology Consultants, www.wildlandhydrology.com/register.htm (accessed June 13, 2012).

10. C. Dean, "Follow the Silt," *New York Times*, June 25, 2008.

11. D. Malakoff, "The River Doctor," *Science* 305 (2004): 937–39.

12. N. Gordon, *Summary of Technical Testimony in the Colorado Water Division 1 Trail: General Technical Report RM-GTR-270* (Fort Collins, CO: U.S. Forest Service, Rocky Mountain Forest and Range Experimental Station, 2005).

13. Lave et al., "Privatizing Stream Restoration in the US."

14. "Short Course Schedule — 2012," Wildland Hydrology Consultants, www.wildlandhydrology.com/html/courses.htm (accessed July 16, 2012).

15. National Research Council, *Restoration of Aquatic Ecosystems: Science, Technology and Public Policy* (Washington, DC: National Academy, 1992).

16. D. L. Rosgen and H. L. Silvey, *Applied River Morphology* (Pagosa Springs, CO: Wildland Hydrology, 1996).

17. D. L. Rosgen and B. L. Fittante, "Fish Habitat Structures — A Selection Guide Using Stream Classification," in *The Fifth Trout Stream Habitat Workshop: Proceedings of a Workshop, August 12–14, 1986, Lock Haven University*, ed. J. Miller, J. Arway and R. Carline (Lock Haven, PA: Lock Haven University, 1986), 165.

18. "QG&G Ad Hoc Committee on Applied Fluvial Geomorphology: Position Statement on Applied Fluvial Geomorphology," Geological Society of America, March 22, 2004, www.geo.wvu.edu/~kite/QG&GFluvGeomPositionStatement22March2004 .html.

19. "Introduction to Sediment and River Stability," U.S. Environmental Protection Agency, http://water.epa.gov/scitech/datait/tools/warsss/sedsource_index.cfm (accessed July 20, 2012).

20. Lave et al., "Privatizing Stream Restoration in the US."

21. Dawson, "The Stream Saver."

22. Malakoff, "The River Doctor," 937.

23. R. A. Lave, "The Controversy over Natural Channel Design: Substantive Explanations and Potential Avenues for Resolution," *Journal of the American Water Resources Association* 45 (2009): 1519–32.

24. S. Gillilan et al., "Challenges in Developing and Implementing Ecological Standards for Geomorphic River Restoration Projects: A Practitioner's Response to Palmer et al. (2005)." *Journal of Applied Ecology* 42 (2005): 223–27.

25. R. A. Lave "The Rosgen Wars and the Shifting Political Economy of Expertise" (PhD Diss., University of California Berkley, 2008).

26. D. L. Rosgen, "The Cross-Vane, W-Weir and J-Hook Vane Structures . . . Their Description, Design and Application for Stream Stabilization and River Restoration," in *Proceedings of the Wetlands Engineering and River Restoration Conference* (Reno: American Society of Civil Engineers, 2001), 1–22.

27. Note the tables for structure-use suitability in Rosgen and Fittante, "Fish Habitat Structures — A Selection Guide Using Stream Classification, 163–79; Rosgen and Silvey, *Applied River Morphology*.

28. M. E. Seehorn, *Fish Habitat Improvement Handbook* (Atlanta, GA: Technical Publication, R8-TP 7 Southern Region, U.S. Forest Service, 1985); Rosgen also referenced another commonly cited paper: R. J. White and O. M. Brynildson, *Guidelines for Management of Trout Stream Habitat in Wisconsin: Technical Bulletin No. 39* (Madison, WI: Department of Natural Resources, 1967). Numerous oft-cited articles were published in Wisconsin by R. L. Hunt that included R. L. Hunt, "A Long-Term Evaluation of Trout Habitat Development and Its Relation to Improving Management-Related Research." *Transactions of the American Fisheries Society* 105 (1976): 361–64.

29. D. M. Thompson, "The Long-Term Stability and Morphologic Influence of the Use of Instream Structures in Channel Restoration Design," in *Managing Watersheds for Human and Natural Impacts*, ed. G. E. Moglen (Williamsburg, VA: American Society of Civil Engineers, 2005), 1–9.

30. M. E. Seehorn, *Stream Habitat Improvement Handbook* (Atlanta, GA: Technical Publication R8-TP 16, Southern Region, U.S. Forest Service, 1992).

31. G. H. Reeves and T. D. Roelofs, "Rehabilitating and Enhancing Stream Habitat: 2. Field Applications," in *Influence of Forest and Rangeland Management on Anadromous Fish Habitat in Western North America, General Technical Report PNW-140* (Portland, OR: Pacific Northwest Forest and Range Experiment Station, U.S. Department of Agriculture, 1982), 1–33.

32. Design referenced in Rosgen and Fittante, "Fish Habitat Structures — A Selection Guide Using Stream Classification," and Rosgen and Silvey, *Applied River Morphology*, with the original design referenced in Reeves and Roelofs, "Rehabilitating and Enhancing Stream Habitat: 2. Field Applications."

33. Lave, The Controversy over Natural Channel Design."

34. Lave et al., "Privatizing Stream Restoration in the US."

35. M. W. Doyle and D. Shields, "Compensatory Mitigation for Streams under the Clean Water Act: Reassessing Science and Redirecting Policy," *Journal of the American Water Resources Association* 48 (2012): 494.

36. T. K. BenDor, J. Sholtes, and M. W. Doyle, "Landscape Characteristics of a Stream and Wetland Mitigation Banking Program," *Ecological Applications* 19 (2009): 2078–92.

37. M. A. Palmer et al., "River Restoration in the Twenty-First Century: Data and Experiential Knowledge to Inform Future Efforts," *Restoration Ecology* 15 (2007): 472–81.

38. S. M. Smith and K. L. Prestegaard, "Hydraulic Performance of a Morphology-Based Stream Channel Design," *Water Resources Research* 41 (2005): W11413, doi: 10.1029/2004WR003926; A. Simon et al., "Critical Evaluation of How the Rosgen Classification and Associated "Natural Channel Design" Methods Fail to Integrate and Quantify Fluvial Processes and Channel Response." *Journal of the American Water Resources Association* 43 (2007): 1117–31; D. A. Schmetterling and R. W. Pierce, "Success of Instream Habitat Structures after a 50-Year Flood in Gold Creek, Montana." *Restoration Ecology* 7 (1999): 369–75.

39. S. L. Niezgoda and P. A. Johnson, "Improving the Urban Stream Restoration Effort: Identifying Critical Form and Processes Relationships." *Environmental Management* 35 (2005): 579–92; W. C. Hession et al., "Influence of Bank Vegetation on Channel Morphology in Rural and Urban Watersheds." *Geology* 31 (2003): 147–50; Simon et al., "Critical Evaluation of How the Rosgen Classification."

40. E. S. Bernhardt et al., "Synthesizing U.S. River Restoration Efforts," *Science* 308 (2005): 636–37.

41. D. M. Thompson, "The Effects of Large Organic Debris on Sediment Processes and Stream Morphology in Vermont," *Geomorphology*, 11 (1995): 235–44.

42. F. J. Magilligan et al., "The Geomorphic Function and Characteristics of Large Woody Debris in Low Gradient Rivers, Coastal Maine, USA," *Geomorphology* 97 (2007): 467–82.

43. "Proposed Amendments to the Inland Wetlands and Watercourses Act Sections 22a-36 to 22a-45a, H.B. No. 5820, An Act Conserving Natural Vegetation Near Wetlands and Watercourses," Submitted to the Environment Committee February 23, 2010.

TEN. THE ECONOMY OF SCALES

The epigraph is from J. J. Armistead, *An Angler's Paradise and How to Obtain It* (Scarborough, UK: The Angler Limited, 1895), 4.

1. A. Harris, "Trout Fishing in 2006: A Demographic Description and Economic Analysis," Addendum to the *2006 National Survey of Fishing, Hunting, and Wildlife-Associated Recreation, U.S. Fish and Wildlife Service Report* 2006-6 (2010): 1–21.

2. D. M. Johnson et al., "Economic Benefits and Costs of Stocking Catchable Rainbow

Trout: A Synthesis of Economic Analysis in Colorado," *North American Journal of Fisheries Management* 15 (1995): 26–32.

3. S. D. Hamilton, *Economic Effect of National Fish Hatchery Trout Production in the Southeastern U.S.* (Atlanta, GA: U.S. Fish and Wildlife Service, 2001).

4. T. Turner and L. Gaumnitz, "Wild Rose Hatchery Celebrates New Trout, Salmon Facilities," *Fox River Current* 11 (2009): 6–7.

5. "Brown Trout," Missouri Department of Conservation, www.conservation.mo.gov/discover-nature/field-guide/brown-trout (accessed May 15, 2012); Kruse et al., "A Plan for Missouri Trout Fishing," Missouri Department of Conservation, last modified October 9, 2003, http://mdc4.mdc.mo.gov/Documents/25.pdf.

6. "Castalia State Fish Hatchery Celebrates $7 Million Renovation," Ohio Department of Natural Resources, last modified April 17, 2012, http://ohiodnr.com/tabid/18276/default.aspx.

7. Harris, "Trout Fishing in 2006."

8. "Castalia State Fish Hatchery Celebrates $7 Million Renovation," Ohio Department of Natural Resources.

9. "Welcome to Norfork National Fish Hatchery," U.S. Fish and Wildlife Service, www.fws.gov/norfork/ (accessed May 15, 2012).

10. "Wolf Creek National Fish Hatchery: Linking the Biological Health of the Nation's Aquatic Resources with the Economic Health of the Nation's Human Communities," U.S. Fish and Wildlife Service, www.fws.gov/wolfcreek/pdf/2011EconomicImpact.pdf (accessed May 23, 2012).

11. "Dale Hollow National Fish Hatchery: Linking the Biological Health of the Nation's Aquatic Resources with the Economic Health of the Nation's Human Communities," U.S. Fish and Wildlife Service, www.fws.gov/dalehollow/dale%20hollow%202010%20econ%20fact%20sheet.pdf (accessed May 23, 2012).

12. "Welcome to the Chattahoochee Forest National Fish Hatchery," U.S. Fish and Wildlife Service, www.fws.gov/chattahoocheeforest/ (accessed May 15, 2012).

13. "Welcome to the Greers Ferry National Fish Hatchery," U.S. Fish and Wildlife Service, last updated June 5, 2012, www.fws.gov/greersferry/.

14. "Brook Trout Fishing Study Summary: Great Smoky Mountains National Park," National Park Service, www.nps.gov/grsm/naturescience/upload/fishing-study.pdf (accessed May 23, 2012).

15. Harris, "Trout Fishing in 2006."

16. Harris, "Trout Fishing in 2006," 13.

17. J. Caudill, *The Economic Effect of Rainbow Trout Stocking by Fish and Wildlife Service Hatcheries in FY 2004* (Arlington, VA: Division of Economics, U.S. Fish and Wildlife Service, 2005).

18. M. Reisner, *Cadillac Desert* (New York, Penguin, 1986); D. Turner, "A First Look at a Modern Legal Regime for a 'Post-Modern' United States Army Corps of Engineers," *Kansas Law Review* 52 (2004): 1285–325.

19. P. E. Roberts, "Benefit-Cost Analysis: Its Use (Misuse) in Evaluating Water Resources Projects," *American Business Law Journal* 14 (1978): 73–84.

20. R. J. Behnke, "From Hatcheries to Habitat? Look Again," *Trout* 32 (1991): 55–58.

21. D. B. Wood and J. J. Kennedy, "Effects of Stocking Albino Trout on Angler Utility," *Journal of Leisure Research* 15 (1983): 179–83.

22. G. E. Whelan, "A Historical Perspective on the Philosophy Behind the Use of Propagated Fish in Fisheries Management: Michigan's 130-Year Experience," *American Fisheries Society Symposium* 44 (2004): 307–15.

23. "Strategic Plan for Management of Trout Fisheries in Pennsylvania 2010–2014," Pennsylvania Fish and Boat Commission, last modified October, 2009, www.fish.state.pa .us/pafish/trout/trout_plan/troutplan2010.pdf.

24. "Fisheries Management in Public Waters," Georgia Wildlife Resources Division, www.georgiawildlife.com/node/931 (accessed May 14, 2012).

25. "Stocked Trout Program: Cost Report," Pennsylvania Fish and Boat Commission, last modified March, 2009, http://fishandboat.com/pafish/trout/stocked_cost _study2009.pdf.

26. M. Goodwin, *Trout Streams of Eastern Connecticut* (Ledyard, CT: Trout Unlimited, Thames Valley Chapter, 2004).

27. "Stocking Program: Nevada Hatcheries," Nevada Department of Wildlife, http:// ndow.org/fish/stocking/hatch/index.shtm (accessed June 20, 2012).

28. "New Fish Hatchery Constructed (1971)," Connecticut Department of Energy and Environmental Protection, www.ct.gov/dep/cwp/view.asp?a=2688&q=456432&depNav _GID=1511 (accessed June 20, 2012).

29. "Oden State Fish Hatchery," Michigan Department of Natural Resources, www .michigan.gov/dnr/0,4570,7-153-10364_28277-22423 — ,00.html (accessed June 20, 2012).

30. "Castalia State Fish Hatchery Celebrates $7 Million Renovation," Ohio Department of Natural Resources.

31. "Renovation of Wisconsin's Wild Rose State Fish Hatchery," National Shooting Sports Foundation, http://wsfr75.com/content/renovation-wisconsin%E2%80%99s-wild -rose-state-fish-hatchery (accessed June 22, 2012); Turner and Gaumnitz, "Wild Rose Hatchery Celebrates New Trout, Salmon Facilities."

32. S. Minkkinen, "The History of Trout Hatcheries in Maryland," Maryland Department of Natural Resources, www.dnr.state.md.us/fisheries/recreational/articles/ historytrouthatchery.html (accessed June 22, 2012).

33. Whelan, "A Historical Perspective."

34. Johnson et al., "Economic Benefits and Costs of Stocking Catchable Rainbow Trout."

35. K. W. Hagos, "The Status of Fish Hatcheries in Rhode Island: A Scheme for Improving Effluent Quality at Lafayette Trout Hatchery," Rhode Island Department of Environmental Management, last modified March 31, 2009, www.ci.uri.edu/ciip/ Publications/Hagos_RI_Fish_Hatcheries_final.pdf.

36. R. Cordes, W. Sayler, and M. Barnes, *McNenny State Fish Hatchery 2002 Annual Production Report* (Pierre: South Dakota Department of Game, Fish and Parks, 2002).

37. J. B. Dunham, D. S. Pilliod, and M. K. Young, "Assessing the Consequences of Nonnative Trout in Headwater Ecosystems in Western North America," *Fisheries* 29 (2004): 18–26.

38. "Strategic Plan for Management of Trout Fisheries in Pennsylvania 2010–2014."

39. "Stocked Trout Program: Cost Report," Pennsylvania Fish and Boat Commission.

40. Johnson et al., "Economic Benefits and Costs of Stocking Catchable Rainbow Trout."

41. "The Fish Hatchery Game — An Interactive Math & Science Resource," Colorado Department of Natural Resources, last modified December 27, 2011, http://wildlife.state. co.us/Education/TeacherResources/FishHatcheryGame/Pages/HatcheryManager.aspx.

42. Cordes et al., "McNenny State Fish Hatchery 2002 Annual Production Report."

43. "Stocked Trout Program: Cost Report," Pennsylvania Fish and Boat Commission.

44. C. Lemon, "Celebrating 100 years of the Hackettstown Fish Hatchery," *New Jersey Freshwater Fishing Digest*, January (2002): 11.

45. J. M. Hinshaw, "Trout Production: Feeds and Feeding and Methods," *Southern Regional Aquaculture Center Publication*, No. 223 (1990): 1–2.

46. "Berkley PowerBait Hatchery Formula Trout Nuggets," Cabela's, www.cabelas.com (accessed on June 8, 2012).

47. D. McCullough, *The Johnstown Flood* (New York: Simon and Schuster, 1968).

48. J. Brooks, *Trout Fishing* (New York: Sedgewood, 1985), 45.

49. "Reader Demographics *Trout* Magazine," Trout Unlimited, www.tu.org/sites/www .tu.org/files/documents/TroutMagDemographics_0.pdf (accessed April 4, 2008).

50. A. Lee, *Fishing Dry Flies for Trout on Rivers and Streams* (Champaign, IL: Human Kinetics, 1988), 288.

51. "Trout Lures Many to State Streams," *New York Times*, August 25, 1907.

52. J. Bailey, *Ultimate Freshwater Fishing* (New York: DK Publishing, 1998), 164.

53. D. Whitlock, *L.L. Bean Fly-Fishing Handbook* (New York: Lyons, 1996).

54. R. L. Eshenroder et al., *Fish Community Objectives for Lake Michigan* (Ann Arbor: Great Lakes Fisheries Commission, 1995).

55. "TIC School Directory," Pennsylvania Trout in the Classroom, http:// patroutintheclassroom.org/MapofTICSchools.aspx (accessed February 20, 2013).

56. "Philadelphia County, Pennsylvania," U.S. Census Bureau, last modified January 10, 2013, http://quickfacts.census.gov/qfd/states/42/42101.html.

57. "Chester County, Pennsylvania," U.S. Census Bureau, last modified January 10, 2013, http://quickfacts.census.gov/qfd/states/42/42029.html.

58. "Reader Demographics *Trout* Magazine."

59. C. DeNavas-Walt, B. D. Proctor, and J. C. Smith, *Income, Poverty, and Health Insurance Coverage in the United States: 2010* (Washington, DC: U.S. Government Printing Office, 2011).

60. "Reader Demographics *Trout* Magazine."

61. Harris, "Trout Fishing in 2006," 13.

62. Harris, "Trout Fishing in 2006."

63. "Reader Demographics *Trout* Magazine."

64. "Reader Demographics *Trout* Magazine."

65. Harris, "Trout Fishing in 2006."

66. "Reader Demographics *Trout* Magazine."

67. "Reader Demographics *Trout* Magazine."

68. "Brook Trout Fishing Study Summary: Great Smoky Mountains National Park," National Park Service, www.nps.gov/grsm/naturescience/upload/fishing-study.pdf (accessed May 23, 2012).

69. "Strategic Plan for Management of Trout Fisheries in Pennsylvania 2010–2014."

70. Harris, "Trout Fishing in 2006."

71. "Reader Demographics *Trout* Magazine."

72. "Reader Demographics *Trout* Magazine."

73. J. Gierach, *Still Life with Brook Trout* (New York: Simon and Schuster, 2005), 204.

74. P. Brunquell, *Fly-fishing with Children* (Woodstock, VT: Countryman, 1994), 160.

75. Brunquell, *Fly-fishing with Children*, 160.

76. "A Message from the Founder," Spring Ridge Club, www.springridgeclubs.com/about/index_spring_ridge_club.html (accessed June 26, 2012).

77. D. Weisberg, "Lawsuit over Access to Fish Little Juniata River Resolved," *Pittsburgh Post-Gazette*, February 8, 2008, www.post-gazette.com/stories/local/uncategorized/lawsuit-over-access-to-fish-little-juniata-river-resolved-379673/.

78. "Homewaters," Homewaters Club, www.homewatersclub.com/ (accessed May 23, 2012).

79. Brooks, *Trout Fishing*, 6.

80. J. Shapiro, "Fly-Fishing Club Casts Line for Liquor License," DNAinfo.com, last modified January 5, 2011, www.dnainfo.com.

81. Shapiro, "Fly-Fishing Club Casts Line for Liquor License."

82. Shapiro, "Fly-Fishing Club Casts Line for Liquor License."

83. G. Torresola, "Comunique No. 3," Fuerzas Armadas de Liberación Nacional, January 24, 1975, http://nothingtobegainedhere.wordpress.com/2012/02/01/ (accessed December 14, 2012).

84. E. S. Bernhardt et al., "Synthesizing U.S. River Restoration Efforts," *Science* 308 (2005): 636–37.

85. "Railroad Brook Fish Habitat Restoration Project: Success Stories," Connecticut Department of Environmental Protection, last modified December 2000, www.ct.gov/dep/lib/dep/water/nps/success_stories/rrhabit.pdf.

86. Department of Environmental Protection, "Facing Our Future: Fisheries Adapting to Connecticut's Changing Climate," *DEP-Climate-FS-005* (2009): 1–6.

87. Restoration costs ran $464/meter in New York State and $2300/meter in urban areas as reported in: G. Nagle, "Evaluating 'Natural Channel Design' Stream Projects," *Hydrologic Processes* 21 (2007): 2539–45.

88. "Railroad Brook Fish Habitat Restoration Project: Success Stories," Connecticut Department of Environmental Protection.

89. "Railroad Brook Fish Habitat Restoration Project," Connecticut Department of Environmental Protection, www.ct.gov/dep/lib/dep/fishing/restoration/railroad.pdf (accessed, June 11, 2012).

90. Data provided on July 16, 2012, by B. Murphy, Connecticut Department of Energy and Environmental Protection.

ELEVEN. REEL RETREATS RESTORED TO REAL PLACES

The epigraph is from H. A. Ingraham, *American Trout Streams* (New York: The Anglers' Club of New York, 1926), 12.

1. D. A. Hendrickson and M. M. Stewart, "Clark Hubbs," *Copeia* 2000 (2000): 619–22.

2. Plastic sheeting, wire for gabions, steel rods, and tires were all mentioned in: G. H. Reeves and T. D. Roelofs, "Rehabilitating and Enhancing Stream Habitat: 2. Field Applications," in *Influence of Forest and Rangeland Management on Anadromous Fish Habitat in Western North America, General Technical Report PNW-140* (Portland, OR: Pacific Northwest Forest and Range Experiment Station, U.S. Department of Agriculture, 1982), 1–33: Tar paper was utilized by Hewitt: E. R. Hewitt, *Hewitt's Handbook of Stream Improvement* (New York: Marchbanks, 1934).

3. J. S. Van Cleef, "How to Restore Our Trout Streams," *Transactions of the American Fisheries Society* 14 (1885): 51.

4. E. Van Put, *Trout Fishing in the Catskills* (New York: Skyhorse Publishing, 2007).

5. W. H. Armistead, *Trout Waters Management and Angling* (London: A&C Black, 1920), 5.

Selected Bibliography

BOOKS

Armistead, J. J. *An Angler's Paradise and How to Obtain It.* Scarborough, UK: The Angler Limited, 1895.

Armistead, W. H. *Trout Waters Management and Angling.* London: A&C Black, 1920.

Arthur, M. B. *Fish Stream Improvement Handbook.* Washington, DC: U.S. Forest Service, 1936.

Bailey, J. *Ultimate Freshwater Fishing.* New York: DK Publishing, 1998.

Barry, J. M. *Rising Tide: The Great Mississippi Flood of 1927 and How It Changed America.* New York: Simon and Schuster, 1998.

Behnke, R. J. *Trout and Salmon of North America.* New York: Free Press, 2002.

Brooks, J. *Trout Fishing.* New York: Sedgewood, 1985.

Davis, H. S. *Methods for the Improvement of Streams.* Washington, DC: U.S. Department of Commerce, Bureau of Fisheries, 1935.

———. *Culture and Diseases of Game Fish.* Los Angeles: University of California Press, 1967.

Duncan, D. J. *The River Why.* New York: Bantam, 1984.

Egan, T. *The Worst Hard Times: The Untold Stories of Those Who Survived the Great American Dust Bowl.* New York: Houghton Mifflin Harcourt Publishing, 2006.

Gee, M. A. *Stream Improvement Handbook.* Washington, DC: U.S. Forest Service, 1952.

Gierach, J. *Still Life with Brook Trout.* New York: Simon and Schuster, 2005.

Goodwin, M. *Trout Streams of Eastern Connecticut.* Ledyard, CT: Trout Unlimited, Thames Valley Chapter, 2004.

Halverson, M. A. *An Entirely Synthetic Fish: How Rainbow Trout Beguiled America and Overran the World.* New Haven, CT: Yale University Press, 2010.

Harvey, G. W. *Techniques of Trout Fishing and Fly Tying.* Belleville, PA: Metz Hatchery, 1985.

Hewitt, E. R. *Telling on the Trout.* New York: Charles Scribner's Sons, 1930.

———. *Better Trout Streams.* New York: Charles Scribner's Sons, 1931.

———. *Hewitt's Handbook of Stream Improvement.* New York: Marchbanks, 1934.

———. *Those Were the Days.* New York: Duell, Sloan and Pearce, 1943.

———. *A Trout and Salmon Fisherman for Seventy-Five Years.* New York: Charles Scribner's Sons, 1948.

———. *Days from Seventy-Five to Ninety.* New York: Duell, Sloan and Pearce, 1957.

Hubbs, C. L., J. R. Greeley, and C. M. Tarzwell. *Methods for the Improvement of Michigan Trout Streams.* Ann Arbor: University of Michigan Press, 1932.

Ingraham, H. A. *American Trout Streams: A Discussion of the Problems Confronting Anglers in the Preservation, Management, and Rehabilitation of American Trout Waters.* New York: The Anglers' Club of New York, 1926.

Karas, N. *Brook Trout: A Thorough Look at North America's Great Native Trout—Its History, Biology and Angling Possibilities*. Guilford, CT: Lyons, 2002.

Lee, A. *Fishing Dry Flies for Trout on Rivers and Streams*. Champaign, IL: Human Kinetics, 1988.

Mares, B. *Fishing with the Presidents*. Mechanicsburg, PA: Stackpole, 1999.

Martin, S. *Izaak Walton and His Friends*. London: Chapman and Hall, 1903.

McCullough, D. *The Johnstown Flood: The Incredible Story Behind One of the Most Devastating Disasters America Has Ever Known*. New York: Simon and Schuster, 1968.

McPhee, J. *The Founding Fish*. New York: Farrar, Straus and Giroux, 2002.

Merwin, J. *The New American Trout Fishing*. New York: MacMillan, 1994.

Montgomery, D. R. *Dirt: The Erosion of Civilizations*. Berkeley: University of California Press, 2007.

Mottram, J. C. *Trout Fisheries: Their Care and Preservation*. London: Herbert Jenkins, 1928.

National Research Council. *Restoration of Aquatic Ecosystems: Science, Technology and Public Policy*. Washington, DC: National Academy, 1992.

Nevins, A. *Abram S. Hewitt with Some Account of Peter Cooper*. New York: Harper & Brothers, 1935.

Quinnett, P. G. *Pavlov's Trout: The Incompleat Psychology of Everyday Fishing*. Kansas City, MO: Andrews McMeel, 1998.

Pinchot, G. *Fishing Talk*. Harrisburg, PA: Stackpole Books, 1936.

Platts, W. C. *Trout Streams: Their Management and Improvement*. London: Harmsworth, 1977.

Pool, L., and A. J. Pool. *Izaak Walton: The Compleat Angler and His Turbulent Times*. Lunenburg, VT: Stinehour, 1976.

Reisner, M. *Cadillac Desert: The American West and Its Disappearing Water*. New York, Penguin, 1986.

Rosgen, D. L., and H. L. Silvey. *Applied River Morphology*. Pagosa Springs, CO: Wildland Hydrology, 1996.

Rust, M. B., F. T. Barrows, R. W. Hardy, A. Lazur, K. Naughten, and J. Silverstein. *The Future of Aquafeeds*. Silver Spring, MD: NOAA/USDA Alternative Feeds Initiative, 2010.

Say, A. *A River Dream*. Boston: Houghton Mifflin, 1988.

Schneider, P. *The Adirondacks: A History of America's First Wilderness*. New York: Henry Holt, 1997.

Seehorn, M. E. *Fish Habitat Improvement Handbook*. Atlanta, GA: Technical Publication, R8-TP 7 Southern Region, U.S. Forest Service, 1985.

———. *Stream Habitat Improvement Handbook*. Atlanta, GA: Technical Publication R8-TP 16, Southern Region, U.S. Forest Service, 1992.

Shor, E. N., R. H. Rosenblatt, and J. D. Isaacs. *Carl Leavitt Hubbs 1894–1979*. Washington, DC: National Academy of Sciences, 1987.

Squeri, L. *Better in the Poconos: The Story of Pennsylvania's Vacationland*. University Park: Pennsylvania State University Press, 2002.

South Side Sportsmen's Club. *Officers, Members, Constitution and Rules of the South Side Sportsmen's Club of Long Island, Oakdale*. New York: C. C. Burnett and Company, 1907.

Walton, I. *The Compleat Angler*. Edited by J. Major. New York: T. Y. Crowell, 1898.

Whitlock, D. *L.L. Bean Fly-Fishing Handbook*. New York: Lyons, 1996.

Wohl, E. E. *Virtual Rivers: Lessons from the Mountain Rivers of the Colorado Front Range*. New Haven, CT: Yale University Press, 2001.

Van Put, E. *The Beaverkill: The History of a River and Its People*. New York: Lyons & Burford, 1996.

———. *Trout Fishing in the Catskills*. New York: Skyhorse, 2007.

ARTICLES

Allendorf, F. W., R. F. Leary, N. P. Hitt, K. L. Knudsen, L. L. Lundquist, and P. Spruell. "Intercrosses and the U.S. Endangered Species Act: Should Hybridized Populations Be Included as Westslope Cutthroat Trout?" *Conservation Biology* 18 (2004): 1203–13.

Anderson M. E., M. W. Ackerman K. D. Hilwig, A. E. Fuller, and P. D. Alley. "Evidence of Young Humpback Chub Overwintering in the Mainstream Colorado River, Marble Canyon, Arizona, USA." *The Open Fish Science Journal* 3 (2010): 42–50.

Ball, R. C. "A Summary of Experiments in Michigan Lakes on the Elimination of Fish Populations with Rotenone 1934–1942." *Transactions of the American Fisheries Society* 75 (1948): 139–46.

Bernhardt, E. S., M. A. Palmer, J. D. Allan, G. Alexander, K. Barnas, S. Brooks, et al. "Synthesizing U.S. River Restoration Efforts." *Science* 308 (2005): 636–37.

Blinn, D. W., C. Runck, D. A. Clark, and J. N. Rinne. "Notes: Effects of Rainbow Trout Predation on Little Colorado Spinedace." *Transactions of the American Fisheries Society* 122 (1993): 139–43.

Brown, C., and R. L. Day. "The Future of Stock Enhancements: Lessons from Hatchery Practices from Conservation Biology." *Fish and Fishes* 3 (2002): 79–94.

Brown, C., and K. Laland. "Social Learning and Life Skills Training for Hatchery-Reared Fish." *Journal of Fish Biology* 59 (2005): 471–93.

Clark, F. H. "Pleiotropic Effect of the Gene for Golden Color in Rainbow Trout." *The Journal of Heredity* 61 (1970): 8–10.

Davis, H. S. "The Purpose and Value of Stream Improvement." *Transactions of the American Fisheries Society* 64 (1935): 63–67.

———. "Stream Improvement in National Forests." In *Proceedings of the North American Wildlife Conference*, 447–453. Washington, DC: U.S. Government Printing Office, 1936.

Deibler, O. M. "Stream Improvement in Pennsylvania and Its Results." In *Proceedings of the North American Wildlife Conference*, 439–43. Washington, DC: U.S. Government Printing Office, 1936.

Dobosz, S., K. Kohlman, K. Gorykczo, and H. Kuzminski. "Growth and Vitality in the Yellow Forms of Rainbow Trout." *Journal of Applied Ichthyology* 16 (2000): 117–20.

Dunham, J. B., D. S. Pilliod, and M. K. Young. "Assessing the Consequences of Nonnative Trout in Headwater Ecosystems in Western North America." *Fisheries* 29 (2004): 18–26.

Gillilan, S., K. Boyd, T. Hoitsma, and M. Kauffman. "Challenges in Developing and Implementing Ecological Standards for Geomorphic River Restoration Projects:

A Practitioner's Response to Palmer et al. (2005)." *Journal of Applied Ecology* 42 (2005): 223–27.

Halverson, M. A. "Stocking Trends: A Quantitative Review of Governmental Fish Stocking in the United States, 1931–2004." *Fisheries* 33 (2008): 69–75.

Harris, A. "Trout Fishing in 2006: A Demographic Description and Economic Analysis." *Addendum to the 2006 National Survey of Fishing, Hunting, and Wildlife-Associated Recreation*, U.S. Fish and Wildlife Service Report 2006–6 (2010): 1–21.

Hession, W. C., J. E. Pizzuto, T. E. Johnson, and R. J. Horwitz. "Influence of Bank Vegetation on Channel Morphology in Rural and Urban Watersheds." *Geology* 31 (2003): 147–50.

Hewitt, E. R. "Shall We Let Vermin Steal Our Trout?" *Outdoor Life* 76 (1935): 22–23, 64.

Hites R. A., J. A. Foran, D. O. Carpenter, M. C. Hamilton, B. A. Knuth, and S. J. Schwage. "Global Assessment of Organic Contaminants in Farmed Salmon." *Science* 303 (2004): 226–29.

Hubbs, C. L. "Fisheries Research in Michigan." *Transactions of the American Fisheries Society* 60 (1931): 182–86.

———. "The Improvement of Trout Streams." *American Forests* 38 (1932): 394–431.

———. "Opening Remarks: Stream and Lake Improvement." In *Proceedings of the North American Wildlife Conference*, 428–29. Washington, DC: U.S. Government Printing Office, 1936.

———. "Planting Food for Fish." In *Proceedings of the North American Wildlife Conference*, 460–64. Washington, DC: U.S. Government Printing Office, 1936.

———. "Fish Management: Looking Forward." *Transactions of the American Fisheries Society* 66 (1937): 51–55.

Hubbs, C. L., C. M. Tarzwell, and R. W. Eschmeyer. "C.C.C. Stream Improvement Work in Michigan." *Transactions of the American Fisheries Society* 63 (1933): 404–14.

Hubbs, C. "An Evaluation of the Use of Rotenone as a Means of 'Improving' Sports Fishing in the Concho River, Texas." *Copeia* 1963 (1963): 199–203.

Hurd, T. M., S. Jesic, J. L. Jerin, M. W. Fuller, and D. Miller. "Stable Isotope Tracing of Trout Hatchery Carbon to Sediments and Foodwebs of Limestone Springs Creek." *Science of the Total Environment* 405 (2008): 161–72.

Johnson, D. M., R. J. Behnke, D. A. Harpmen, and R. G. Walsh. "Economic Benefits and Costs of Stocking Catchable Rainbow Trout: A Synthesis of Economic Analysis in Colorado." *North American Journal of Fisheries Management* 15 (1995): 26–32.

Krumholz, L. A. "The Use of Rotenone in Fisheries Research." *Journal of Wildlife Management* 12 (1948): 305–17.

Latta, W. C. "The Early History of Fisheries Management in Michigan." *Fisheries* 31 (2006): 230–34.

Lave, R., M. W. Doyle, and M. Robertson. "Privatizing Stream Restoration in the US." *Social Studies of Science* 40 (2010): 677–703.

Leonard, J. W. "Notes on the Use of Derris as a Fish Poison." *Transactions of the American Fisheries Society* 68 (1939): 269–80.

Littauer, G. A., J. F. Glahn, D. S. Reinhold, and M. W. Brunson. "Control of Bird

Predation at Aquaculture Facilities: Strategies and Cost Estimates." *Southern Regional Aquaculture Center Publication* 402 (1997): 1–4.

Magilligan F. J., K. H. Nislow, G. B. Fisher, J. Wright, G. Mackey, and M. Laser. "The Geomorphic Function and Characteristics of Large Woody Debris in Low Gradient Rivers, Coastal Maine, USA." *Geomorphology* 97 (2007): 467–82.

Moore E., J. R. Greeley, C. W. Greene, H. M. Faigenbahm, F. R. Nevin, and H. K. Townes. "A Problem in Trout Stream Management." *Transactions of the American Fisheries Society* 64 (1934): 68–80.

Palmer, M. A., J. D. Allan, J. Meyer, and E. S. Bernhardt. "River Restoration in the Twenty-First Century: Data and Experiential Knowledge to Inform Future Efforts." *Restoration Ecology* 15 (2007): 472–81.

Parkhurst, J. A., R. P. Brooks, and D. E. Arnold. "Assessment of Predation at Trout Hatcheries in Central Pennsylvania." *Wildlife Society Bulletin* 20 (1992): 411–19.

Pinchot, G. "The Relation of Forests to Stream Control." *Annals of the American Academy of Political and Social Science* 31 (1908): 219–27.

Pretty, J. L, S. S. C. Harrison, D. J. Shepherd, C. Smith, A. G. Hildrew, and R. D. Hey. "River Rehabilitation and Fish Populations: Assessing the Benefit of Instream Structures." *Journal of Applied Ecology* 40 (2003): 251–65.

Rosgen, D. L. "The Cross-Vane, W-Weir and J-Hook Vane Structures . . . Their Description, Design and Application for Stream Stabilization and River Restoration." In *Proceedings of the Wetlands Engineering and River Restoration Conference*, 1–22. Reno, NV: American Society of Civil Engineers, 2001.

Rosgen, D. L., and B. L. Fittante. "Fish Habitat Structures — A Selection Guide Using Stream Classification." In *The Fifth Trout Stream Habitat Workshop: Proceedings of a Workshop*, August 12–14, 1986, Lock Haven University. Edited by J. Miller, J. Arway, and R. Carline, 163–79. Lock Haven, PA: Lock Haven University, 1986.

Schill, D. J., R. S. Griffith, and R. E. Gresswell. "Hooking Mortality of Cutthroat Trout in a Catch-and-Release Segment of the Yellowstone River, Yellowstone National Park." *North American Journal of Fisheries Management* 6 (1986): 226–32.

Schill, D. J., and R. L. Scarpella. "Barbed Hook Restrictions in Catch-and-Release Trout Fisheries: A Social Issue." *North American Journal of Fisheries Management* 17 (1997): 873–81.

Shetter, D. S., O. H. Clark, and A. S. Hazzard. "The Effects of Deflectors in a Section of a Michigan Trout Stream." *Transactions of the American Fisheries Society* 76 (1949): 248–78.

Simon, A., M. W. Doyle, G. M. Kondolf, F. D. Shields, B. Rhoads, and M. McPhillips. "Critical Evaluation of How the Rosgen Classification and Associated "Natural Channel Design" Methods Fail to Integrate and Quantify Fluvial Processes and Channel Response." *Journal of the American Water Resources Association* 43 (2007): 1117–31.

Tarzwell, C. M. "Progress in Lake and Stream Improvement." *Transactions of the Twenty-First American Games Conference*, 119–34. New York: American Game Association, 1935.

———."Experimental Evidence of the Value of Trout Stream Improvements."
Transactions of the American Fisheries Society 66 (1936): 177–87.

———."Lake and Stream Improvement in Michigan." In *Proceedings of the North
American Wildlife Conference*, 429–34. Washington, DC: U.S. Government Printing
Office, 1936.

———."An Evaluation of the Methods and Results of Stream Improvement in the
Southwest." In *Transactions of the Third North American Wildlife Conference*, 339–64.
Washington, DC: American Wildlife Institute, 1938.

Thompson, D. M."Long-Term Effect of Instream Habitat-Improvement Structures on
Channel Morphology along the Blackledge and Salmon Rivers, Connecticut, USA."
Environmental Management 29 (2002): 250–65.

———."The Long-Term Stability and Morphologic Influence of the Use of Instream
Structures in Channel Restoration Design." In *Managing Watersheds for Human and
Natural Impacts*. Edited by G. E. Moglen, 1–9. Williamsburg, VA: American Society of
Civil Engineers, 2005.

———."Did the Pre-1980 Use of Instream Structures Improve Streams? A Reanalysis of
Historic Data." *Ecological Applications* 16 (2006): 784–96.

Van Cleef, J. S."How to Restore Our Trout Streams." *Transactions of the American
Fisheries Society* 14 (1885): 50–55.

Whelan, G. E."A Historical Perspective on the Philosophy behind the Use of Propagated
Fish in Fisheries Management: Michigan's 130-Year Experience." *American Fisheries
Society Symposium* 44 (2004): 307–15.

Wulff, L."Edward Hewitt." *Rod & Reel* (November/December 1983): 59–60.

About the Illustrations

Index